When Housing Markets Meet Shadow Banking

Bubbles, Mortgages, Securitization, and Fintech

When Housing Markets Meet Shadow Banking

Bubbles, Mortgages, Securitization, and Fintech

Rose Neng Lai
University of Macau, Macao S.A.R

Robert A Van Order
George Washington University, USA

World Scientific

NEW JERSEY • LONDON • SINGAPORE • BEIJING • SHANGHAI • HONG KONG • TAIPEI • CHENNAI • TOKYO

Published by

World Scientific Publishing Co. Pte. Ltd.
5 Toh Tuck Link, Singapore 596224
USA office: 27 Warren Street, Suite 401-402, Hackensack, NJ 07601
UK office: 57 Shelton Street, Covent Garden, London WC2H 9HE

Library of Congress Cataloging-in-Publication Data
Names: Neng Lai, Rose, author. | Van Order, Robert, author.
Title: When housing markets meet shadow banking : bubbles, mortgages, securitization, and fintech / Rose Neng Lai, University of Macau, Macao S.A.R, Robert A Van Order, George Washington University, USA.
Description: New Jersey : World scientific, [2024] | Includes bibliographical references and index.
Identifiers: LCCN 2023042121 | ISBN 9789811283871 (hardcover) | ISBN 9789811283888 (ebook) | ISBN 9789811283895 (ebook other)
Subjects: LCSH: Real estate business--United States. | Real estate business--China. | Nonbank financial institutions--United States. | Nonbank financial institutions--China. | Asset-backed financing--United States. | Asset-backed financing--China.
Classification: LCC HD255 .N46 2024 | DDC 332.63240973--dc23/eng/20231012
LC record available at https://lccn.loc.gov/2023042121

British Library Cataloguing-in-Publication Data
A catalogue record for this book is available from the British Library.

For any available supplementary material, please visit
https://www.worldscientific.com/worldscibooks/10.1142/13611#t=suppl

Desk Editors: Nimal Koliyat/Geysilla Jean

Typeset by Stallion Press
Email: enquiries@stallionpress.com

To Meagan and Pan, and Ava and Nil

Preface

The first two decades of the millennium have been a roller coaster ride for both housing and mortgage markets in both the West and Asia. They have encountered housing bubbles, new forms of funding such as securitization and shadow banking, the Global Financial Crisis, the emergence of the Chinese economy, the evolution of financial technology, the COVID-19 pandemic, and the Ukraine war. Having been researching housing markets and shadow banking in the U.S. and China, we got the urge to share our understanding and thoughts with you and hope you will find at least some parts of the book insightful.

We have been interested in real estate markets and housing finance by "training and by inclination" (one of us was drawn to them in the PhD study and another earned a living for a long time by researching them). We have been much intrigued by the housing bubbles that appeared to have been blown bigger because of securitization and the boom of shadow banking. Hence, both became very natural topics for our book. The fascinating part for us is trying to link the two topics, which can be individual books themselves, into one and yet not losing the "dance" among the parts. The dance was within the boundaries of two quite different countries rather than between them. It started before the beginning of the millennium and is still continuing albeit not to the same rhythms.

The main features of this book are two-fold. First is the evolution of the connection between the housing market and shadow banking stories in the U.S., which start from the basics of housing demand and supply forces, then affect mortgage markets, shadow banking, securitization, and in turn feed back into price growth, etc., creating momentum, destroying the shadow banks that they had created, eventually leading to the Global Financial Crisis. The second feature is how China took a similar but different route. It mostly stayed with shadow banks supplying funds, without the panic, but not without stress. It had rapid price growth, but not a bubble burst. It also had fiscal stimulus along with heavy-handed regulation. There is evidence of China slowing down, probably raising risks we don't know about.

During the course of writing the book, several "rare events" happened. As if the COVID-19 pandemic is not enough, the Russian invasion of Ukraine has caused interest rate hikes in many countries. To keep the story as up-to-date as possible, we also cover the impacts of financial technology and the COVID-19 pandemic.

The book is not meant to be a textbook or a treatise. It is meant for general readers, non-finance academics and their friends, students and policymakers. We have purposely laid out the structure of the book in a way that readers with different backgrounds can read in different sequences. It is not our intent to assess blame across or within countries. Our work has been to try to find out how things evolve. We hope this book distinguishes itself from others as a clear illustration of how housing markets and shadow banking are intertwined and how they will continue to affect each other's development in the future. With that, we offer some analysis of regulatory policies to tackle overheated markets and poor regulations. But our main goal is analyzing the "dance".

About the Authors

Rose Neng Lai is Professor of Finance and Dean of the Honours College at the University of Macau. She runs the Executive Director Office for the Asian Real Estate Society, for which she was the President in 2007. She is one of the Founding Directors and past President (2012) of the Global Chinese Real Estate Congress. She has also sat on various committees in international academic associations and academic search/promotion committees. Her research in real estate finance and economics, behavioral finance, and risk management has been published in a range of academic journals. She won the 2019 International Real Estate Society Achievement Award and the 2017 Edwin Mills Best Paper Award. She is currently the Executive Editor of the *International Real Estate Review*. She has also led several government consultancy projects, joined think-tanks and committees for expert opinions, and is consulted by international bodies.

Robert Van Order holds the Oliver Carr Chair in Finance and Real Estate at George Washington University and is Professor of Finance and Economics. He was Chief Economist at Freddie Mac from 1987 to 2002. He has taught at Purdue, USC, UCLA, Penn, Michigan and Aberdeen Universities, and worked at the U.S. Department of Housing and Urban Development. He has published in a range of academic journals, primarily in modeling credit risk, location theory, house prices and financial institutions. He received the George Bloom Distinguished Service Award in 2007 and the 2017 Edwin Mills Best Paper Award (both awards were from the American Real Estate and Urban Economics Association).

Acknowledgments

The list would get extremely long, covering major countries around the globe, if we include everyone who has taught, inspired, supported, and/or just been a friend (which can mean much more than anything at times). That said, we still want to mention a few whom we can never miss, no matter what.

Special thanks from Rose goes to Ko Wang and Su Han Chan for their relentless care (and love, if she may) and guidance, and always being there throughout her career development. Others are Tyler Yang, Robert C. Merton, Sheridan Titman, James Mirrlees (who is no longer with us), Timothy Riddiough, and James Shilling, who have inspired her so much and are whom she always looks up to time after time.

Robert has a lot of people to thank but is sticking to several involved in Housing Finance who have been co-authors and/or co-conspirators. First, from the Department of Housing and Urban Development (HUD): Bob Buckley, Ann Dougherty, Mike Lea, Beth Preiss, and Kevin Villani. Second, from Freddie Mac: Ed Golding, Arnold Kling, Vanessa Perry, Ann Schnare, and Peter Zorn. Third, from Academe: Dennis Capozza, Yongheng Deng, and Pat Hendershott. And finally, special acknowledgements to three gentlemen and scholars who are no longer here: Chet Foster (HUD), Frank Nothaft (Freddie Mac), and John Quigley (Academe).

Regarding our research and studies related to this book, we would like to thank Zongyuan Li and Nicole Ruihui Xu for providing excellent research assistance to our earlier work, and Man Cho and Thies

Lindenthal for always remembering our passion for researching housing bubbles.

Our final acknowledgment goes to the team at World Scientific Publishing Co Pte Ltd. We are especially grateful to Angela Lixi Dong who previously worked at the publisher and invited us to write this book. Our collaboration with her was succeeded by Geysilla Jean T Ortiz who has also been very helpful throughout the publication process. Both Angela and Jean have been particularly considerate in working along our delays due to our sometimes busy schedules. Finally, we thank Nimal Koliyat and the book editing team for their excellent editing.

Contents

Introduction

Where were you in 2020? In 2022? How have the COVID-19 pandemic and the war between Russia and Ukraine affected you? How about interest rate hikes, for seven times, or around 4.5% in 10 months in the U.S., and still rising? How much do you know about housing bubbles? Shadow banking? The Global Financial Crisis (GFC) in 2008? What can you think of when all these questions are put together? In a global context? What has been happening over the last 25 years with all these together?

It has been a longish and somewhat strange trip for housing and housing finance. House prices have grown rapidly and sometimes crashed. New forms of housing finance have emerged, and expanded rapidly both in volume and in a wider array of products, and many of them crashed in the U.S. In China, prices grew rapidly around the time of the crash in the U.S., and new mortgage lenders, shadow banks, which were outside the regular banking system, grew along with house prices, but there was no crash (so far).

Shadow banks have evolved in both the U.S. and China, but done differently. In the U.S., the most explosive shadow banks were related to both the housing boom at the beginning of the millennium, and the newer brands of securitization that, despite looking like good ideas, were often toxic. They stimulated the growth of the shadow banks that held them, and the two together fed back into the boom. In China, the shadow banks were not tied to securitization. Instead, they were a part of an expansion that at first looked like a market-oriented boom heading for a bust. It didn't bust, but the market orientation part is fading.

Background and Summary

Financial market expansion has been greatly aided by the advancement of technology. As the size and volume of the markets have increased, so has their liquidity and efficiency. The expansion has opened up new sources of funding and ways of managing investment, enhanced by improvements in technologies to move money around faster and gather more information. Along with this have been innovations in understanding and pricing financial assets, starting from the Black–Scholes–Merton option-pricing model, due to Fischer Black and Myron Scholes (Black and Scholes, 1973), and Robert C. Merton (1973), and the application of contingent-claims analysis to corporate debts and financial intermediation by Robert C. Merton (Merton, 1974, 1989, 1990). However, it has not been all good; information asymmetry, which often happens with newness, has led to moral hazard (lying and cheating), spoiling important elements of what might have been market efficiency.

Unlike financial markets, housing markets are not liquid and are subject to costly and complicated transactions. They too involve moral hazard. Trading assets in real estate and in mortgage markets have become polar opposites in the U.S. Due largely to innovations alluded to above, mortgages can be traded like bonds and can be used relatively easily to finance real estate transactions, even if the transactions themselves are slow to move. That both housing and financial markets can be plagued with moral hazard explains some of the institutions, public policies and market structure of both markets.

Since the 1970s, the world has seen strong demand (with a few bumps along the way) for housing, for both investment and consumption purposes, enabled by the development of mortgage markets through an enlarging financial system. This came largely from banking systems in Europe, from shadow banking systems in China, and from securitization as well as shadow banking in the U.S. Much of this is migration away from the traditional banking sector, which has for some time been highly regulated and somewhat sleepy.

Our special interest is in the evolution, side by side, of U.S. and China housing and mortgage markets. This is in part because they are the two most important economies in the world and also because their evolutions have been both similar and different in ways that we find illuminating. We spend more ink on the mortgage market and its interactions with housing than we do on housing alone because its evolution has been a stranger trip.

Sources and Insights

Why did shadow banks play a central role in the crash in 2008 while the regular banking system largely stayed open for business? Why not in China? Are banks inherently fragile?

We have two important sources (both short explanations of long lines of research) to acknowledge and exploit. The first reference comes from Douglas Diamond of University of Chicago, who has made a career of developing models of banking and bank runs.[1] The second is by Gary Gorton of Yale University, who hit the nail on the head early on when he saw the crash as a version of a generic sort of bank panic[2]; but it was a run on shadow banks, and not the old-fashioned kind that the U.S. had about once a decade in the 19th century, and on steroids in the 1930s. We exploit these two authors, along with their coauthors, in order to save us from having to be original.

First is Diamond and the Diamond-Dybvig story about bank runs.[3] Homeowners generally need mortgages to buy houses.[4] However, a major impediment is a moral hazard (see Chapter 5) in the form of investors in the loans getting stuck with bad loans on bad terms because of not knowing as much as borrowers. This is also a problem in secondary markets where the banks know more about the loans they sell than the buyers. A market rampant with moral hazard can end up with a degenerate situation where buyers end up expecting that sellers will deliver only bad stuff, and both sides get

---

[1]See Diamond (2023). Two Contracts That Are Central to the Financial System, A Nobel Winner Explains His Groundbreaking Research. CBR — Finance, January 26, 2023.

[2]Gorton, Gary, "Misunderstanding Financial Crises", *Financial Times*. Available at: https://ftalphaville.ft.com/2012/10/25/1223861/misunderstanding-financial-crises-a-qa-with-gary-gorton/.

[3]This is from his seminal paper with Philip Dybvig (his joint Nobel Prize recipient), in Diamond and Dybvig (1983).

[4]Even people who own but have no mortgage now probably had one earlier. A large majority of Americans are exposed to the mortgage market at least once.

what they expect at a price consistent with only bad stuff, a kind of self-fulfilling prophecy. But there are buyers who want to buy good loans and some sellers would like to sell them, and the market leaves them out: a classic case of market failure. These are sometimes called *lemons* problems in reference to the notion of used car dealers selling lemons — the worst cars. How can financial markets solve this ubiquitous problem, which is at the core of understanding financial markets?

The survey article by Diamond points to two important vehicles (contracts) for controlling the moral hazard and expanding markets beyond lemons. The first is to tackle the difficulty of direct lending from one person to another because people do not know one another. A solution is to put loans into pools and then carve (*structure*) them and sell pieces, rather like parts of a chicken, so that different investor types can take on different risk types (Chapter 8). It is also a version of *securitization*, which uses securities markets to raise money and leaves the risk to the investors.

The other is financial intermediation. Intermediation happens when an institution like a bank acquires assets (like mortgages) or lends money and funds them with deposits, which are claims promised to investors that are independent of the assets' performance. This transformation of assets into liabilities is the essence of intermediation. It requires less information of investors, making it easier to deposit their money.[5] The deposits are "liquid" in the sense of being convertible to cash or transfer on demand, even though the assets backing them are not.

The promise by banks to redeem deposits at par is a selling point and is usually not a problem as long as depositors think other depositors are not about to make large-scale withdrawals. But what if they do, for instance, because of a belief that the bank is about to "go under"? Because the bank assets are not liquid and banks do not carry enough reserves to pay off the withdrawal rapidly, there is a run. A way around this is guarantees, like deposit insurance by a government agency, which take away the need to rush.[6] The source

[5]This combination of information insensitivity and liquidity for investors is also at the center of the Gorton story.

[6]Not all deposits are insured; there can be problems with uninsured deposits and short-term debt.

of bank runs is short-term liabilities, such as deposits, that have to be "rolled over" for the bank to stay in business. Banks funded with long-term debt can certainly become insolvent, but that (like most bankruptcies) does not have the immediacy of a bank run.

Gorton's line reinforces the notion of banks' short-term debt and panic. It develops a common interpretation of the GFC in the U.S. It focuses on *securitized banking*, meaning shadow banks that hold pieces of securitization deals as their assets. This type of banking was both a stimulus to housing demand and a result of it via house price growth that makes almost all loans look good. The problem is that the securitized banks held pieces of structured deals about which information was quite poor, and the pieces were rich in moral hazard and sensitive to shocks about the information. The shadow banks did not have deposit insurance and were subject to *silent bank runs* (via wire transfers rather than irate depositors), which happened in 2007 and 2008 when asset quality was revealed to be much worse than expected. There is of course more than this, which we try to cover in Chapters 8 and 9.

China's trip was different. It requires a broader discussion of its banking system and its wide variety of tools (see Chapters 7 and 10). A central characteristic is the broad usage of new technologies and platforms, raising the possibility of emerging, but unknown, risks.

House Price Dynamics (When Are There Bubbles?)

We think of homeowners as landlords renting to themselves. Our measure of rent is the measure of the value of services provided. Then we take the price of housing to be the discounted value of that income stream (see Chapter 3), in the same way we would think of the value of any marketable asset. Since housing markets do not adjust as fast as stock markets or Treasury markets, we can think of the dynamics as a kind of moving average of discounted values. This gives us three versions of where price changes come from: changes value for services, high interest rates (e.g. Fed policy), and momentum from past changes based on recent history rather than from its "fundamentals". It is the momentum that gets us into bubbles.

A complication is that more than one thing can happen simultaneously or sequentially. A shock to rental markets or interest rates can affect house prices before the bulk of the shock has happened to rents, and lack of foresight can induce all sorts of projections of future prices, subsequently inducing momentum, which can become a bubble ready to burst. We think of two important reasons for rapid price growth: first is space becoming increasingly expensive, with prices chasing the rents, and second is momentum that ignores rent projections, with prices chasing prices. It looks like the U.S. and China had different versions of each.

Two Dances: An Overview

The relationship between housing and mortgage markets and shadow banking has been intertwined in different countries for different reasons. This relationship can be thought of as symbiotic, or maybe just a variety of dances, albeit to different music. China had a simpler dance. It was shadow banking, but not short-term deposits, and interactions with housing. The shadow banks are not a part of the *regular* banking system and may or may not have implicit guarantees. This is an archetypical example of shadow banking (more like the Diamond-Dybvig story, but without short-term debt and bank runs). The U.S. had two parts to its dance: securitization and then shadow banks, eventually dancing with each other and with housing (the Gorton story).

The evolution of shadow banks in both countries came from many of the same reasons. In particular, they entered into niche areas that were not done (or not done well) by the regular system. This is called "regulatory arbitrage". In the U.S., it entered in places where bank regulations made it difficult for regular banks to enter, and also in the securitization market, where it provided private deals that the three government-related Agencies could not easily enter. In China, it entered as a line of business that the major (big four) banks did not compete much.

Outline

The structure of the book falls into four phases.

The first phase presents background and overview of housing and mortgage markets. Chapter 1 in the U.S. and the "West" and Chapter 2 in China are largely descriptive. A common characteristic of the two has been rapid growth in house prices, but the aftermath of the growth varied.

The second phase is an introduction to models of housing and mortgages and some tools for analyzing them. Chapter 3 is about housing markets and dynamics and why deep understanding of the dynamics of house prices, and that spotting the bubbles is more or less impossible. Chapter 4 discusses mortgage mathematics and pricing. It covers somewhat complicated tools to analyze mortgage pricing and mortgages rates, and the behavior of mortgage borrowers, for instance, reasons why they default. These two chapters can be skipped if desired. But we'd rather you read them.

The third phase is the core. Chapters 5–8 are about mortgage markets and their structures. Chapter 5 is about the mortgage markets in the U.S. We bring in two concepts and a theorem: *moral hazard* and *regulatory arbitrage*, and the *Modigliani−Miller irrelevance theorem* (M−M).*−Miller irrelevance theorem (M–M)* The first two have been discussed above. M−M asks a very important question: So What? Why do any of the structures we talk about matter if they are just different liability structures that receive payments from the same assets?

We discuss shadow banking in the U.S. in Chapter 6 and shadow banking in China in Chapter 7. We describe how regulatory arbitrage stimulated securitization markets in the U.S. and the rise of shadow banks to support them. Wall Street's arbitrage was both in extending the securitization model and in creating shadow banks that took up functions, which regular banks could not (easily). Regulatory arbitrage in China was about shadow banks developing outside the big banks.

In Chapter 8, we discuss the rise and fall of *private label* securitization (Wall Street version) in the U.S. There became a plethora of financial structures that look alike, but have turned out to be significantly different. We discuss them and the problems they tried to address, especially moral hazard problems.

The last phase is recent history in light of phase 3. It begins in Chapter 9 with the GFC and the breakdown in securitization and securitized banking. This follows Gorton's analysis. In Chapter 10, we cover China, which was not much affected by the GFC, but it had a sharp increase in property values and changes in institutional structures and regulatory crackdowns, as well as a move away from market models. In Chapter 11, we discuss the post-GFC period. We look at housing affordability around the world and the acceleration of shadow banks and their "fellow travelers" in China. Perhaps one of the hottest spices we added here is the evolving role that technology has played in the dances of shadow banking and housing markets.

More recently, new developments from the Chinese property developers, the Big Techs in China, the development of the COVID-19 pandemic, the Russia–Ukraine war and stagflation, have individually and collectively brought a lot more flavor and spice to our story. We therefore end the book with an epilogue to cover the spice colors, like different shades of yellow to red in a spice shop in India or Mexico, but with a distinctly sour taste.

Looking Forward

The dance has continued, but it has changed. In the U.S., it has gone from something like the agitated sounds of Pink Floyd (We don't need no education ...) to something more like the cool moods of Frank Sinatra (... and one more for the road). In China, the music is about the same, but the instruments have changed.

Chapter 1

Housing Markets: The West

At the time of writing this book, the world has been hit hard by the COVID-19 pandemic and then the Russian Invasion of Ukraine, which led to inflation and interest rate hikes. Many countries have experienced lockdowns in 2020. Several major cities in China were both the earliest, Wuhan being the first, and the latest to undergo lockdowns; although it finally opened up as 2022 ended. The latest massive lockdown was for six weeks in Shanghai, starting at the end of March and running through to the beginning of May. It induced a lot of reassessment of what basic necessity meant to individual households. New terms such as staycation and work-from-home (WFH) sprung up. As a result, the needs and preferences of both homeowners and renters also underwent fundamental changes. New waves of increased housing costs seem to be hitting many countries at the same time.

Housing units can be rented or owned, forming two distinct, but intertwined, markets: the residential rental market and the property sales market. Most countries have both markets, differing only in size and scope. However, because both serve the same function of providing shelter and space for people to live in, owners of housing units are essentially tenants of their own possession, paying for the service of the housing units as shelters. More of this will be covered in Chapter 3.

If you ask why people want to own housing units and not just "consume" the units, two common answers would be "I want to own my own home; it is mine, it means everything to me," or "Simple! Housing prices will rise in the future. I need to hedge against rent increases and inflation by buying now." The former answer is more sentimental; the latter is more about housing serving both consumption and investment purposes. It is this latter reason that makes housing markets important for the overall economy as well as investment and capital markets. When individuals gain handsome profits from booming stock markets, they might want to diversify and/or spend their windfall on consumption, or they might be more interested in investing in housing. Hence, when studying housing markets, one cannot ignore the details of the corresponding economies.

Thinking of the differences in housing across the globe, people often have presumptions that housing units in the U.S. are larger in size, while those in Asia are smaller, not to mention the "shoebox apartments" in Singapore, or the "nano flats" in Hong Kong. Also stuck in many people's minds is the notion that being tenants is better than being homeowners, such as in some European countries, while it is a tradition to own a home in Asia as well as the U.S.. Due to worldwide differences in ownership preferences and choices, and housing policies, it is worth taking up some pages to discuss the major markets in the world before starting more in-depth discussions of the theme of this book.

Housing markets are inefficient compared to financial markets because of their illiquidity, high transaction costs, and differences in features of the housing units. Think of buying and selling some shares of a stock. All you need is to sign in to your trading account, and the transaction would be made almost immediately. Even 20–30 years ago, all you needed was to make a phone call to your agent or broker (provided they were available; it was often the case that several investors called the same agent at the same time when the market was rising or falling sharply). Now consider the lengthy process of buying a housing unit. You need first to search among different housing units that are listed on the market. Then you usually will visit the chosen unit for a thorough look, sometimes a few times, before you decide if that is what you want. You then meet up with the seller, or his/her agent/representative, and discuss with your bank how to finance it, and so on. That can easily take a month before you can finally possess the unit. This is an example of how unique the housing market is from other investment markets.

Now consider housing developments like those in Asia with many, relatively homogenous, units in one high-rise building. The developer of the building will decide to build when he/she thinks there is demand and the price will be stable or rise. Think of the construction time of 2 years. By the time the building is completed, the market has already moved up or down for 2 years. Sales are made at the price at completion, which can be quite different from what the developer anticipates.[1] Suppose the price was at a peak when the developer started building. Then he/she will have to sell all the units at prices lower than anticipated. If the building consists of hundreds of units, such bulk supply into the market will push the price further down. Prices continue to drop to a level where homebuyers find housing units cheap enough to attract purchases. Prices start to grow again when more homebuyers join the market. Then production starts to increase again. Does this sound familiar? This is how a housing market cycle is created.

These cycles can be further amplified as momentum becomes "bubbles," which are, for a while, self–fulfilling prophecies. That is, the price rises because people expect them to rise and do not want to miss out on a good chance by waiting. Then at some point after they stopped being self-fulfilling when people realize that the price increase cannot last, they become self-fulfilling in the other direction, and there is a crash.

Albert Saiz has suggested that land-constrained cities can have lower housing supply elasticities as well as higher house prices.[2] Many researchers have found that housing prices continue to grow for extended periods of time. From this "momentum," it is possible to generate abnormal returns based on changes in returns, as shown by Karl E. Case and Robert J. Shiller in the U.S. housing markets, at least in their studies for the period of 1970–1990.[3] Others have also shown that buyers' and sellers' overconfidence is a cause

[1]It is common practice for developers in Asia to sell the housing units before they are completed. In some cases, they were sold even before any development began. However, there had been incidents of incomplete projects, or projects that were never started, causing losses to buyers, that governments nowadays approve presale only upon completing certain proportion of the projects. Therefore, developers still face uncertainty of the selling prices from the time they start building to the time they could sell the units.

[2]Saiz (2010).

[3]Case and Shiller (1989, 1990).

of momentum. For instance, Shiller argues that the housing boom leading to the latest Financial Crisis was due to overconfidence that prices would continue to rise, fueling the momentum, and leading to the housing price bubbles.[4]

How can one distinguish a bubble market from the peak of a normal market cycle? With great difficulty![5] This should be clearer after the next few chapters where we consider the mathematics of pricing housing units and the difficulty of drawing before-the-fact influences. This chapter serves to provide some background on different markets around the world.

While we would like to cover as many markets as possible, we limit our geographical footage to two economic models for two reasons. First, housing demands and supplies are broadly similar within models in fundamentals, both in theory and practice. Even if some markets tend to be more volatile than others, while others might have stickier prices than the rest, markets tend to move in similar cycles. Second, a majority of countries in the western world follow similar free, not too overregulated, market models, like those of the U.S.

On the other hand, China is highly regulated. Chinese markets have a relatively short recent history, which covers the transformation from a socialist type of housing to some mechanisms similar to capitalist markets. But still, government policies have played very major roles in controlling (or, more accurately, trying to prevent) significant swings from boom to bust.

Other Asian markets are in between, albeit with less periodic government intervention. We have decided to focus on the housing markets of the two largest economies in the world, the U.S. and China, and touch base with other markets, which are representatives of some features of the markets.

1.1. The Economies: Shocks and Crises

Here we discuss some of the major movements in the world economy because they are very closely linked to housing markets. More about the economies of individual countries will be covered later when their

---

[4]Shiller (2007, 2008).

[5]If we knew how to do that, we would not be writing about it.

housing markets are discussed. We discuss major economic shocks over the past 30 years or so. We choose this relatively short period for two main reasons. First, the 30-year period includes the recent very major Global Financial Crisis (GFC), which started in mid-September 2008. Second, it is a period that brings out differences between the U.S. and China, even in shadow banking.

This was an era that shook up the world, during which people experienced "black swan" events. The GFC began in the U.S., triggered by one relatively small part of the financial system that became contagious and spread to other seemingly stable parts, eventually triggering a debt crisis in Europe. Nothing similar happened to financial systems in Asia; although they did experience recessions from trade connections. Seldom before (since the 1930s) had there been so many countries at the edge of bankruptcy. Finally, the end of this period is also an unprecedented encounter of the COVID-19 pandemic that, despite all economies moving on strongly, businesses, industries, and traveling have suddenly come to a halt for unpredictably and unforeseeably long.

Some of the major shocks over the past 50 years originated in the U.S. and rippled through to other parts of the world because of its economic dominance and connectedness. Notable examples are the high inflation period of the late 1970s and 1980s and the Black Monday on October 19, 1987, when the Dow Jones crashed and rippled to other stock markets in the world, leaving unprecedented drop within just hours after the market opening. The last major shock of the last century was the dot-com crisis at the turn of the millennium. The most recent one, as of the time this book is completed, was the subprime mortgage crisis that started in 2006–2007, eventually leading to the Global Financial Crisis. We shall cover this latest crisis in detail in Chapter 9 because it was directly caused by housing markets and shadow banking.

To better represent the financial conditions of countries, the International Monetary Fund (IMF) started to introduce the financial conditions indices (FCIs) in the April 2017 Global Financial Stability Report (GFSR).[6] Methodologies for finding the FCIs have been

---

[6]Annex 3.1 of Chapter 3 "Are Countries Losing Control of Domestic Financial Conditions?" of the IMF (2017b) *Global Financial Stability Report*, April 2017.

studied by various academics as early as 2000.[7] The GFSR model is meant to standardize the measures so as to allow comparison across 43 countries, both advanced and emerging economies. The details can be found in Chapter 3, Annex 3.1, of the April 2017 Report. FCIs are based on ten financial variables that cover a broad array of financial segments: corporate spreads, term spreads, interbank spreads, sovereign spreads, the change in long-term interest rates, equity returns, changes in house prices, equity return volatility, change in market share of the financial sector, and credit growth. FCIs are interpreted as follows. A positive index value implies that the country's financial condition is tighter than the average of all countries (i.e. common dynamics across countries, or global financial conditions). Similarly, a negative index value means that the country's financial condition is looser than average. This is why the data are in standard deviations from the mean.

Figure 1.1 depicts the FCIs of China, the Euro Area, and the U.S. released by the IMF in the World Economic Outlook, January 2022 Update, which is according to the October 2021 Global Financial

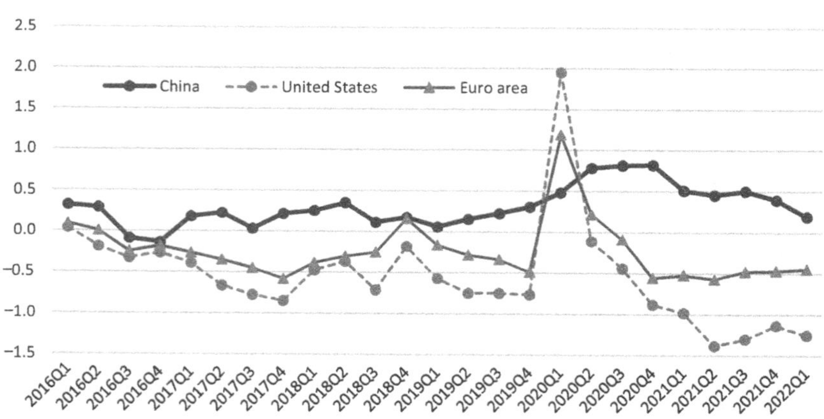

Figure 1.1 Financial Conditions Indices of the U.S., Euro Area, and China

Source: World Economic Outlook January 2022 Update (more positive means more tightening, more negative means more loosening).

[7]The earliest one, according to the GFSR 2017, p. 100, is Dudley and Hatzius (2000).

Stability Report. It shows that financial conditions in China have been tighter than the average of the 43 countries since 2017, while those of the Euro area and the U.S. were mostly on the loose side until the outbreak of the COVID-19 pandemic in the first quarter of 2020. Exactly also because of the pandemic, both regions have significantly loosened financial conditions by providing several stimulus packages. For instance, the Federal Reserve (Fed) of the U.S. cut interest rates, bought long term loans and assets, launched several lending programs to help businesses, and established new policies such as lowering bank reserve requirements. The European Central Bank adopted more or less the same approach.

Similar measures were used by other countries. On the other side of the world, China as the first country to have an outbreak of COVID-19 took swift economic measures in cutting interest rates and increasing liquidity in the economy, and issuing consumption vouchers to residents to boost spending. Loans were extended, and rents were reduced. Since it was able to achieve a complete lockdown of a whole city or community, it was able to contain the pandemic very quickly. Life was back to usual as early as the beginning of summer in 2020, but only for a while.

The government decided to take a "cautious approach" to reduce and eventually withdraw the policies supporting the economy during the pandemic. The peak of its FCI in the fourth quarter of 2020 overlaps with the time when the Chinese government decided to implement much-tightened regulations on its technology sector on data protection and antitrust. Simultaneously, the troublesome peer-to-peer lending (P2P) sector was completely shut down. Billions of dollars of market values of the tech giants evaporated. For example, Alibaba's stock price dropped from its peak on October 23, 2020, at USD 309.92 to USD 111.96 on December 3, 2021, and ended at USD 88.09 on December 30, 2022.[8] As a consequence, many players in the financial market were caught off-guard, and the economy slowed down. One year later, this tightening was finally associated with looser financial conditions, albeit still tighter than average.

[8]It reached USD 76.76 on March 15, 2022, USD 113.68 on June 30, and then USD 63.58 on October 31, 2022.

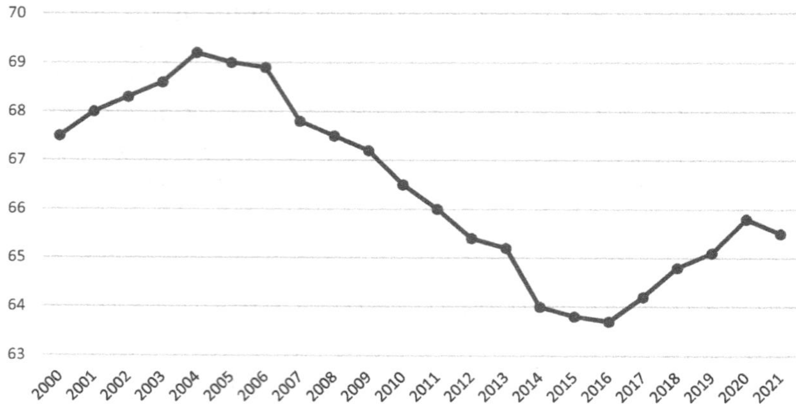

Figure 1.2 Homeownership Rate in the U.S. for the Period 2000–2021
Source: U.S. Census Bureau.

We now turn to the U.S., followed by Europe. China will be discussed in Chapter 2.

1.2. United States

Homeownership in the U.S. has been relatively stable since the surge after World War II ended in the 1960s. The percentage of American homeowners in 1990 was 64.1%, and then 65.1% and 67.5% in 1995 and 2000, respectively, according to the U.S. Census Bureau. More recently, as shown in Figure 1.2, the homeownership rate at the end of each year between 2000 and 2021 has been within the range of 63% and 70%. The figure shows that the peak is at the housing market boom resulting from the low borrowing costs, eventually leading to the crisis. Homeownership dropped gradually thereafter because of foreclosure when a lot of subprime mortgagors defaulted. It was not until more than a decade later that homeownership started to pick up again.

1.2.1. House Prices

Figure 1.3 shows the S&P CoreLogic Case–Shiller U.S. National Home Price Index, which covers the nine U.S. census divisions, with

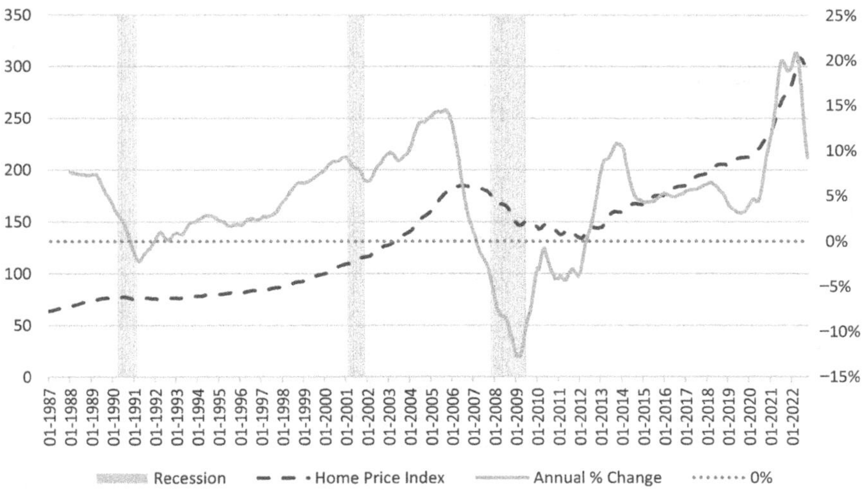

Figure 1.3 Case–Shiller U.S. National Home Price Index
Note: The base year is January 2000 = 100. Data are seasonally adjusted. The three shaded periods represent recessions.
Source: Federal Reserve Economic Data (FRED).

January 2000 as the base year with 100 index points.[9] The period covered is January 1987 to October 2022. The annual percentage changes are also plotted on the right axis. The fine horizontal dotted line shows where changes are zero. The house price index shows an almost continuous increase in the period covered, except the big swings in the three periods shaded in grey, representing the three recent recessions, the last of which covers the subprime mortgage crisis that led to the GFC.

More about the Crisis will be covered in Chapter 9. For now, a short preview is that households have always been encouraged to own their homes, not that they always needed to, but partially because they found easier ways to borrow. Simultaneously, house prices grew very rapidly, and lax borrowing standards allowed borrowers to obtain mortgages of various, and sometimes dubious, sorts. Among these were the not fully documented, Alt-A, loans as well

[9]A reason for its widespread use is that the index sample is constructed rather like a stock price index, which makes it better able to capture house price changes separately from housing quality changes.

as so-called subprime mortgages, which looked good for lenders in a time of rapid house price growth. Alt-A mortgages are generally mortgages deemed as good (like "A"-grade mortgages) on paper but without documentation for things like income and source of down-payment. Subprime loans could also be "low-doc" (for low documentation) made to high-risk borrowers — even if fully documented. Alt-A loans had default rates higher than prime loans, but lower than subprime. Since they provide less real information, Alt-A loans are susceptible to moral hazard. Demand was built up, leading to the surge in housing prices that started around 2000, until 2006, coupled with a peak of subprime mortgage issuance, triggering the crisis that lasted from 2007 to 2009 and into 2010.

It took some time for households to recover from the GFC. Prices once again went up afterward and experienced another local maximum growth of 10.83% in October 2013. Growth subsequently moderated and was at its slowest in August 2019. Just when the growth seemed to have slowed down, the COVID-19 pandemic kicked in globally in early 2020. The demand for homeownership picked up again, this time at a much faster pace, which, however, did not last long. The growth significantly slipped in the second quarter of 2022. We shall have more details about both the subprime crisis in Chapter 9 and this new round of surge of homeowners in Chapter 11. For now, we shall see which parts of the U.S. are more (or less) affordable over the past 30 years.

The lines in Figure 1.4 show regional data on house prices of the nine regions of the U.S. from the Federal Housing Finance Agency (FHFA). The regional patterns are similar to the changes in the national house price index in Figure 1.3. Note the thickest line somewhere in the middle of the line bundle is the change in the overall price index. The States included in each of these nine regions are listed and mapped in Appendix.

The biggest oscillations, with the highest peak by the end of 2004 and the worst trough by the end of 2008, were recorded in the Pacific, i.e. West Coast, a region where major cities like Los Angeles and San Francisco are situated. The other two regions with big, but more moderate, swings are the Mountain and South Atlantic regions. The Mountain region includes states such as Arizona, Nevada, and Wyoming. House prices in these States are not very high. Yet, the price index of this region is the highest among all, especially after

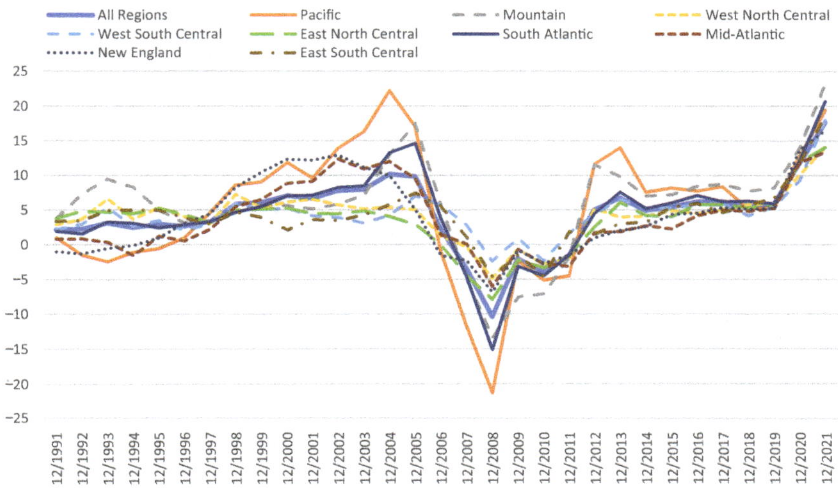

Figure 1.4 Percentage Change in House Price Index in U.S. Regions

Source: Federal Housing Finance Agency.

2006, because all the price indices start at 100 index points in January 1991 together. Hence, their movements are only relative to 1991. In any case, homebuyers experienced the biggest changes in these States. Interestingly, the decline from the GFC did not seem to scare off housing market growth, probably because the financial system stayed strong. In fact, the house price index climbed at an even faster pace since the COVID-19 pandemic started in March 2020.

1.2.2. Borrowing Costs

Lax borrowing standards, which sometimes go along with innovative mortgage products, were both causes and effects of the last boom. A reason for the house price increases was low borrowing costs as can be seen from Figure 1.5. Panel (a) shows a mostly decreasing trend of the 30-year fixed-rate mortgage (FRM) rates over the past 35 years, until the end of 2021 after which it spiked quite sharply. From Panel (b), the few years after the turn of the millennium saw a continuous drop and then stable rates until interest rates, represented by the Fed funds rates (1/1990–12/2022), went up again in 2006. The rest was the crisis and the recovery from it, with a generally continuous drop of interest rates again.

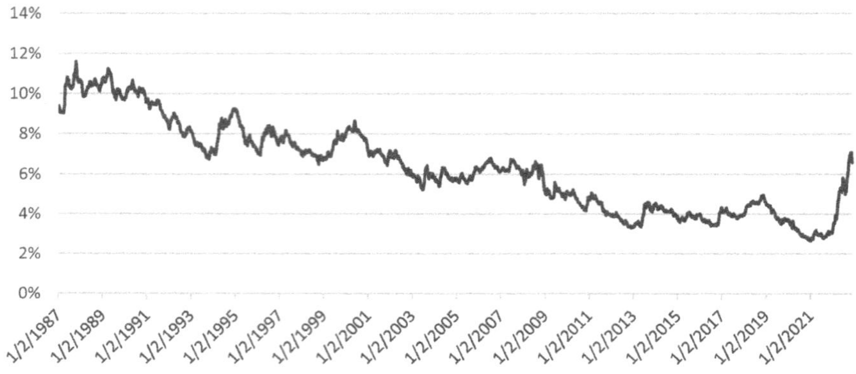

(a)

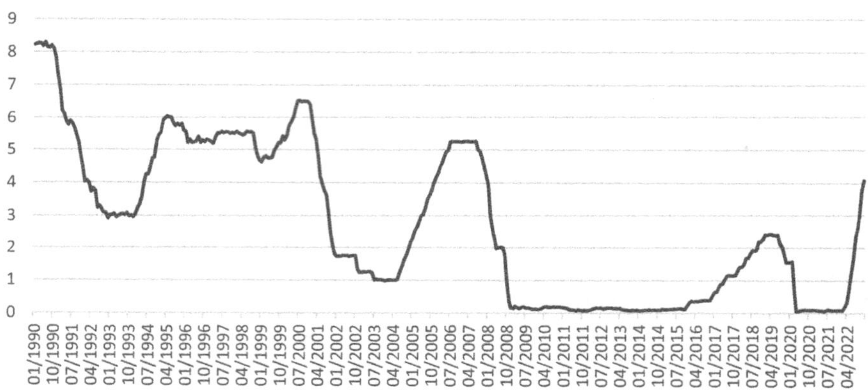

(b)

Figure 1.5 U.S. Interest Rates. Panel (a) 30-year Fixed Rate Mortgage (FRM) Rates. Panel (b) Effective Fed Funds Rate

Source: (a) Freddie Mac. (b) Board of Governors of the Federal Reserve System and St. Louis FED Economic Research.

The COVID-19 pandemic lockdown in China (mainly the megacities of Shanghai and then Beijing) starting in late March, and extending through May, as well as the Russian Invasion of Ukraine starting at the end of February 2022, seriously affected the global supply chain and production of both for manufactured goods (mostly from China) and raw materials and crops (mostly from Russia and Ukraine, as Ukraine is a very crucial supplier of metal and crops). An extensive war would mean that it would take a long time before agriculture and manufacturing could pick up again, let alone the length of the war. This has led to a series of increases in interest rates in order to combat inflation, with no end in sight at the end of 2022.

In response, the Federal Reserve (Fed) increased the Effective Fed Funds Rate (EFFR) by 0.5% (the biggest increase since 2000) to between 0.9% and 1% on May 5, 2022 (after the 0.25% increase on March 17), and then four more times in the following 6 months, by 0.75% each, another 0.5% in December and 0.25% in January; and more to come to combat inflation, which peaked (year-on-year) at 9.1% in June.[10] Inflation was then slowing down, which is behind the smaller rate hikes. The current question is whether inflation can revert to the 2% long-run goal with a "soft landing." Maybe, maybe not. Probably not easily.[11]

1.2.3. Affordability

Low borrowing costs do not necessarily translate into more homeownership if house prices are too high. Figure 1.2 shows a stable homeownership rate. Why is ownership not higher? The choice of owning versus renting is complicated by the inflexibility for households to switch from renting to owning and vice versa in most cases. In the U.S., many households have spells of both: e.g. renters at first, owners later, and renters later on. Such decisions depend on factors like demographics, tax benefits and credit availability, and rent regulations, which vary a lot across countries. A common reason is affordability. There are many ways of measuring affordability. The cash-flow burden of carrying a house in the form of mortgage payments relative to income is an important one. An alternative is house price relative to income. Neither of these includes the investment

[10]See "Implementation Note issued May 4, 2022" and "Implementation Note issued November 2, 2022" by the Federal Reserve. Available at: https://www.federalreserve.gov/newsevents/pressreleases/monetary20220504a1.htm#:~:text=In%20a%20related%20action%2C%20the,%2C%20effective%20May%205%2C%202022, and https://www.federalreserve.gov/newsevents/pressreleases/monetary20221102a1.htm#:~:text=The%20Board%20of%20Governors%20of,%2C%20effective%20November%203%2C%202022.

[11]We expand this in both Chapter 11 and the Epilogue.

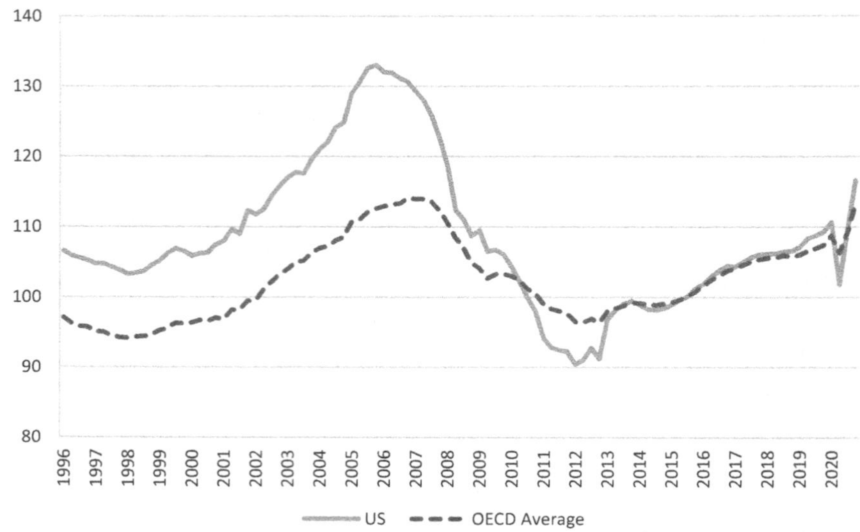

Figure 1.6 Price-to-Income Ratio of Housing in the U.S. and OECD

Source: OECD (2021).

aspect of ownership, which we address as *user cost*, in Chapter 3 (Equation 3.17).

The OECD (2021) mentioned that while there is no standard definition, affordable housing should clearly be tied to the house price-to-income ratio and housing-expenditure-to-income ratio. Too high a house price relative to income means it is more difficult for households to be homeowners unless interest rates are low. The OECD definition extends further to housing quality as an indicator, which suggests that low affordability also implies only low-quality housing can be bought for an affordable price. Figure 1.6 is a plot of a readily available measure of affordability across countries, the housing price-to-income ratio of the U.S., with 2015 as the base year (i.e. ratio in 2015 = 100). Compared to the OECD country average, housing in the U.S. is more or less affordable at the same levels over the past 10 years, but was way less "affordable" before the Crisis according to the plot.

However, the period before the Crisis was also a period with high home purchases and a housing boom, which contradicts "less affordability", because the investment (capital gain) dimension (leading to a bubble) was strong. Another interesting observation is the relatively less stable price-to-income ratios in the U.S. until 2013, particularly during the U.S. bubble period, after which they moved in tandem with the OECD average.

The 2022 Demographia International Housing Affordability report provides another source that measures housing affordability by the "median multiple,"[12] which is the ratio of median house price to the pre-tax gross median household income, and classifies housing as "affordable" if the multiple is 3.0 or below, 4.1–5.0 as "seriously unaffordable," and anything at 5.1 or higher as "severely unaffordable". In the case of the U.S., the median multiple of 56 major housing markets chosen for measurement is 5.0 in 2021. Only 1 U.S. market is classified as affordable and 9 as moderately unaffordable. The others are seriously (19), and severely (27) unaffordable, the latter has increased from 14 in 2019. The least affordable metropolitan market is San Jose, followed by Honolulu, San Francisco, and Los Angeles, with multiples of 12.6, 12, 11.8, and 10.7, respectively. Furthermore, according to the National Association of Realtors (NAR, 2020), the five least affordable Metropolitan Statistical Areas (MSAs) in the third quarter of 2019 are, in the order from most to less unaffordability, San Jose-Sunnyvale-Santa Clara, Anaheim-Santa Ana-Irvine, Lost Angeles-Long Beach-Glendale, San Francisco-Oakland-Hayward, and San-Diego-Carlsbad, all of which are in California. The next two MSAs are in Florida, namely Naples-Immokalee-Marco Island and Miami-Ford Lauderdale-West Palm Beach.

Figure 1.7 plots household savings and household expenditure on housing as a percentage of disposable income in the U.S. There are two plots of household spending, one using the left axis to compare with the household savings, and the other one (the dotted line) using a smaller scale on the right axis to show the oscillations more clearly. In general, household spending on housing has always been between 14% and 17% over the past 50 years. There was indeed a "sharp" increase in household spending by 2% (the dotted curve) into the 1980s. Back then, there were two rounds of recession, in 1980 and 1981–1982, which were coupled with extremely high inflation rates,

[12]Cox (2022).

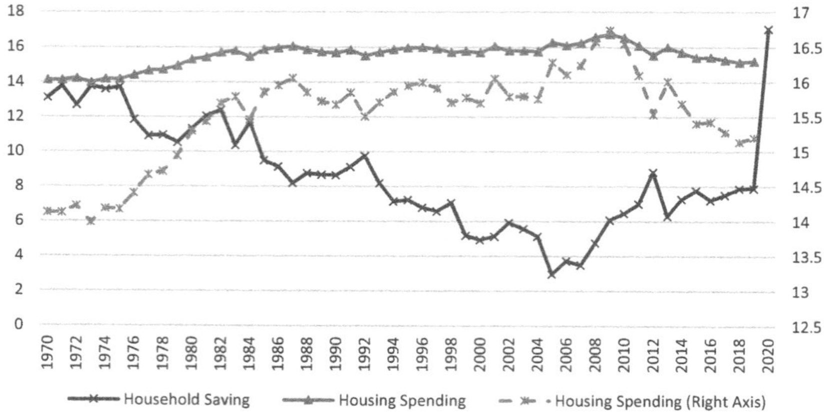

Figure 1.7 Household Savings and Housing Spending in the U.S. as a Percentage of Household Disposable Income

Source: OECD (2022).

and therefore interest rate hikes. The unemployment rate at the beginning of 1980 had reached 7%. Simultaneously, inflation hit 11%! To combat inflation, Paul Volcker, then Fed chairman, increased the Fed funds rate to 20% at the end of 1980, marking the beginning of the recession. By the end of 1982, unemployment even reached 11%; that of the residential construction industry was 22%. Finally, inflation fell to 5% by October 1982, and interest rates started to drop. While painful, Volcker's persistence in tightening the money supply and maintaining high interest rates prevented the double-digit inflation from coming back.[13]

In general, housing costs have been almost stable since the 1981–1982 recession, fluctuating within 1% difference until the outbreak of the GFC when it shot up to 16.8%, and dropping thereafter. U.S. households saved (or were able to save) less and less until government transfers shot up and were only gradually spent. As expected, household savings and housing expenditure series in the figure are negatively correlated. Higher housing costs would eat up savings in the net disposable income when all other expenses were held constant. Household saving was lowest at the peak of the housing price

[13]Sablik (2013).

bubble in 2005; and when the housing expenditure is high, savings start to increase, reaching a maximum of 16.74% in 2009.

In Chapter 11, we will cover how the pandemic has changed household tenure choice, offering further discussion about household spending on housing costs.

1.3. European Markets

It might be of interest to see what others encountered besides the U.S. Selected European countries are chosen for discussion in this section because they were also directly hard hit by the Global Financial Crisis, leading to the European debt crisis that lasted from 2008 to 2012.

1.3.1. Housing Costs

Housing costs in the United Kingdom (U.K.) are notably higher than other European countries. Panel (a) in Figure 1.8 shows that household expenditure for housing is always over 20% of the household disposable income in 1995–2020. Even Switzerland, a famously expensive country, is second only to the U.K. Housing costs in some Nordic countries shown in Panel (b) are similarly high.

Panel (c) shows the household expenditure for housing for the PIIGS countries, the acronym for Portugal, Ireland, Italy, Greece, and Spain, used during the GFC for their extremely troubling financial situations. Housing in Greece had the biggest price surge among the PIIGS countries after the crisis. This is also the country that got itself in really big trouble during the crisis. The other members also experienced a significant increase in housing costs relative to disposable income. Interestingly, except Ireland, all the other four, PIGS, are in Southern Europe, along the Mediterranean Sea, offering gorgeous weather and beautiful scenery all year round. A major proportion of the housing markets there are vacation homes, which are the second homes for many Northern European households. This is why, unlike primary homes that households live in, these vacation homes will be the first to be sold when market prices drop. As a result, the housing markets in the PIIGS countries boomed the fastest when economies were good, but were also hardest hit when prices went south.

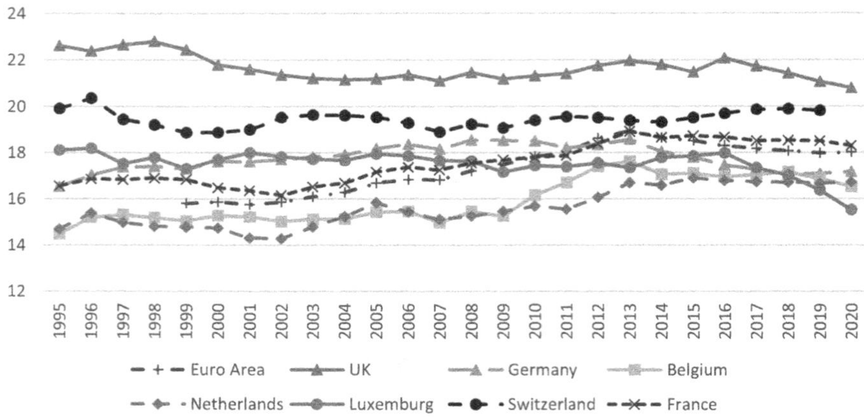

(a)

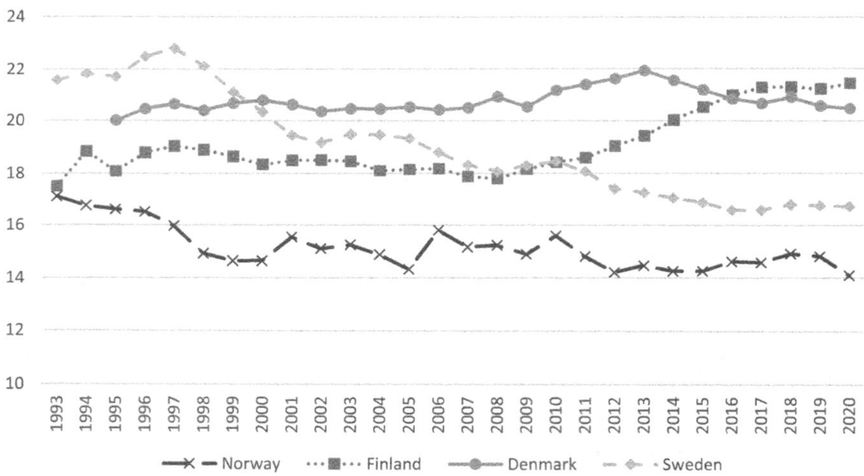

(b)

Figure 1.8 Household Expenditure on Housing as a Percentage of Household Disposable Income. Panel (a) Major European Countries and the Euro Area. Panel (b) Nordic Countries. Panel (c) The PIIGSs. Panel (d) Selected Central European Countries

Note: Data for Iceland are not available.
Source: OECD (2022).

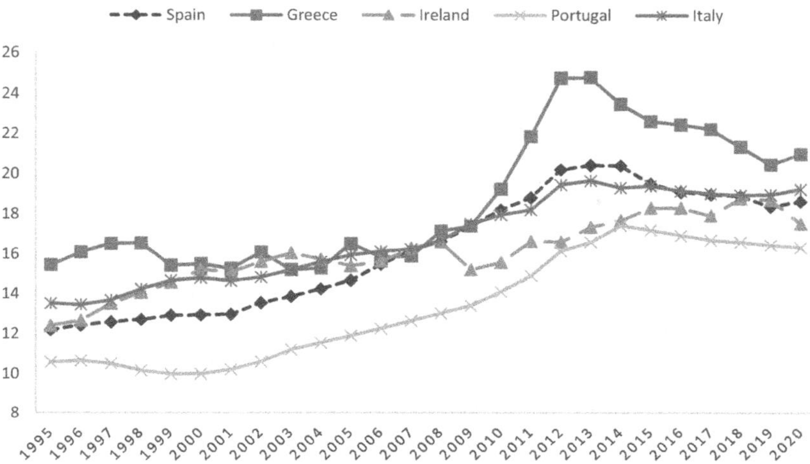

(c)

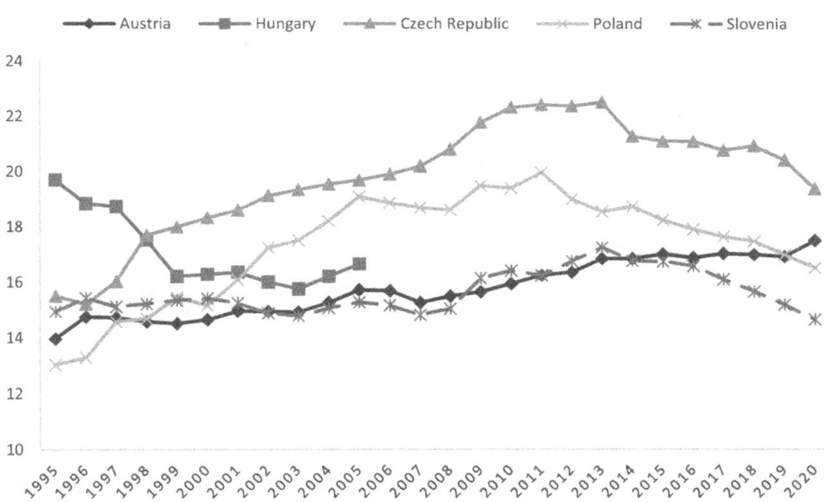

(d)

Figure 1.8 (*Continued*)

As for Central European countries, Panel (d) shows that the Czech Republic is the most expensive among the few countries shown, especially in the years after the Crisis. Figure 1.9 shows a few other countries for comparison. Unsurprisingly, Japan is expensive, although New Zealand is relatively even more expensive. We do not include the house price series here because we aim to focus

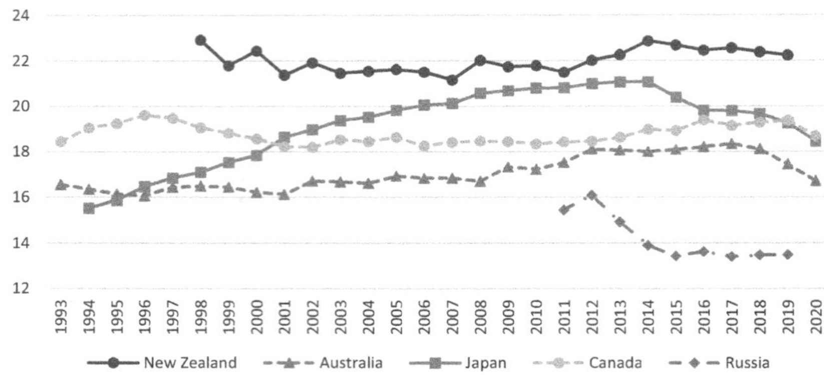

Figure 1.9 Household Expenditure on Housing as a Percentage of Household Disposable Income — Selected Other Countries

Source: OECD (2022).

on how the cost of housing affects the consumption of households. We will touch on house prices in Chapter 9 when we talk about the housing bubbles.

1.3.2. Homeownership Rates

The comprehensive social welfare systems across many European countries, which include free higher education, health care, social protection, and public housing are well known. Availability of housing is almost never an issue. The question for households is always the tenure choice. In some countries, households choose to rent because ownership is unaffordable. An example is the U.K. In other cases, renting is preferred; quality of living (or tax implications) without homeownership is not much affected. Typical cases are Switzerland and Germany. Table 1.1 lists the homeownership rates of selected European Countries.

The last row is the overall average across the European Union, not including the U.K., which completed Brexit in February 2020. Compared with this overall average, the homeownership rate in Norway is significantly higher than the other three Nordic countries. The Mediterranean countries within the PIIGS group all have above-average rates. People in Central European countries also tend to own their homes. Exceptions are Austria, Germany, and Switzerland. Households usually opt for renting rather than owning probably because there are fewer advantages to owning there.

Table 1.1 Homeownership Rates of Selected European Countries

	2011	2012	2013	2014	2015	2016	2017	2018	2019	2020
Western Europe										
Belgium	71.8	72.4	72.3	72.0	71.4	70.9	72.4	72.3	71.3	71.1
France	63.1	63.7	64.3	65.0	64.1	64.9	64.4	65.1	64.1	64.0
Netherlands	67.1	67.5	67.1	67.0	67.8	69.0	69.4	68.9	68.9	69.1
U.K.	67.9	66.7	64.6	64.4	63.5	63.4	65.0	65.2	65	
Nordic Countries										
Denmark	68.7	66.0	64.5	63.3	62.7	61.7	62.2	60.5	60.8	59.3
Finland	74.1	73.9	73.6	73.2	72.7	71.6	71.4	71.6	71.1	70.7
Norway	84.0	84.8	83.5	84.4	82.8	82.9	81.5	81.3	80.3	80.8
Sweden	65.7	66.1	66.3	65.6	66.2	65.2	65.2	64.1	63.6	64.5
Central Europe										
Austria	52.4	57.5	57.3	57.2	55.7	55.0	55.0	55.4	55.2	55.3
Czech Republic	80.1	80.4	80.1	78.9	78.0	78.2	78.5	78.7	78.6	78.9
Germany	53.4	53.3	52.6	52.5	51.9	51.7	51.4	51.5	51.1	50.5
Hungary	89.3	89.8	88.7	88.2	86.3	86.3	85.2	86.0	91.7	91.3
Luxembourg	68.2	70.8	73.0	72.5	73.2	73.9	74.7	71.2	70.9	68.4
Poland	82.1	82.4	83.8	83.5	83.7	83.4	84.2	84.0	84.2	85.6
Slovenia	77.5	76.2	76.6	76.7	76.2	75.1	75.6	75.1	74.8	74.6
Slovakia	90.2	90.4	90.5	90.3	89.3	89.5	90.1	91.3	90.9	92.3
Switzerland	43.8	43.8	44.0	44.5	43.4	42.5	41.3	42.5	41.6	42.3
The PIIGS										
Greece	75.9	75.9	75.8	74.0	75.1	73.9	73.3	73.5	75.4	73.9
Ireland	70.2	69.6	69.9	68.4	69.6	69.5	69.5	70.3	68.7	69.3
Italy	73.2	74.2	73.3	73.1	72.9	72.3	72.4	72.4	72.4	75.1
Portugal	75.0	74.5	74.2	74.9	74.8	75.2	74.7	74.5	73.9	77.3
Spain	79.7	78.9	77.7	78.8	78.2	77.8	77.1	76.3	76.2	75.1
European Union (No U.K.)	70.8	71.0	70.7	70.7	70.2	70.1	70.0	69.9	69.8	70.0

Source: Eurostat.

1.3.3. House Prices Relative to Income

According to the 2022 Demographia International Housing Affordability Report ("Demographia" hereafter),[14] Ireland and the U.K. are the only two European countries on the list of places with unaffordable housing, of which one Irish city is severely unaffordable, while there are one moderately, nine seriously, and 11 severely unaffordable in the U.K.[15]

[14]Cox (2022).
[15]Table ES-2 on page 1 of Cox (2022).

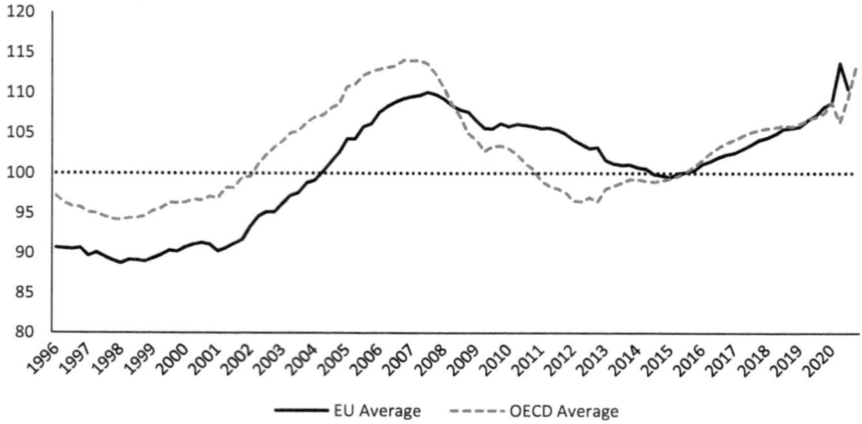

(a)

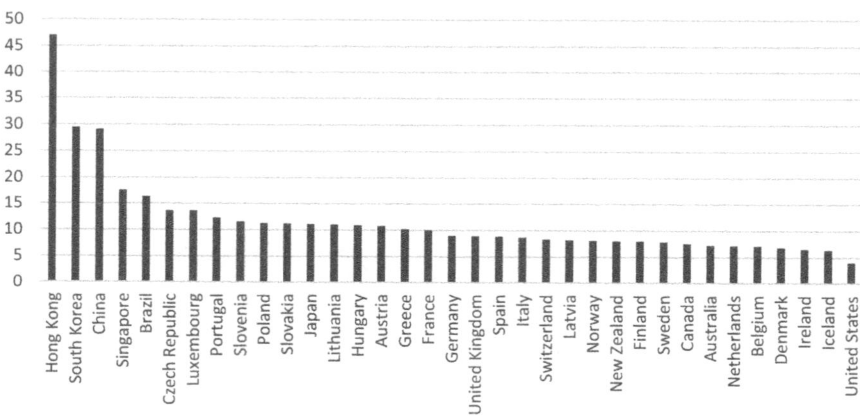

(b)

Figure 1.10 House Price-to-Income Ratios. Panel (a) Overall Average of European Union Countries and OECD Across Time. Panel (b) Ratios of Different Countries/States/City in 2022

Source: (a) OECD (2021). (b) Numbeo.[16]

[16]Even though Numbeo is a private online provider, has been widely cited by global media. Available at: https://www.numbeo.com/property-investment/rankings_by_country.jsp.

Relative to 1997, most of the median house price to the median income in these U.K. cities have doubled, meaning that house price surge is way more than income increase. The most serious price increases were in London. Since there are different ways of measuring housing affordability, we take note of the house price to income ratio as in Figure 1.6 and plot the average across all countries in the European Union versus that of the OECD in Panel (a) of Figure 1.10.

The OECD country average was higher before the GFC but not afterward, although the second half of the last decade saw both intertwined. Panel (b) shows the ratios across different countries in 2022. Depending on the type and size of housing units used for the price-to-income ratio, this can be quite different from those recorded in OECD (2021). As a reference, some non-European countries/states/cities are also included for comparison. For example, the most unaffordable place in the world both in Figure 1.10 and Demographia is Hong Kong. Its affordability multiple in Demographia is 23.2, meaning its median house price is 23.2 times the pre-tax gross median household income. The other four chosen as having the least affordable housing are China and South Korea, and the city-state, Singapore, all of which are in Asia, and Brazil.

In general, housing in central European countries is more unaffordable than in western or southern Europe. One can see from Figure 1.8 that housing cost relative to disposable income in Norway is indeed lower than the other three members in the group, which may be the reason for the higher homeownership. However, interest rates in Austria and Germany are not high enough to explain the homeownership difference. This is especially the case for Switzerland. Switzerland has the lowest homeownership rate among all countries listed in Table 1.1. Yet, from Figure 1.10, it is easy to see that the low ownership rate is not because of unaffordability, but more because of the different benefits from renting versus owning.

Figure 1.11 shows the cost burden of different tenure choices across several OECD countries in 2019.[17] Cost burden is defined

[17]OECD (2021).

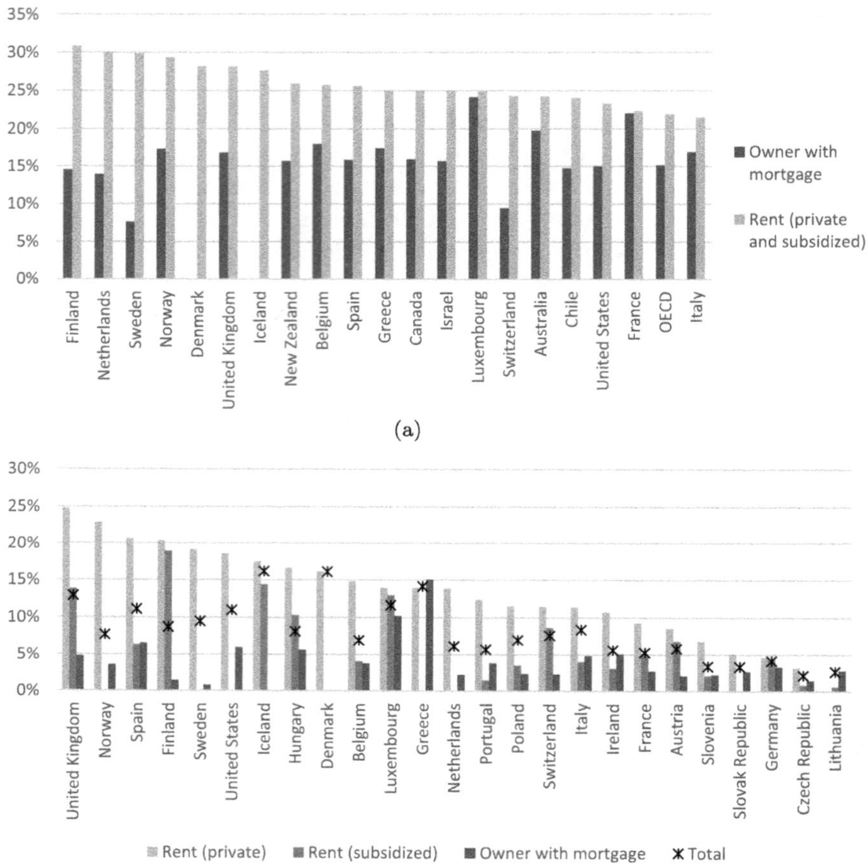

Figure 1.11 Housing Cost Burden of OECD Countries in 2019. Panel (a) Median Housing Cost (Mortgage or Rent) as a Share of Disposable Income. Panel (b) Percentage of Population Spending over 40% of Disposable Income on Housing Cost

Source: OECD (2021). Available at: https://www.oecd.org/housing/data/affordable-housing-database/housing-conditions.htm.

as the median mortgage burden for homeowners, which includes principal repayment plus interest, or median rent for tenants both in private rental and subsidized rental markets. Switzerland is among those with relatively lower housing payment burden for both homeowners and tenants (both private and public housing). Yet, more Swiss choose to rent than to own.

The OECD (2021) takes a further step in listing the share of the population that needs to spend 40% or more of their disposable income on housing costs, the so-called "overburden rate". This is depicted in Panel (b) of Figure 1.11, with the rates from renting (private and subsidized) and owning with mortgages separately shown. The asterisks in the figure represent the overall rate. Housing cost burden to households in Denmark and Iceland are the highest, with "overburden rates" of 16.1% and 16.2%, respectively. That of Greece is 14.2%, and 12.9% for the U.K. That of Switzerland is 7.6%. Hence, even though it is obvious that affordability is an important consideration for homeowners, preferred tenure choice is the dominant factor for homeownership in some countries.

1.4. Summary

We have introduced some data and some concepts about housing markets in the U.S. and various Western countries in terms of prices and affordability according to household income. We shall cover economic models of house prices and rents more formally in Chapter 3.

Appendix: Table and Map Showing the Regions and States in the U.S.

Pacific (West Coast)	Mountain	West North Central	West South Central	East North Central	South Atlantic	Mid-Atlantic	New England	East South Central
California	Arizona	Iowa	Arkansas	Illinois	North Carolina	New York	Connecticut	Alabama
Oregon	Colorado	Kansas	Louisiana	Indiana	South Carolina	Pennsylvania	Maine	Kentucky
Washington	Idaho	Minnesota	Oklahoma	Michigan	Georgia	New Jersey	Massachusetts	Mississippi
Alaska	Montana	Missouri	Texas	Ohio	Florida	Delaware	New Hampshire	Tennessee
Hawaii	Nevada	Nebraska		Wisconsin	Virginia	Maryland	Rhode Island	
	New Mexico	North Dakota			West Virginia	District of Columbia	Vermont	
	Utah	South Dakota						
	Wyoming							

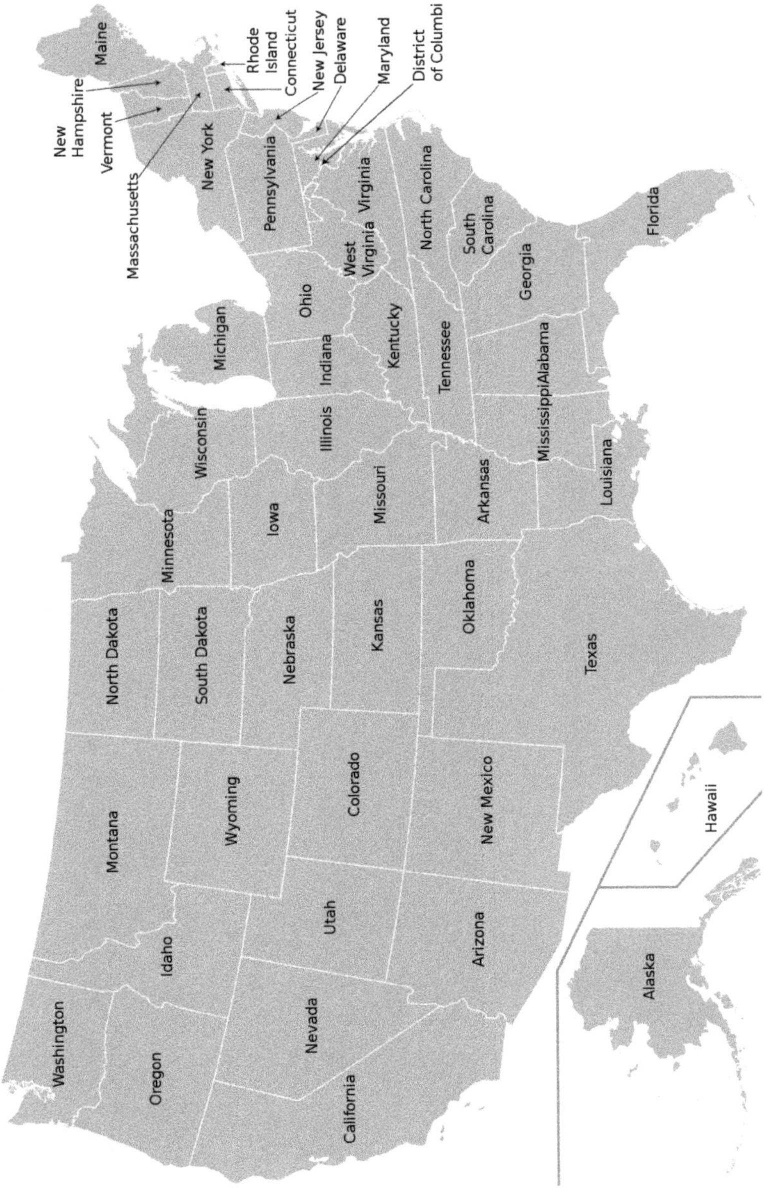

Source: The map is downloaded from 50States.com at https://www.50states.com/us.htm.

Chapter 2

Housing Markets: China

Since the establishment of the People's Republic of China (PRC) in 1949 and until recently, housing has always been supplied by the government via employment units, which were mainly State-owned. While it might sound good to have housing provided by the employment units, the system encountered a lot of the problems that often go along with publicly supplied housing. There were shortages of supply, low investment due to unattractive returns, corruption-led unfair allocation in geographical and amount of distribution, and poor management, not to mention the poor living quality.

The idea to change from welfare housing to private homeownership started when Deng Xiaoping initiated the Reform and Opening-up of China starting in 1977. It took several years into the early 1990s for the housing system to be reformed, aiming to commercialize the housing units. But it was not until 1998 that the old system with employer-distributed housing was completely replaced. Occupants were encouraged to purchase their occupied units at very affordable prices. The housing reform allowed low-income groups to rent, low- to medium-income groups to purchase "affordable housing", and high-income groups to buy "commercial housing".[1] Consequently, housing markets in China were fully commercialized, with housing units built

[1]State Council (1998), The Circular of the State Council on Further Deepening the Urban Housing System Reform and Accelerating Housing Construction, No. 23.

by commercial developers rather than employers. Housing finance and insurance systems were simultaneously established.

The development of the real estate markets was further enhanced by the State Council, from which "economically affordable housing" was distinguished from "commodity housing".[2] The former, also called "policy commercial housing", would ensure affordable housing for homeowners to live in, not for investment. The costs for development, neighborhood infrastructure, and loans and taxes for such housing projects are strictly controlled. For example, the developers were allowed to sell the units only at 5% higher than the construction costs. The sizes of these housing units must be small to medium sizes, with sales prices strictly monitored.

At the same time, the supply of housing units increased speedily according to market demands. Special statements were also made for reduction in administration costs and construction costs, and maintaining housing prices that should be reasonable and affordable to most families. Along with this is the availability of cheap rental housing units to meet the demand from urban families with minimal income. As a result, private companies were able to profit from selling properties in open markets and at market price.

The 10 years of full commercialization of the Chinese housing markets demonstrated the determination of the Chinese Central government to establish a "socialist economy with Chinese characteristics", a mixture of capitalism with socialism. The market was initially filled mostly by small developers at the beginning of the century. Some prospered and expanded to become large developers. We will come back to the story of these notoriously indebted large developers in Chapter 10. Housing markets nowadays are mostly market driven, while low-income families, particularly those in cities, have been guaranteed affordable housing, both for renting and for purchasing. China's housing has improved greatly, mainly from lifting constraints on, and/or supporting, markets and income growth.

Accompanying this was the development of a very fast-growing economy for the two and a half decades after Deng Xiaoping's Reforms. In just 30 years, China overtook Japan to become the

[2]State Council (2003), The Circular of the State Council on Promoting the Continuous and Healthy Development of the Real Estate Markets, December 8, 2003. CLI.2.49316.

world's second largest economy in 2010. Its GDP based on purchasing power parity constituted only 2.26% of the world's total in 1980, but reached 18.91% by October 2022. Its real GDP grew by 8.1% in 2021, contrasting the 5.9% of global growth, and compared to 5.6% of the U.S.[3] A major factor in the growth was Chinese housing.[4]

There have, however, been questions about the accuracy of China's GDP data for some time, for instance, because of incentives to overstate output growth at the local government level. There is a body of research that has looked at this. Some check official numbers against proxies for growth, and some look at more exotic variables, such as changes in nighttime illumination in cities. While the research is mixed, it looks like there is a consensus that GDP growth has been overstated. A study by the Brookings Institute (see Chen *et al.*, 2019) suggests that the overstatement has been on the order of 2%, which is probably a "middle of the road" type estimate. In what follows, we use the data for GDP that we have, but we need to keep in mind that it has to be taken with a grain of salt.

2.1. Economic Performance: GDP

Figure 2.1 shows the growth in the official measure of China's GDP over the period from 1980 to 2021, and the estimated change for 2022 to 2027, as released by the World Economic Outlook Database (October 2022) of the International Monetary Fund (IMF). It suggests that China has had strong economic growth for 40 years, even if it might be overstated by 2% per year. China was also affected by the GFC, mainly because its exports had significantly shrunk. As a result, the central government introduced the largest stimulus package ever, injecting RMB4 trillion into the market, equivalent to roughly USD 564 billion (USD 1.00 $\approx$ RMB7.088 at the end of 2022), and the downturn at the end of 2008 lasted for only a short time. GDP moved with double-digit growth since 2003 and reaching 14.2% in 2007 to only 9.6% in 2008 has quickly restored in 2009, eventually

[3]World Economic Outlook Update from IMF (2022a, 2022b), and https://www.imf.org/en/Countries/CHN#data.

[4]As mentioned below there are caveats about the GDP numbers. Nevertheless, they do not appear to be enough to change overall rankings significantly.

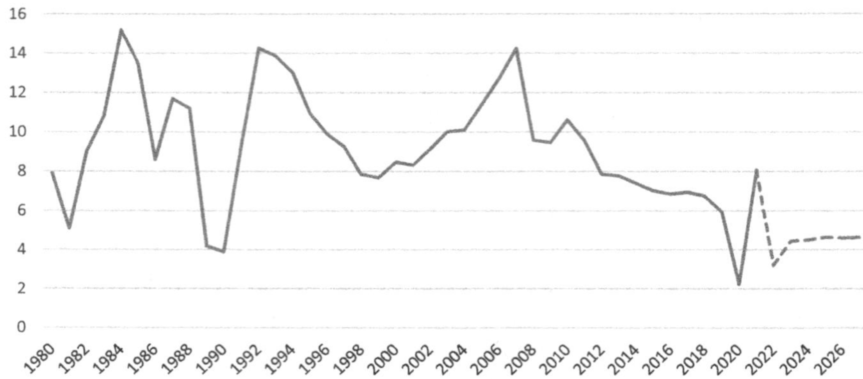

Figure 2.1 Growth in GDP in China

Note: The dotted curve represents estimates after 2021.

Source: World Economic Outlook Database (October, 2022).

reaching double-digit growth of 10.4% again in 2010.[5] In fact, a closer look would reveal that the GDP growth in the last quarter of 2008 was only 6%, but already 8% in the second quarter of 2009, and then 10% in the third quarter of the same year. At the same time, it surpassed Japan to become the second largest economy in the world and is now one of the BRICS (Brazil, Russia, India, China, and South Africa) countries.[6]

Likewise, as in Figure 2.2, GDP per capita (in USD) depicts an exponential increase over the past 42 years and was estimated to continue in the next 5 years into 2027. The growth in GDP per capita depicted in Panel (b) (inferred from Panel (a)) has been positive since 1995. When comparing with the growth rate of GDP in Figure 2.1, the per capita GDP growth in Panel (b) of Figure 2.2 shows more fluctuations. And despite a positive GDP growth all along, per capita

[5]Wong (2011) and Lin (2011) offered valuable discussions about how China has managed to recover from the Global Financial Crisis very rapidly by covering the issues of the Fiscal Stimulus Programme of China.

[6]The BRICS countries were driving up the global economy when other European and North American countries were still in the financial mess. However, extending through the decade, none of these BRICS countries continues to grow well except for China.

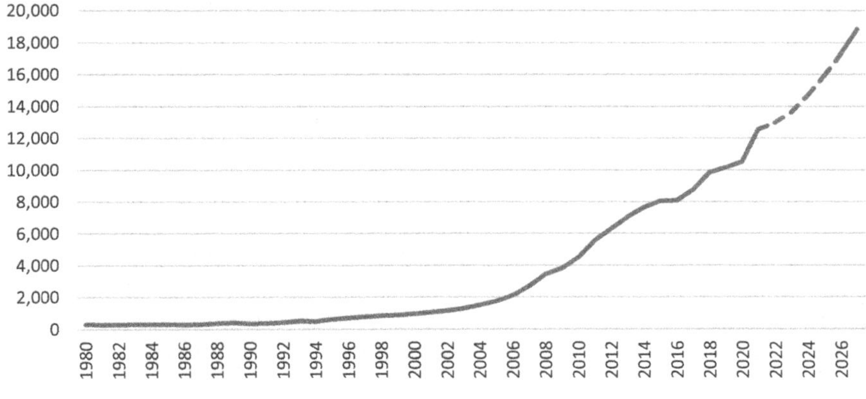

(a)

(b)

Figure 2.2 GDP per Capita of China (1980–2021, Estimates till 2027). Panel (a) GDP Per Capita in USD. Panel (b) Growth in GDP per Capita in percent per year

Source: (a) World Economic Outlook Database (October, 2022). (b) World Economic Outlook Database (October 2021) and author's calculations.

growth was actually negative in 1981, 1982, 1985, 1986, 1990, and 1994. That said, it has rarely gone below 5% since then, except in 2016, 2019, and 2020.

2.2. Where Does Housing Demand Come From?

Several factors have contributed to housing growth. Here are the ones that seem most important.

2.2.1. Rising Income

Housing demand growth is almost always either income-driven or finance-driven. Financial conditions of the people in China have become significantly better lately. So is income. Figure 2.3 shows per capita disposable income of China. In particular, Panel (a) shows per capita disposable income in the urban areas versus the rural areas, and compared to the overall average. The trends show more or less exponential increases. The income in 2021 of RMB35, 128 is 8.63 times that of 20 years ago (RMB4,070.38 in 2001), and is almost 9.5 times that of RMB3,721.34 in 2000.

Economic growth is obvious even in rural areas. Although people in rural areas generally earned less than those in urban areas, the gap between the two has widened even more over the years. If one focuses on the overall average, however, it is also obvious that the average is closer to the urban income than the rural income. This is very likely because more cities have been formed, and more of the population has moved from rural areas to urban cities. According to the National Bureau of Statistics of China,[7] the median per capita disposable incomes of the whole country, urban areas, and rural areas are RMB29,975, RMB43,504, and RMB16,902, respectively. Interestingly, the median incomes are 85.33%, 91.76%, and 89.28% of the averages for the three groups, respectively. This means that the increase in average per capita income is not because of a few really rich individuals.

Panel (b) of Figure 2.3 provides another view of the situation. Even though people in urban areas tend to earn more, the amount of disposable income in the rural areas actually grew faster after 2008, which is the time when the Chinese government injected the RMB 4 trillion financial stimulus. In fact, households in rural areas

[7]The "Household's Income and Consumption Expenditure in 2021" is released by the National Bureau of Statistics of China on January 18, 2022.

benefited from the initial success of the Chinese open economy in the 1990s, with higher growth in income than urban counterparts. Nevertheless, these growth rates are still not enough to lead them to incomes comparable with urban households. Both groups show

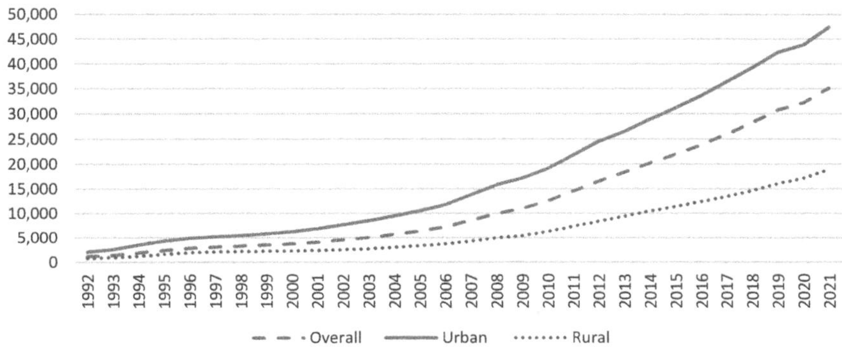

(a)

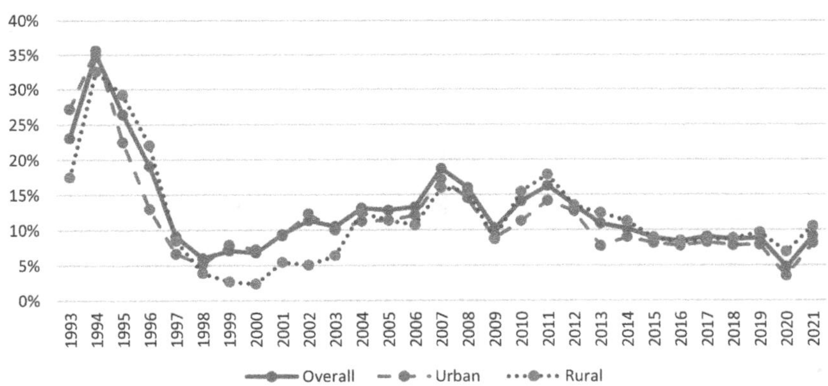

(b)

Figure 2.3 Per Capita Disposable Income China. Panel (a) Overall Average, and Rural versus Urban Areas (in RMB). Panel (b) Growth in Disposable Income, Overall Average, and Rural versus Urban Areas (in percentage). Panel (c) Urban to Rural Per Capita Disposable Income Ratio. Panel (d) Percentage Change in Urban-Rural Per Capita Disposable Income Ratio

Note: The earliest Per Capita Disposable incomes for urban and rural areas are available starting from 1993.

Source: National Bureau of Statistics of China and CEIC Data, https://www.ceicdata.com/en.

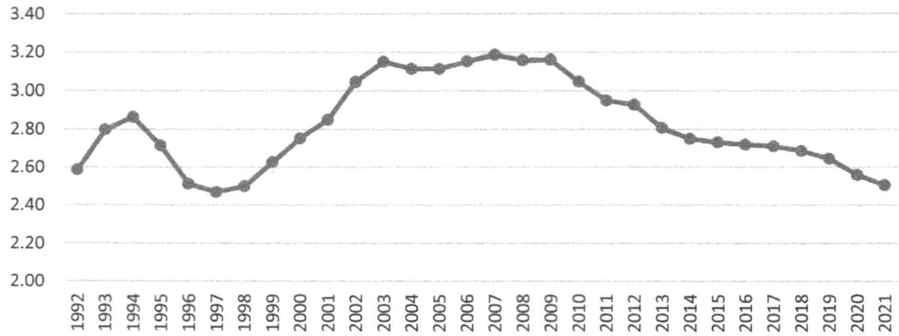

(c)

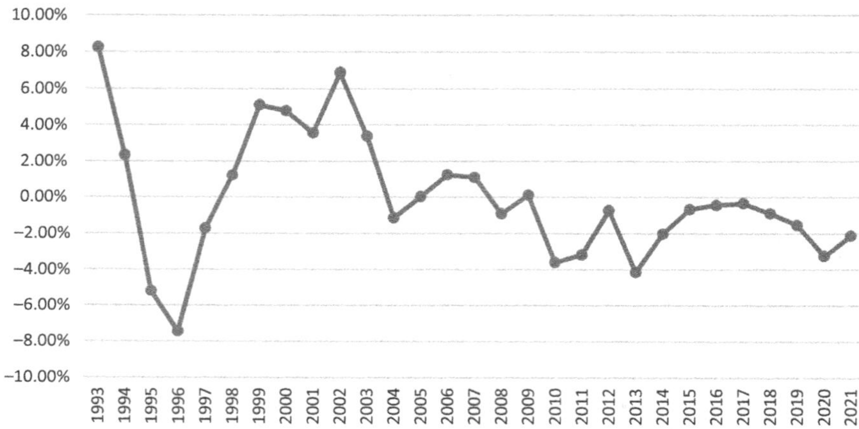

(d)

Figure 2.3 (*Continued*)

the highest growth of income in 1994, within which is a period of double-digit growth until 1997. Double-digit growth started again around 2002 (2004 for the rural areas) for slightly more than 10 years. Even though it has gone to single digits, the official number was never below 7% until 2020, the COVID-19 pandemic year, after which China was the first economy in the world to recover from the pandemic and reached 8.16% for urban areas and 10.5% for rural areas, or 9.13% overall. Panels (c) and (d) provide even clearer pictures by showing the ratio of disposable income per capita and its percentage change, respectively. The ratio has been between 2.4 and 3.2 over the past 30 years, peaking in the first decade of the century, but gradually dropping since, implying that people in rural areas have been earning more than before. Panel (d) displays this phenomenon in percentages.

No matter which countries they live in, Chinese are famous for saving a lot and spending little. Figure 2.4 shows the per capita consumption of China. In particular, Panel (a) of shows the per capita consumption income in the urban areas versus the rural areas, and compared to the overall average. There seems to be almost no difference in consumption regardless of where people lived, until 1988 when consumption in urban regions started to deviate from those in the rural areas. However, the enlarged graph at the bottom pane of

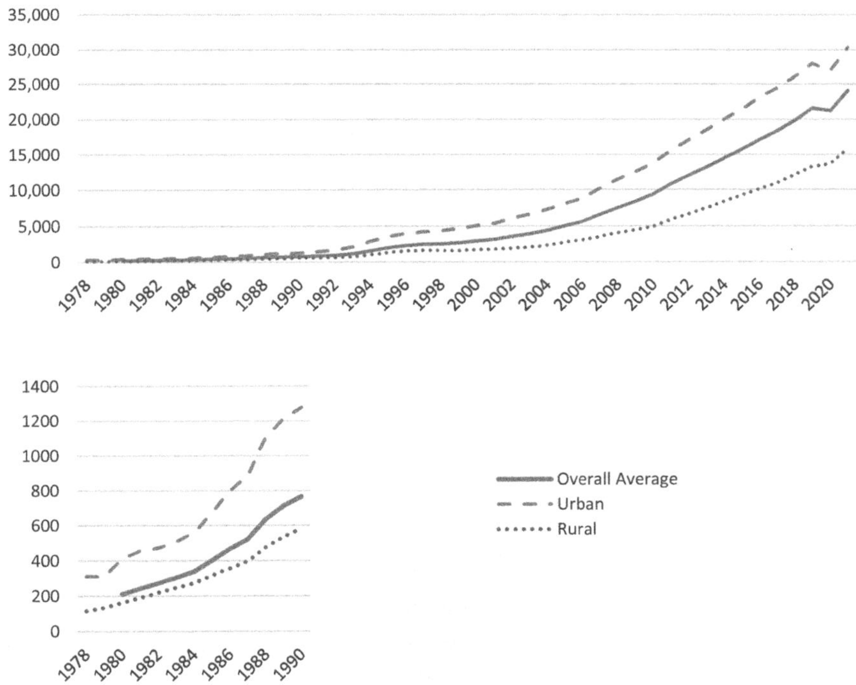

(a)

Figure 2.4 Per Capita Consumption in China. Panel (a) Overall Average, Urban and Rural Areas (in RMB). Panel (b) Ratio of Urban to Rural Per Capita Consumption. Panel (c) Growth in Consumption for Overall Average, Urban and Rural Areas (in percentage)

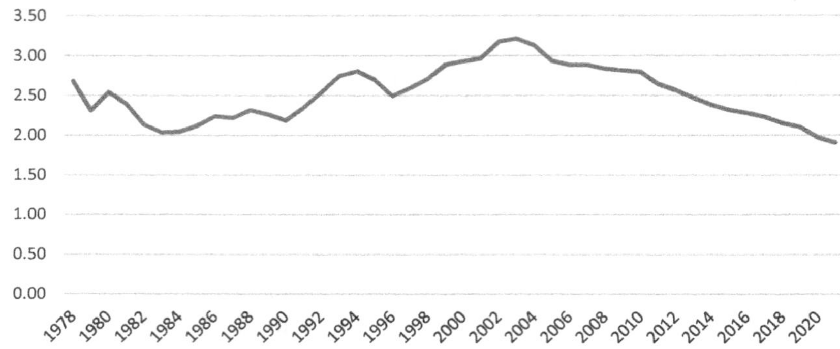

(b)

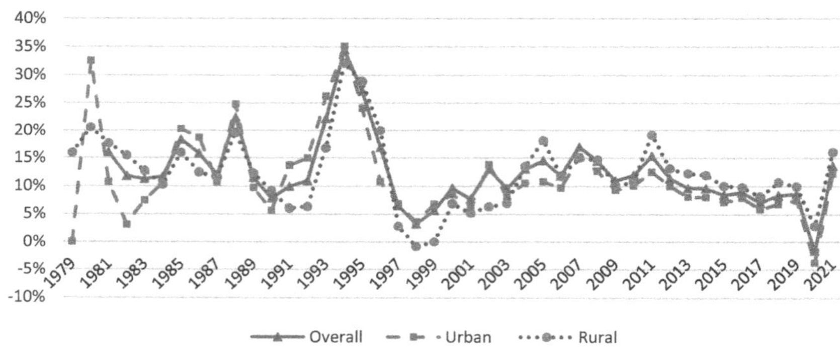

(c)

Figure 2.4 (*Continued*)

the Panel (a) shows that there is still a relatively big gap between the consumption levels of the two areas before 1988.

That overall average consumption is closer to rural consumption implies that there were more people in rural areas than in urban areas. This trend started to change in 1996 when the average began to pull away from the rural area consumption as more people migrated to urban areas. Per capita consumption in urban areas was 2.68 times that of rural areas in 1978, and was highest in 2003 at 3.21 times (see Panel (b)). The ratio gradually declined thereafter. This is also around the time the average per capita consumption is closer to the urban consumption than the rural counterpart, which means more people are now in the urban areas.

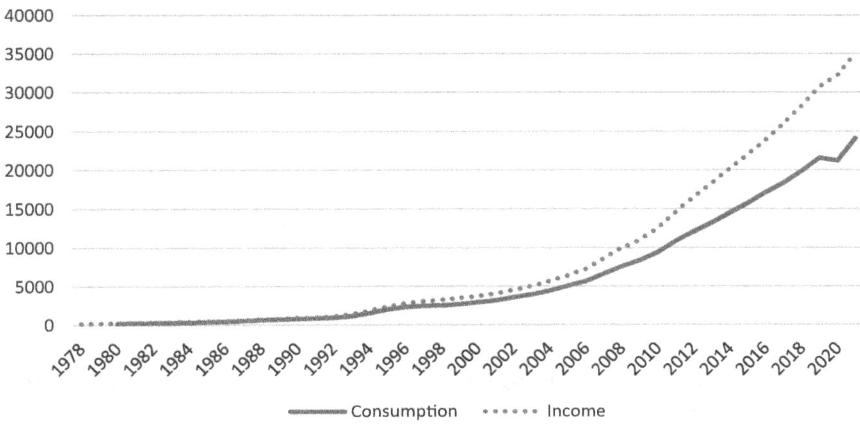

Figure 2.5 Per Capita Income versus Consumption

Panel (c) of Figure 2.4 shows the growth of per capita consumption. Overall, changes (positive or negative growth) underwent big swings until 1998, although almost all changes are positive, implying growth. Over the past 20 years, annual growth in consumption in urban areas always ranged between 5% and 15%; whereas that in rural areas was between 10% and 20%. This explains why households living in rural areas have steadily increased their amount of consumption faster than those living in cities. However, there is no detailed information about whether they bought more to enjoy better living, or because of inflation that made everything they consumed more expensive. The stimulus package after the GFC resulted in a bigger jump in the growth rate in 2011.[8] In any case, these figures provide some idea of the increase in household consumption over the years, which is of course due to increased household wealth.

Combining income and consumption, Figure 2.5 shows that households spent almost all that they earned before 1990. Gradually, however, the gap continues to widen thereafter. In fact, the ratio between income and consumption had stayed at a little over 1.1 until 1990 and then grew to about 1.5 by 2021.

[8]Details of the issues related to the Fiscal Stimulus Programme can be found in Wong (2011).

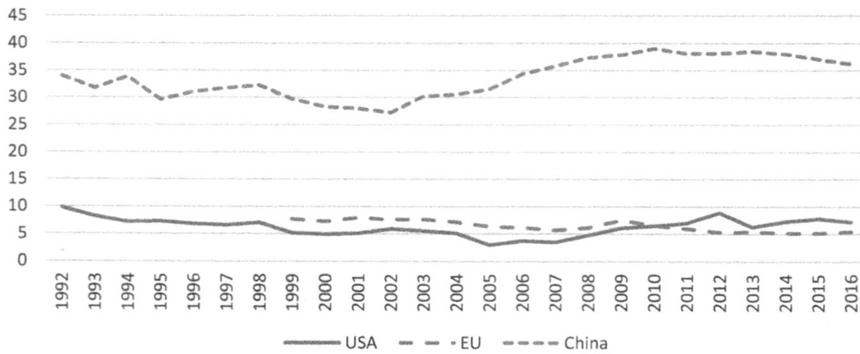

Figure 2.6 Household Savings Rates — China, European Union, and the United States

Source: World Economic Outlook, IMF.

Figure 2.6 depicts household savings rates as percentages of household disposable income for China, the European Union, and the U.S. Contrasting the 3%–10% in the U.S. and 5%–8% in the European Union, the savings rates for households in China of about 30%–40%, except the few years between 1999 and 2003, are quite high.[9] The habit of saving most of their income after spending on necessities has been very common in Asian culture; although this is changing among the younger generation. All data point to the increased affordability of homeownership.

Yet, another more crucial factor related to Chinese culture that helps support a big homeownership market has always been the widespread preference for owning one's bricks and mortar, both as shelter and as store of wealth.

2.2.2. Urbanization and City Tiers

The next issue is where, geographically, the housing markets are. The demand for housing has been continuously growing since the privatization of the housing markets, especially because of the Chinese central government's determination for urbanization. The number of cities has increased from 226 in 1981 to 687 by June 2020, classified

[9]Because the GDP is over-estimated as explained in Section 2.1, and consumption is probably not, the household savings is probably overestimated as well.

into 6 provincial-level cities, 293 prefectural-level cities, and 388 county-level cities. The 6 provincial-level cities include 4 Tier 1 cities, consisting of Beijing, Shanghai, Guangzhou, and Shenzhen,[10] and two Special Administrative Regions, being Hong Kong and Macao. Prefectural-level cities are classified into other tiers according to different criteria from different agents. For example, *YiCai Financial News Agency* is a leading agency in classifying cities into New Tier 1 cities, Tier 2, Tier 3, and Tier 4.[11] A list of these 4 Tier 1 cities, 15 New Tier 1, 30 Tier 2, and 70 Tier 3 cities from *YiCai* is provided in Appendix. Its classification criteria include the level of resource allocation for commercial activities, scope as urban hub, degree of people's activeness, degree of lifestyle diversity, and adaptability to future changes.

It is essential to know the tier system of China because market demands in Tier 1 cities are so much different and stronger than in other tiers. Housing demand in Tier 2 cities is also different from that in Tier 3 cities, and so on. The two Special Administrative Regions (SARs), Hong Kong and Macau, are surely well-developed and very important strategically and politically, too. But because of the "One Country Two System" policy, we shall not include these two SARs in the discussions about China.[12] The 4 Tier 1 cities are the most developed cities in China, with the biggest transportation system and city infrastructure, and are major political and cultural centers.

Naturally, young people are lured to these big metropolitan areas to find their careers and better living standards. The immigration rate to large cities was 30% for the period of 1998 to 2009.[13] Housing demand is huge. Given the limited land for development, these

---

[10]South China Morning Post, in its "China's Cities Classification" article, classified Beijing, Shanghai, Chongqing, Guangzhou and Tianjin as the 5 Tier 1 cities based on the criteria of having population of more than 15 million, GDP of over USD 300 billion, and that there are directly controlled by the Central Government. Information is retrieved from https://multimedia.scmp.com/2016/cities/.

[11]https://www.yicai.com/.

[12]The two SARs have their own legislature, currencies, and area codes, for example.

[13]Page 313 of Wang, Songtao, Su Han Chan, and Bohua Xu (2012). The Estimation and Determinants of the Price Elasticity of Housing Supply: Evidence from China, *Journal of Real Estate Research*, 34(3), 311–344.

cities have grown in size too, while the housing supply remains quite inelastic. Housing prices and rental rates are high as expected. Other city tiers are also subject to continuous development and an increasing degree of urbanization, with housing prices growing by 47% from 1998 to 2009. In the same period, the East, West, and Central regions experienced 36%, 24%, and 20% of overall price appreciation, respectively. That said, the housing markets in Tier 1 cities (all in the East) are uniquely different. According to Statista, when the housing markets slowed down significantly in other cities, these four cities still recorded growth of 4% in March 2019 to 6% in July 2021 in housing costs.[14]

Figure 2.7 depicts quarterly per capita disposable income and consumption of the country's average, Beijing and Shanghai, and the Guangdong province in Chinese yuan (RMB) for the period of 12/2012 to 12/2021. The data are from the National Bureau of Statistics (NBS) of China, which reports the data of the other 2 Tier 1 cities, Guangzhou and Shenzhen, within the Guangdong province. This is why the average per capita disposable income of the Guangdong province in Panel (a) is higher than the country average, although still far below that of Beijing and Shanghai. The graph shows distinct seasonality in disposable income with lower income in the second and third quarters but higher in the other two. The gap between the two quarters widened in time. It is worth noting that the disposable incomes of the 2 Tier 1 cities are always double that of the country average. That of Beijing is between 2.05 and 2.25 times, and that of Shanghai is between 2.20 and 2.36 times. Given this much higher income, no wonder young people opt for moving to big cities for better career development.

One might ask how could there be enough wealth for homeownership if living costs are also high, especially in Tier 1 cities? Panel (b) of Figure 2.7 shows the per capita consumption. Comparing consumption to disposable income would generate similar ideas to those shown in Figure 2.5 except that the lines there are not as oscillating because they are year-on-year, thus avoiding the seasonal effect within the year. According to the National Bureau of Statistics of China, "residence" constitutes 8.2% of the nationwide per capita

[14]Buchholz (2021) Chinese Housing Boom Slowed Outside Main Cities.

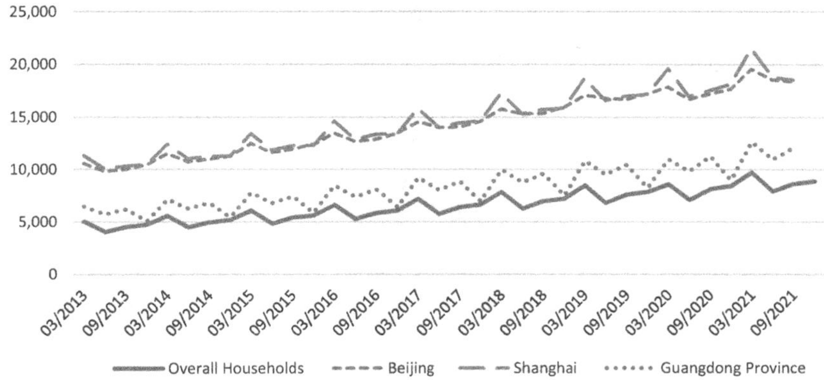

(a)

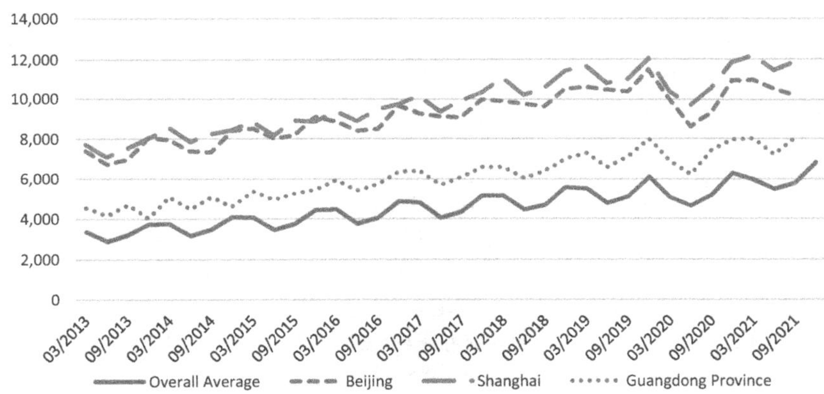

(b)

Figure 2.7 Income and Consumption — Overall Average versus Tier 1 Cities. Panel (a) Per Capita Quarterly Disposable Income (in RMB). Panel (b) Per Capita Quarterly Consumption (in RMB)

Source: National Bureau of Statistics of China.

expenditure in 2021, amounting to RMB5,641.[15] Urban households spent RMB7,405, which is 6.4% of per capita expenditure. On the other hand, rural households spent less, at RMB3,315, but representing 11.9% of their total expenditure.

[15]From the press release entitled "Households' Income and Consumption Expenditure in 2021" by National Bureau of Statistics of China on January 18, 2022.

So, one can easily guess that income and consumption patterns between the Tier 1 cities and the rest could be very different. In fact, the two groups have been described as "a tale of two property markets" in which the year-on-year price increase of new housing units in Shenzhen in February 2016 reached an astonishing 72% (45% for Beijing and 28% for Shanghai), while the average price increase of Tier 2 cities was only 1.5%; other cities actually experienced a drop of 0.1%.[16] We shall cover more about the housing market dynamics in the next section.

2.2.3. Residential Properties as Household Investments

According to the data from the China Index Academy, the general housing prices in China have surged from RMB1,934 in March 1998 to RMB10,396 in December 2021 (see Panel (a) of Figure 2.8). Notice that these prices are for the "commodity housing", which, as recalled, are the ones bought and sold for investment purposes. The corresponding growth rate plotted in Panel (b) shows a very clear seasonal pattern, with spikes in January every year (followed by a slight drop in the following month) as Chinese people tend to buy new homes before the Chinese New Year, which is anywhere between mid-January and mid-February. Panel (c) shows that the prices of RMB5,000 or less per square meter for the Tier 1 cities at the end of the last century to staggering levels of RMB56,844 in Shenzhen, RMB42,684 in Beijing, RMB36,741 in Shanghai, and RMB27,112 in Guangzhou in 2020. The country's overall average has also gone from as low as RMB1,857 in 1999 to RMB10,396 at the end of 2021. Note that the 2003–2013 period is classified as the "golden age" of the real estate industry in China when many new development companies were established, while 2014 onwards is called the "new normal" when China was starting to undergo slower but with better quality economic growth.[17] Interestingly, this period segmentation can also

[16]In "China Property, Tier-1 vs the rest" on 10 March, 2016 of *Financial Times*, by David Keohane.
[17]Zhang *et al.* (2016).

be seen in Panel (c) of Figure 2.8, with prices increasing at steeper rates in the "new normal" period.

More crucially, the growth rates of housing prices shown in Panel (d) are mostly positive, contributing to the almost ever-increasing housing prices. The highest growth of the Tier 1 cities of 37.2% to 51.1% happened in 2007, with the exception of Shanghai,

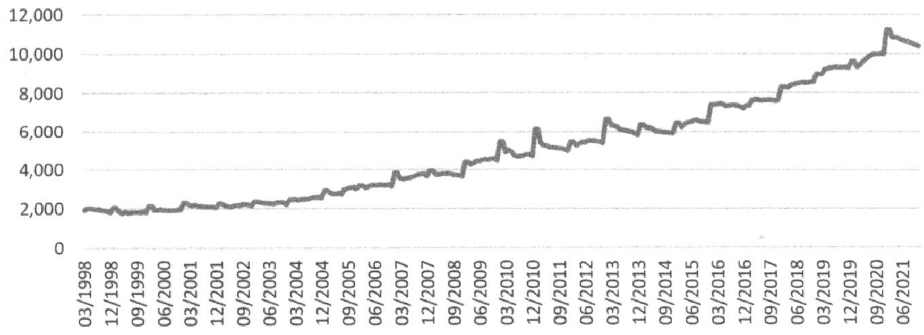

(a)

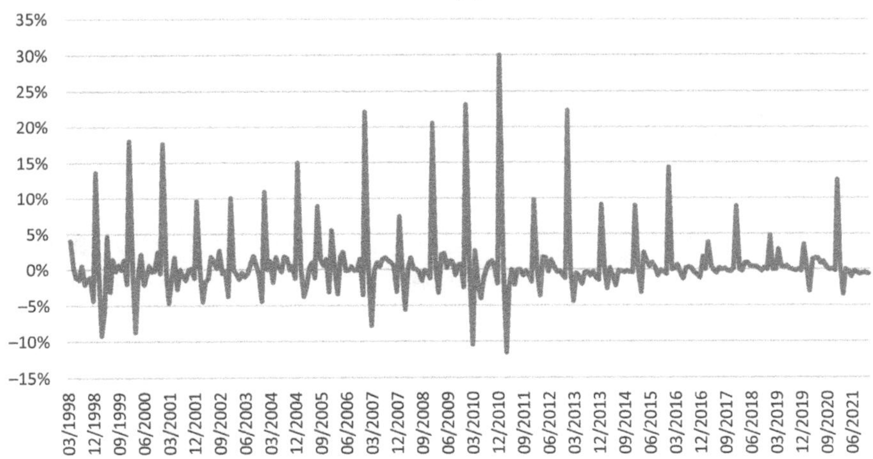

(b)

Figure 2.8 Chinese Residential Housing Prices. Panel (a) Average Price in Chinese Yuan (RMB) Per Square Meter. Panel (b) Percentage Change in Prices. Panel (c) Prices Per Square Meter (in RMB) in Tier 1 Cities Versus Country Average. Panel (d) Percentage Change in Prices in Tier 1 Cities versus Country Average

Source: (c) Chinese Index Academy.

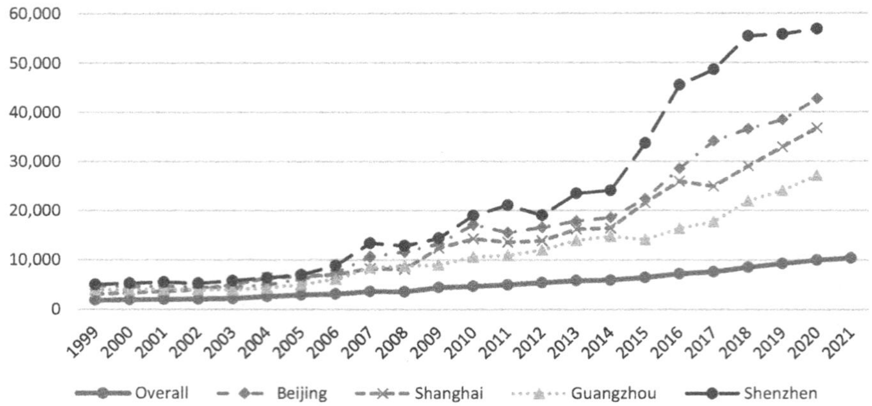

(c)

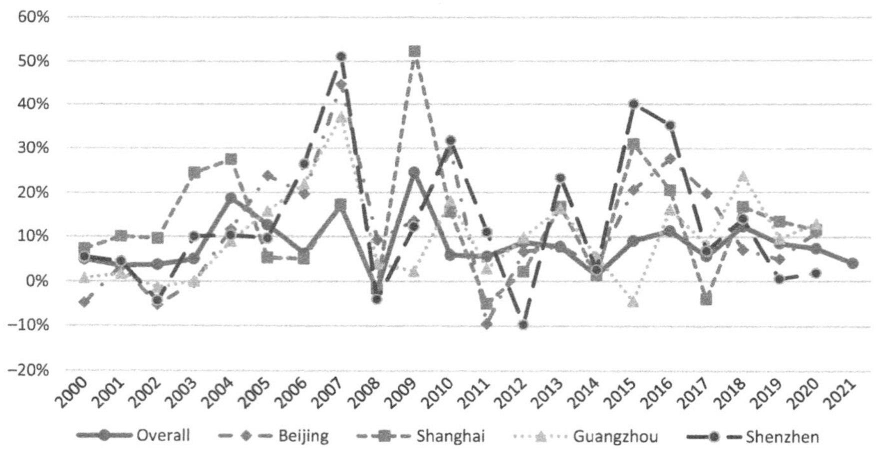

(d)

Figure 2.8 (*Continued*)

with which the growth of 52.4% occurred 2 years later, the same year when the overall country growth rate also peaked at 24.7%. The growth rates did not really die down even after the highly impactful policy measures in 2015. The slow-down occurred only after 2018. The housing markets in general still experienced growth during the COVID-19 pandemic turmoil in 2020; it was the second half of 2021 that really saw big corrections of the Chinese housing markets, which will be further discussed in later chapters.

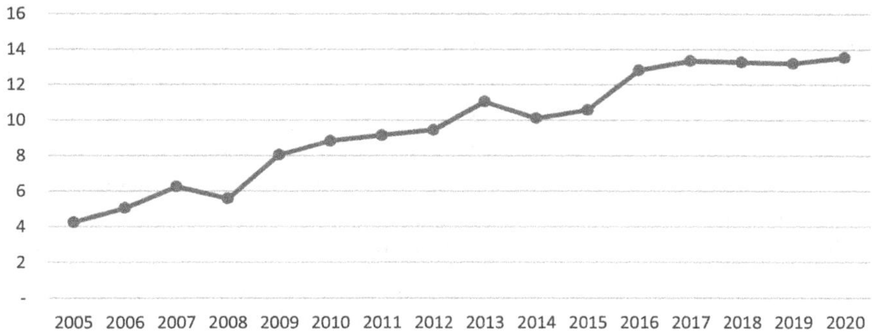

(a)

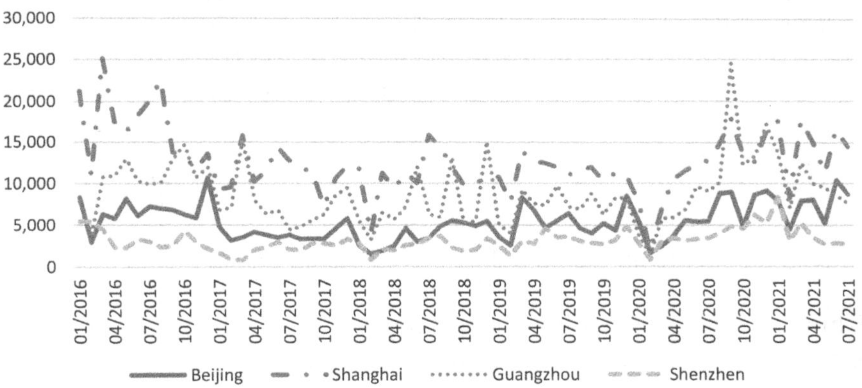

(b)

Figure 2.9 Number of Residential Units Sold Each Year. Panel (a) Total Units Sold in China (in Million units). Panel (b) Units Sold in Tier 1 Cities between 01/2016 and 07/2021

Source: CEIC Database.

Surging prices are mostly a result of continued demand growth. Most Chinese believe that it is due to what they call "rigid demand", that is, there are always people buying housing units, either as shelter or the Asian tradition of "bricks and mortar" investment to preserve wealth, and not for speculation. The former source of demand can be supported by the increased number of households from 329,088 in 1994 to 423.27 million in 2009, and then 494.157 million in 2020, according to the CEIC Database. The increase in just 2020 alone is 18.142 million. In the same year, a total of 13,555,925 units were sold, as shown in Panel (a) of Figure 2.9. This is only 3-quarters of the additional number of households in the same year, not to mention that a noticeable proportion of these sales include second homes, a lot of which are left vacant rather than being rented out or occupied. Also interesting is the phenomenon that these second homes are usually in the same cities where the owners live; the idea of a "vacation home" is almost non-existent for most households.

Panel (b) shows the number of housing units sold in the 4 Tier 1 cities, although the available data is only from January 2016 to July 2021 (from CEIC). All four cities experienced major drops in 2016, 2018, and 2020, all in February. The drop in 2020 is unsurprisingly due to the COVID-19 pandemic, which caused city lockdowns during the Chinese New Year that lasted from mid-January to the whole of February. The other 2 years reflect the period of major policy changes and economic downturns. Also noteworthy is that there are way fewer housing units sold in Shenzhen than in the other three Tier 1 cities. This perhaps explains why the prices are highest in Shenzhen, as demand is way higher than supply.

2.3. How about Supply?

China is big and has a lot of land, but not always in the right place. Urbanization and income growth ensure that people move into cities for jobs, better jobs, and better living. This has made the supply of space in cities, especially Tier 1 and other major cities, inelastic. Land is relatively scarce in these places. The cities have undergone expansion and merging with the neighboring townships as a result.

To provide an idea of how densely populated these prime cities are, just consider the population of, for example, Shanghai and Beijing of over 24.24 and 21.54 million, respectively, in 2018, according to the 2019 China Statistical Yearbook published by the National Bureau of Statistics of China, and an astonishing 31.02 million population in Chongqing. A Google search of the "ten most densely populated cities in China" will prompt several different websites that show you similar, but different, numbers. This is because there is a "floating population" of people moving around from location to location, or moving to cities where their "hukou" (i.e. documentation as legal residents of particular areas/cities) are not registered. The "hukou" system is a major reason why households buying second homes tend to choose properties in the same cities where they reside.

This is because one of the policies frequently adopted to cool down the housing markets is to prohibit households without their hukou from purchasing housing units from the same cities.

Having "hukou" means having access to a lot of benefits and rights in the city with "hukou", such as public services and social protection, which is why people moving to cities would like to register for their "hukou", much like successfully getting a "green card" in the U.S., although the definitions and functions are not really comparable.[18]

The huge demand for housing and an inelastic supply in the really populated cities have kept housing costs high. Moving away from the city centers, or to other second (or lower) tier cities, one could still easily see the ongoing construction of residential projects up to the beginning of the COVID-19 pandemic, but also with a lot of vacant flats. While the inventory of housing space grew from 4 billion square feet in 2011 to over 10 billion square feet in 5 years, the growth in Tier 1 cities was only from 310 billion to 390 billion in 2014 and then dropped slightly in 2015, according to Ed Glaeser and his co-authors.[19] On the other hand, that of the Tier 3 cities grew from 940 million to 3.45 billion in the same 5-year period. They also estimated that there were 20 square feet per capita of vacant real estate in Tier 1 cities using the Urban Household Survey from 2012. This is in contrast to the 37 square feet per capita in Tier 2 cities and 30 square feet per capita in Tier 3 cities. Interestingly, they also deduce the proportion of vacant areas between investors and developers. For instance, the ratio in Tier 1 cities would be 2 to 1, while that in other cities is closer to 50:50.

2.4. Summary

We have introduced the transformation of the housing markets in China in this chapter. We also pointed out the serious demands in top-tier cities, but huge supply in lower-tier cities. One can sense problems here. We will cover the story of imbalance, and how the various policies change the direction of the "scent" in Chapters 7, 10, and 11.

[18]It is extremely difficult to change the "hukou" from one city to another.

[19]Highlighted in Glaeser *et al.* (2017).

Appendix: Top 3 Tiers of Prefectural-Level Chinese Cities

Tier 1 Cities				
Beijing	Shanghai	Guangzhou		Shenzhen
New Tier 1 Cities				
Chengdu	Hangzhou	Chongqing	Xi'an	Wuhan
Nanjing	Tianjin	Zhengzhou	Changsha	Dongguan
Foshan	Qingdao	Shenyang	Ningbo	Suzhou
Tier 2 Cities				
Hefei	Kunming	Wuxi	Xiamen	Jinan
Fuzhou	Wenzhou	Dalian	Harbin	Changchun
Quanzhou	Shijiazhuang	Nanning	Jinhua	Guiyang
Nanchang	Changzhou	Jiaxing	Zhuhai	Nantong
Huizhou	Taiyuan	Zhongshan	Xuzhou	Shaoxing
Taizhou	Yantai	Lanzhou	Weifang	Linyi
Tier 3 Cities				
Langfang	Shantou	Baoding	Haikou	Yangzhou
Huzhou	Zhenjiang	Tangshan	Ürümqi	Luoyang
Yancheng	Hohhot	Jiangmen	Ganzhou	Xianyang
Jieyang	Taizhou	Jining	Zhangzhou	Wuhu
Yinchuan	Guilin	Handan	Zunyi	Zhanjiang
Fuyang	Lianyungang	Huaian	Hengyang	Putian
Liuzhou	Sanya	Mianyang	Zibo	Nanyang
Zhaoqing	Shangrao	Cangzhou	Ningde	Xinxiang
Yichang	Chuzhou	Jiujiang	Qingyuan	Shangqiu
Yueyang	Xinyang	Chaozhou	Weihai	Zhuzhou
Xiangyang	Ma'anshan	Suqian	Xingtai	Heze
Zhoukou	Yichun	Lishui	Bengbu	Maoming
Zhoushan	Anqing	Anshan	Daqing	Zhumadian
Sanming	Qinhuangdao	Jingzhou	Liuan	Dezhou

Source: This is from YiCai Global in 2021. Available at: https://www.yicai.com/news/101063860.html.

Chapter 3

Housing Dynamics and House Prices

This chapter provides a framework for analyzing housing markets, particularly rents and house prices, as well as the determination of mortgage rates and prices in the mortgage markets that usually fund housing markets. Formally, a mortgage is a debt instrument that is secured by the real property, in which, subject to regulations, the owner of the mortgage has the right to take the property if the borrower defaults. We paint with a broad brush, focusing on the U.S. market as an illustration of many of the mortgage markets in Europe and elsewhere. Recall from Chapter 1 that there are two distinct functions for housing: one is a provider of housing services, and another is a real asset that can accumulate wealth and which can be traded. These two functions are separate for rental housing but are bundled together for home-owners. However, because homeowners have the option of living in their housing unit or renting and investing elsewhere, they can be thought of as making separate choices for consumption and investment.

Before we begin, we need to emphasize our abstractions. Most important is that we think of homeowners as landlords who rent to themselves, and we use tenant rent or *owner-imputed rent* (rent on a comparable property) as an indicator of the value of services produced by owner-occupiers for themselves. We also make the abstraction of not distinguishing among housing types or locations, ignoring important differences among housing types and users. These abstractions save us from having to model more complicated housing markets.

We divide a typical housing market into three components:

1. Rental and owner-occupancy markets providing housing services measured by rents;
2. The price of housing as an asset, pricing with the value of the rental services from housing; and
3. House price adjusting over time: momentum and bubbles, and long-run fundamentals.

We use rent as a summary statistic that measures service flows for an average household, so we can move on to analysis of housing markets in a simple, but hopefully illuminating, way.

3.1. Housing, Rent, and House Prices

Housing is an important part of any economy. Income from housing services, real and imputed rent, in the U.S. is around 15% of its GDP. The value of the housing stock as a share of national wealth is around 40%. Housing is different from most consumer goods. It is a very important part of people's well-being, and it is very durable. Durability is beneficial to users, but it causes the production of housing inherently unstable. For instance, housing production generally varies in the range of 3%–5% of GDP in the U.S., which is not especially big. However, given an overall value of housing stock of around 200% of GDP, the two percentage point range indicates a large level of industry volatility. Small changes in the demand for housing will generate large percentage changes in production. For example, a 1% drop in demand for the stock of housing from 200% of GDP to 199% could lead to a 25% change in housing production (from 4% to 3%) if the gap were closed in one year. A burp in the demand for housing services can cause a recession for builders. With this in mind, we now turn to some theory, spiced up with some description/evidence later.

3.1.1. The Spot Market for Housing Services

Here we look at the structure of supply and demand in the housing market using the notions from a first course in economics. We begin with the rental market, a place where people buy housing services

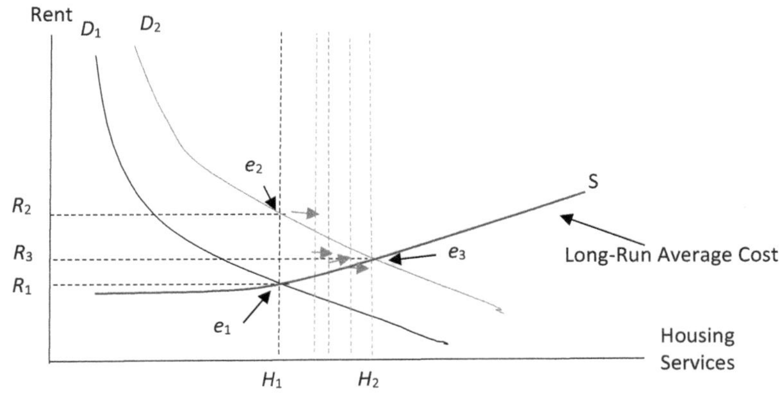

Figure 3.1 Rental Markets

for a short period of time. We can think of rent as the *spot price* of one unit (e.g. rent per square foot for 1 month) of housing services. The market can be represented by the standard demand and supply model. We assume that the supply of housing services in the short term is fixed by the available stock of housing. Demand for housing services falls when rents go up. This is depicted in Figure 3.1 by the two downward-sloping demand curves, D_1 and D_2. The demand curve D_1 is the point of departure. H_1 is the current fixed supply of housing; equilibrium is at e_1 with price R_1. The flatter curve, S, is the long-run supply curve, which represents rent levels that allow landlords to make enough returns to be in business. Production will go up when rents are above S, and down when they are below. Its position depends on input costs, taxes, zoning, etc. We ignore depreciation to make the calculations easier to see.

The demand curve can shift outward from changes in income, wealth, family structure, age, and other reasons. Let's assume that income increases and the curve shifts to D_2. Rents will increase to R_2 given that supply is still at H_1, and short-run equilibrium is at e_2. However, because rents at e_2 are well above profitable levels, the output will increase, as represented by the gradual shift of the light-dotted vertical lines to the right, depicting a gradual increase in housing stock, and a correspondingly gradual decrease in rents along the curve D_2. The increase in housing stock will stop when

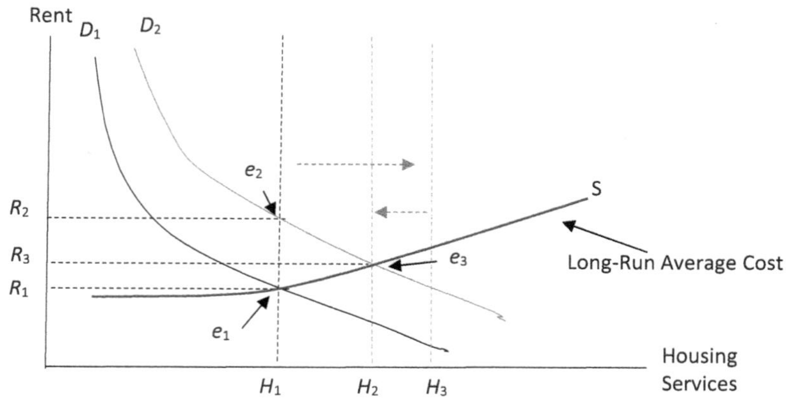

Figure 3.2 Overshooting in the Rental Market

the rent has descended to R_3 at the equilibrium point, e_3, which will be the long-run equilibrium. How much time this takes depends on the time needed to build different types of housing as well as on the extent to which builders saw the boom starting and tried to produce more sooner. So, even such a simple model can be complicated in reality.

Production usually reacts with lags which are different not only for different housing types, but also due to regulations, land accumulation, and so on. A problem is that the production of assets need not be coordinated. In the case of office buildings and big developments, for instance, it is possible that too many will be started simultaneously, leading to overproduction later. This is depicted in Figure 3.2, where there is supply overshooting from H_1 to H_3 before returning to the long-run equilibrium at e_3. Note in this case that the increases are not gradual. Increases come easily from production, but it is difficult to "un-produce" housing, and the decline from H_3 to H_2 has to wait for depreciation, use changes, or demolition, which will take very long, as one can imagine.

Several phenomena are buried in the pictures. For instance, different types of housing shift supply at different times. The first shift to the right might be from restoring or improving existing housing. It may also be converting existing housing or building small projects in places where zoning is easier. The aggregated data that we usually see are only averages of the processes at different lengths and time.

3.1.2. Determination of House Prices

We have only discussed rent so far. To model prices of housing as assets, we use models like those used in pricing shares in corporations. Rent is analogous to dividends from a stock, and owning property entitles the owner to current and future rents (real or imputed) in the same way as owners of the shares of a company are entitled to dividends and other payouts. Converting this stream into up-front values requires two bits of information that are the basis of almost all asset valuation: information about future revenues and the weights attached to those streams. The demand-supply relationship above suggests that given the likely volatility in rents, we should expect housing prices to be volatile, which makes future revenues hard to project and perhaps requires higher expected/average returns to compensate for the risk.

The weights on the future rent streams represent the way we discount benefits in the future. It begins with the time value of money. Future revenue is worth less than current revenue because investors have alternatives that will yield returns in the future. If you can earn 5% interest at a bank for a 1-year deposit, you will pay no more than \$1/1.05 for \$1 in a year. The 1.05 is a *discount factor*, which converts the future value into the present. You will discount at an even higher rate if the borrower is not a good bet to pay the dollar back, i.e. the discount rate includes the return that compensates the risk you take. We elaborate on this in Section 3.2.1.

In order to take all of this into account, our model of pricing dynamics for housing includes the following:

1. Given the currently available housing stock, supply and demand for housing services determines the value of housing services, which is measured by rent, whether real or imputed;
2. Expectations of future rents, or proxies for them (e.g. via forecasting models) are developed;
3. Housing price is the discounted value of all estimated net future rents;
4. Housing production adjusts to the excess supply of housing, measured as either excess profits from renting or excess of current market prices over the cost of production[1];

[1]These are essentially the same if we extend landlord behavior to be forward looking by including expected value of changes in net rent. In both cases, the dynamics of current to long run price are essentially the same.

5. There are lags and cycles in the market, and prices and production can over-adjust and form bubbles, which may or not be identifiable before they happen.

There are two common approaches to empirical work on housing (and other) markets: *structural models* and *reduced-form models*. In *structural models*, the demand and supply curves are estimated separately before being combined to predict rent and output simultaneously. With *reduced-form models*, we assume that there is a solution to an underlying structural model, such that the output of the model can be represented without knowing the details of the structure. The solution to the model can be directly estimated by finding the relationships between outputs (the things we want to know about) and inputs (the underlying factors that drive the model) without showing how they drive the model. Reduced form models are easier to estimate, and avoid technical problems involved in estimating structural models. However, they are *black box* models because they do not usually reveal the details of the structure. Knowing the reduced form does not in general allow us to get back to the structural model which, although esthetically preferable, is not necessary or worth the extra effort in many situations. So, there are tradeoffs. We show the usefulness of both below.

3.2. Asset Pricing: Applications to Housing and Mortgages

Housing is traded less frequently than most assets, which makes its price difficult, but certainly not impossible, to evaluate. Housing value can be estimated using the same methodology for evaluating assets like stocks, except that the "fundamental" value of a property is less likely to reflect the current market price. Nonetheless, obtaining at least the fundamental value is crucial to evaluating housing investments. Valuation is always about best guesses and depends on both insight and available data.

The values of both financial and real investments are generally estimated from the present or capitalized values of the services (often just cash flows) they generate. This begins with estimating service flow values, or a range of possible values, weighting them by when they are received, and adding them up, often with a large margin of error. Here we present basic valuation models as a way of understanding how investors estimate property values, how prices are determined in markets, and as a lead-in to pricing mortgages later in the chapter. We treat the property as either owned by landlords who rent to tenants or by owner-occupiers, who are treated as if they rent to themselves. The materials in this section might be very familiar and/or common-sense knowledge to many of you. Let us do a review nonetheless.

3.2.1. Time Value of Money and Present Value

Valuation models estimate today's value of a stream of *receipts* over time. We refer to the receipts as R_i (for (net) *rent*, *receipts*, or *cash-flows*), paid at the end of period i, ending after period n. The estimates could come from promised payments or from either "best-guess" estimates, or taken from estimates of a distribution of possibilities. We assume initially that investors act as if they are certain to receive (net) R_i from tenants. They have the option of investing in projects with a return given by r. Alternatively, we assume they can borrow at r, where r is adjusted for risk (e.g. AAA vs B credit rating). So, r is the benchmark for *opportunity cost* of doing the project, either in terms of financing costs or missed opportunity elsewhere, and is also the *discount* rate.

Nothing is really risk-free, but the assumption is ok for low-risk projects, like Treasury securities and where investors are indifferent to risk. A version of this is the *certainty-equivalent* approach, where investors use *expected* receipts, rather than promised receipts.[2] We will discuss this in more detail below. The important concept is that we are using a single scenario of the receipt pattern and pretending we are sure of it. Valuing the stream begins with understanding the time value of money.

Suppose you can earn a return of r by putting \$1 in the bank for a year so that you will have $1 + r$ dollars at the end of the year. Alternatively, as mentioned earlier, if someone offers you a dollar in a

[2] For instance, landlords will allow for average vacancy rates or occasional cost overruns.

year, you will pay at most $1/(1+r)$ dollars for it now. In a competitive market, the price of that security would be exactly $1/(1+r)$. Suppose you can reinvest another year at r, then the value of \$1 in 2 years now is $1/(1+r)^2$. More broadly, if you can earn a rate of r_n (% per year) on a comparable project that pays off \$1 in n years, then you will be willing to pay $\frac{1}{(1+r_n)^n}$ for a project that will pay \$1 in n years Then the *present value* of a stream of n payments from the asset beginning at time t is given by

$$P_t = \sum_{j=1}^{n} \frac{R_{t+j}}{(1+r_{t+j})^j}. \tag{3.1}$$

This can be applied to a range of financial assets and property valuation with sufficient tweaks and concerns about risk. Note that this allows interest rates for different periods to be different, although they usually are. So r_{t+j} need not be the same as r_{t+k}. Throughout what follows, we assume value and price are as of the beginning of period t, but rents and other cash flows are paid at the end.

We can simplify Eq. (3.1) by defining the discount factor, D^j, for a payment n period into the future as $D^j = (1+r_{t+j})^j$. Then using summation notation

$$P_t = \sum_{j=t}^{n} \frac{R_{t+j}}{(1+r_{t+j})^j} = \sum_{j=1}^{n} \frac{R_{t+j}}{D^j}. \tag{3.2}$$

Later we will use generalized versions of D to adjust for price growth and depreciation, but the use and the concept of present value will remain the same. For exposition purposes, we will often assume interest rates (and later on growth rates of revenues) are constant. These are reduced-form models in the sense that they are not trying to capture the underlying determinants of rent.

3.2.2. Some Examples

Variations in the discount factor depend on the details of contracts and what we pretend is true. Three common applications are[3]:

[3]The math that follows is somewhat tedious. If you can convince yourself that Eqs. (3.1) and (3.2) are ok and the idea of risk-adjusted present value is ok, you can skim most of the rest of this section and the next one.

1. *Constant discount rate and internal rate of return*

This is the case where the cash-flows are discounted at a constant rate, r_t. That is,

$$P_t = \frac{R_t}{(1+r_t)} + \frac{R_{t+1}}{(1+r_t)^2} + \cdots + \frac{R_{t+n}}{(1+r_t)^n}. \tag{3.3}$$

Although Eq. (3.3) is simpler than Eq. (3.1), it is not quite right because unequal patterns of interest rates, with r_t different for different times, can make a significant difference in valuation. As a result, this requires similarity in cash-flow structures across comparisons. It is often used to solve for r_t given P_t, which gives the internal rate of return (IRR) on the asset and can be compared to returns on comparable investments. This is also where we have higher r_t to compensate for riskier investments — "higher risk, higher return". Note that r_t is also the required rate of return, or, alternately, the hurdle rate.

2. *Balloon payments: Bonds*

With balloon payments, the usual setup is to involve small, mostly constant, amounts throughout and then a big lump sum at the end. If the periodic payments are interest payments, the terminal payment would be interest plus par or face value (the big *balloon payment*), similar to the stream of payments for a standard bond or debenture. The value or price of such a bond or debenture would be:

$$P_t = \frac{R_t}{(1+r_t)} + \frac{R_t}{(1+r_t)^2} + \cdots + \frac{R_t + \text{PAR}}{(1+r_t)^n}, \tag{3.4}$$

where R_t is the constant periodic payment, and PAR is the face or par value. If the discount rate, r_t, is the same as the rate with which PAR is multiplied to get R_t, then the price P_t should be equal to PAR. Also, in the case of bonds (or debentures), r_t is assumed to be the same for all payments of the bonds at any point in time, t, in which case it is the yield-to-maturity at t. Of course, one does not need to rule out the possibility that the discount rate for different periods can be different. That is,

$$P_t = \frac{R_t}{(1+r_{t+1})} + \frac{R_t}{(1+r_{t+2})^2} + \cdots + \frac{R_t + \text{PAR}}{(1+r_{t+n})^n}, \tag{3.5}$$

where r_{t+n} is the rate charge at time t for a payment to be received in n periods.

3. *Constant payments: Annuities*

An annuity refers to the same payment made periodically throughout an agreed period. This is similar to Eq. (3.4) except for the last payment, because there is no balloon payment, PAR. Most U.S. and Asian mortgages have payments structured as annuities. This allows borrowers to pay off their loans evenly over time and have a fixed time when they are paid off.

The value of such an arrangement is:

$$P_t = \frac{R_t}{(1+r_t)} + \frac{R_t}{(1+r_t)^2} + \cdots + \frac{R_t}{(1+r_t)^n}. \tag{3.6}$$

Again, one can assume, hypothetically, that interest rates for future payments remain constant at r_t, and the same argument as in Eq. (3.4) holds. Noting that the sum is of a geometric series in Eq. (3.6), it can be shown that

$$P_t = \frac{R_t}{r}\left(1 - \frac{1}{(1+r)^{n+1}}\right). \tag{3.7}$$

which is less tedious to calculate. It can also be inverted to find the level of R_t needed to get to price P_t. If the payment arrangement is a mortgage, R_t would be the required payment per period to fund a mortgage with balance P_t at time t. It also implies that as n becomes extremely large, the second term inside the parenthesis approaches zero, and the security price approaches

$$P_t = \frac{R_t}{r}. \tag{3.8}$$

This type of security is called a *perpetuity*.[4] It is a useful approximation for long-term bonds.

The classic tools for the valuation of these models are spreadsheets, which add up cash flows of various types by period and use

[4]In the 18th century, Britain consolidated some of its existing debt into Consul Bonds, which paid a fixed amount forever — presumably there would always be an England.

the "bottom line" as input into the present value calculation. This can be used to generate single scenarios as we are here, or simulations of multiple scenarios.

3.2.3. Extensions: Real Rates

Revenues are generally not constant. Investors are drawn to investments that grow in value, which suggests that growth needs to be incorporated explicitly into the valuation. We can convert rents over time into the initial rent, R_t, plus growth rates afterward. Treated in the same way as interest rates, growth rates applied to periods in the future are (geometric) averages of projected period-to-period growth rates over time. More specifically, define g^t as the growth rate from period t to $t+1$. Then the average growth rate projected over t periods, g_t, is defined by $(1+g_t)^t = (1+g^1)(1+g^2)(1+g^3)\cdots(1+g^t)$ (be sure to note the different subscripts and superscripts). It is sometimes the case that simple arithmetic averages give similar answers, particularly if the g^i is small.

Then Eq. (3.6) becomes

$$P_t = \frac{R_t}{(1+r_t)} + \frac{R_t(1+g_t)}{(1+r_{t+1})^2} + \cdots + \frac{R_t(1+g_{t+n-2})^{n-1} + P_{t+n}}{(1+r_{t+n-1})^n}, \quad (3.9)$$

which can be expressed as

$$\begin{aligned}\frac{P_t}{R_t} &= \frac{1}{(1+r_t)} + \frac{(1+g_t)}{(1+r_{t+1})^2} + \cdots + \frac{(1+g_{t+n-2})^{n-1}}{(1+r_{t+n-1})^n} \\ &\quad + \frac{P_{t+n}}{R_t(1+r_{t+n-1})^n} \\ &= \sum_{j=0}^{n-1} \frac{1}{D_j} + \frac{P_{t+n}}{R_t(1+r_{t+n-1})^n},\end{aligned} \quad (3.10)$$

where $D_j = \frac{(1+r_{t+j})^{j+1}}{(1+g_{t+j-1})^j}$.

D_j is the discount rate net of rent inflation. It is greater than one if rents grow slower than the interest rate but will "blow up" otherwise.

As mentioned above the discount rate can be approximated using[5]

$$D_t = \frac{(1+r_t)}{(1+g_{t-1})} \cong 1 + (r_t - g_{t-1}). \tag{3.11}$$

$\frac{P_t}{R_t}$ in Eq. (3.10) is analogous to the price-earnings ratio (P/E) for stocks, and its inverse, R/P, is analogous to what real estate investors call the "cap rate." The value of an indexed perpetuity that pays a fixed amount in "real" (inflation-adjusted) terms (like long-run P/E ratio) is given by $\frac{P_t}{R_t} = 1/(r-g)$. Its inverse is therefore a long-run cap rate. We can incorporate a version of depreciation into the formula by assuming that it causes rent income to grow at a lower rate, which means we can treat depreciation as a reinterpretation (lowering) of the growth rate of rental income. This suggests that D_j should generally be greater than one.

3.2.4. Trading

Equation (3.10) can be thought of as the value to an investor who holds the property, with a focus on using, rather than selling, it. Nevertheless, investors also trade assets and, as speculators, are mostly concerned about capital gains. Here we consider investors who always trade at the end of the period. Then the value over the trading period, t, is receipts plus sale value:

$$P_t = \frac{R_t}{(1+r_t)} + \frac{P_{t+1}}{(1+r_t)} = \frac{R_t}{(1+r_t)} + \frac{P_t(1+\pi_t)}{(1+r_t)}, \tag{3.12}$$

where π_t is price appreciation during the period, i.e. $\frac{P_{t+1}}{P_t} - 1$.

We can project this into the subsequent holding period. Then we have

$$P_{t+1} = \frac{R_{t+1}}{(1+r_t)} + \frac{P_{t+2}}{(1+r_t)}. \tag{3.13}$$

and therefore

$$P_t = \frac{R_t}{(1+r_t)} + \frac{(1+g_t)R_t}{(1+r_t)^2} + \frac{P_{t+2}}{(1+r_t)^2}. \tag{3.14}$$

[5]This is because $(1+r-g) = (1+r-g)\frac{(1+g)}{(1+g)} = \frac{(1+r+(r-g)g)}{(1+g)}$. If the time intervals are small, then $(r-g)g$ is quite small (e.g. $0.01 \times 0.02 = 0.002$ relative to 0.01 or 0.02) and can therefore be approximated by Eq. (3.11).

After continued iteration, we get the same old present value formula for an n period project:

$$\frac{P_t}{R_t} = \sum_{j=0}^{n-1} \frac{1}{D_j} + \frac{P_{t+n}}{R_t(1 + r_{t+n-1})^n}, \tag{3.15}$$

where the last term is the discounted value of the last sale. In other words, even if the asset is going to be traded every period, a forward-looking market (perfect foresight on average) will still charge a price equal to the present value of rents. The discounted terminal value is expected to approach zero as t increases because of the discounting effect. This, therefore, appears to rule out bubbles unless rents are unstable.

While Eq. (3.15) is not an especially realistic model (to be discussed below), it is a good place to start, especially if we are confident that rent projections are at least accurate on average.

Note that Eq. (3.12) implies that

$$(1 + r_t) - \frac{R_t}{P_t} = \frac{P_{t+1}}{P_t} = 1 + \pi_t. \tag{3.16}$$

and therefore,

$$\frac{R_t}{P_t} = r_t - \pi_t. \tag{3.17}$$

and

$$r_t = \frac{R_t}{P_t} + \pi_t. \tag{3.18}$$

Equation (3.17), which is equivalent to the "cap rate" to investors from Eq. (3.10), can be interpreted as a version of imputed rent relative to property value and is usually referred to as *user cost* to the homeowner. It is a broader notion of housing cost than *affordability* measures like payment burden (mortgage payments or ratio of mortgage payments to income) in Chapter 2. The reason is that it includes the investment benefit of owning, π_t. The cost of investment, r_t, includes borrowing cost and opportunity cost of downpayment. It is consistent with the notion that the overall opportunity cost of housing for a homeowner is the rent for a similar house at market rent.[6] Affordability is more of a short run, cash-flow type measure.[7]

It would be nice if pricing were as easy as is implied by Eq. (3.17) or Eq. (3.18). Prices would be the same as the expected present value of rents, and bubbles would be very unlikely in a "rational" system, not a bad first approximation. However, the formulation of π_t is likely to be based on ad hoc modelling of available datasets. That can produce bubbles, as we will see in Section 3.3. To go further, we have to look more at pricing and risk.

3.2.5. Explicitly Incorporating Risk — The Expected Present Value (EPV) Model

In reality, assuming certainty equivalence and single-scenario modeling by assuming only one possible outcome for risky assets like real estate is not quite right. It is sometimes important to consider all possibilities for the rental rates, R's. For instance, a widely dispersed distribution of R's might be worse than a less dispersed with a smaller mean. If investors are indifferent between \$50 with certainty and a coin toss that pays either nothing or \$100, they are said to be risk-neutral because they only care about the expected value of both being \$50.[8] In that case, a security forming a 50-50 chance in a competitive market would be priced at 50, as would a sure 50.

In what follows, we assume risk neutrality because it is easier to manage and does not usually make much difference. Risk neutrality assumes investors are neither risk-averse nor risk-loving among different levels of risk. A way of handling risk aversion is to think of risk as coming from reinterpreting variables being above or below their underlying expected values. For instance, if borrowers needed a

[6]This is the methodology used in the Consumer Price Index, CPI, in the U.S. for calculating housing cost for homeowners.

[7]See Dougherty and Van Order (1982) for a model and an application of user cost.

[8]Risk aversion can be handled in the model, for instance, by having investors concerned with a welfare function that incorporates their own value preferences for $w(\cdot)$. They will then concern about the expected value of this welfare function, $E(w(\cdot))$. This is interesting but does not matter much for what we try to explain.

cushion of 2 to accept the risk, then this could be interpreted as pretending that the mean is 48 instead of 50. We represent the expected or average value of a variable, x, by $E(x)$.

Even with risk neutrality, dispersion in payoffs can still matter. Suppose the present value is determined by uncertain factors, like revenue or interest rates, and its value can only be given by expected present value, which is of course very complicated. But let's simplify by assuming it depends on a single factor, a random variable, x, for instance, the interest rate used in discounting, so that we express the present value as:

$$P_t = E\left[\sum_{j=1}^{n} \frac{R_{t+j}}{(1+r_{t+j})^j}\right] = E\left(V(x)\right), \tag{3.19}$$

where $V(x)$ is a general way of expressing how the present value depends on x. Risk neutrality means that investors care only about the expected present value of their investment, $E(V(x))$. The certainty equivalent method assumes that $E(V(x)) = V(E(x))$, which is generally not the case. This is unfortunate because the latter is easier to calculate. But the difference does matter, as we shall see below.

3.2.6. Why Modeling Risk Matters: Shapes of Things[9] and Convexity

To understand the difference between the expected present value and certainty equivalence, consider a one-period example paying \$1 at the end of the period. The current value is

$$P = E\left(\frac{1}{1+r}\right). \tag{3.20}$$

Figure 3.3 depicts the curve $P(r,t) = 1/(1+r)$. The payoff is risk-free, but the interest rate is random. We assume r is determined by a coin toss with 50–50 chance of being high at $r^* + \Delta$, or low at $r^* - \Delta$, and its expected value is r^*. Assume its possible values are 0.10 and 0.08, respectively. Suppose the information set is simple, such that

[9]Homage to the late, great Jeff Beck.

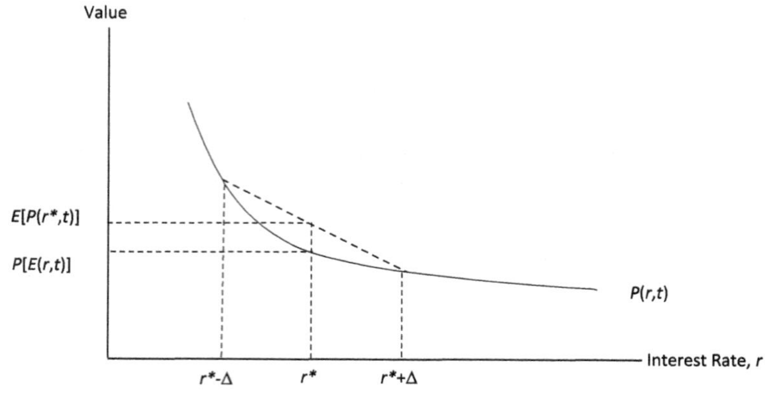

Figure 3.3 Discounting and Expected Present Value

the payoffs are determined by a coin toss, and so the value (and the payoff) is either 1/1.08 or 1/1.10; the corresponding market price would be $(1/1.08 + 1/1.10)/2 = \$0.91751$. The certainty equivalent value with $r = 0.09$ is \$0.91743, which is $P[E(r^*, t)]$ in the figure.

It is clear here that the expected present value, $E[P(r^*, t)]$, is greater than the certainty equivalent value, $P[E(r^*, t)]$. The reason is that the shape of the curve $1/(1+r)$ is such that a drop in interest rates increases value by more than the same rise would decrease value. This property is called *convexity* (i.e. the second derivative with respect to r is positive). It implies that volatility might not be all bad for property owners. It is a common property of bonds. It does not make a big difference here, relative to the certainty equivalent model, because convexity is small at one period out. Note however, that the value of an n-year risk-free pure discount bond with r as the discount rate is $1/(1+r)^n$, which implies that convexity increases as n increases (Check the second derivative!). Certainty equivalence can be very misleading if the R's and r's are correlated. For example, payoffs are lower (e.g. due to higher default rates) when interest rates are increased. We shall see in the next chapter that this is a big deal for mortgages that can be refinanced. The option to refinance can turn the shape from convex to concave, and the option to default can add concavity to the relationship between default risk and mortgage rates.

3.2.7. Monte Carlo Methods

A widely applicable approach to estimating the expected present value for risky assets like the example above is *Monte Carlo* simulation, which uses repeated simulations as follows: Step one is to estimate the probability distributions of the variables to be simulated. Step two is to draw random values from the distributions over the period of the model to obtain a scenario, and then discounting to produce the present value. Both the numerator and denominator can be in probabilistic functions. Step two is repeated for the desired number of times, usually in hundreds (depending on the complexity of the mathematical model and the computing time). Finally, averaging across scenarios gives an estimate of the expected present value.

A simple example can be taken from Figure 3.3, where the distribution is generated by two possibilities, up and down. Tossing coins repeatedly would generate the two points in the figure; averaging across the results would generate point r^*. Of course, most problems are much more complicated and involve messy correlations among variables that are important but not always easy to estimate. As an example, a problem with pricing collateralized debt obligations (CDOs, to be discussed in Chapter 5) before the GFC was the seriously underestimated correlations among default rates.

3.3. Market Prices, Momentum, and Bubbles: Anything Interesting?

Judge Potter Stewart, a former justice on the U.S. Supreme Court, while discussing obscenity once famously gave a non-definition of obscenity, "I shall not today attempt further to define the kinds of material I understand to be embraced within that shorthand description, and perhaps I could never succeed in intelligibly doing so. *But I know it when I see it ...*"[10] Bubbles are rather like obscenity.

[10]Retrieved from "Potter Stewart" by Artemus Ward in *The First Amendment Encyclopedia* of the Middle Tennessee State University. Available at: https://www.mtsu.edu/first-amendment/article/1359/potter-stewart#:~:text=Stewart%20concluded%20that%20criminal%20obscenity,succeed%20in%20intelligibly%20doing%20so.

We cannot really define them ahead of time or predict them. We only know them when we see them burst. Indeed, if we could identify them beforehand they would probably not happen. So how can we see them? Let's start from the basics.

Extending the trading model to incorporate expected present value gives:

$$\frac{P_t}{R_t} = E\left(\frac{1}{1+r_t}\right) + E\left(\frac{1+\pi_t)}{1+r_t)}\bigg|\,\Omega_t\right), \tag{3.21}$$

where the symbol Ω_t denotes the information available to players for estimating future values. Ω_t is symbolically important because it reminds us that we need a lot of information about what people know and how it can/will be used before we can answer valuation questions. It can be anything from a complete set of everything that can be known to just past values of prices. We cannot simply assume that projections of rents will be unbiased estimates (more discussion on the "unbiased" measure of rent is in Appendix).

Iterating as we did to obtain Eq. (3.15), the expected present value is

$$\frac{P_t}{R_t} = E\left(\sum_{j=t}^{n} D^{-j}\,\Bigg|\,\Omega_t\right) + E\left(\frac{1}{{D_{t+n}}^{n}}\bigg|\,\Omega_t\right) \quad \text{and}$$

$$\frac{1}{D^i} = \frac{(1+r_i)^i}{1+d_i} \cong \frac{1}{(r_i - d_i)}. \tag{3.22}$$

To conserve notation, let $\rho_t = \frac{R_t}{P_t}$. Then, in a manner analogous to how we got Eq. (3.17), we can represent Eq. (3.21) as

$$\rho_t = r_t - E(\pi_t|\,\Omega_t). \tag{3.23}$$

This is the current price given future expectations of prices in the same ways as Eq. (3.17) except that the $E(\cdot)$ operator reminds us of the convexity issue in Figure 3.3, and from the presence of Ω_t, that the information set available is important. It is especially complicated because we are dealing with projections from limited information sets, which can lead to very uncertain estimates of future revenues. Furthermore, the items in the income streams can be correlated in all sorts of ways and correlated with interest rates, making it all even more complicated.

An easy case is where Ω_t is big and available to everyone, so that investors estimate the correct expected value of π, and asymmetric information will not be not a problem. Although this is not the same as perfect foresight, at least it means that the traders can estimate a consistent model of future prices, rents, and interest rates.[11] Unfortunately, that is asking for too much. In a property or other markets that are new or where information sets are small, we have to observe how these sets might project expectations. As discussed above, a simple choice is to use models that begin with Eq. (3.23) and work on ways of getting at $E(\pi_t|\,\Omega_t)$. Given the range of possible information sets, this makes for a wide range of possibilities and ways of making mistakes.

So it is messy and with little clear guidance from theory. In the extreme, investors try to buy now to preempt price increases later based on recent price increases and in turn drive prices up, stirring new expectation of prices going up. In this case, where prices feed on themselves, bubbles are formed. But bubbles are "not really bubbles" until their existence is proven by the market crash. We next explore models like this where traders have some information about long-run fundamentals, but the models can still generate momentum and bubbles.

3.3.1. An Approach to Modeling Price Changes: The Problem with History

An acceptable but not tight approach (rather like *meatball surgery* in the television show "Mash") is to find the factors that cause house prices to rise and fall (e.g. interest rates, previous prices or determinants of rents, etc.) and insert their current and past values into the right-hand side of a reduced form model. This implicitly allows for expectations to be formed in backward-looking ways such as past values of price growth affecting current expectations,

[11]By *consistent*, we mean in the classic statistical sense of converging to "true" values as sample size becomes increasingly large.

which can imply momentum. It is also a black box, which may be OK for forecasting but less so for understanding the structure of the problem.

To model momentum mathematically, a version of Eq. (3.23) which only depends on history can (after a bunch of steps) be written as the following:

$$\Delta\rho_t = \alpha\left[\rho_t - \sum_{i=1}^{n} b_i(x_{t-i})\right] - \sum_{i=1}^{n}[a_i(\Delta\rho_{t-i}) + b_i\Delta x_{t-i}], \quad (3.24)$$

where Δx_{t-i} is the change from the previous period $t-i$, and is the difference between the values of variable x in period t and $t-i$. That is, changes in cap rate are given by cap rates and a bunch of other stuff.

A rise in expected property appreciation changes the value of π, causing ρ to fall and property value to increase. This leads to feedback into the next period's price growth. Positive coefficients imply momentum, and negative can imply reversion back to the original level of ρ or negative momentum. A pattern of positive coefficients for $\Delta\rho_{t-i}$, followed by negative coefficients later, implies a cycle. Large enough positive coefficients can imply the process blowing up, in which case we do not have a coherent model. If that were true, all the capital in the economy would be sucked into the housing market. If it were to happen, there would certainly be adjustments in the economy, like increases in interest rates. Such adjustments would not be captured in an estimation model, which would not have initially included any episodes of explosion.

Equation (3.24) breaks the process into two parts: a transitory part and a long-run solution. The long run solution is where the b_i values would lead to $\rho_t = \sum_{i=1}^{n} b_i(x_{t-i})$, i.e. the expression inside the first pair of brackets equal to zero. This will happen when the delta variables in the second part of the equation go to zero. That is, $\rho_t = \sum_{i=1}^{n} b_i(x_{t-i})$ can be construed as the fundamental equation. The second part with the non-zero delta variables forms a transitory part. Empiricists researching housing bubbles using the idea similar to Eq. (3.24) can use econometric models like the autoregressive distributed lag (ARDL) models, which include lagged values of both the regressand (i.e. the dependent variable) and the regressors (the independent variables). Further variations are the mean group estimation and pooled mean group estimations.[12]

If we further restrict our notion of fundamentals to be given by a constant long-run real rate, $(r_t - g_t)$, then Eq. (3.24) can be written as

$$\Delta\rho_t = \alpha[\rho_t - (r_t - g_t)] - \sum_{i=1}^{n}[a_i(\Delta\rho_{t-i}) + b_i\Delta x_{t-i}]. \qquad (3.25)$$

Equation (3.25) also allows for the dynamics (i.e. interactions among the Δ variables) to be quite wild if expectations of price growth are formed by looking at the past. As in Eq. (3.24), cycles become explosive bubbles if the a_i's and b_i's are large. For the system to converge to the long run fundamental, the value of α next to the first pair of brackets has to be negative. This means that the value of ρ declines toward long run equilibrium when it is above the equilibrium. A value of g greater than r, in the long run, will also blow up the pricing system, even if the transitory part does not explode. As above, this is an implausible result because it would surely cause long increases in r to keep the property market from sucking up all the capital in the economy. Unless the model "blows up", this anchors the long run at some level of fundamentals, and one can test whether the fundamentals work as expected (α should be negative for the convergence (recall that g should be interpreted as containing depreciation).[13]

The problem with history, both as data and as personal experience, is that samples are never really good enough by themselves, and people change over time. We can try to force some sense on the data through a theory (or model of a theory) like Eq. (3.25). But still, it relies on history, and it therefore can show bubbles by making projections from unrepresentative data. Although explicit present value models are in many ways preferable, they can be too abstract to be taken seriously or too sophisticated to be applied. There is not much

[12]Note that even though the long run and short run components sound like cointegration models and error correction models (ECM), ARDL are different. We shall leave these technical issues to readers to find their own references to the topics.

[13]See the last paragraph of Section 3.2.3. Assuming cap rate equals real rate plus depreciation is a common assumption, but factors like taxes can spoil that.

we can do about this, except to iterate between the two worlds. Unfortunately, the models people actually use in making decisions about buying and selling, with incomplete history and theory, can lead to bubbles and other nasty problems.

3.4. Comments

This chapter introduced the basics of pricing housing units, regardless of whether they are for investment or consumption. The formulation shows the link between rents and prices, given the necessary information about the market and economic conditions. The simplicity of the formulation allows analogy with stock market pricing. This sets the foundation of pricing market bubbles.

We now have two explanations for rapid house price growth. The first is the "regular" one, which looks like a version of Eq. (3.10) and Figure 3.1. It is a model with well-informed, "rational," foresight with nice properties such as convergence, even in the presence of speculation. Then property values rise because the spot price of space (rent) rises or discount rates decline. At a minimum, this is a good model for long-run trends (provided the economy does not blow up).

The other occurs when expectations are not so rational and are very responsive to recent history. In that case, shocks to any of the variables (such as an increase in current prices or rents) can feed into price expectations and push price growth further up. This generates momentum, which may settle down later or, better yet, fluctuate back to the fundamentals. This is characterized by property values rising faster than rent, and perhaps crash-landing later on as the market discovers that property is overpriced for the service it provides. How do we know which is which ahead of time? We probably do not at first; and if we do notice it, we probably cannot tell when it will be reversed, rather like still seeing people dancing at a party that we know should be ending, but not just yet.

The appearance of bubbles may be smothered by policy-makers' delayed reactions to price surges, and dampening them. As mentioned at the beginning of this section, no one can be sure if there is a bubble until it bursts. The problem is in part because of a great deal of uncertainty about estimated parameters. A simple marker is the behavior of price relative to rent. If that diverges very quickly from its history for no obvious reason, it can signal the beginning of a bubble. We still cannot tell whether a burst bubble was really a bubble in the sense of whether it was the inevitable outcome of momentum or that the market contracted in reaction to policies (e.g. maybe China around 2010).

Oh well!!! This all suggests a need for humility tempered with occasional rationalization.

Appendix: Rents and Rent Data

There are two sorts of measures for durable goods such as housing: new and used. Neither is uniquely correct; it depends on what you want to find out about. The U.S. Consumer Price Index (CPI) collected by the Bureau of Labor Statistics (BLS) includes rent data from surveys of what consumers are paying that month. This gives average cost across all renters, but it mixes old rents and new rents, and actual or imputed, which are different, especially in 2021.

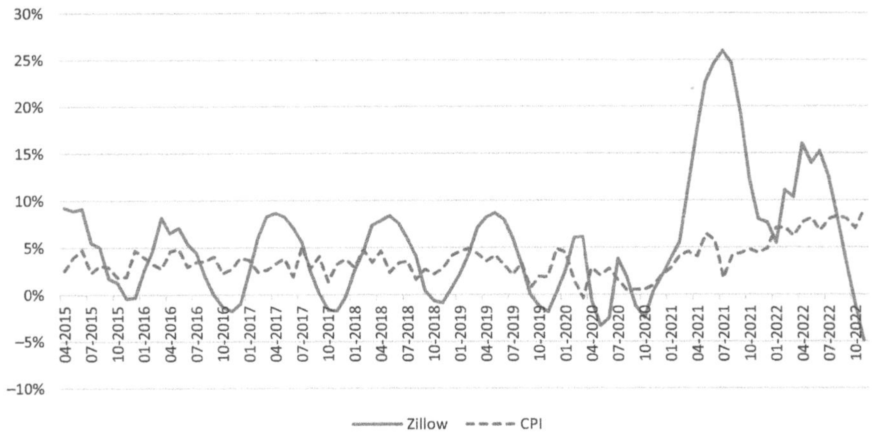

Figure 3A Annualized Changes in Monthly Rent

Source: Zillow rent data is the Zillow Observed Rent Index (Available at: https://www.zillow.com/research/data/), Rent from CPI is the Rent and Shelter U.S. City Average from CPI, obtained from Federal Reserve St. Louis database (Available at: https://fred.stlouisfed.org/series/CUUR0000SAS2RS). See Krugman (2023).

Zillow is a firm that provides real estate data from around the country for newly rented units. Figure 3A[14] depicts the annualized percentage changes of both, monthly, with CPI rent in dotted line and Zillow new rentals in solid line. There is a cyclical pattern to new rents much of the time. Apparently, rents on new units tend to be higher in the summer. That is not especially an important problem, and seasonal adjustments can handle that. But the period beginning around 2021 is different. New rents shot up by way more than average rents (peak at around 25% for Zillow but falling later. That CPI is under 10% but continuing to be high. The timing was also different — CPI's shot up later. Apparently, there were two quite different stories in the news. Both surveys are reputable. So, what does it mean? Which is better? Depends![15]

The one in CPI is better for deflating income or wages in order to estimate average living standards across groups. The second, marginal, measure is good if you want to tell people what they have to pay if they want to rent a new place, which nevertheless affects only a small part of the population during the measurement period (a month). For the purpose of using discounted rents, values from Zillow might be better, except that they can be very volatile and way too high as a starting point for discounting rents over a long period of time. So, we use the rent value in the CPI in our present value equations.

[14]See Krugman (2023).
[15]Krugman (2022) and Adams *et al.* (2022).

Chapter 4

Mortgages, Mortgage Math and Pricing Mortgages

This chapter is about understanding the types and values of mortgages (and associated mortgage rates). The structure of the U.S. mortgage market has changed and grown rapidly after World War II. A centerpiece of the changes has been the shift from savings banks funded with deposits to securitization funded by bond market investors. We address these changes in more detail here. We note that the types of mortgages have evolved along the structure of the markets. We discuss mortgage types and values as if the institutional changes did not matter. We present some theory and empirical price/mortgage rate models along with some data.

4.1. Mortgage Lending: Products and Values

A mortgage is a contract that specifies details of what the borrower must do to keep the house he/she bought. There are three classic mortgage types:

i. *Fixed rate mortgages* (FRMs): These constitute well over half of the U.S. market.
ii. *Adjustable rate mortgages* (ARMs): With these, rates are changed periodically according to an index, such as indexed to the 1-year Treasury rate plus 2.50% margin once a year, and usually with limits on how much rates can be changed.

iii. *Hybrids*: These come with adjustable rates at longer intervals, such as fixed for the first 5 years and adjusted every year thereafter, indexed to Treasury rates (5/1), or fixed for 2 years and adjusted for the next 28 years (2/28); the former is more associated with prime mortgages and the latter with subprime mortgages.

The last two types above typically begin with low rates (*teaser* rates) for some period and then adjusted to the index plus a premium. They have two types of principal payoffs:

i. *Balloon* (like a bond): This requires that interest be paid periodically, and a lump sum payment of principal at some later date.
ii. *Amortized*: In these, payments are fixed so that the loan principal is fully paid off at the end of the term as a type of annuity.

While most loans in the U.S. are fully amortized, some (e.g. hybrids) have balloon payments.

Mortgages are generally classified by credit quality in the following categories:

i. *Prime* loans are mortgages with good credit history and downpayment or with private mortgage insurance (PMI) to cover most of the loss if there is a foreclosure.
ii. *Federal Housing Administration and Veterans Administration (FHA/VA)* mortgages include government insurance; FHA loans have low downpayments, easier underwriting and limits on loan size.
iii. *Subprime and Alt-A (non-prime)* mortgages are conventional loans (loans not insured by the government are referred to as *conventional*) with flaws (e.g. with poor documentation).

Recalling from Chapter 1, Alt-A mortgages are usually with less than full documentation (aka low-doc), but are otherwise ok; subprime mortgages can be low and poor credit history plus low-doc. Both had especially expanded through 2006 and were very much a part of the 2007 crash. They have become rare since then.

The characteristics of a mortgage can be expressed mathematically. Mortgage rates move up and down with Treasury securities, and ARMs are indexed to Treasuries. We will discuss both theory and evidence on how mortgage rates are determined relative to the

Treasury benchmark in Chapter 5. Here, we focus on some definitions and notation by applying variants of the present value approach in Chapter 3.

First, consider a fully amortized FRM with a series of monthly fixed payments, labeled *pmt*, and a balance to be paid off over a fixed period of time, typically 30 years, or 360 months (15 or 20 years are less typical), and a fixed interest rate, I, in a way that pays off the initial balance, B, by the end of the loan period. It is an annuity with some complications. The initial balance is given by

$$B = pmt\left[\frac{1}{\left(1+\frac{i}{12}\right)} + \frac{1}{\left(1+\frac{i}{12}\right)^2} + \frac{1}{\left(1+\frac{i}{12}\right)^3} + \cdots + \frac{1}{\left(1+\frac{i}{12}\right)^{360}}\right], \tag{4.1}$$

where $n = 360$ months at origination. This can be simplified to

$$B = \frac{pmt}{\frac{i}{12}}\left[1 - \frac{1}{\left(1+\frac{i}{12}\right)^n}\right]. \tag{4.2}$$

Note that the annual rate, the one that is usually quoted, is divided by 12 because the payments are monthly. This can be "inverted" to find the payment, *pmt*, necessary to pay off the loan in n months, that is,

$$pmt = \frac{B}{\frac{12}{i}} \frac{\left(1+\frac{i}{12}\right)^n}{\left[\left(1+\frac{i}{12}\right)^n - 1\right]}. \tag{4.3}$$

Given B and *pmt*, i is the internal rate of return on the mortgage contract. Taking the difference between the balances at month t and $t+1$ gives

$$pmt_t = B_t - B_{t+1} + \left(\frac{i}{12}\right) B_t. \tag{4.4}$$

That is, the payment is divided between the monthly interest and the principal pay-down (amortization). It is clear from Eq. (4.4) that amortization is small at the beginning of the loan because the constant payment, *pmt*, covers both the amortized principle and the interest payment, and the interest payment is large when the balance at the beginning is high. Over time, the loan balance shrinks, and less interest payment is paid. These relationships define important parts of the mortgage contract.

Note, however, that market relationships also matter because the mortgage can be traded like almost any asset. Therefore, its market value, M, can change along with the changes in rates on comparable mortgages. In particular, if the market return on a comparable mortgage is r, then what it would sell for in a competitive market is the value of the mortgage, which is

$$M = pmt\left[\frac{1}{\left(1+\frac{r}{12}\right)} + \frac{1}{\left(1+\frac{r}{12}\right)^2} + \frac{1}{\left(1+\frac{r}{12}\right)^3} + \cdots + \frac{1}{\left(1+\frac{r}{12}\right)^{360}}\right]$$
$$= \frac{pmt}{\frac{r}{12}}\left[1 - \frac{1}{\left(1+\frac{r}{12}\right)^n}\right]. \quad (4.5)$$

It is clear that $M = B$ if $r = i$, and the mortgage is worth less than the balance ($M < B$) if $r > i$, and *vice versa.*

Two points to note. First, we will describe in Section 4.3 that there is more to consider than Eq. (4.5) because of borrower options. Second, as hinted earlier, much of the evolution of the mortgage market has come from the facilitation of trading mortgages and the securities containing them.

4.2. Borrowers' Behavior

We have already seen that mortgages are investments that provide cash flows like annuities or bonds. Pricing mortgages and bonds would be relatively easy if interest rates remained more or less constant. We could use the certainty equivalent method discussed in Section 3.2 as a good approximation to the expected present value by discounting expected cash flows at the current constant market interest rate, which is a common tactic going into the 1980s.

However, life is not that easy, more so in the case of mortgages because of important correlations between market rates and mortgage cash flows. Suppose you just bought a house financed with an FRM for 30 years, and then the borrowing rate decreased by, say, 3%. The payments on a new, lower-rate, mortgage will be smaller. You will probably want to pay off the mortgage and refinance your house with a mortgage bearing the lower borrowing rate. This will harm the owner of the original mortgage (i.e. the lender or investor) by the amount you benefit.

In other cases, particularly during economic downturns, the borrower might not have enough income to continue the payments because of, say, loss of job. Alternatively, if the property market value drops by enough, the current mortgage value can be higher than the value of the property securing the mortgage. The borrower is said to have *negative equity* (or the mortgage is *underwater*). Both cases could induce the borrower to think about default on the mortgage, and the two together make default more likely. The connection for credit risk is indirect. Declining interest rates may mean a stronger economy and higher house prices along with less unemployment and fewer defaults. However, because low interest rates are sometimes an indicator of a weak economy, it may suggest more defaults. Hence, it is important to consider *why* rates are moving the way they are. How do we take options like these into account when deciding mortgage prices? We can think of these borrower choices as modified versions of exercising options on other securities. For example, a *prepayment* option allows the borrower to choose to "buy back" the mortgage, like a callable bond being called. The homebuyer settles the prepayment with his/her own savings or by taking on a new mortgage at a lower rate and using the proceeds borrowed to buy back the first mortgage. The latter is called *refinancing.*

On the other hand, a *default* option allows the borrower to clean up the household balance sheet by getting rid of an underwater mortgage. It has become common for researchers in mortgage pricing at least since the 1980s to view prepayment and default explicitly as contracts that can be priced with option-pricing methodologies for stock and bond options.[1] Applying option pricing is not as applicable in the case of default because of the more serious "exercise" costs for the borrower.

The great insight of the contingent claims/option models comes from determining prices by imposing only the conditions of zero

[1]See Black and Scholes (1973), Brennan and Schwartz (1977), Cox, Ingersoll, and Ross (1985), and Merton (1973). Kau and Keenan (1995) present a discussion of rigorous applications of these techniques to mortgages.

arbitrage profits and rational, wealth-maximizing, exercise of options. Such models provide exact predictions about prices using relatively few parameters, and the central proposition is that the value of a security is the risk-adjusted expected present value of its cash flows. Although still doable, using this technique becomes more complex when transaction and other costs are incorporated. Also, the models can sometimes be unrealistic because they are usually based on the strong assumption that the price of the underlying asset follows a lognormal distribution. This means that its return follows a normal distribution, which often seriously underestimates the tail risks, i.e. the likelihood of loss in extreme cases. Nevertheless, they represent an important element of truth and are a good reference to start with.

4.3. Interest Rate Risk

Here we consider effects of changes in interest rates in a fancier model than the one we developed for real estate pricing in Chapter 3. The option-based approaches specify probability distributions rather than projected levels of interest rates and evaluate the effects of the randomness of interest rate changes on mortgage values. This method has two advantages. First, it requires predicting only the probability of changing rates and not the rates themselves. Second, upon addressing the borrower's prepayment option, it shows how the sheer volatility (and hence the unpredictability) of interest rates affects pricing. Perhaps, more importantly, it allows us to model correlations among variables and cash flows. We apply the method to prepayable (callable) mortgages and then compare them to those non-prepayable cases. This reveals some important differences in their price/interest-rate relationships.

We assume that the risk-free rate (e.g. Treasury rate) changes randomly and will either go up or down by the amount Δ, and the changes are independent over time. The probability that it will rise is p; so, the probability of falling is $1 - p$. Suppose the initial rate is 10%. Next, suppose there is equal chance of going up or down, i.e. $p = 1 - p = 0.5$, like tossing a coin. If Δ equals 1%, the rate will either go up to 11% or down to 9%. This change can go on and on. Figure 4.1 shows how rates can change over the next three periods. For instance, starting from the beginning at the "10%" node, the rate will either go up to the "11%" node or down to the "9%" node at the end of period 1. This process is not entirely realistic because it implies that interest rates can be negative.[2]

We next consider a loan or a bond subject to this interest rate process. To simplify the illustration and make use of a mortgage type we previously introduced, we assume the instrument matures at the end of three periods and has a balloon payment, such that the borrower pays periodic interests and the balance at the end. While this assumption is not essential, it is helpful for exposition purposes because amortization over a longer period complicates things without really adding much insight into the results.

For reasons that will be clearer later when bringing in prepayment, we solve the problem by starting at the end and working back toward origination. Suppose a bond maturing in four periods pays a \$10 coupon at the end of the first three periods and the coupon plus \$100 in principal (its par or face value) at the end of period 4. This is roughly the same as a 10% FRM that has a balloon payment setting and is paid off after four periods. Assuming the interest rate movement is as in Figure 4.1, the corresponding bond price at the end of each period given a certain interest rate can be obtained as a one-period present value. At the end of period 3, no matter which of the four nodes in Figure 4.1 is realized, the subsequent outcome of the remaining one-period bond paying \$110 remains (i.e. 10% coupon plus \$100 par value at the end of period 4). There are four possible one-period rates at this point: 7%, 9%, 11%, and 13%. There is no further interest rate uncertainty once the rate in the last period is known, and the last payment can be priced easily. For example, if the rate is 13% (top right node), the one-period bond will be worth $\frac{\$100+\$10}{(1+13\%)} = \$97.35$. If rates have fallen to 7%, the bond will be worth \$110/1.07 or \$102.80. Figure 4.2 shows all possible rounded-up bond prices at the end of period 3, with one period to maturity. This is like the *binomial decision tree* used for option pricing in general.

[2]Like the option-pricing models assuming changes in underlying asset prices follow continuous stochastic processes, various researchers have modeled interest rate processes as stochastic processes in different forms, some could result in negative interest rates, while others like the Hull–White model due to Hull and White (1990) would not.

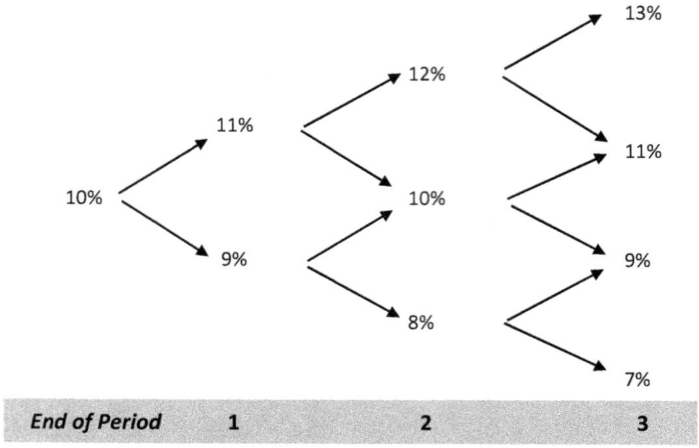

Figure 4.1 Distribution of Interest Rates Over Three Periods

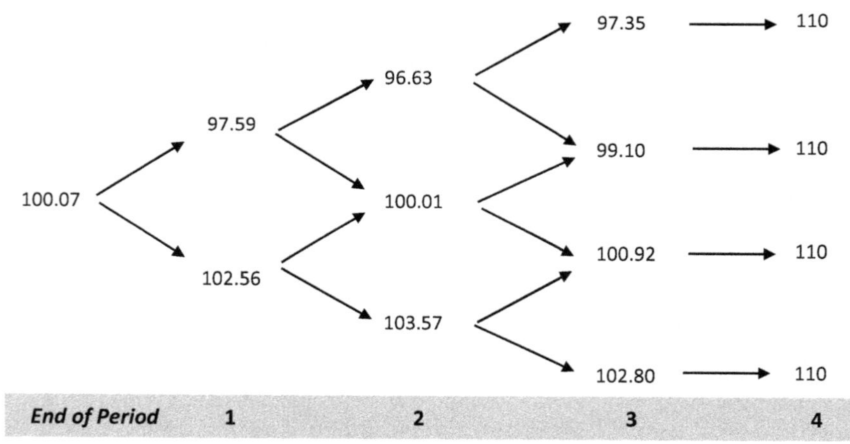

Figure 4.2 Bond Pricing

With 2 years to maturity, the problem is more complicated because of uncertainty. For instance, suppose the current one-period interest rate is 12% (i.e. "12%" node at the end of period 2 in Figure 4.1). The rate will either rise to 13% in the following period, in which case the bond will be worth \$97.35, or fall to 11%, and the bond will be worth \$99.10. Both cases have equal chance of happening; the \$10 coupon will be paid regardless. The value of the bond at the end of period 2 with 12% is the expected present value of the two possible outcomes, each with 50% chance, plus the $10 coupon:

$$\frac{0.5(\$97.35) + 0.5(99.10) + \$10}{(1 + 12\%)} = \$96.63.$$

Since the 12% interest rate exceeds the 10% coupon rate, the bond's value is below par ($100).

We can use the same procedure to evaluate the bond for the other two possibilities (8% and 10%) at the end of period 2. With these three possible bond prices and working backward, we can obtain two prices, $97.59 and $102.56, for the possible rates of 11% and 9%, respectively, at the end of period 1. Iterating the procedure backward, we can find the initial price of the bond as $100.07. Iterating the above calculation (by changing the coupon payment until you get an answer equal to 100) generates an initial bond price of $100 if the coupon rate is 9.98%, which is the mortgage rate, like internal rate of return on housing investment in Chapter 3.

The extra $0.07 in price corresponds to the convexity of the bond curve in Figure 3.3, i.e. interest rate decreases have a bigger effect on the bond value than do increases. This increases the value of the bond, but not by much, and the price could be loosely approximated with a certainty equivalent measure. Note that this problem is solved by starting from maturity and working backward. This approach, while illustrative, is not essential. We could have arrived at the same solution by searching over all possible interest rate paths, computing the present value of each, and then averaging across these. This is like the Monte Carlo approach described in Section 3.2.7. The backward induction model serves as a good warm-up for the same model with the borrower choosing prepayment.

4.4. Prepayment Risk as a Ruthlessly Exercised Call Option

What about prepayment? U.S. mortgages are generally prepayable at any time before maturity, analogous to the owner of the mortgage selling a callable bond to the mortgagor. The call (prepayment) can be either from selling the house or wanting to pay off the mortgage early. The latter is usually because of two motives. One is to take out equity after property values have gone up by taking out a new mortgage with a bigger balance and pocketing the difference. Another is to take out a new mortgage with a lower mortgage rate. In either case, there is a particular decision-making process all along.

Our focus here is on the latter because it is the most consequential for mortgage rates, and it is analyzed in a way similar to analyzing callable bonds.[3] The shapes of the relationships among prices, interest rates, and volatility for callable bonds look quite different from those for non-callable bonds. We use a backward-solving model as in the previous section. This is necessary because borrowers make choices along the way that require consideration of future possibilities and probabilities in this case.

When should the borrower prepay the mortgage in a way that maximizes wealth? How is it priced? Intuitively, we expect borrowers to prepay the mortgage when interest rates fall and to hang on when they go up. This means that certainty equivalence is likely to be a bad approximation because cash flows and interest rates will be correlated due to the borrowers' prepayment choices. Luckily, modeling a mortgage as if it were a callable bond is relatively simple. By making the bond in Figure 4.2 callable at $100 (analogous to the mortgage principal) at every payment node, the borrower determines whether continuing or paying off increases expected wealth. We leave out transaction costs for now.

The complication with the borrower's decision-making is that he/she has to take account of the fact that he/she could prepay next period if he/she does not prepay now; and if not, then the period after, etc. That is, future exercise possibilities need to be considered. The solution is again to start at the *end*, as with the non-callable bond in the previous section. This is a *structural* model because it takes account of the structure of the underlying choice problem.

Let's see how it works. The choices with reference to Figures 4.1 and 4.2 are depicted in Figure 4.3. The final payments are all $110 (principal plus interest) provided the mortgage has not been prepaid. Suppose rates have risen from 10% at origination to 13% at the end of period 3 (the next to last payment) as in Figure 4.1. The mortgagor

[3]Of course, the decision to sell a house also comes from a decision-making process. However, here, we want to focus on the call option part of the mortgage.

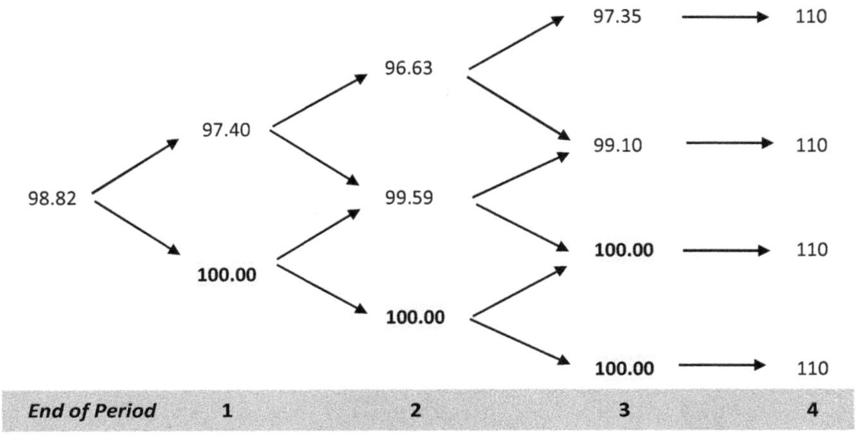

Figure 4.3 Mortgage Pricing

can either make the final balloon payment of the $110 at the end of period 4, which in the present value term costs him $97.35, or prepay it by buying it back for $100, the principal. Clearly, being a wealth maximizer, the borrower will not want to pay $100 for something worth only $97.35. No prepayment occurs. But suppose rates have fallen to 7%. The present value of carrying the loan for another period is $102.80. Obviously, the borrower increases wealth by paying off the $100 loan and refinancing the housing with a 1-year loan at the new market rate. The prepayment option is exercised, and the mortgage is terminated.

Suppose the interest rate is 10% at the end of period 2. The mortgage will be worth either $99.10 or $100 if called. The expected present value of these two possibilities plus the coupon is $99.59. Compare this with the non-callable bond at the same node in Figure 4.2 where the value of the bond going forward is 100.01. The possibility of prepayment in the following period or later causes the mortgage to have a lower value than the non-callable bond at the same interest rate even before prepayment. That is, the valuation anticipates future prepayment. Solving backward gives a mortgage value at origination of $98.82, which is $1.25 less than the value of the non-callable bond of $100.07 (or mortgage without prepayment option). This $1.25 represents the market's implied value of the call option. The $1.18 difference between $100 and $98.82 is often referred to as the "points" charged upfront on the mortgage. The "upfront" of the call option of \$1.25 is slightly bigger because of the convexity of the non-callable bond. The shaded "\$100" nodes in Figure 4.3 are where prepaying the mortgage is better than continuing.

We could also calculate the coupon rate that makes the present value of the promised payments equal to \$100 by iteration, as with the non-callable case above. The answer is 10.28%. The 30 basis-point spread between this and the 9.98% for the non-callable bond represents the value of call option, which is added to the coupon rate rather than paid upfront. This difference is sometimes called the *option-adjusted spread* (often called the OAS). In this case, we do not need to know what the borrower does to replace the mortgage. The borrower can replace the old mortgage with a new, smaller, one with the same payments and pocket the difference, or take out a new mortgage with a lower coupon, or take out a mortgage that is not callable. All three strategies will have the same expected present value.[4]

Solving such a problem is not always easy, particularly as the number of choice variables and period becomes large, although computers help. The borrower does not really need a computer and a degree in finance to make the complicated backward-solving present value calculations. He/she only needs to know the market value of the loan versus the balance (or the rate on a new loan with identical maturity). The market will make the expected present value calculations by incorporating the borrower's call strategy. This is complicated, and practitioners almost always perform the calculations using Monte Carlo simulations with more behavioral rather than backward-looking/explicitly optimizing models of prepayment.

Panel A of Table 4.1 lists the values of the non-callable and callable mortgages given different initial values and changes in market interest rate values and volatilities using the additive volatility model as in Figure 3.3. The last set of columns shows the differences between the non-callable price and the callable price which gives

[4]There can be a friction in the real world if mortgages only have a small number of terms to maturity. That is, one cannot take out a 28-year mortgage after paying off a 30-year mortgage 2 years after the old mortgage is initiated. However, one can take out a 30-year mortgage and make extra principal payments so that it pays off in 28 years. That will be pretty close.

Table 4.1 Values of Bonds (Rounded to the Nearest 10th) with Different Parameters

	Non-callable Bonds				**Callable Bonds**				**Price Difference**			
	Volatility				**Volatility**				**Volatility**			
	0.5%	**1.0%**	**1.5%**	**2.0%**	**0.5%**	**1.0%**	**1.5%**	**2.0%**	**0.5%**	**1.0%**	**1.5%**	**2.0%**
Interest (%)					*Coupon Rate at 10%*							
Panel A Additive Changes in Interest Rate												
8	106.7	106.7	106.8	106.9	100.0	100.0	100. 0	100.0	6.7	6.7	6.8	6.9
9	103.3	103.4	103.4	103.5	100.0	100.0	100.0	99.5	3.3	3.4	3.4	4.0
10	100.1	100.1	100.1	100.3	99.0	98.8	98.3	97.7	1.1	1.3	1.7	2.6
11	96.9	97.0	97.0	97.0	96.9	96.6	96.2	95.9	0.0	0.4	0.8	1.1
12	93.9	94.0	94.0	94.2	93.9	93.9	93.7	93.4	0.0	0.1	0.3	0.8
	Non-callable Bonds				**Callable Bonds**				**Price Difference**			
	Volatility				**Volatility**				**Volatility**			
	5%	**10%**	**15%**	**20%**	**5%**	**10%**	**15%**	**20%**	**5%**	**10%**	**15%**	**20%**
Interest (%)					*Coupon Rate at 10%*							
Panel B Multiplicative Changes in Interest Rate												
8	106.6	106.5	106.3	106.1	100.0	100.0	100.0	100.0	6.6	6.5	6.3	6.1
9	103.2	103.1	102.9	102.6	100.0	100.0	99.9	99.3	3.2	3.1	2.9	3.3
10	100.0	99.9	99.7	99.4	99.9	98.7	98.0	97.3	0.1	1.1	1.7	2.1
11	96.9	96.7	96.6	96.3	96.9	96.4	95.8	95.2	0.0	0.4	0.8	1.1
12	93.9	93.8	93.6	93.3	93.9	93.7	93.2	92.6	0.0	0.1	0.4	0.7

the values of the call (prepayment) option. The basic results are as follows:

1. While the values of both types of mortgages decrease in interest rates and increase in coupon rates, the prepayable mortgage is always worth less than the non-prepayable, and the difference represents the non-negative option value for the borrower to prepay the mortgage.
2. Borrowers are unlikely to prepay when interest rates are high or mortgage borrowing rates (coupon rates) are low. That is, the call option is "out of the money". In plain words, the mortgage is cheap, so why give it up?
3. There is a basic asymmetry that callable mortgage value does not go above 100 when initial interest rates fall but can drop sharply if rates rise, which implies negative convexity. That the upper limit is \$100 means that the market anticipates the possibility of exercising the prepayment option before it actually occurs.
4. The non-callable mortgage exhibits *positive convexity*, and increased volatility increases price. The callable mortgage exhibits *negative convexity* when rates are high and when they are low. At high interest rates, the callable mortgage looks like a non-callable mortgage.
5. Analogous to volatility increasing values of options, the values for the non-callable mortgage also increase with volatility. However, interest rate volatility lowers the callable mortgage value as the value is closer to par because of anticipation of prepayment.

These are the most important implications of positive and negative convexity.

Modeling the interest rate process with equal increases and decreases can result in negative interest rates if we wait long enough, and that is not very realistic. An alternative is to replace the additive change with a more realistic multiplicative change, such that the increase is $u = e^{\Delta}$ and decrease is $d = e^{-\Delta}$. This approach is often used in practice. The interest rate pattern is different. It is depicted in Figure 4.4.

The pricing is listed in Panel B of Table 4.1. Note that using a multiplicative shift in our illustration has not made much difference in values or in call premia, but it now has a more pronounced negative

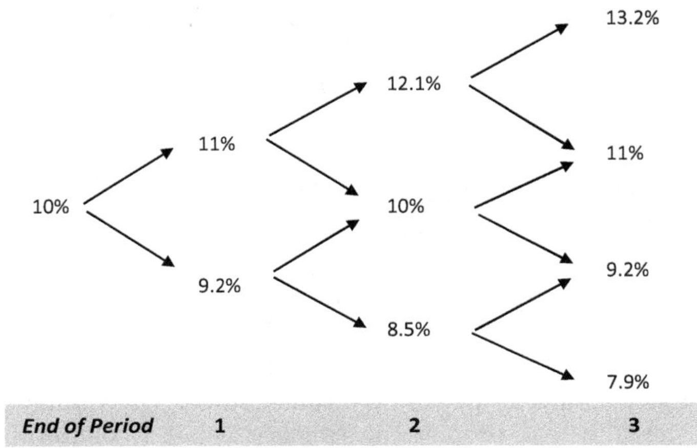

Figure 4.4 Distribution of Interest Rates over Three Periods: Multiplicative Changes

response to volatility. Note the asymmetry relative to Figure 3.3. In particular, rates fall less rapidly and will never reach zero. This mitigates the convexity that appears in the additive model because the compression at low rates offsets the larger increase when rates fall. This can be seen, for instance, in the non-callable section of Panel B where the value falls as volatility increases across the rows.

In reality, most borrowers do not prepay as "ruthlessly" as in the model, perhaps because of transaction costs and/or general inertia.[5] The model can be modified to conform more closely to real behavior by modifying the option approach. For example, we can add a transaction cost to refinancing, which drives a wedge between what the borrower pays and what the investor gets. Alternately, we can use reduced-form models that estimate the effects of the important variables on default without having a specific theory or resort to the backward-solving models. These models estimate the probability of prepaying as a function of the difference between the existing mortgage rate (the coupon) and the current market interest rate, or on the difference between the value of the mortgage today and the outstanding mortgage balance (these are almost mirror images of each other) as well as other variables that might explain shifts in the probability.

[5]See, for instance, Deng *et al.* (2000) for a model with sluggish prepayment behavior and heterogeneous borrowers.

Then we can use Monte Carlo models as in Section 3.2.7 to obtain the expected present value. We will explain some reduced-form models of default in the following section.

4.5. Understanding Mortgage Default in Not-Very-Ruthless Models

The most important characteristic of mortgages is the property acting as collateral, which could be seized if the borrower fails to make payments, i.e. the borrower defaults. Rules for taking over the property once defaults take place vary considerably by country and by state in the U.S. The property in concern being a collateral lessens default costs and leads to lower mortgage costs. However, the level of cost saving depends on the ability to take the property, evict the borrower and sell the property. The rules for this vary considerably by jurisdiction.

Borrower default can be compared to exercising an option to exchange the house for the mortgage. It is of course a "sloppy" option. First, it is costly for the borrower to default. Also, many borrowers do not have enough "liquidity" to borrow or draw down savings when their homes are still worth more than the mortgage's value. Nonetheless, the option approach does appear to be useful as it suggests, for instance, that borrower's equity, or lack of it, is an important predictor of default. It also suggests the presence of asymmetry in option models in that the lender benefits very little when property values go up, but is at risk for large losses from foreclosure when they go down, like the lender selling a put option to the borrower, but with exercise costs. We now discuss the probability of default in a reduced-form model with option-like variables as explanatory variables.

The option-based approach leads to a relationship between homeowner's equity and default that suggests the following:

1. The borrower is less likely to default as equity accumulates. He/she will do whatever is possible to raise money to protect the investment and likely sell the property and keep the equity rather than turning it over to the lender.

2. Even if he/she does default with positive equity, the lender might recover costs after selling the property.[6]

Hence, focusing on negative equity and thinking of default behavior akin to exercising an option is a good way to begin because only in states of the world with negative equity where a "rational" borrower chooses to exercise the default option will it become a serious problem to the lender. Of course, there is more to default than just negative equity. Most analysts and researchers believe that a good first approximation to default behavior is that default comes from the intersection of three events: (1) negative equity, (2) a "trigger event" such as illness or job loss, and (3) lack of resources to survive the trigger event.

It is possible that default can occur without such an intersection. For example, the equity might be so far negative that the borrower wants to clear his/her balance sheet by defaulting without a trigger event and/or choosing not to survive a trigger event even if resources exist. Detailed analysis of *how* these interact is generally not possible with most datasets. Hence, analysts generally must be satisfied with proxies for these factors and *ad hoc* empirical models. Recent research suggests that although credit history and equity are both very strong predictors of the probability of default, there is no good way of predicting *which* borrowers will default.

Here, we use two datasets in the U.S. that illustrate situations of default. The first includes data aggregated by state with loan-to-value ratios (LTVs) of around 80% and depicts default rates as a function of price appreciation of individual states. The second sample is narrow in terms of available explanatory variables, as it does not have, for instance, borrower credit history. Nevertheless, it covers the late 1970s when the economy went through an important market cycle. The focus is on borrower's equity, given initial LTVs and the strength of the economy. We discuss the third and more striking dataset in Chapter 9 when we look at the GFC. It has aggregated

---

[6] An important issue when default happens is the lost interest and neglect of the maintenance during the time between stopped payments and disposing of the house.

data on credit scores which allows analysis of differences in default among mortgage products before and after the GFC.

4.5.1. Equity, Property Appreciation and Default

The first dataset depicts results for loans purchased by Freddie Mac from 1985 to 1995 and followed for their first 7 years. More about Freddie will be covered in detail in Chapter 5. For now, just understand it as a U.S. government-sponsored enterprise. Figure 4.5 depicts default experience by state (and nationally) for a fixed initial LTV ratio of 79%–81% against state house price appreciation (the grey diamonds) and for the nation as a whole (the black squares). The horizontal axis depicts cumulative house price changes over the 7 years and the vertical axis depicts cumulative foreclosure rates. The grey diamonds represent the experience of a particular state-origination year. For instance, the AK diamond represents the experience of loans originating in Alaska in 1986.

The scatters are as we should expect. States with rapid property appreciation had low default rates, and those with price declines had big ones. As the option model predicts, the results are asymmetric.

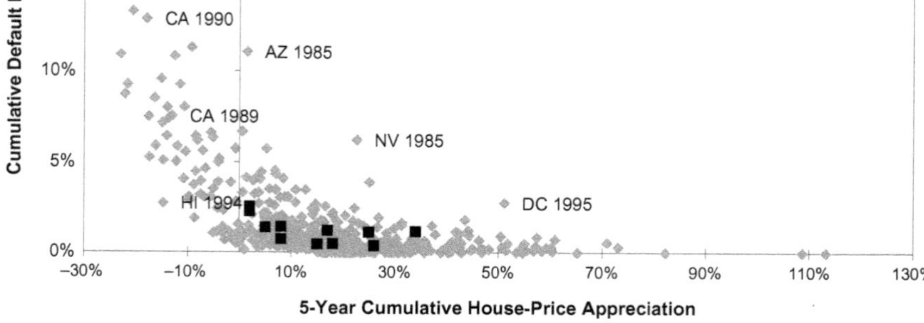

Figure 4.5 Default and House Price Growth in U.S. for the Period of 1975–1985

Source: Hendershott and Van Order (2005).

Default accelerates and lenders lose money when property values fall, but simply clusters at zero when values go up, like the lenders selling put options to the borrowers. An important note is that the U.S. has in general experienced small national recessions but occasionally large regional recessions. Low house price growths in bad times have a strong effect on default, and there has been a great deal of regional variation in house price growths, but much less nationally. This causes large differences in experience across states. The tighter clustering of the black squares shows benefits of nation-wide diversification.

4.5.2. Likelihood of Default Given LTV and Market Cycle

The second dataset comes from quantifying the effects of LTVs to default for the period of 1976–1983 comparable to the first dataset. Let's call it Model 1 from Van Order (1990). Table 4.2 depicts defaults from Model 1 by LTV (Panel A) and origination year (Panel B) by averaging across those categories in the dataset. The coefficients are interpreted as "multipliers" relative to what happened in the 1979 vintage (the base year). For instance, a loan with an LTV greater than or equal to (mostly equal to) 95% will default about eight times as often as one with an LTV at 80% or below. Given the same LTV, one that originated in the recession year, 1981, will default about 2.5 times more frequently than that originated in 1979, and about 25 times more frequently than that originated in 1976, which was a boom year in the middle of sharply rising property values. The model *assumes* that the multipliers are independent, so that a 95-LTV originated in 1981 is about 72 times more likely to default than an LTV below 80 in 1976; that assumption may not be accurate for big differences.

The last column in Panel B shows the price appreciation for the 2 years after the origination year, which verifies that slow market growth will lead to more defaults. The evidence here suggests that default does indeed vary with LTV and economic fluctuations. The model is thin in that we cannot tell how rates vary across different borrower types (e.g. the dataset does not include information about borrowers' credit history). It does however cover an important cycle in house prices.

Table 4.2 Effects of LTV and Origination Year on Annual Default Rates (Model 1)

Panel A

LTV Class (in %)	Effect (Multiplier)
≤80	1.0
81–90	3.9
91–94	5.7
≥95	8.1

Panel B

Year of Origination	Effect (Multiplier) Effect (Multiplier)	Price Growth After 2 Years (%)
1976	0.1	12
1977	0.2	10
1978	0.5	4
1979	1.0	0.60
1980	1.9	−0.40
1981	2.5	1.40
1982	2.1	2.50
1983	1.4	4

Notes: "Multipliers" are relative to default rates in the base year 1979. "Price Growth After 2 Years" represents the average price growth rate in the 2 years after origination. See Van Order (1990).

Models like Model 1, which generates the default rates in Panel B of Table 4.2, can lead directly to a "pricing matrix". For instance, we could assume that each of the 8 origination years is equally likely in Model 1. To get the expected costs, we need more assumptions about default severity and a baseline default profile. Here, the baseline scenario is assumed as a loan in the "below-80%" LTV category having a 1% chance of ever defaulting. Furthermore, although not very realistic, we can also suppose that the loss per default in present value terms is constant at 25% of the loan balance. Then the expected credit cost as a percentage of the mortgage for each LTV bucket and year is depicted in Table 4.3. The bottom row gives the breakeven prices by LTV, assuming the data are a good enough sample of behavior.

Model 1 also illustrates model risk. The model uses a large sample in which millions of loans are aggregated into the categories in

Table 4.3 Pricing Matrix: Default Costs (as Percentage of Mortgage) from Model 1

	LTV ≤ 80	81–90	91–94	≥ 95
1976	0.025	0.10	0.14	0.20
1977	0.05	0.20	0.29	0.41
1978	0.13	0.49	0.71	1.01
1979	0.25	0.98	1.43	2.02
1980	0.48	1.85	2.71	3.85
1981	0.63	2.44	3.56	5.06
1982	0.53	2.05	2.99	4.25
1983	0.35	1.36	2.00	2.83
Average	0.30	1.18	1.73	2.46

Table 4.3. However, if the model had been estimated through 1979 to predict defaults, it would have only been through one upswing even though it would still have had a large sample, thus greatly underpredicting subsequent default costs. This appears to have happened with models estimated before the GFC. More formal discussions about the Great Crash will follow in Chapter 9 (see Table 9.1). Models estimated during the housing boom had little data with high default rates and underestimated the effects of shocks like a large decline in property or deterioration in underwriting standards. *Caveat Emptor.*

4.6. Summary

This chapter covers the pricing of mortgages that fund home purchases. Pricing mortgages is, as a first approximation, similar to pricing bonds and annuities. We introduce models for pricing mortgages when the borrower's behavior affects cash flows from when he/she might default or prepay. These in turn determine mortgage rates relative to risk-free rates. Now that we are equipped with the foundation needed for pricing in housing and mortgage, we can move on to understanding the markets. Awkward as it was.

Chapter 5

Where Does the Money Come From?

The Structure of U.S. Mortgage Markets

Now that we know about how mortgages are priced, we should find out who the investors are, and the structure of the mortgage markets. The U.S. mortgage market has been on a long strange trip, from a sleepy market dominated by low-key savings banks to a securitization-oriented market dominated by Federal Agencies, to a go-go Wall Street-oriented market with impenetrable structured deals, to collapse, and then back to the agencies and banks. With the exception of the go-go market in 2002–2007, it has been dominated by government-sponsored institutions, regulations, subsidies, and guarantees, and market share has been largely about tradeoffs between low-cost sources and government-guaranteed sources.

This chapter is about the pros and cons of different types of mortgage markets, how they compete with one another, and how they fit in. We introduce the notions of *moral hazard* and *agency cost*, which occurs when an *agent* acts in some capacity for but does not have incentives to act in the interest of, a *principal*. This is common to financial markets, more so in mortgage markets where mortgages are originated to then be sold to someone else, and the seller acts as an agent for the buyer. We use agency costs and different transaction costs among sources of funds, as well as taxes and subsidies, to explain the existence of rather different aspects of the system.

5.1. U.S. Homeownership and Size of the Mortgage Market

As introduced in Chapter 1 (Figure 1.2), the homeownership rate in the U.S. has been between 63% and 70% over the past two decades. Many renters either will own later or did own in the past, which means that the share of the population being owners at some point in time is on the order of 80%. Figure 5.1 extends Figure 1.2 to depict homeownership rates since 1900. The big story is rather the sharp run-up from World War II till the early 1960s. Not much has happened since. Most of the post-war increase was clearly driven by demographics — a surge in birth rates and household formation along with almost steady economic growth from the end of the war until the crash in 2007.

Almost all homeowners begin homeownership with a mortgage. The surge in ownership as in Figure 5.1 was enabled by mortgage market expansion. The U.S. mortgage market is large and has changed in structure over time, moving from bank-type lending toward securitization. Government policies since the end of World War II were generally meant to expand mortgage markets, particularly via programs like government-insured loans, deposit

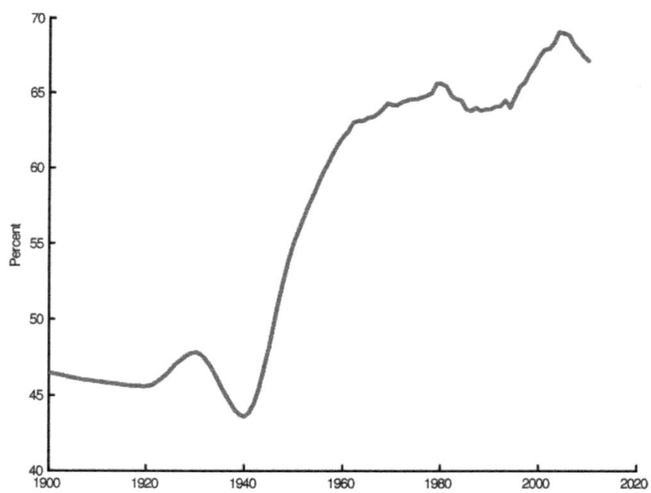

Figure 5.1 U.S. Homeownership Rate Since 1900

Source: U.S. Census (Data through 1960 are from decennial censuses).

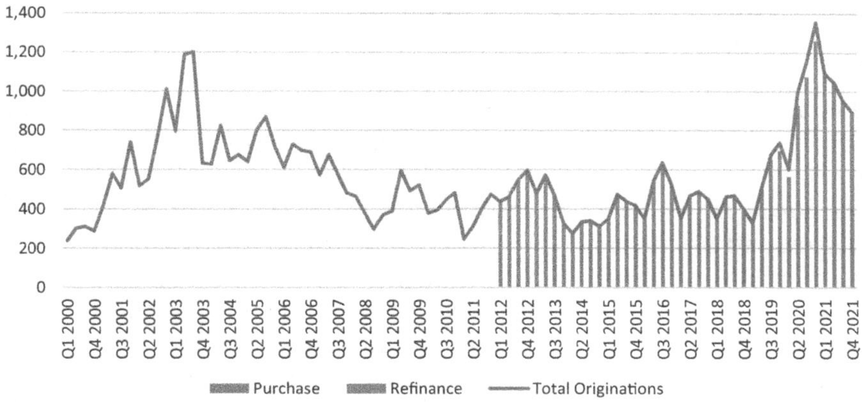

Figure 5.2 Total Mortgage Originations in the U.S. for 2000–2021 (in billion USD)

Source: https://www.statista.com/statistics/205937/us-mortgage-originations-since-1990/ and https://www.statista.com/statistics/275722/mortgage-originations-in-the-united-states/.

insurance which supports bank lending with money raised in deposit markets, the Federal Housing Association (FHA), which insures credit risk, and various government "Agencies" that promote secondary mortgage markets.

Figure 5.2 depicts the number of annual mortgage originations over the last 20 years. Given the source of the data, the amount can further be classified as originations for purchase and for refinancing for 2012–2021.[1] The biggest fluctuations are in loans to refinance existing loans. Since they are fixed-rate mortgages (FRM, which constitute most American mortgages), borrowers can reduce their borrowing costs through refinancing when interest rates fall, as discussed in Chapter 4. Originations are big when interest rates are low. People are enticed to own houses. Homeowners who have accumulated a lot of equity in their houses can refinance to take out equity, all of which were especially strong around 2002–2004 and 2020–2021 as shown in the figure.

[1]The total amount can also include home equity lines of credit (HELOC). Unfortunately, this is not available from our accessible data source.

5.2. How Are Mortgages Funded?

There are two archetypical models of markets that fund mortgages. The first is the traditional *portfolio lender model*, in which banks or other intermediaries (e.g. savings banks) originate loans, fund them (mainly with deposits) and hold them while accepting the risk that the loans might default. Traditionally, transactions tend to be in-person and all-inclusive. For instance, a would-be homebuyer would go to a bank to discuss the possibility of getting a mortgage, and the terms therein, typically and most importantly having the housing unit as collateral. The bank would evaluate the financial background of the homebuyer to see if he/she has the capability to make periodic payments to the bank before a mortgage is approved. Once approved, the borrower obtains the loan, buys the house, and makes periodic payments to the bank directly. If the borrower fails to pay and therefore defaults, the mortgage is said to be delinquent. Depending on state regulations, the house can be foreclosed by the bank and sold. U.S. banks (regular banks that is, see Chapter 6) have deposit insurance, which makes them easy to attract and keep deposits.

The second is the *securitization model*, in which banks or other lenders (e.g. mortgage banks) originate loans and put them into pools like mutual funds, and sell shares of the pools into capital markets. As with collateral for mortgages in the portfolio lender models, the housing units serve to "back" the mortgage securities, which is why the securities are called mortgage-backed securities (MBS). Typically, sellers transfer most of the risks to the buyers or outside guarantors. We will cover the mechanisms of securitization in Chapter 8, but its function as a funding source here. Most of the world outside the U.S. uses versions of the portfolio lender model.

There are tradeoffs between the two models. Securitization generally sells into more efficient capital markets where funds can be raised more quickly than in deposit markets. However, banks are likely to be closer to loan-level information than are bond market investors. This creates a *moral hazard* problem (aka lying and cheating) for buyers, to be discussed in Section 5.5.

The portfolio lender model and securitization model are just archetypes. The relationship between different parts of the mortgage market and the connection with housing and housing prices means there are multiple causation routes, with markets acting together as a kind of symbiosis — or a *dance*. For instance, some forms of securitization leave some credit risk with the institutions (e.g. banks) that originated the loans, and some forms of bank fundraising, such as *covered bonds* (see Chapter 8 for details), are similar to securitization in that they raise money in bond markets and set aside a pool of mortgages that acts as collateral for the sale of bonds to the bond market. That both archetypes have existed and still exist suggests benefits and costs for both.

We next present a brief recent history of the U.S. mortgage market. We then discuss a theory that suggests that all of these market structures are just different ways of carving up assets, and they do not matter to housing. We then cover the development of moral hazard/agency cost concerns, which suggests the structures (along with different costs) could matter after all.

5.3. A Brief History of the U.S. Mortgage Market: The 1980s and Beyond

There are three major *channels* for connecting borrowers with lenders/investors in the U.S.:

1. *The "Agency" market*: Mortgages were funded mainly through mortgage-backed securities (MBS), issued by the three Government Sponsored Enterprises (GSEs). The Federal National Mortgage Association (Fannie Mae, FNMA) and the Federal Home Loan Mortgage Corporation (Freddie Mac, FHLMC) were privately owned corporations that deal largely in conventional markets. The Government National Mortgage Association (Ginnie Mae, GNMA) is a government-owned enterprise that securitizes government-insured loans and is an "Agency", but not a GSE. These pools tend to be made up of fixed-rate mortgages. A point to note is that what makes an Agency an agency is government support; what makes a "GSE" is private ownership. Ginnie Mae has an explicit Federal guarantee on its payments to investors, and the GSEs have implicit guarantees. In this sense, banks are like GSEs because of deposit insurance and the possibility of bailouts.
2. *Private label securities (PLS)*: Mortgages are also funded by the issuance of "non-agency" MBS, i.e. without Agency guarantees.

The loans are either too big for the agencies by regulation (the so-called Jumbo loans) or are riskier than in the Agency market. These pools contain both FRMs and ARMs, although most are made up of ARMs during the PLS boom (2002–2006). The PLS market operates in the same sorts of markets as those of the Agencies, although it does not have guarantees or special charters. Its niches mostly come from less stringent regulation, relatively free entry, and information differences, so that it can compete with the big guys (Agency guarantees). This can produce adverse selection against investors, who are not always good at understanding what they are buying. We will return to this market and its discontents in Chapter 8.

3. *Banks*: Mortgages are originated or purchased and held (in portfolio) mostly by banks and institutions like pension funds and life insurance companies. These financial institutions deal primarily in conventional loans, although they also buy and hold Agency securities. They are the major source of ARMs. Banks are also players in the securitization markets, both selling and buying. The bank function presented here is the traditional bank lending model funded by deposits.

The three agencies and the PLS market are examples of the securitization model, while banks are examples of the portfolio lender model. But there is also overlap. For instance, the GSEs also hold mortgages in their portfolios, usually by buying back their own MBS. This allows them to sell something cleaner than pass-through securities, like bank intermediation. The "arbitrage" is that it does intermediation in bond markets by providing close substitutes for Treasury bonds and by managing the unique characteristics of mortgages (see Chapter 8). Banks also set up securitization deals, and they also buy PLS and their derivatives (see Chapter 8).

An alternative way to distinguish among channels is by strategy: between *buy and hold* and *originate to distribute* strategies. These two channels vary in subsidies, agency costs, and regulations. Fannie and Freddie are publicly traded institutions having unique charters that allow them to act as profit-maximizing institutions and sell into the bond market, with implicit guarantees from the government on their securities, subject to regulations. Banks have guarantees (mainly through deposit insurance and possible government bail-outs), charters that were, however, not unique (with essentially free entry), and are subject to regulations. They usually have the best information about loans because they see them first, which allows them to impose agency costs on the rest of the market by dumping the worst loans and keeping the best ones.

Ultimately, the fall-out from the GFC has changed the markets, in some ways, to be back to where they were in the 1990s when banks funded ARMs to manage interest rate risk and sold FRMs to the agencies, while the agencies were mostly stuck to FRMs and selling into bond markets. The PLS market has now largely quit selling riskier pools, suggesting that the regulatory arbitrage which PLS enjoyed (aside from loan size) was not as important as the moral hazard.

We next discuss the banks and the agencies in more detail.

5.4. Portfolio Lenders: Banks and Intermediation

Here we show the balance sheet of a typical portfolio lender — a bank. A bank is a corporation with which the liabilities have a pecking order with equity being the residual that takes the first hit if losses cannot be covered by revenues. Its balance sheet structure is shown in Figure 5.3, which is very similar to that of a typical corporation, an ongoing business with flows in and out of the balance sheet. While banks have different assets and earn income from fees, for instance from loan guarantees, we only focus on mortgages as assets here.

Asset	Liabilities
Mortgages Other assets Income streams (e.g. value of loan guarantees)	Deposits Other debt Subordinated debt Present value of insurance premiums
Other assets (Present value net of deposit insurance)	Equity

Figure 5.3 Balance Sheet Structure of a Portfolio Lender: A Bank

Banks have both benefits and costs. The main benefit in the U.S. and many other countries is deposit insurance (or access to bailouts or loans from the Fed or central banks). They can borrow at low rates, although not as nimbly as can capital market sellers. The limitations on where they can use their benefits leave room for regulatory arbitrage. There is also potential for imposing agency costs because banks can exploit mispriced insurance. For instance, banks can start by taking lots of risk and getting the upside when business goes well, but turning whatever the banks have left over to the insurers when failed, without the need of paying depositors for the risk. or being charged efficient premiums for the insurance. We recognize this by adding the present value of the deposit insurance, net of insurance premia to the FDIC. Clearly, efficiently priced insurance could solve the problem, but there would still be the moral hazard and agency costs (e.g. from the need for audits and regulation).

The structure in Figure 5.3 is applicable to two important extensions. One is real estate investment trusts (REITs). While some REITs do hold mortgages, assets are mostly real investments. The other is securitized banking, a term used by Gorton and Metrick (2010). This is done by shadow banks (see Chapter 6). The structure is a bank-like institution that holds securities rather than loans, and funds them with deposit-like debt. Versions of this are Repurchase Agreements (Repos) which are short-term (e.g. overnight) borrowing that are secured by highly rated securities, and money market funds which hold securitized commercial papers funded with short-term debt. These are discussed later in the chapter.

5.5. The Three Agencies

The three agencies have primarily been about guaranteeing pools of MBS, like insurance companies. Fannie and Freddie have also operated portfolios of MBS funded with their own debt, like hedge funds. Both are still primarily insurers now, but the hedge fund content of their businesses has varied over time.

Fannie Mae, Fannie in short, was established in the 1930s and is the oldest of the agencies as a secondary market for newly-created loans insured by the Federal Housing Administration (FHA) insured by the government. It had trouble gaining acceptance by investors during the Great Depression. For much of its history, until the 1980s, it operated like a hedge fund that was in some ways like a national savings and loan, gathering funds by issuing its own short-term debt (rather than deposits) and buying mortgages that were held in portfolio. Since it held government-insured mortgages, it accepted almost no credit risk. This was a particularly useful function during credit crunches when deposit rate ceilings limited the ability of savings and loans to raise money. It also avoided restrictions on bank operations across states. In 1968, the originally government-owned Fannie was moved off the budget to be set up as a private, government-sponsored enterprise (GSE). At the same time, it was allowed to deal in conventional loans, which do have credit risk, and which have dominated its activities since then.

Ginnie Mae, or Ginnie in short, was created as a successor to the old Fannie to handle Fannie's policy-related tasks and to provide a secondary market for government-insured loans. It is owned by the government as part of the U.S. Department of Housing and Urban Development (HUD), largely responsible for developing the major innovation in secondary markets, the mortgage-backed security (MBS).

Ginnie developed an important contract with its servicers that they guarantee the payment of interest and principal of the Ginnie pool even if the borrower defaults. The issuer is covered with government insurance for almost all of the foreclosure costs. Ginnie also guarantees timely payment even if the issuer does not make the payments. Hence, the Ginnie guarantee is on top of the federal insurance on FHA loans and the issuer's guarantee. This has proven to be valuable in marketing government-insured loans, and it tends to align the incentives of Ginnie originators with those of Ginnie. Since it simply enhances other guarantees, its costs are small and has actually made money from the fee it charges. A reason for its success is that it *requires* servicers to take a servicing fee of 75 basis points, which is much larger than the cost of servicing.[2] This creates value in the rights to service pools. Ginnie has the right to seize the servicing if servicers do not fulfill their obligations. Fannie and Freddie have

[2]Servicers would rather get their income up-front and not, in effect, use the value of servicing fees as performance bond to protect the government.

similar arrangements. But unlike these two, Ginnie is generally not allowed to hold mortgages or mortgage-backed securities.

Freddie Mac, Freddie in short, was created in 1970 to be a secondary market for conventional loans. Like Fannie, it is a private GSE, and it too is off-budget. It originally dealt only with savings banks, like savings and loans, and Fannie dealt with mortgage banks which are largely "dealers" that originate loans in order to sell them. Now both institutions deal with the same originators. It initiated the first MBS program for conventional loans in 1971. Fannie began its conventional MBS program in 1981. The MBSs of all three agencies are similar in protecting investors against credit risk but not interest rate risk. Neither Fannie nor Freddie does more than a small amount of federally insured mortgages, as these almost always go into Ginnie pools.

Since Ginnie is on the government budget, its securities have a "full faith and credit" Federal guarantee. On the other hand, Freddie and Fannie are private corporations, and therefore neither has an explicit guarantee. Since both are GSEs, investors believe that the government would protect debt-holders if these institutions failed, albeit without clear *legal* obligation.[3] This has allowed the two GSEs to borrow or sell MBSs at lower interest rates than otherwise.

5.5.1. Risks and Strategies of Fannie and Freddie

Fannie and Freddie operated quite smoothly from the late 1980s until around 2007. There were always concerns about capital levels, but they generally had quite low credit costs. The major concerns in 2007 were over debt funding and interest rate risk. The concern turned out to be misplaced. It was credit losses that caused the problems in 2007.

Fannie's and Freddie's business strategies, especially regarding risk-taking, have evolved over time as markets and regulations have changed. As discussed above, there is an overlap between GSEs and portfolio lenders. GSEs have hedge fund businesses that hold

[3]The GSEs sometimes argued that they did not have a real guarantee, but lobbied hard to keep it.

mortgages or MBSs funded with their own agency debt. The debt has an implicit guarantee and is more transparent to investors than MBS. They are traded very much like government bonds at a low spread over Treasury securities. The GSEs portfolios can have interest rate risk, as well as credit risk because, unlike with MBS, their cash flows from assets need not be the same as payments promised by borrowers.

Originally Fannie funded FHA loans with its own debt, typically short-term, and was effectively the only national savings bank. However, the interest rate risk got into trouble in the late 1970s and early 1980s, when its funding costs rose sharply as the Fed raised interest rates in order to control inflation. The rates on the interest income were more or less fixed, but their cost of funds went way up. As a result, Fannie was essentially insolvent, although it eventually evolved with considerable forbearance. After that, it limited its interest rate risk by moving into securitization and funding its portfolio with longer-term debt, often callable, to match up with borrower prepayments.

Freddie was almost entirely in the securitization business until the late 1990s. It was initially tied to the Savings and Loan industry and specialized in pooling mortgages in growing regions with excess demand for mortgage credit and selling them in slower regions with excess savings. It was essentially a way of getting around regional branch-banking restrictions, as well as deposit rate ceilings, which sometimes made it very hard to attract deposits. The ceilings were eliminated in the early 1980s. However, Freddie survived, and by the end of the 1980s, Fannie and Freddie had almost identical charters and customer bases. They are now more or less out of the portfolio lender business.

In the late 1990s, the U.S. federal government began running surpluses; safe Treasury debt became scarce and was priced at below risk-free rates. Freddie began buying back its own MBS and selling its debt that looked like Treasury debt but at higher prices than otherwise, in order to arbitrage the low Treasury rates. Buying back existing securities, rather than keeping some loans and securitizing others, was to handle a moral hazard problem because purchasers of the MBS might (probably would) believe they were being selected against and damage the MBS market. Hence, buying existing MBS maintained the credibility of the MBS market.[4] Since it was not entirely match-funded it was exposed to interest rate risk, but much of it was controlled with hedging. A way of hedging short funding is swapping cash flows from their short-term liabilities for the cash flow from someone else's long-term payouts. Sometimes this is supplemented with "swaptions" that offset the prepayment option embedded in fixed-rate mortgages (see Chapter 4). This is not always easy.

Although both Fannie and Freddie look like shadow banks (to be covered in detail in Chapter 6) as well as securitizers, they were not, based on our definition above, because they have a (conjectured but real) guarantee and are regulated rather like banks. In 2007, both GSEs began piling up losses and there was concern about whether there was a guarantee. Some international investors began selling off GSE debt, making it harder for them to roll over their debt. Was this the beginning of a run? It could have been if the Treasury had not intervened to remove the conjectures.

5.5.2. The GFC and Conservatorship

The conjecture of a guarantee finally turned out to be true. After property markets crashed and defaults increased dramatically in 2007 and 2008, both GSEs began losing money from default costs. In September 2008, in conjunction with the Treasury Department and the Federal Reserve, the Federal Housing Finance Agency (FHFA) placed the two GSEs under conservatorship,[5] in which the treasury guaranteed GSE liabilities by recapitalizing the two by injecting over $180 billion via preferred stock, which was essentially loans that paid a 10% dividend.

Both GSEs are still currently in conservatorship and operate more or less like public utilities. Their securitization operations are

---

[4]Both GSEs have separate groups that make the purchases of their MBS. These parts of the companies do not have access to loan level data and are supposed to have only information that the rest of the market has. There have been concerns about the lack of data access, although this appears not to have been a factor in limiting the MBS market.

[5]Frame *et al.* (2015) discusses the conservatorship and some background and implications.

relatively the same as before conservatorship, though perhaps for different purposes. Ultimately, taxpayers made money on the capital injections by earning a spread between the 10% that the GSEs paid and the close to 0% rate that the treasury paid to raise the money to fund them, and the capital was paid off.[6] At the time of writing, it is not clear what will happen to the two in the future.[7] Since conservatorship, at the direction of regulators, the two have now almost completely out of the portfolio/hedge fund business and are sticking to the MBS business.

5.5.3. Dueling Charters and Market Share

Since some time in the 1970s, the mortgage market could be described as one of "Dueling Charters", between the banks (and savings banks) as archetypical portfolio lenders, and the agencies as the archetypical securitizers.[8] As discussed above, the big trade-off is the efficiency of bond markets versus the moral hazard against them and the roles of guarantees in both markets. There has been considerable policy and political debate around this about which charter is better and/or worthier of subsidies. It has paid the salaries of many lobbyists and consultants. To have some idea of how market shares have evolved, Figure 5.4 depicts mortgage market shares by outstanding balance over time.

The big story from the figure is that securitization did not catch on until the 1980s and then grew steadily. Portfolio lenders (especially savings banks) dominated the market until the agencies cut into their market. Securitization was almost entirely done via the Agencies. The GSE (Fannie and Freddie) shares increased steadily from the 1980s into the new millennium, until 2003. This was due to the Federal guarantee, which gave agency MBS better than an AAA rating, so

---

[6]See Wall (2014) for a discussion of what was paid back. Since 2012, dividend payments have stopped and treasury takes all the net income.

[7]This is a standoff between Republicans, who generally want to eliminate their charters (or greatly revise them), and Democrats, who tend to want to keep them inside the government, or redirect them more toward social goals.

[8]See Van Order (2000). Dueling Charters is a variation on a notion originating with Michael Lea (1986).

they could compete with deposit insurance and exploit bond markets as a better way of funding fixed-rate mortgages. This was the big change; the GSEs had won the duel. The figure also shows the evolution of the Agency markets in the 1990s.

The other story is that the private label business exploded after the millennium. A reason was the boost from rising house prices substituting for Agency guarantees, making bad loans taste good by building equity up so rapidly that defaults were low everywhere. PLS offered risky, but not horribly risky, securities with higher promised yields than did Fannie and Freddie. This lost market share for the Agencies was most likely a factor for their upping their credit risk exposure.

The Agencies (still in conservatorship) came back after the crash and eliminated the competition. Currently, Agency MBS occupies over 90% of the securitization market and over 60% of the overall mortgage market (about 70% of residential mortgages are securitized). Figure 5.4 also shows the evolution of Agency portfolios in the 1990s. The charters were still dueling, without much interference in the private market, and with the GSEs still ahead of the banks.

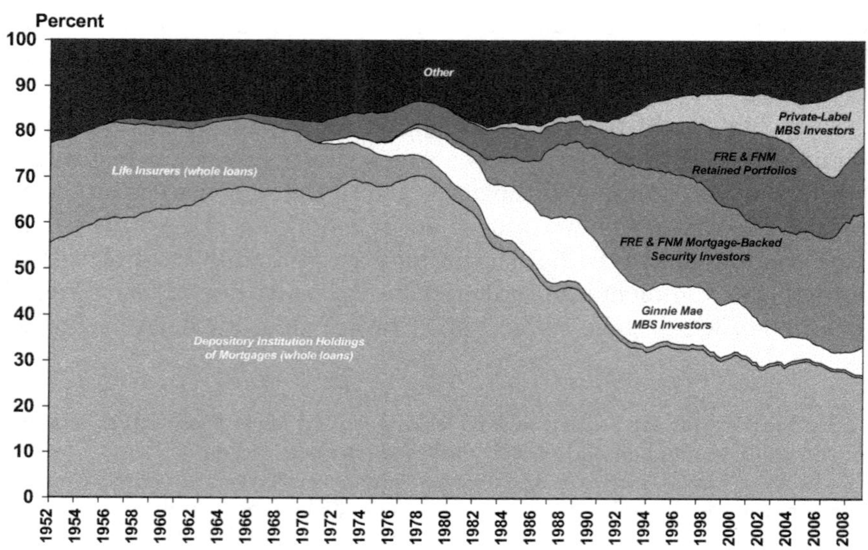

Figure 5.4 Mortgage Market Shares

Source: Federal Reserve Board; Data as of 2Q 2009: Courtesy Ed Golding.

Before moving on, we need to think about the usefulness of all this fuss about securitization and different types of conduits when we have banks to begin with. What value do they add when all they do is pass on cash flows from the same sorts of assets and pay up for the cost of doing the deals?

5.6. Modigliani–Miller Theorem: Does Anything Matter?

A guy phones a pizza store to order a pizza to be delivered to his house. The receptionist taking the order asks, "Would you like it cut into six pieces or eight". The guy says, "Eight pieces,[9] I'm hungry tonight". Sounds silly, doesn't it? Or does it? This is a simple example of a major topic in finance: dividing portfolios into separate pieces, and why that might or might not matter. It is the much-celebrated "Modigliani–Miller Irrelevance Theorem" (henceforth "M–M", by Franco Modigliani and Merton H. Miller)[10] that is a bedrock of finance theory.[11]

5.6.1. The Theorem

Briefly, the theorem holds under a set of assumptions that define "perfect markets", which assumes competitive markets without transaction or bankruptcy costs, widely agreed on information (but not perfect information), and no taxes/subsidies or other differences in holding or trading costs. The liability structure of the firm (financial or not) is irrelevant according to the model in the sense that changing the way it finances its assets will not affect its "all-in" cost of funds, nor will it affect the firm (or structure) value, which is also the sum of its liabilities (including its share price).

This is because different liability strategies are simply different ways of rearranging (or slicing) the same cash flows from the firm's assets (or the store's pizzas); and in a well-informed, competitive

[9]Finance guys would call them *tranches.*

[10]Modigliani and Miller (1958).

[11]Adapted from Yogi Berra and the M&M Proposition, *Journal of Applied Corporate Finance*, 7(4), 1995, p. 6. By way of Arnold Kling.

market, trading and competition will assure that all structures will be priced so that none has an overall advantage. Otherwise, there will be exploitable profits from buying the liabilities and restructuring them, which can happen quickly. For instance, if an eight-slice pizza costs more than a six-slice one, the pizza guy could buy a cheaper six-piece but identical-size pizza, cut each piece in half, and have him and his three friends each have three pieces.[12]

The theorem applies to all sorts of financial and business liability structures (as well as pizzas). For instance, consider a bank putting a pool of mortgages for sale. In a competitive market, the value of the pool will be the sum of the values of the individual mortgages. If these are turned into a fund, like a mutual fund, the sum of the values of the shares in the fund will equal the value of the mortgages in the pool. If the pool is structured by breaking it into the debt and equity pieces, the value of both pieces together equals the value of the assets, according to the theorem, no matter what their shares of debt and equity are. If this were literally true, there would be no motivation for the structures in the first place. There must be some frictions or costs that make selling the mortgage pool pieces profitable. A softer version is that the frictions are small, and the liability structure is relatively unimportant in determining mortgage rates.

M–M is one of those ideas that is obvious when you think about it, given its assumptions of perfect markets. However, it is mostly wrong. Asymmetric information can easily ruin a competitive market, and transaction costs can vary across markets, which is a major reason for the existence of different financial intuitions. Tax and subsidy differences can affect market structure too.

Nevertheless, M–M is a good place to start because it makes us ask the right question: why should we expect one institutional setup to be better than another at financing a particular set of cash flows when they all compete in the same overall financial system? It suggests that some rationales for securitization, like "getting assets off balance sheet", "the high cost of capital relative to debt", or "allowing banks to shed the risk of low downpayment loans" (risk should be the same

[12]This is pretty much what the structured securities business does. The pizza guy would sell the pieces to his three friends and make money off the spread.

to the buyer of the loans who will pay the market price) are suspect, pending further information.

5.6.2. Reasons for M–M Failure: Costs, Moral Hazard, and Lemons

There are two especially important violations of M–M in financial markets, even in competitive markets and with no excess profits. First, not all traders have the same information and costs. Sources of funding may have low costs because they are further removed from the information. Second, different sources have different taxes and subsidies. The most interesting motive of the sources is moral hazard.

5.6.2.1. *Moral hazard*

Information differences can cause a *principal-agent (or agency)* problem between buyers/investors (the principals) and the lenders/sellers (agents) who put the deals together. The principals rely on agents to act in their interest when it is not always in the interests of the latter. Banks (more generally loan originators) can dump the worst loans into securitization deals. This is *moral hazard.* It introduces distortions into the market (e.g. higher cost loans and a smaller market). Principals will tend to assume the worst because they know they are being selected against, leading to a kind of self-fulfilling prophesy – that the worst loans are delivered as they are expected — limiting the size of the market to the extent that contracts cannot do all the work at low cost. It also introduces *agency costs* from trying to monitor or control agents' incentives, e.g. by using contracts. Many of the policies involved in regulating and promoting mortgage markets and financial firms revolve around managing agency costs (or exploiting them).

5.6.2.2. *Lemons*

A classic example of moral hazard is the case of used car markets explained by George A. Akerlof.[13] Sellers know more about cars than

[13] Akerlof (1970).

buyers and will tend to dump the low-value cars (lemons[14]) first. Buyers know this, of course, but are limited in how they can handle it because they can only know at best the average value of cars in a pool for sale. Sellers will exploit this information asymmetry and dump cars until the last (marginal) car sold has a price equal to the average cost of the cars in the pool. Consequently, buyers will get cars that are in general worse than the price paid. This is unsustainable, and will tend toward a situation where only bad cars are traded at bad car prices; good cars cannot be traded because buyers cannot tell the good from the bad. This is of course inefficient! It blocks mutually beneficial trades. The agency costs come from this market distortion and from costs used to get better valuations of the cars, e.g. independent inspections.

5.6.2.3. *Agency costs and pizza*

Back to the pizza guy. As above, if he is sharing the pizza with three friends, then the eight-slice strategy really is preferable because it is more easily shared by four. However, because it is so easy to make slices, the slicing "structure" would have no effect in the cost of pizza even though some "structures" might be more popular than others without much reason or benefits from the structures. Suppose, however, that there is a tax on pizza based on the number of slices. Then there would be a noticeable cost to having eight slices and might encourage an inefficient switch to six or fewer. Both cases induce agency costs, either from tax or from re-slicing the pizza.

Regarding moral hazard, this pizza tax issue presents a principal-agent problem for the tax collector. Suppose the pizza place is supposed to collect taxes for the government. It can avoid the tax by selling unsliced pizza and having customers use their own slicers, or selling to the pizza guy to be restructured and sold (arbitraged) in the secondary market. This imposes costs, in place

[14]A term coined by George A. Akerlof, the Nobel Laurate, in his paper entitled "The Market for "Lemons": Quality Uncertainty and the Market Mechanism", in Akerlof (1970). "Market for lemons" refers to markets in which all the best items would have been picked, leaving the worst that are not supposed to worth, and therefore priced, as much.

of tax, on customers to buy slicers and on pizza guys (aka investment bankers) to worry about their deliveries. There is probably nothing the tax collector can do except to have a more sensible tax system.

In real-world cases, the costs may be from monitoring the assets, as with inspections for used cars, or buybacks from sellers (refunds) for poorly performing securities. It may involve costly regulation, such as bank inspection and capital requirements.

5.6.3. Solutions

Moral hazard is inevitable in finance, at least in any part that involves contracts and/or trust. In the mortgage market, whoever takes the risk needs to try to align the incentives of originators and servicers with their own. Ginnie Mae's contracts with servicers are a good example. Otherwise, they'd better obtain more accurate information on risk. An important substitute for good information is the use of collateral, such as the housing unit in the case of a mortgage, because the owner of collateral takes the first hit in a loss situation, limiting losses to investors. It is sometimes said that collateral is rather like ketchup — enough of it can make a bad meal tolerable.

M–M fails in financial structures (see Chapter 8) of firms (or banks) where investors have different information and risk tolerance. A piece of the liability structure may be set up to absorb risk and another safer piece for other more risk-averse investors. For instance, equity holders of corporations absorb risk first, and debt holders second. In banks, equity capital protects depositors. This allows distinctly different investor types to be involved in funding. If a bank has insurance, the bank capital protects the insurer more than the depositors.

Finally, note the two big ideas here, beyond the pepperoni. First, moral hazard does not just produce costs. It leads to a smaller market where only the worst stuff gets traded. For instance, the sale to buyers who want perfectly good cars are blocked; they cannot get the cars because of market failure. Second, M–M leads us into a lot of interesting directions and forces us to ask questions about things we might have otherwise taken for granted.

5.7. Summary

This chapter looks at the traditional mortgage market in the U.S., which is composed of both bank portfolio lender models and securitization models. The focus here is the part of the system with a government guarantee. We have posed some reasons for current markets in terms of the Modigliani–Miller irrelevance theorem and the trade-off embedded in its violations. Market share hinges on balancing between information differences (and hence agency cost problems) and the willingness of investors to pay up for protection against different risks.

It was widely understood that what ultimately led to the GFC was the U.S. subprime mortgage crisis, which was caused by poor underwriting and a fall in housing prices. But blaming it solely on the subprime mortgages is inaccurate. The culprits were also the complicated shadow banking system and its interconnectedness with the larger financial system, which led to new types of bank runs. We cover all these in the following chapters.

Chapter 6

Shadow Banking

Banking without Banks

The term *shadow banking* was not widely used until the Global Financial Crisis (GFC). It has however existed for centuries, albeit under different names, such as "non-bank banking" not too long ago. In any event, shadow banking refers to bank-like financial institutions that act *in the shadow* of "regular" banks, mimicking what they do, but without bank charters. That is, banking without banks. There is no widely accepted notion of what the shadow banking system is, except that we know it is not the regular banking system. This is a start, albeit vague. To understand what shadow banking covers, we should understand what traditional banking does. Banks are special financial institutions with special charters and provide two defining and complementary functions, *liquidity provision* and *financial transformation.*[1] As Gorton puts it, "banks exist to create debt that is used for transactions".[2] The debt is created from borrowing, in the form of loans or deposits.

Banks collect funds from depositors, who can demand the cash back on short notice (*liquidity provision*), and they transform these

[1]Of course, you also go to a bank to transfer money to accounts in other places, exchanging foreign currencies, and other "banking services". These services are, however, not unique to banks.

[2]Page 5 of Gorton (2015).

funds into risky loans that may take longer to be paid back (i.e. not liquid) and are difficult to sell (*financial transformation*). When the loans do default, banks run the risk that depositors, who are generally not in a good position to evaluate default risk, will try to withdraw all their money at once (aka *bank runs*) if deposit insurance is absent, i.e. the Diamond–Dybvig story.

Regular banks are also subject to constraints, such as regulatory restrictions on the types of assets they can hold and on the amount of leverage, they can take. They also often have portfolio restrictions for public policy purposes. For instance, they have incentives to provide funds to underserved borrowers and to promote financial inclusion. Offsetting this, banks benefit from guarantees like deposit insurance and other implicit guarantees (usually from central banks) that allow them to raise money from depositors at low interest rates.

Shadow banking in the U.S. largely replicates the liquidity provision and financial transformation function of regular banks but is not subject to the same regulations and scrutiny. Actually, before the advent of bank regulations, deposit insurance, and government guarantees, banks were about the same as shadow banks are now. Not all financial intuitions that compete with banks are shadow banks though. Lots of other financial institutions that are neither banks nor shadow banks perform some of the functions mentioned above. A firm that helps its customers buy and sell shares of company stocks or exchange dollars for euros is a financial institution that acts as a broker between customers, but it is neither a bank nor a shadow bank, and private lending platforms supporting it are not the same as shadow banking. Platforms are more like auctioneers. Private conduit lending connecting lenders to borrowers has the shadow, but not the bank.

We discuss shadow banking in the U.S. in this chapter. We are brief about the development of U.S. shadow banking because it has already been very extensively covered by many books since the GFC. Instead, we have devoted a whole Chapter 7 to the shadow banking structure in China because it has had a different and very rapid development, for different purposes, with different clientele, different implications, and less popular coverage. Whereas U.S. shadow banking has been associated with the advent of securitization and expanding sources of funds, China's has been more about extending banking to areas not well covered by the main banking system, and is less about new institution types.

6.1. Why Is There Shadow Banking, and Where Is the Arbitrage?

The Financial Stability Board in 2011 characterized shadow banking as follows:

> The 'shadow banking system' can broadly be described as 'credit intermediation involving entities and activities outside the regular banking system.
>
> ... The term started to be used widely at the onset of the recent financial crisis, reflecting an increased recognition of the importance of entities and activities structured outside the regular banking system that perform bank-like functions ("banking"). These entities and activities provide credit by themselves or through a "chain" that transforms maturity or liquidity, and builds up leverage as in the regular banking system. They also typically rely on short-term funding from the markets, such as through repos and asset-backed commercial paper (ABCP).[3]

Why operate outside the regular system? After all, banks get a lot of benefits from their charters. Nevertheless, they are also heavily regulated, and the cost of some regulations for some activities is bound to be higher than the benefits of low-rate borrowing, leaving an opening for competitors with lower costs or higher returns in those activities. Warren Buffett posed the issue as:

> Shadow banking is mostly a reflection of the official mispricing in the regular banking market. The more severely the banks' interest rates deviate from the "fair" and equilibrium interest rates, the more outrageous the shadow banking interest rates will be.[4]

This is sometimes referred to as "regulatory arbitrage." For instance, in the U.S., if deposit insurers misprice their coverage, banks can exploit their insurance rates by taking on riskier loans, while still getting to borrow at low rates. In such cases, they have something akin to an option because they can "roll the dice" and only get the upside of their decisions, with the deposit insurer taking the downside.[5] Shadow banks pay higher interest rates on their debt, and

---

[3]Financial Stability Board, October 17, 2011 (pages 1 and 2).

[4]Page 124 of Zhang (2014).

[5]There is more to it than just that. Banks are inclined to wait until something big happens, such as losing a lot of money and on the verge of losing their "franchise value". Then they can "Gamble for Resurrection."

have to find niches less profitable for banks. The size variation of the shadow banking markets across countries is largely due to the differential costs of regulations (resulting in different levels of regulatory arbitrage). China's regulations have many different relative costs from those in the U.S. and so have a different arbitrage.

We should note that the implications of the shadow banking setup are not themselves bad. It has long been argued that trying out new activities outside the formal system might be a good idea, as long as the system is not at risk, eventually laying the costs on shadow bank investors. However, shadow banks that create liquidity are prone to the same bank-run-like problems as afflicted regular banks before the existence of deposit insurance. Bank runs can cause significant disruptions that spread beyond the shadow banking system itself. This was true both during the Great Depression in the 1930s without deposit insurance and during the GFC with runs on shadow banks.

6.1.1. Shadow Banks and Securitization

Shadow banks have played a significant role in the securitization market, sometimes as sellers and sometimes as buyers. Securitization has been briefly introduced in Chapter 5 when covering the GSEs. More details can be found in Chapter 8. For now, the question is: Why would shadow banks want to do securitization? Simple! By doing so, they can write loans like banks, earn income without all of the regulatory costs and provide liquidity in ways regular banks don't (and enjoy the regulatory arbitrage).

The Global Monitoring Report on Non-Bank Financial Intermediation 2019, also released by the Financial Stability Board (2020, page 64), shadow banks are

> ... entities that are involved in securitization-based credit intermediation (such as CLOs) or funding of financial entities through investment funds (or other similar structures, such as trust companies) to finance illiquid assets by raising funds from markets. Both bank and non-bank financial intermediaries use securitization for funding (with or without the transfer of assets and risks from the securitization entities), to improve their lending portfolios and for capital management. By facilitating the transfer of credit risk off balance sheet, securitization reduces funding costs for both bank and non-bank financial entities, and facilitates the availability of credit to the real economy.

In most countries, shadow banking takes the form of non-bank financial intermediaries, including money market funds, investment banks, mortgage lenders, insurance companies, hedge funds, and private equity funds. It can also include legal entities called Special Purpose Vehicles (SPVs, or SPEs for special purpose entities), or conduits that are formed by banks and financial institutions to manage funds and enforce the rules of the securitization deals and to own the assets. It looks like there are unlimited ways for shadow banks to profit as long as they are good at obtaining sources of funding. This also opens up the possibility of selecting against the "depositors" by putting lemons (as in Chapter 5) into the bank's portfolio, which is mispriced in a way that buyers do not understand (see Chapter 8).

Figure 6.1 depicts the total amount of assets held globally by non-bank financial intermediation (NBFI) and those by banks in trillions of U.S. dollars. Also shown are their proportions in the total global financial assets. It is clear from the figure that the amount of shadow banking assets has already surpassed that of traditional banks since 2003, except for a couple of GFC years. It did not take long to grow again starting in 2021, this time with even bigger increase. NBFI assets have become a larger and larger share of the total global

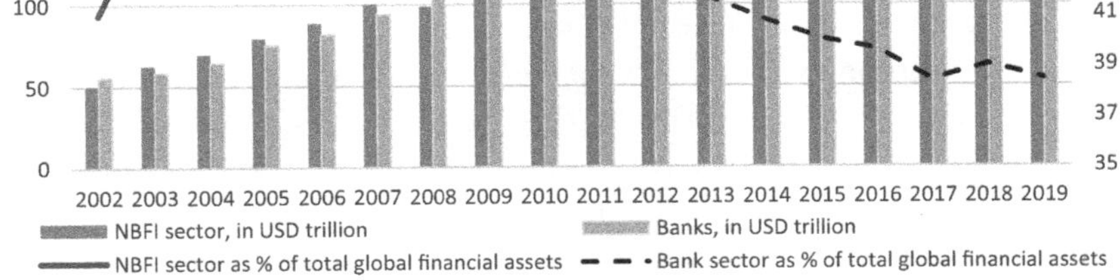

Figure 6.1 Assets Held by Non-Bank Financial Intermediation versus Banks (Left Axis), and as Percentages of Total Global Financial Assets (Right Axis)

Source: Financial Stability Board (2019). *Global Monitoring Report on Non-Bank Financial Intermediation 2018*, 4 February 2019. Available from: https://www.fsb.org/wp-content/uploads/P040219.pdf and authors' calculations.

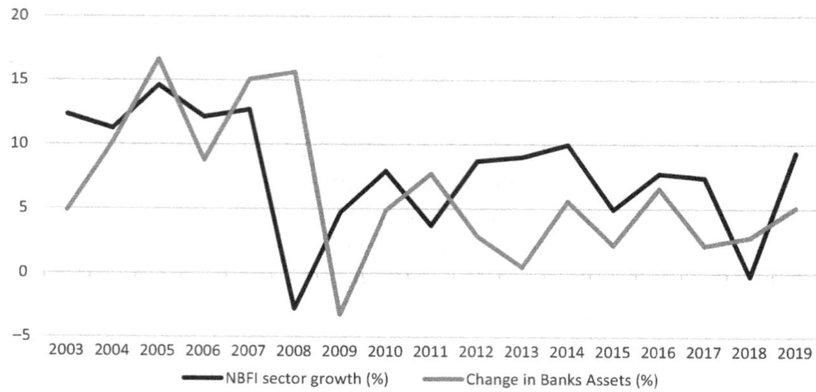

Figure 6.2 Growth in Non-Bank Financial Intermediation versus Growth in Banks

Source: NBFI sector growth is from Financial Stability Board (2019), Change in Banks Assets are authors' calculations.

financial assets, while assets of banks have shrunk continuously, from a gap between NBFI assets and bank assets of −4.46% (40.99% versus 45.45%) in 2002 to NBFI assets surpassing that of banks by 3.76% (46.74% versus 42.98%) in 2006, then reversed to a gap of −4.28% (42.31% versus 46.55%) in 2008, and finally to a widened gap of 11.06% (49.53% versus 38.46%) in 2019. Figure 6.2 further shows the growth of both asset values. While both grew in similar trends over the 2003–2019 period, the NBFI assets generally grew faster after the Crisis years.

Structures for shadow banking can include Repos and Asset-Backed Commercial Papers (ABCP) (to be covered later in this chapter), and securitization products (details in Chapter 8). The financial sector has become ever more creative in new financial products with so many acronyms especially during the first 10 years of the new century, like a bowl of "alphabet soup". Whether it is tasty depends. What is correct for sure is that its complex taste of sweetness at the beginning, then spicy later, and very bitter in the end with the GFC.

6.1.2. Examples of Shadow Banking and Liquidity Creation

Shadow bank assets include Asset-Backed Commercial Paper (ABCP) and securities used in repurchase agreements (repos).

ABCPs are short-term money-market securities for banks usually for maturities of 90 to 270 days, and are backed by collateral that would generate future payments, such as credit card payments and student loans. Unlike normal commercial papers, which borrowers write to the lenders directly, ABCPs are issued by structured finance operating companies (SFOC) that collect the collateral from participating banks and financial institutions. Typical investors of ABCPs are Money Market Mutual Funds (MMMFs, used interchangeably with money-market funds) or other mutual funds. Other forms of SFOCs that also issue ABCPs are the Structured Investment Vehicles (SIVs), which are also shadows of banks performing dynamic asset/liability management in their risks. All these create liabilities that look like deposits in traditional banks in terms of liquidity.

MMMFs are shadow banks not only because they invest in shadow banking instruments and enhance liquidity creation, but also because, like conduits issuing ABCPs, they are not entitled to deposit insurance. MMMFs are open-ended mutual funds investing in highly liquid investments with minimal credit risk such as U.S. Treasury bills, short-term debts of GSEs (discussed in the previous chapter) in the case of the U.S., banker's acceptances, commercial papers, repos, certificates of deposits, with varying maturities to cater investors' redemption of shares at any time, and paying investors periodic dividends. According to the Global Monitoring Report on Non-Bank Financial Intermediation 2019 issued by the Financial Stability Board (2020, page 47), the two largest holders of global MMFs assets in 2018 are the U.S. and China, occupying 53% and 18% of total global assets, with growth rates of 5% and 13%, respectively.

6.1.3. Repurchase Agreements

An archetypical version (e.g. in Gorton's work) of a shadow bank is a repurchase agreement. A repo is essentially an overnight (sometimes longer) deposit at a bank (maybe an investment bank) that is collateralized by assets in the bank's portfolio. In creating repos, banks, and other financial institutions, bundle Treasury securities or corporate or other loans which they hold, including AAA-rated securitization deals, and use them as collateral for short-term borrowing. This is a typical way for corporations or other institutions such as other banks, money market institutional investors, mutual funds, pension funds, and insurance companies to park their idle cash for a while and earn higher returns than from regular deposits.[6] The repurchase part comes from the sale of the securities used as collateral at a discount and then repurchases at a higher price. The difference in the two prices determines the overnight borrowing rate. The bank transfers the collateral to the "depositor" and must repurchase or have the depositor roll it over for another night. Other types of similar arrangements are, for instance, MMMFs putting out what are essentially demand deposits secured by loans to businesses.

Repos are a favorite example of securitized banking because they were more at the center of the GFC. This is also an example of securitized banking. The structure has deposit-like liabilities, and assets constituting securities rather than loans. The size of the market at one point was almost as big as the value of all bank assets.

For the repo market to work, the buyers/depositors have to be confident that the sellers (banks) can buy back their collateral. Banks sometimes take a "haircut", meaning they have to own some of the pool to make the depositors happy, rather like capital for a bank. The amount of haircut depends on the riskiness of the securities, which depends on the volatility and liquidity of the collateral. A significant part of the GFC began after banks put highly rated MBS into these collateral bundles, and haircuts went way up as the ratings of the securities fell. This became a bank run as the bank had to scramble to find cash to cover the bigger haircut.

Figure 6.3 shows the net positions (i.e. Repo assets minus Repo liabilities) for the 29 Jurisdictions from which the FSB collects data. Other Financial Intermediaries (OFIs) are still the major provider of funds in 2020, albeit smaller in percentage compared to the recent peak in 2014.

6.1.4. A Mock Description of a Structure with Shadow Banking and Securitization

Figure 6.4 provides a generalized structure of securitization and securitized banking from the viewpoint of the trades involved.

[6]Deposit insurance is not so helpful for really big investors as there is a maximum size on insured deposits.

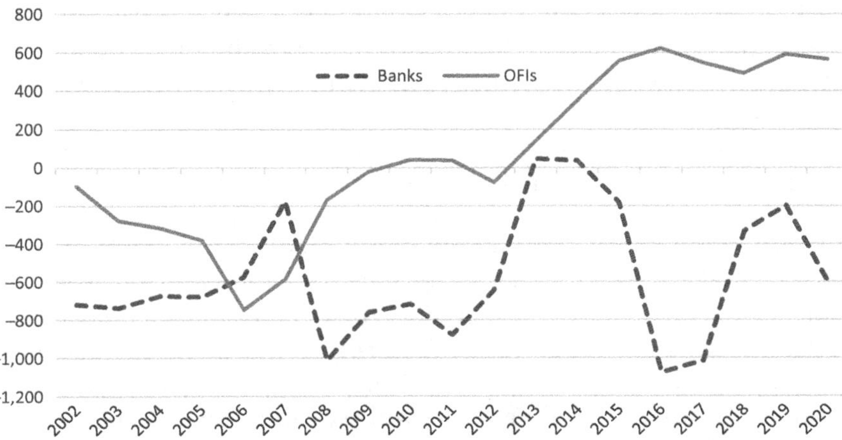

Figure 6.3 Net Positions in Repos for 29 Jurisdiction Groups (in Billion USD)

Source: Financial Stability Board "Underly data for graphs" of the Global Monitoring Report on Non-Bank Financial Intermediation 2021. Available at: https://www.fsb.org/wp-content/uploads/Underlying-data-for-graphs-2021.xlsx.

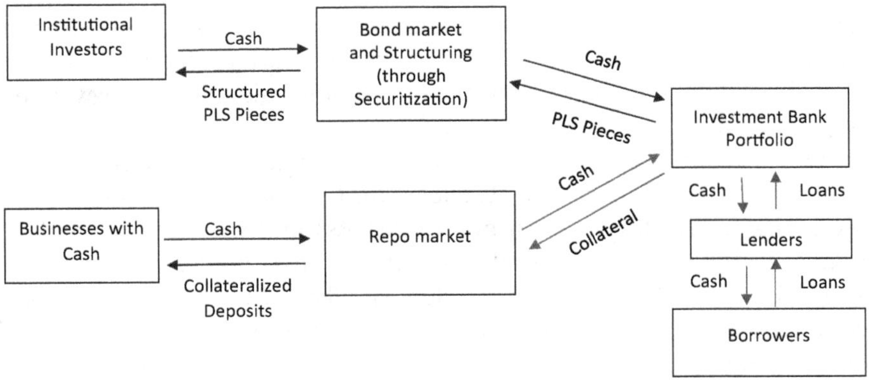

Figure 6.4 Simplified Structure of a Securitized Banking Set Up

It is adapted from Figure 6.2 of Gorton and Metrick (2010), which provides an excellent illustration of the structure of shadow banking. We do not present what is in a bank's portfolio, but rather purchases and sales moved in and out. To provide some sharper color, we limit the choices for the bank. Let's call the investment bank "Lerman", ("Investment Bank Portfolio" box in Figure 6.4), and let's narrow the options to loans put into pools that are turned into securities.

The players in the Lerman story are borrowers, loan originators, and Lerman. Let's call the loan originator that lends the money and sells the loans to Lerman and then services them "County-wide" ("Lenders" box in the figure). Lerman is an investment bank that does not take in retail deposits or make loans directly (at least not mortgage loans). Rather, it considers doing two things with the pool of loans. It can package and sell slices of the pool, the so-called tranches of the deal, into the bond market (as will be discussed in Chapter 8). Institutional investors will pay up if the piece of the deal has a good (AAA) rating and provides some extra yield. Lerman can also keep some of the deal for its yield and for the option to fund them in the repo market.[7] In this case, the repo structure is a securitized bank (Gorton model).

Note that the investment bank has two choices. It can both create securities and be a shadow bank (the repo structure) that owns some of the securities. With the latter, it provides liquidity to investors who can withdraw their "deposits" by not rolling over the repos. All these are similar to what regular banks do, but all done outside the banking system with similar securities and options to buy or sell. What Lerman chooses to do depends on balancing the revenues coming from the two choices as in Figure 6.4.

Oversimplifying a bit, we think of securitization as a process by which institutions (like the Agencies and investment banks) create securities for trading (e.g. in bond markets) and we think of shadow banks as largely unregulated institutions that hold some of these securities funded with uninsured deposit-like debt. This is the classic comic book story of U.S. shadow banking over the last 30 years. Some banks have a bit of both; e.g. having uninsured deposits in regular banks is much like establishing a shadow bank subsidiary. Other countries have different types of shadow banks with different arbitrages.

[7]Keeping them as marketable securities makes them better collateral for the repos.

6.2. Global Shadow Banking

The Financial Stability Board started conducting monitoring exercises on the non-bank financial intermediation/institutions (NBFIs) in 2011 and has since published the Global Shadow Banking Monitoring Report, which has later been changed to Global Monitoring Report on Non-Bank Financial Intermediation. NBFIs include life insurance companies, pension funds, investment funds, and other financial intermediaries (OFIs). "Banks" refers to "all deposit-taking corporations". "FIs" refers to all other "public financial institutions" not identified above. Shown in Panel (a) of Figure 6.5 is the size of the NBFI sector, growing significantly within 1 year in 2003, and then plummeted due to the GFC, and then slowly picking up again in the following 12 years, eventually reaching 48.3% in 2020, compared to 42% in 2008. Due to its size, which is now larger than banks plus financial institutions, it could pose a considerable systemic risk if it has too much leverage from the maturity and liquidity transformation.

Assets of FIs have almost doubled, from USD 11.93 trillion in 2002 to USD 19.87 trillion in 2020. Assets of banks have grown by a factor of 3.5, from USD 57.52 trillion in 2002 to USD 180.38 in 2020. Yet, banks plus financial institutions added up to 55.49% in 2002, but only 42.72% in 2020. Panel (b) of Figure 6.5 shows the contribution of pension funds, insurance corporations, and the OFIs to the growth of the NBFIs that led to the growing proportion of NBFIs in the overall financial assets in Panel (a).

Of the different types of NBFIs, OFIs refer to different financial entities, as broken down in Figure 6.6. They are money market funds (MMFs), hedge funds (HFs), investment funds other than MMFs (OIFs), real estate investment trusts (REITs), trust companies (TCs), finance companies (FinCos), broker-dealers (BDs), structured finance vehicles (SFVs), Central counterparties (CCPs), captive financial institutions and money lenders (CFIMLs) which can be subsidiaries of non-financial corporations used for capital pass-throughs, "others identified", and "others". "Others identified", not to be confused with "others", are entities that do not fit in the above categories. Finally, "others" includes the important part that we are due to cover — microfinance companies and peer-to-peer (P2P) lenders, especially in the case of China.

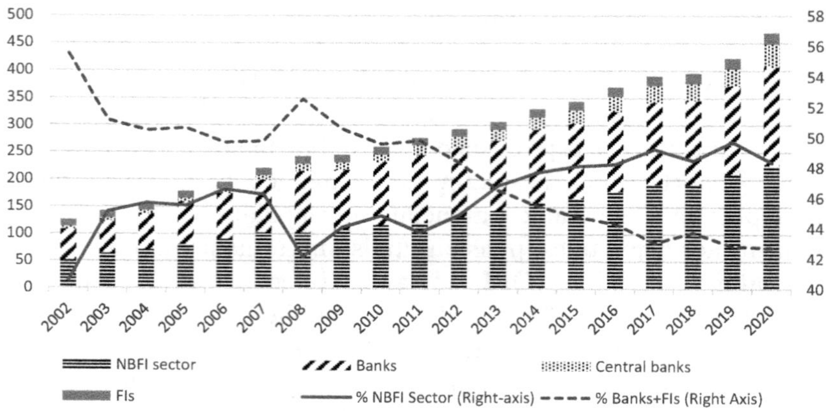

(a)

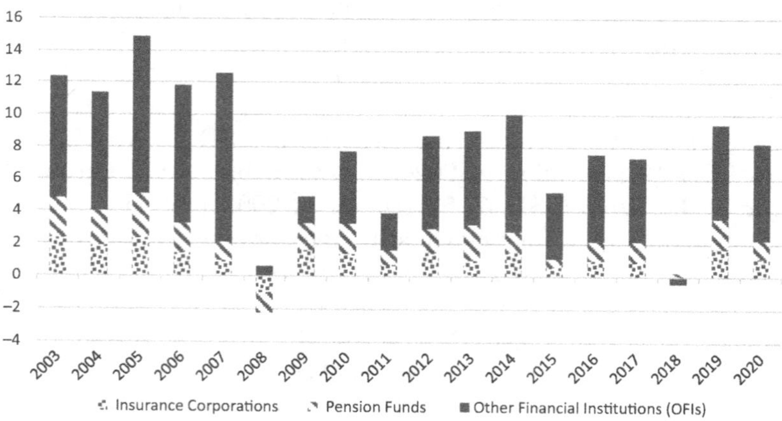

(b)

Figure 6.5 Global Financial Institution Assets. Panel (a) Bank and Non-bank Financial Institutions, Amount in Trillion USD and Proportion in Percentage. Panel (b) Contribution to NBFI Sector Growth in Percentage

Source: Financial Stability Board "Underly data for graphs" of the Global Monitoring Report on Non-Bank Financial Intermediation 2021. Available at: https://www.fsb.org/wp-content/uploads/Underlying-data-for-graphs-2021.xlsx.

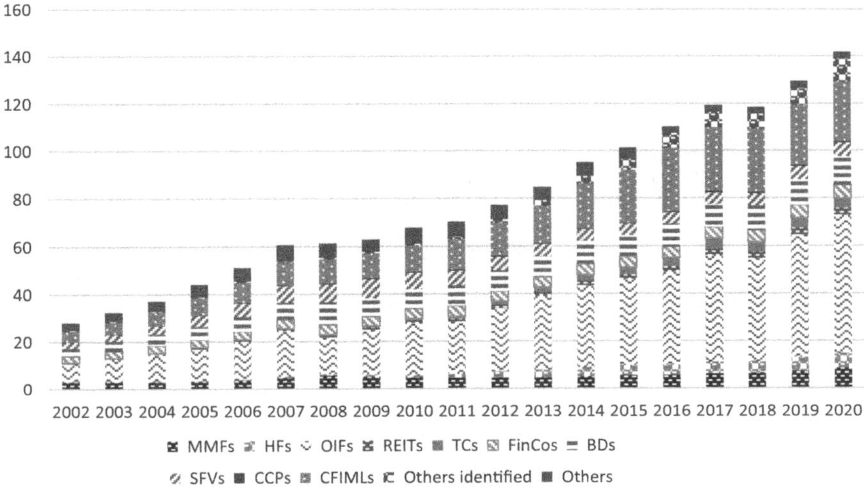

Figure 6.6 Breakdown of Other Financial Intermediaries (OFIs) (in Trillion USD)

Source: Financial Stability Board "Underlying data for graphs" of the Global Monitoring Report on Non-Bank Financial Intermediation 2021. Available at: https://www.fsb.org/wp-content/uploads/Underlying-data-for-graphs-2021.xlsx.

In terms of the invested amount, Financial Stability Board (2021a) classifies the funds into groups of five Economic Functions (EFs) plus "unallocated". Panel (a) of Figure 6.7 shows the amount of non-bank financial activities according to the five economic functions (EFs) classified by FSB. EF1, which groups all collective investment vehicles that are susceptible to runs, composes the largest amount of this grouping of shadow banking activities. Between 2007 and 2020, only EF1 has positive annual growth (Panel (b) of Figure 6.7), while all other economic function groups experienced some negative growth in different periods. In particular, loan provisions dependent on short-term funding (EF2) decreased mostly after the beginning of the GFC in 2008–2009, and did not grow until 2013. Insurance of financial products (EF4) is mostly having positive growth except dropping briefly in 2009 and 2016–2017. However, this does not mean very much because the total amount of EF4 is really relatively small, only about USD 0.17 trillion in 2020.

EF3 representing broker-dealers accounts that depend on short-term funding are the ones that dropped the most in the wake of

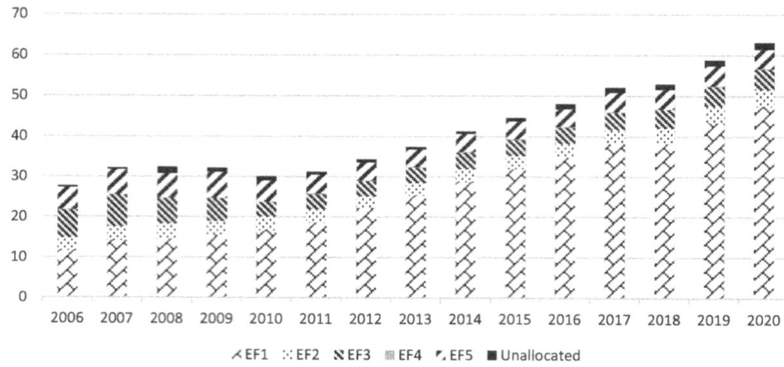

(a)

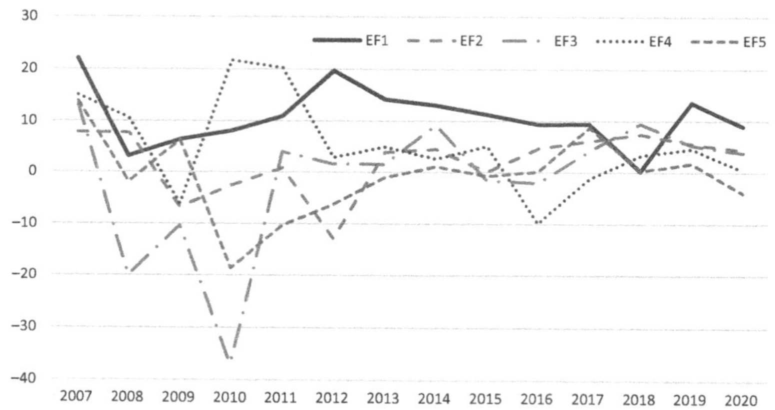

(b)

Figure 6.7 Non-Bank Financial Activities according to Economic Functions. Panel (a) Amounts in Trillion USD. Panel (b) Percentage Change in Values of Activities. Panel (c) Values of Various Entities within Economic Function 1 (EF1)

Note: EF1 represents collective investment vehicles susceptible to runs. EF2 includes loan provisions that are dependent on short-term funding. EF3 are market activities such as broker-dealers and custodial accounts that depend on short-term funding. EF4 is insurance and guarantees of financial products. EF5 is credit intermediation through securitization.

Source: Financial Stability Board "Monitoring Dataset" of the Global Monitoring Report on Non-Bank Financial Intermediation 2021. Available at: https://www.fsb.org/wp-content/uploads/Monitoring-Dataset-2021.xlsx.

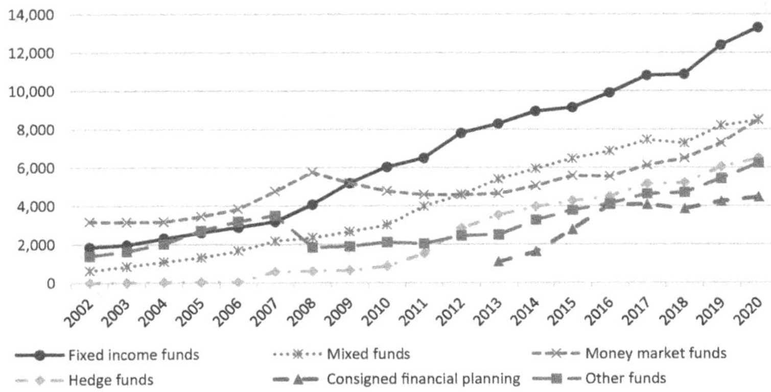

(c)

Figure 6.7 (*Continued*)

the GFC, lasted till 2011. Interestingly, securitization (EF5) which is perceived as the major problem during the Crisis only reduced briefly by 1.9% in 2008, and then more after 2009 (with a drop of 18.64% in 2010, and then 10.3% in 2011); and did not experience any growth until 2014. Also interesting is that all of the EFs grew in 2020 except the amount of securitization of credit, which dropped by 4%. In terms of EF1, the two largest components are the MMFs and fixed-income funds (Panel (c) of Figure 6.7). And although all funds either slowed down or actually dropped (significantly for "Other Funds") in response to the GFC, all picked up momentum quite quickly. Even during the sudden hit by the COVID-19 pandemic at the end of quarter 1 of 2020 when there was a flight to safety, all funds still continue to grow. One interesting point to note, though, is that, just as China is a major holder of the U.S. Treasuries, Chinese institutional investors are also attracted to the Collateralized Loan Obligations (CLOs) of the U.S.

6.3. Financial Technology and Financial Inclusion

The story of shadow banking cannot be complete without mentioning financial technology (fintech). Since the GFC, more innovations beyond securitization have emerged, leading to what is broadly called fintech. Two very important breakthroughs of non-bank banking — microfinance and fintech — have provided access to banking services, that is, "financial inclusion", for instance, for those in remote areas where physical banks do not exist, either because these places are difficult to reach or because the population is too scattered to make having a branch there profitable and for minorities and low-income families.[8] Fintech is not really innovation; neither the "fin" nor the "tech" part is new. It is simply using "tech" to change the mode or enhance the mechanisms of doing "fin". In its simplest form, a fintech firm can be a neobank (also called digital bank, online bank, or challenger bank, the last term is more common in the U.K.) offering exactly just what banks do — financial services — completely online, without physical locations.

The innovation lies in the new ideas of how to apply the relevant and contemporary technology to pertinent components of finance, either to speed up the services significantly or to reach users who would have otherwise been left out. Technology applied to the financial sector, directly or indirectly, to concepts, processes, methodologies, transactions, and products, within the sector, or spilling over to related sectors, has been taking place all along. However, it is the turning of the century, specifically after the GFC, that much more attention is turned to fintech.

Like other innovations, there have been many innovations in finance that helped change and improve our lives. Many of these innovations existed together with other inventions, very often with mathematical or economic theories. Perhaps one recent iconic financial innovation is the automated teller machine (ATM) in the 1960s; at least that is what Paul Volcker, the former Chairman of the Federal Reserve, said when criticizing how financial innovations called credit default swaps (CDS) and collateralized debt obligations (CDO) "took us right to the brink of disaster" and destroyed the global economy.[9]

"Innovation" is certainly not the synonym of "useful"; and not all innovations guarantee continuous positive outcomes. For example,

---

[8]Brett King wrote two excellent books, *Bank* 3.0 (King, 2013) and *Bank* 4.0 (King, 2019), to explain how we all need banking, but not banks, and how banking has transformed, particularly in the new era with financial technology and smart phones.

[9]*Wall Street Journal* London (December 8, 2009). "Volcker Praises the ATM, Blasts Finance Execs, Experts. *Wall Street Journal.* https://www.wsj.com/articles/BL-MB-14786.

the original purpose of CDS (more details in Chapter 8) and structuring securitization deals was to transfer risk to those who are more capable of managing risk from entities who could focus on their own strength or businesses. The analogy is similar to seat belts — they were invented to protect people from car crashes, but people with seatbelts on feel safer and tend to drive faster, and therefore have a higher probability of crashing.[10] In the book edited by Michael Haliassos, financial innovation is described as ... *a product of the complex interaction between and among the saving and borrowing needs of households, the financing needs of firms, the need to manage risks, developments in financial theory and related fields, and the profit motives of the financial sector* and *Even a long history of good past use is no safeguard against poor future use.*[11]

Fintech has improved financial inclusion by allowing people living in remote areas where banks are not available to have access to banking services. The availability of mobile phones has doubtlessly changed our lives. What people living in developed countries might not have realized is that, in many developing countries, the development of communication has skipped fixed-line analog phones to using mobile phones directly. According to the report released by the Global System for Mobile Communications Association, GSMA, of 96% of the developing countries, less than one-third of the population have a formal bank account.[12] Furthermore, 1.4 billion adults do not have bank accounts because of a lack of money, distance to financial institutions, and/or inadequate documents.[13]

Hence, the availability of mobile money accounts has enhanced financial inclusion for this group of population through accessible banking services. Enhanced financial inclusion because of advancement in technology not only results in lower transaction costs, but

---

[10]The analogy used by Robert C. Merton, 1997 Nobel Laureate in Economic Sciences, when explaining options, meant to be a good tool for hedging risks, could bring more risk because investors take more risks.

[11]Pages viii and ix, respectively, in Haliassos (2013).

[12]Andersson-Manjang and Naghavi (2021). See also Awanis *et al.* (2022) for more about mobile payments enhancing financial inclusion.

[13]The Global Findex Database 2021 by the World Bank Group (Demirgüç-Kunt *et al.*, 2022).

also leads to better analysis of data, which in turn reduces, or better evaluates, credit risks. This also makes countries adopting digital currency for financial inclusion all the more alert about regulating data usage and handling.[14]

A lot of the functions of financial inclusion are done through NBFIs. Fintech has been pushed into "fast forward" due to the pandemic. Digital payments and finance have never been as crucial during the lockdowns in many parts of the globe. Big Tech also took a big role here. Stark examples are India and China. We next move on to Chapter 7 about shadow banking in China.

[14]IMF (2021).

Chapter 7

Shadow Banking with Chinese Characteristics

We have presented forms of shadow banking in the U.S. and Europe in Chapter 6. Microfinance is a form of shadow banking in developing countries. It enhances financial inclusion and market efficiency. The case in China is different. Shadow banking has gone beyond microfinance and has taken on a more comprehensive, but less complicated, form. It too has had much room for regulatory arbitrage. Its shadow banking system has been made up of (1) bank sales to transfer liability burdens out of the banks and free up cash, and (2) conventional shadow banking by non-bank financial intermediaries that transfer money from investors to borrowers.[1] Whereas shadow banking in the U.S. is largely about creating liquidity, only the former (bank sales) is related to liquidity. Chinese shadow banking has enhanced the growth of economic functions by supporting the individually small, but collectively large, small and medium enterprise (SMEs) sector.[2]

7.1. A Brief History of Shadow Banking in China: Since the 1990s

Starting from the 1990s, and expanding into the 2000s, microfinance took up a big market share in financing SMEs. Unlike its more

[1]Sun (2019).
[2]Collier (2017).

developed counterparts that were undergoing recession from the GFC, China performed relatively well, generating positive GDP growth (albeit at lower rates than before). The RMB4 trillion stimulus package initiated the use of Local Government Financing Vehicles (LGFVs) by municipal governments. LGFVs are essentially State-Owned Enterprises (SOEs) owned by municipal governments. Their functions are to borrow from banks for the municipal governments and to issue municipal corporate bonds (MCBs), the latter of which are usually bought by shadow banking funds. Businesses that cannot borrow from banks can rely on entrusted loans. Chinese households started to become obsessed with Wealth Management Products (WMPs). Finally, when other countries were still recovering from the Crisis, China had developed mobile payments extensively and has become the leader in the usage of fintech (financial technology). Big Tech giants like Alibaba and Tencent also joined the fintech financing fleet.

Securitization occupies only a minor role in China's shadow banking, although it has existed for some time. All the developments in the shadow banking family in the context of the Chinese markets will be discussed one by one in the following. What stands out is the huge size of shadow banking sector in China. For instance, entrusted loans have become 82% of China's GDP by the first half of 2016, which was double of that in 2011, and has been the largest sector of shadow banking in China, until surpassed by WMPs in 2014.[3,4]

The shadow banking system in China is enhanced by investors' belief in government implicit guarantees (as with Fannie and Freddie in the U.S.).[5] This is not without good reason. Consider LGFVs belonging to the local governments, WMPs bought from banks, many of them state-owned, and financial products from Big Techs. Individual investors believe that these investments will be a sure win! Any problem (like a run) on these products would almost certainly be

[3]Allen *et al.* (2019).

[4]Books like Zhang (2014), Sheng and Soon (2016), and Collier (2017) offer some very good and detailed references of the development of shadow banking in China. Also informative is the report by the Asian Development Bank (2014) and other reports and papers such as Hachem (2018).

[5]From page 279 of the book of IMF entitled The Future of China's Bond Market (Zhu *et al.*, 2019).

stifled by the Chinese government because they are issued by local governments, or SOEs, and Big Techs. Deposit insurance has been available in China since May 2015.

To see the size of shadow banking in China, we refer to the Global Shadow Banking Monitoring Reports by the Financial Stability Board (see Section 6.2 for comparison). On page 17 of the 2016 Report, the number of OFIs in China has grown by 29% in 2016, which has become the main driver of global OFI growth.[6] Then according to the 2019 Report (Financial Stability Board, 2020, p. 14), the amount of OFI assets in China reached USD 11.2 trillion in 2018, making China the third largest country in the share of global OFI assets, after the U.S. and the Euro Area.

Moody's Investors Service also produces Quarterly China Shadow Banking Monitor Reports. According to the ones released on August 7, 2017 and April 1, 2022, the asset value of shadow banking in 2021 shown in Panel (a) of Figure 7.1 has decreased by RMB2.19 trillion to RMB57 trillion. Due to the rapid economic growth in the same year, its shares as a percentage of GDP and percentage of bank assets has reached a record low of 49.8% and 16.9% since 2013.[7] Panel (b) is a breakdown of the different shadow banking products as percentages of the total banking assets. The largest shadow banking assets are now funded by WMPs and Asset Management Plans (AMPs), which were only a small amount in 2012. On the other hand, the undiscounted bankers' acceptances continued to shrink.

Where does the supply of shadow banking funds come from? As mentioned in Chapter 2, household savings in China have always been high. However, the lack of investment channels has left households with limited choices, except for investing in housing. For those who already own housing units and perhaps do not have mortgages, second homes are alternatives. If the amount of savings is not enough for buying housing units, WMPs are an attractive alternative. While the growth of pension funds in advanced economies has slowed down in 2019–2021, growth in China experienced continuous double-digit growth, being 20% in 2019 (Financial Stability Board, 2020, p. 14)

[6]Financial Stability Board (2018).

[7]Moody's Investors Service (2017, 2022a).

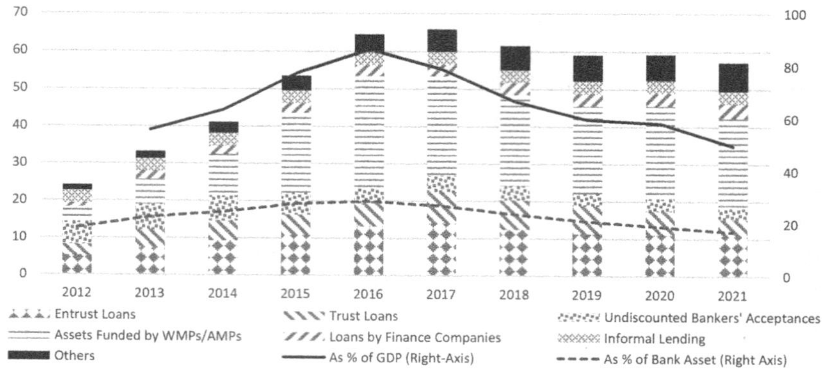

(a)

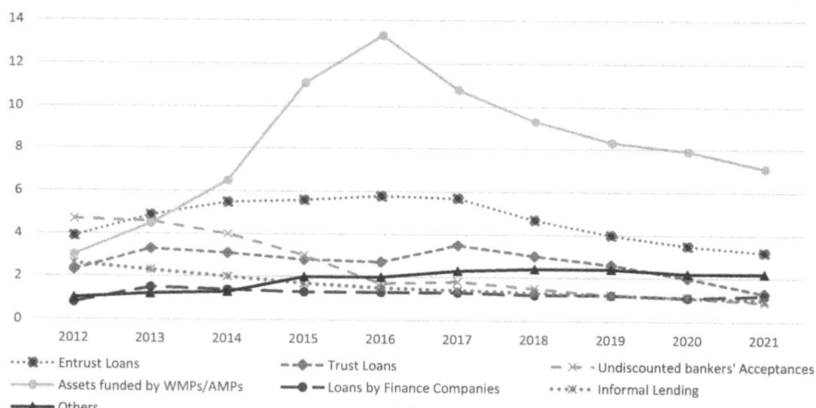

(b)

Figure 7.1 Asset Values of Shadow Banking in China. Panel (a) Breakdown of Products, and Shadow Banking as a Percentage of GDP. Panel (b) Breakdown of Shadow Banking Products as a Percentage of Banking Assets

Source: Moody's Investors Service (2017, 2022a).

and 26.6% in 2021 (Financial Stability Board, 2021b, p. 11). Also, trust funds in China constitute 80.2% of all assets owned by global trust companies in 2020.[8]

Following the introduction of shadow banking instruments in China, it is not difficult to see how these instruments and their

[8]Page 13 of the 2021 Report (Financial Stability Board, 2021) and page 65 of the 2019 Report (Financial Stability Board, 2020).

providers became quite intertwined. While there is a huge demand for funds, there is also a huge supply, both from household investors who try to get away from the low deposit rates and from institutional investors who have abundant funding but limited channels of investment.

7.2. Microfinance

Microfinance, or microcredit, is the provision of banking services to those that do not have easy access to banking services. The clientele often includes low-income groups, people living in remote areas, or others who have limited access to banking services. Microfinance dates back to the 19th century or earlier for similar but not exact forms of financing for the poor. Its current form is a system due to Muhammad Yunus, who was awarded the Nobel Peace Prize in 2006.[9] It helps promote financial and business education for some developing regions.

Microfinance qualifies as shadow banking because microfinance institutions provide loans (in small amounts) in addition to other bank-like services such as taking deposits from people, private equity, loans from banks, and other institutions. Interest rates on microfinance loans are usually lower than those from regular commercial banks. Like banks, they are run like corporations, even though the basic aim is to provide financial inclusion. Although it is a type of shadow banking, what happened to the GFC has nothing to do with microfinance. Some research criticizes the labeling of microfinance because shadow banking dwarfs the contribution of microfinance to financial inclusion, especially in developing countries. Microfinance loans are usually short term in nature and hence do not present maturity mismatch issues (although some microcredit institutions provide housing finance, meaning longer-term loans).[10]

The early 1990s marked a big leap in economic development in China, from a completely socialist country that had slowly recovered from the aftermath of the Cultural Revolution to one of "socialism

[9]See the Nobel Prize official website: https://www.nobelprize.org/prizes/peace/2006/summary/.

[10]Lyman *et al.* (2015).

with Chinese characteristics", and more market-oriented. More and more people set up their own micro and small enterprises (MSEs). There were over 42 million SMEs and MSEs by the end of June 2007, of which 38 million were established by individual proprietors.[11] Additionally, 23.1 million township and village enterprises (TVEs) were formed by the end of 2006. Almost all these TVEs are SMEs and MSEs requiring credit, which was not available from large banks that specialize in loans to SOEs or other large corporations. This forms the niche, or arbitrage, for microfinance. Microcredit was supplied in China by microfinance institutes of non-government organizations (NGO MFIs) starting in 1993 to mid- and low-income people without collateral.[12] The amount of the loans was generally small with annual interest rates ranging from 3% to 18%.[13]

The Agricultural Bank of China (ABC) started providing microcredits in 1996, and the interest rate was only 2–3%. Soon afterwards, Rural Credit Cooperatives (RCC), Rural Mutual Credit Cooperatives (RMCCs), village/township banks, and lending companies established by commercial banks have started to provide microcredits. Microcredit companies (MCCs) offered loans with the highest interest rates, ranging from 14% to 28%. Commercial banks offer loans of up to several tens of thousands.[14] Many of these were pilot projects of the China Banking Regulatory Commission (CBRC). It was only in 2008 that CBRC formally legalized the microcredit sector, after which over 5,000 MCCs were established.[15] CBRC merged with the China Insurance Regulatory Commission (CIRC) to form the China Banking and Insurance Regulatory Commission (CBIRC) in April 2018.

Wenzhou, a city famous for its entrepreneurship culture, situated in the coastal Zhejiang Province, has a relatively large

[11] He (2010).
[12] Du (2010a).
[13] Table 1a of Du (2010a).
[14] Table 2a of Du (2010b).
[15] According to Zhang (2014). Also, Riecke (2014) wrote, *the number of providers is a few thousand higher, spanning nonprofit institutions, government programs, microcredit companies, commercial banks, rural credit cooperatives and banks, village and township banks, and P2P lenders. Even Alibaba, China's internet giant, is involved. ... through its AliFinance arm, launched in 2011.*

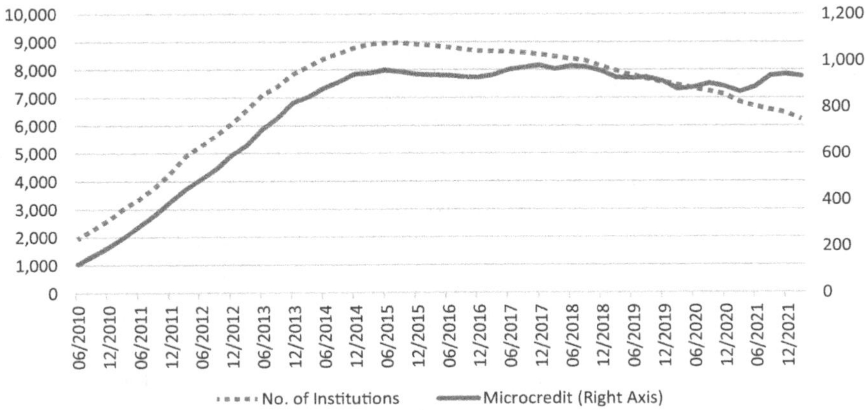

Figure 7.2 Amount of Microcredit (in Billion RMB) and Number of Microfinance Institutions in China

Source: CEIC Database based on data from the People's Bank of China.

microfinance sector. Typical private lending rates according to the People's Bank of China in April 2011 was 19.52%, and peaked in March 2012 at 21.71%, with a mean of 20.77% over the 1-year period. According to Standard & Poors, there were 9,704 microfinance firms in China at the end of 2019, with a total loan balance of RMB1.004 trillion.[16] Figure 7.2 plots the amount of microcredit loans and the number of such institutions in China. Both values in 2019 from the figure are smaller than the S&P measures, probably due to variations in definitions of which institutions are in microfinance.

7.3. WMPs: Heating Up and Cooling Down

Outside of microfinance, funding the Chinese shadow banking system by individual investors is mostly via Wealth Management Products (WMPs), which are similar to selling units of trust funds by commercial banks. Due to the scope of products, types of issuing financial institutions, and involvement by different types of investors, including many individual investors, we explain them here first.

[16]See Chong (2020).

From 2008 to 2010, there was an emergence of alternative investments to individual investors in China in the form of WMPs. The investors were individuals and households who chose the products over bank deposits for higher interest rates, normally guaranteed, and usually with shorter maturities.[17] The deposit rate caps, which resulted in unattractive deposits, have helped boost the deposit-like WMP market.[18] The growth of the amount of this product was very strong, from RMB3.5 trillion in all of 2008–2011 to RMB2.5 trillion in just 2012, and RMB3.1 trillion in 2013.[19] In December 2016, 62% of the funds for the municipal corporate bonds (MCBs) come from the WMPs.

The problem with WMPs is that many of them do not have clear statements of what instruments they are invested in (moral hazard). Ironically, in many cases, investors do not really care, as long as they get periodic returns during the promised period. After all, investors assume, maybe falsely, that banks need to maintain good reputations, and will therefore not let investors lose their investments. The large size of the sector and its potential risk could affect the financial sector as well as the wealth of individual investors. The CBRC enacted a regulatory policy in November 2017 requiring trust companies (especially the single trusts, which are essentially funding vehicles for financial institutions, similar to special purpose vehicles) not to provide conduit services to financial institutions in order to avoid regulatory arbitrage.[20]

Studies have shown that secured pension schemes and the preference for wealth accumulation have incentivized female Chinese investors to take on risky investments. In any case, a "gambling" mentality in investing creates more opportunities for high-risk projects to obtain funding, perhaps at the cost of more volatile markets. As a result, the People's Bank of China (PBoC) included WMPs in the "Macro-Prudential Assessment (MPA)" for the first time in early 2017.[21] The immediate consequence has been a large reduction in new issuance of off-balance sheet WMPs.

[17]Hachem (2018) describes WMPs as "asset-backed term deposits".
[18]Page 124 of Zhang (2014).
[19]Chen *et al.* (2018).
[20]Financial Stability Board (2021).
[21]Page 6 of IMF (2017a).

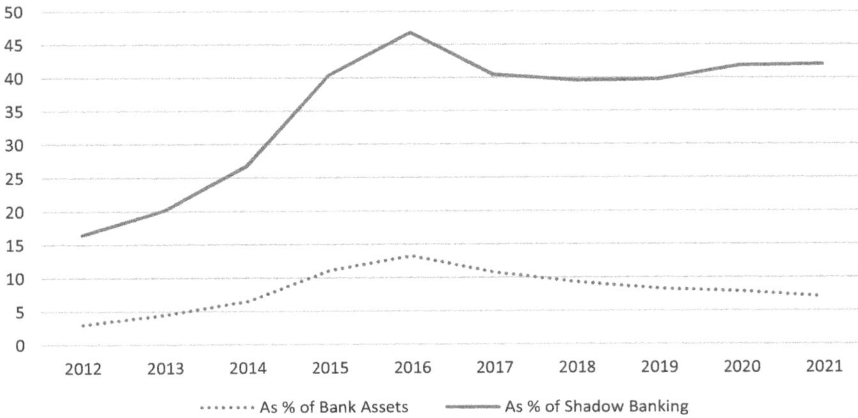

Figure 7.3 WMPs as Percentages of Bank Assets and Total Shadow Banking

Source: CEIC Database.

The category "Assets funded by WMPs/AMPs" in both Panels of Figure 7.1 was smaller in amount than "Entrusted Loans" and "Undiscounted Banker's Acceptances" in 2012, but it surpassed them to become the largest group of shadow banking investments in 2014. Since WMPs dominate the group, we treat "Assets funded by WMPs/AMPs" as the amount of WMPs due to a lack of more detailed information. Figure 7.3 compares the amount of WMPs as a percentage of bank assets (like Panel (b) of Figure 7.1) and as a percentage of total shadow banking (which is the sum of all the items in Panel (b) of Figure 7.1). Although WMPs as a percentage of bank assets show a downward trend in recent years, which is in line with all shadow banking instruments, the proportion of WMPs in shadow banking has constantly constituted at least 40% of all shadow banking instruments.

WMPs are further classified as principal-guaranteed and nonprincipal-guaranteed WMPs. Non-principal-guaranteed WMPs have been described as "shadow deposits".[22] Issuance details are depicted in Figure 7.4: in units in Panel (a), in amount in Panel (b), and in units from the various financial institution

[22]Page 296 of Hachem (2018).

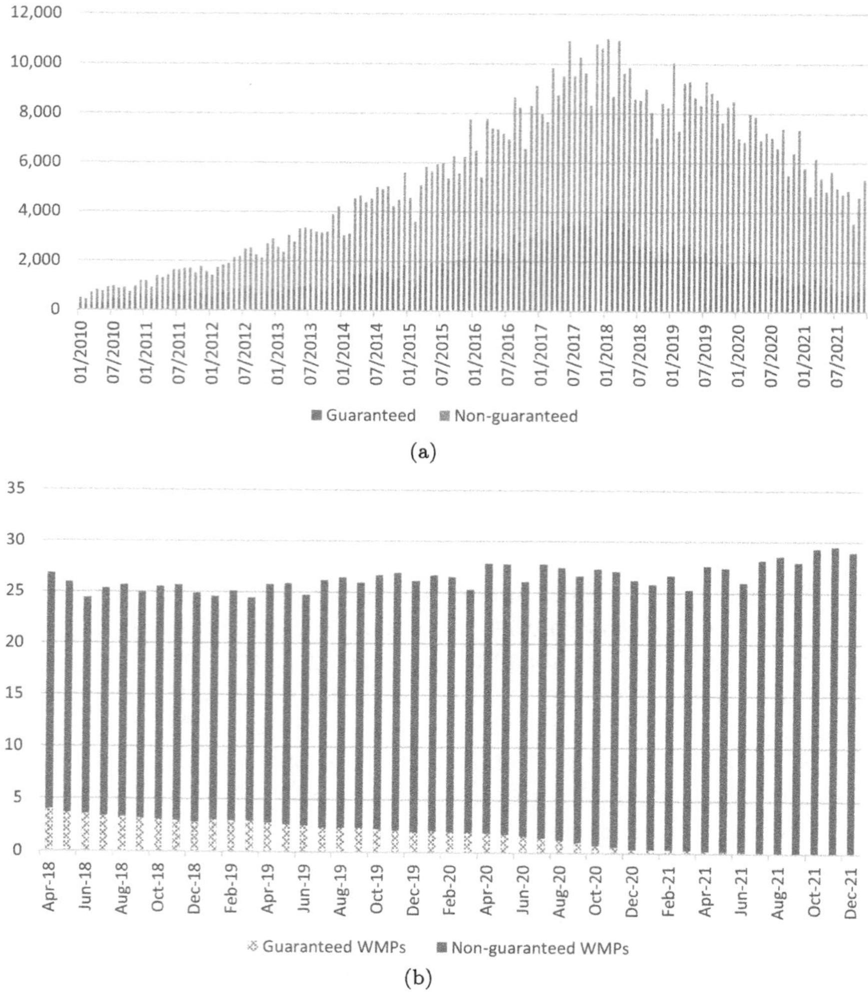

Figure 7.4 Issuance of WMPs: Principal-Guaranteed versus Nonprincipal-guaranteed Funds. Panel (a) Total WMPs with Principal-Guaranteed versus Nonprincipal-Guaranteed Funds (in units). Panel (b) Values of WMPs Issued, with Principal-guaranteed versus Nonprincipal-guaranteed Funds (in trillion RMB). Panel (c) Guaranteed Funds by Issuer Categories (in units). Panel (d) Non-Guaranteed Funds by Issuer Categories (in units). CEIC Database

Source: (a, c, d) CEIC Database. (b) Banking Wealth Management Registration and Custody Center.

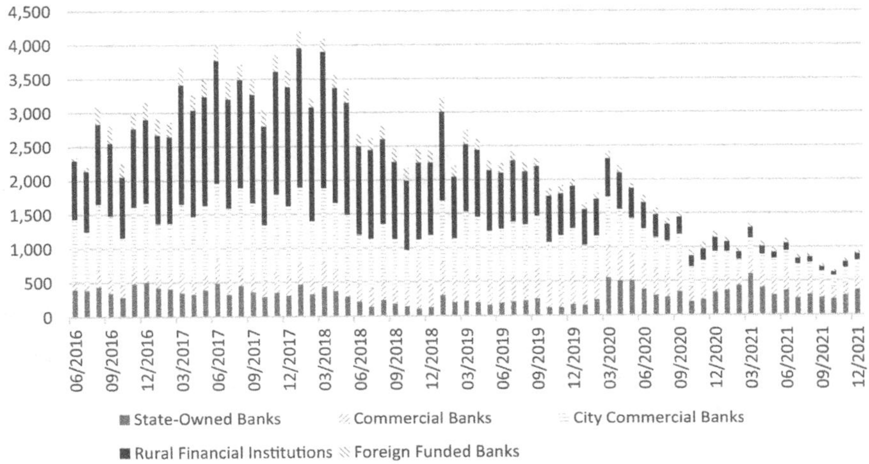

(c)

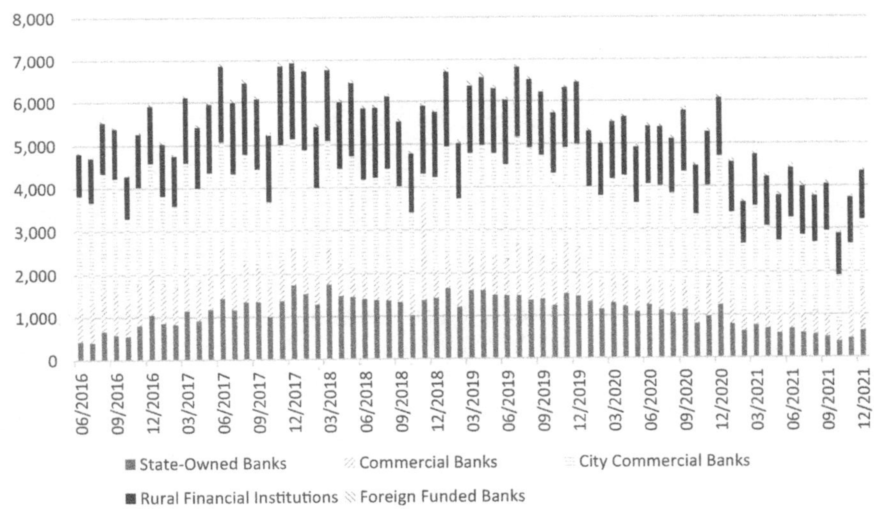

(d)

Figure 7.4 (***Continued***)

categories (Panel (c) for principal-guaranteed and Panel (d) for non-principal-guaranteed). Nonprincipal-guaranteed WMPs have considerably out-numbered principal-guaranteed in proportion, especially after the 2017 policy change. It indicates that banks prefer not to guarantee the principal of the "deposits" used to buy the WMPs, in which case the funds do not need to be listed on the balance sheet. Instead, they are usually passed through to trust companies. This is how WMPs are linked to single-trust and collective-trust products. With WMPs under single-trust funds, the banks do provide implicit guarantees and instruct the trust companies on investment strategies. On the other hand, those on collective-trust funds will not be associated with bank guarantees, explicit or implicit.

Despite the gradual reduction in units issued after the 2017 policy, the amount of issuance has been steadily increasing, again mainly from the nonprincipal-guaranteed WMPs. In fact, even the units issued picked up starting at the end of 2021. As of the end of quarter 1 of 2022, 268 financial institutions issued 7,717 units of WMPs, raising a total of RMB25.14 trillion, according to the Banking Wealth Management Registration and Custody Center. Simultaneously, 321 financial institutions renewed the products of up to RMB28.37 trillion. Panel (c) shows that the dominating issuers of principal-guaranteed WMPs used to be rural financial institutions, and later changed to state-owned banks and city commercial banks. Nonprincipal-guaranteed WMPs (Panel (d)) are mainly dominated by city commercial banks.

In terms of value appreciation, Panel (a) of Figure 7.5 shows the percentages of value transformation of WMPs from different types of financial institutions, being SOE banks, urban commercial banks, and rural financial institutions. The trends show increases in the values of the products over time, with the fastest increases in value from the state-owned banks, while those from rural financial institutions have slower value accumulation, although they also picked up by the second half of 2021. Similarly, the changes in value transformation shown in Panel (b) reflect riskier WMPs from rural financial institutions (in terms of bigger swings in the changes), and lower growth rates for those from the state-owned banks.

Figure 7.6 shows the performance of the various WMP products, including fixed income, hybrid, and cash management products. The overall performance is depicted as "Benchmark" in the figure. Performance of the different products has converged to steadier rates of between 3% and 5% in response to the policy change in 2017. Nevertheless, the highly fluctuating hybrid WMPs continue to show

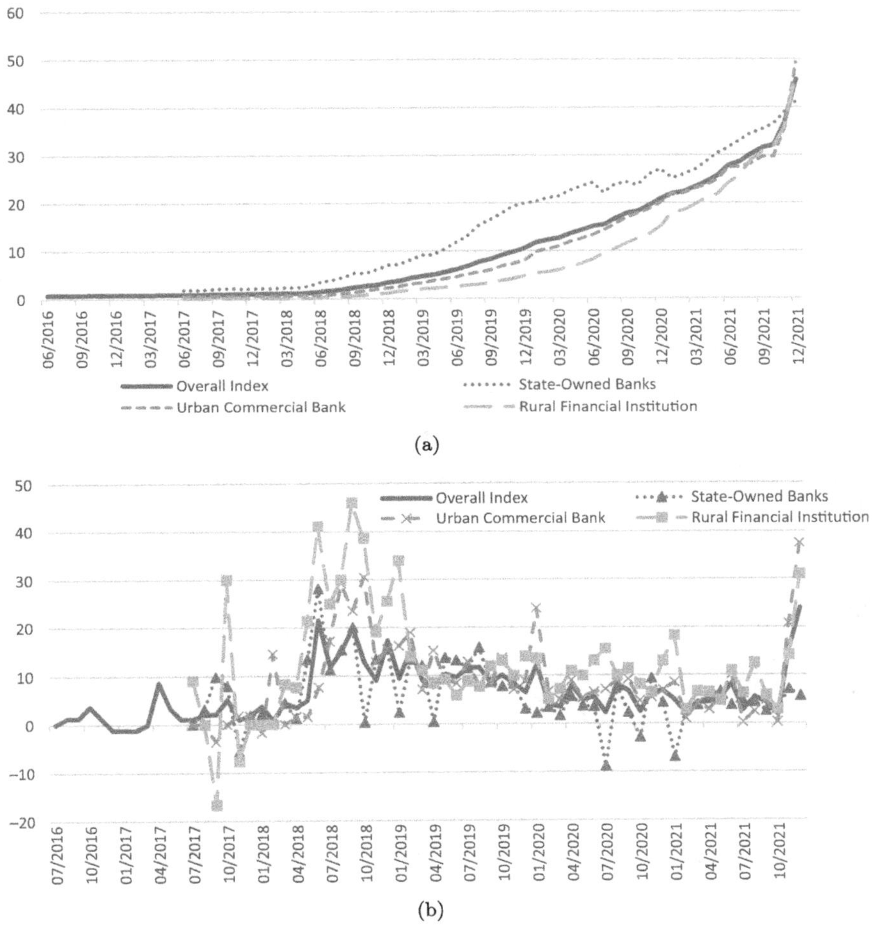

Figure 7.5 Net-Value Transformation of WMPs. Panel (a) Net-Value Transformation, in Percentages, Across Bank Types. Panel (b) Percentage Changes in Net-Value Transformation across Bank Types

Source: CEIC Database.

more volatile performance. Furthermore, Figure 7.7 shows some noteworthy details. First, the issuance index is another way of interpreting the drop in overall WMP issuance as in Figure 7.4. Second, closed-end WMPs are always more expensive than open-end WMPs.

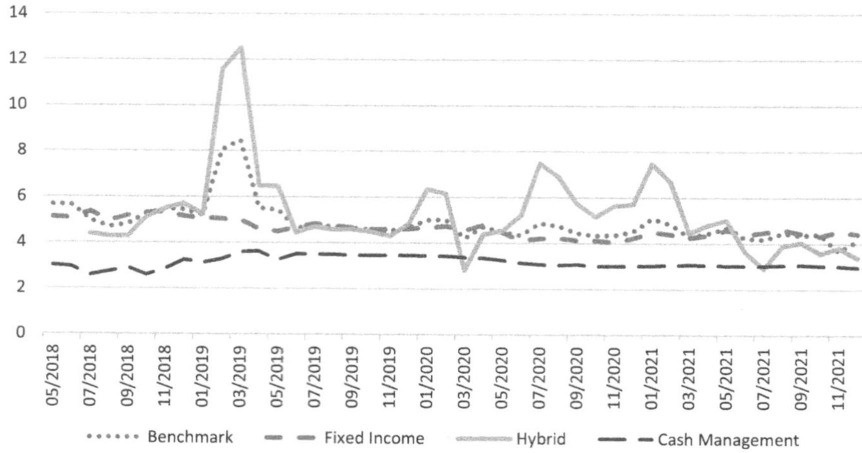

Figure 7.6 Performance of Various Net-Value of WMPs (in percentages)

Source: CEIC Database.

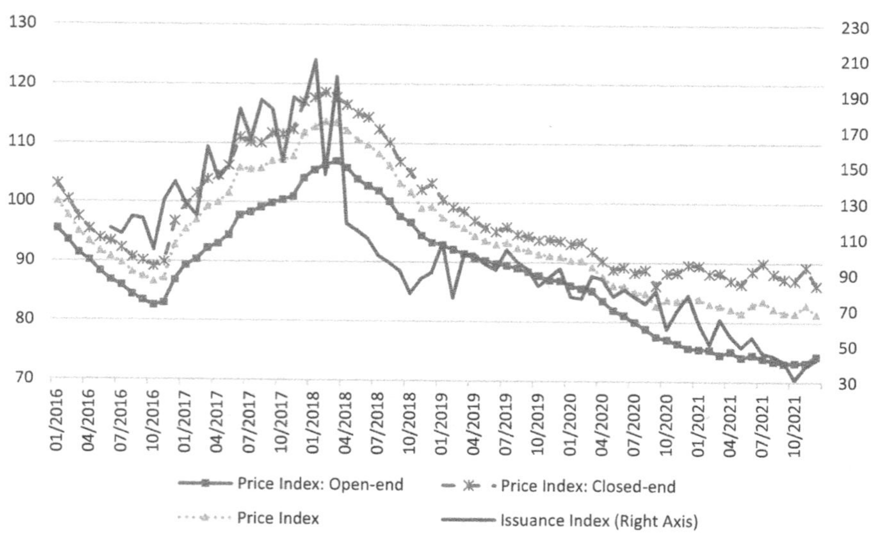

Figure 7.7 WMP Issuance Index and Price Indices, Including Open-End and Closed-End Funds (February 2016 = 100 index points)

Source: CEIC Database with data from Puyi Standard, which provides "Evaluation of Comprehensive Asset Management Ability", and various index series in Chinese WMPs (with February 2016 as the base with 100 index points).

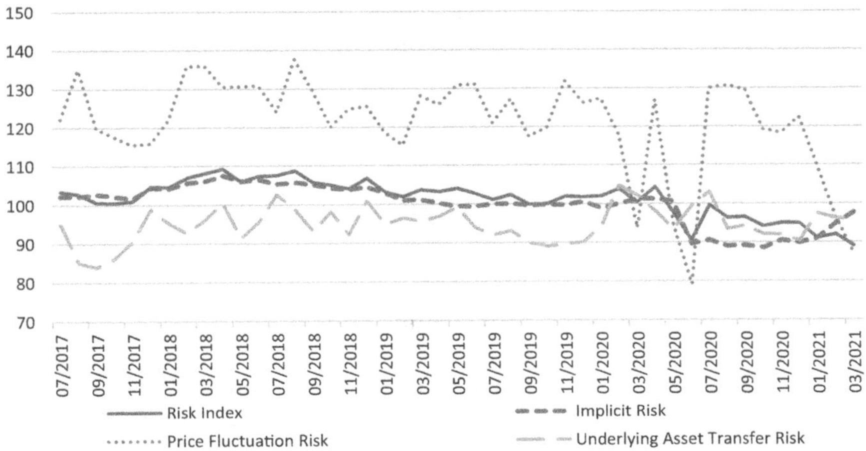

Figure 7.8 WMP Risk Indices (February 2016 = 100 Index Points)

Source: CEIC Database.

More importantly, both types of WMPs dropped by about 35 index points at the end of 2021 from their peaks in March 2018 (after the implementation of the 2017 policy change).

Finally, according to the indices in Figure 7.8, WMP risk fluctuated significantly, plummeting during the serious COVID-19 pandemic periods (quarter 1 and end of quarter 2 of 2020), and the beginning of 2021. The overall risk has been between 100 and 110 index points for most of the time shown in the figure until quarter 2 of 2020, which has stayed below 100 since. These fluctuations were mainly due to price fluctuations, implicit risk, and underlying asset transfer risk shown in the figure. The implicit risk mostly follows overall risk until after quarter 2 of 2020, while the underlying asset transfer risk more or less offsets the implicit risk.

All of the above verify what the Research Announcement of Moody's Investors Services (2021) covered. Specifically, there is a heavy concentration of fixed income WMPs. Even though fewer and fewer principal-guaranteed WMPs have been issued, more banks have set up subsidiaries to issue nonprincipal-guaranteed WMPs, pointing towards the transformation of handling WMPs to something like mutual funds. Cash management WMPs, which are short-term products investing in assets with longer maturities, have grown to 29% of total WMPs in quarter 1 of 2021. This poses problems of maturity mismatch. To be fair though, the amount of interbank WMPs has continued to decrease. The 2017 policy change has helped regulate the WMP market to reduce contagion risks.[23] Products have included fewer non-standard assets, and transparency has been enhanced. WMPs were only equal to 25% of nominal GDP at the end of 2021, significantly lower than the 36% at the end of 2017.

7.4. Entrusted Loans and Trust Funds

Entrusted loans are credits between two non-financial corporations done through banks, because direct borrowing between non-financial corporations is not allowed in China. Essentially the banks are just "middlemen", servicing the loans, and are therefore not liable for the credit risk. Franklin Allen and his team find that entrusted loan lenders are usually SOEs having good access to traditional bank loans, lending to their subsidiaries, customers or suppliers, or partners in joint ventures, especially in periods of tight credit.[24]

Other corporations that have excess cash but not much growth make unaffiliated loans as alternative investments to earn interest, which could be as high as 13.9%. In comparison, affiliated loans only generate 6% interest. For example, minimum and maximum rates for affiliated loans range from 5.1% for the hotel and tourism sector to 9.1% for real estate and construction (which is the largest group in their sample, or 394 out of a total of 2373 loans). In contrast, the minimum and maximum for non-affiliated loans are 6.9% for the textile and garment industry and 16.1% for paper and printing. That for real estate and construction is also quite high, at 15.5%, and is also the largest sector, with 269 loans out of 587 loans.[25] Figure 7.9 shows the exponentially increasing trend of entrusted loans since December 2002, which peaked in 2017 (Panel (a)) and then decreased quite sharply for some time, stabilizing only in 2021.

---

[23]Fitch Ratings (2022).

[24]Allen *et al.* (2019).

[25]Allen *et al.* (2019) listed the interest rates charged for the affiliated versus non-affiliated entrusted loans in their Table 4.

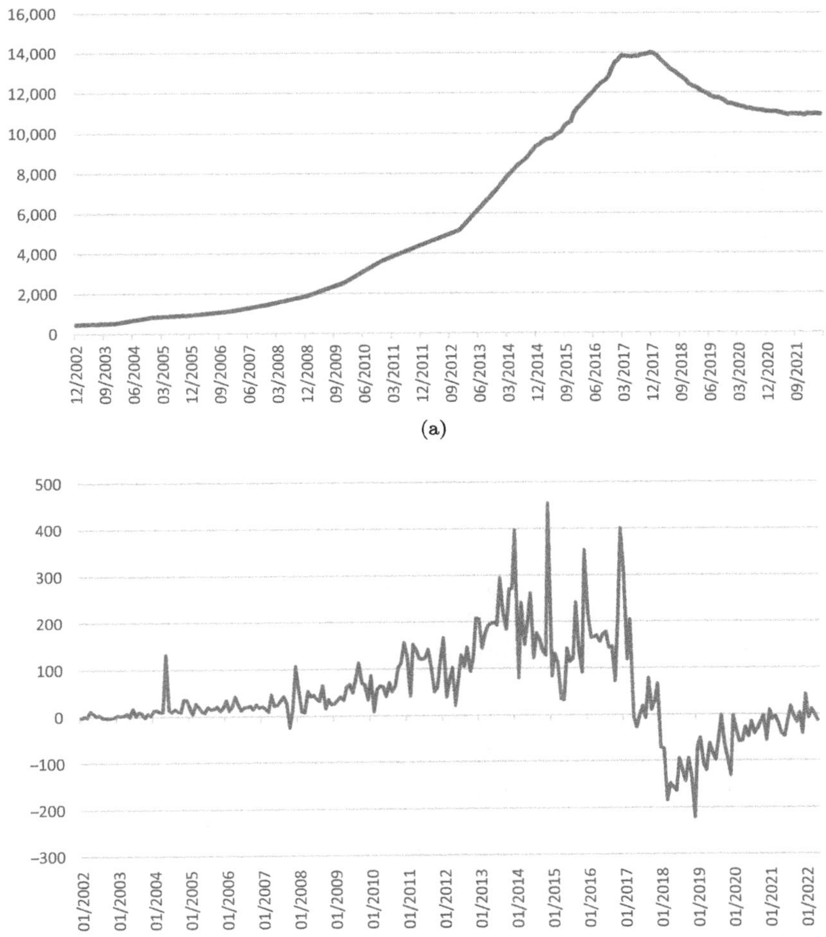

Figure 7.9 Entrusted Loans in China. Panel (a) Amount in Billion RMB. Panel (b) Change in Entrusted Loan Amounts (in Billion RMB)

Source: CEIC Database.

Later in 2004, trust companies started lending to short-term borrowers who failed to meet the loan requirements of banks, borrowers who had already borrowed from banks and needed additional loans, and those who were in urgent need of loans. These trust companies have replaced banks as the middlemen, collecting funds from customers and loaning to those who need funds but could not pass banks' lending requirements. They only need to maintain a reserve of 5%, relative to 12.5%–14.5% for banks.[26] Since they could raise 1,000 times their capital base, they could have funds to support their profitable merchant banking activities, and therefore attract funds from many investors. Being the funding vehicles for financial institutions, these trust companies have facilitated a bank-trust cooperation to allow banks to use their on-balance sheet or off-balance sheet funds (such as WMPs) to invest in financial products that they could not otherwise touch, such as lending to those they could not lend to. This is successful because Chinese are accustomed to trust developed from personal relationships.

Trust companies do more than lending to individuals. Single-trust products are set up for pools of funding from individual institutional customers, of which 80% are banks according to FSB,[27] and invested in financial products or loaning to enterprises or individuals as short-term financing. Collective-trust products are financed by the funding that they themselves pooled, usually from their own WMPs. These products have an average maturity of 1.7 years and are usually invested in fixed-income or mixed financial products. Note that the WMPs usually have shorter maturities than trust fund products, and therefore create maturity mismatch. Property trusts are for managing non-monetary assets for clients.

The Global Monitoring Report on Non-Bank Financial Intermediation 2021 noted that the amount of trust funds in China constitutes 80.2% of all assets owned by global trust companies in 2020, which is already a decline from 2018 due to the CBRC 2017 regulatory policy on trust companies. Panel (a) of Figure 7.10 shows the total amount of trust funds in China, whereas Panels (b) and (c) show the total amount and the increase in amounts of collective-trust products and single-trust products by quarters invested in loans and real estate, respectively. Unlike overall trust funds, which peaked in 2017, trust funds for real estate peaked only in mid-2019, and the amount invested in collective-trust products surpassed single-trust products by five-fold in mid-2020.

[26] Allen *et al.* (2019).
[27] Financial Stability Board (2018).

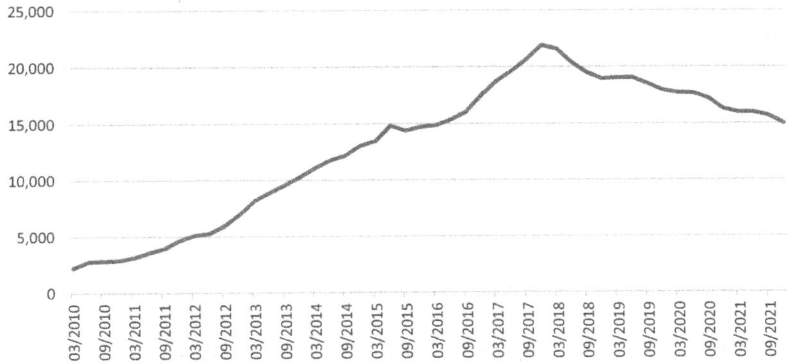

(a)

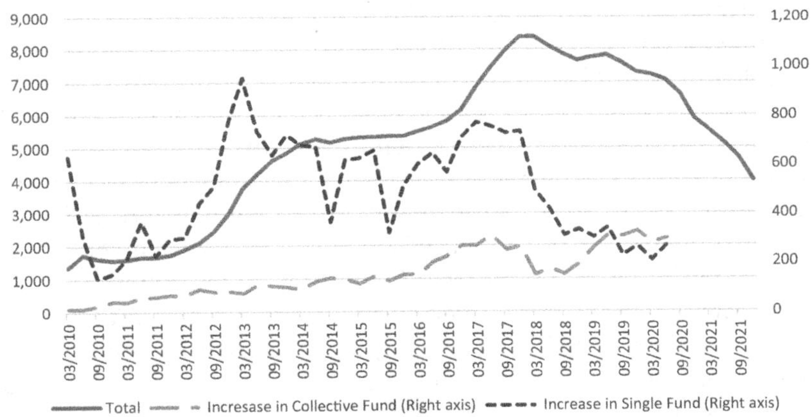

(b)

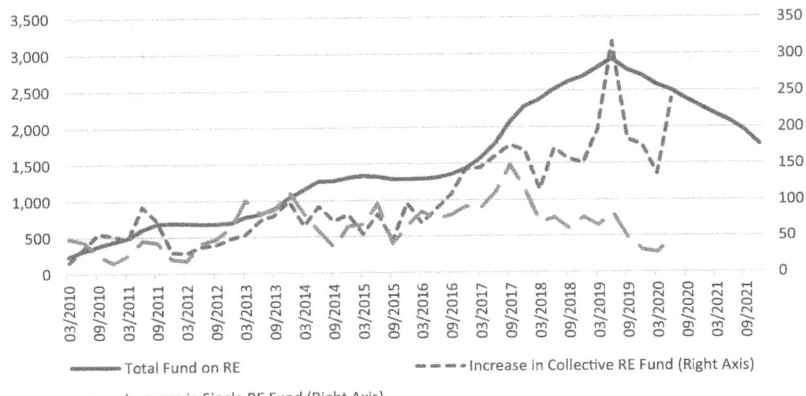

(c)

Figure 7.10 (*Continued*)

Figure 7.10 Trust Funds in China (in Billion RMB). Panel (a) Total Amount of Trust Funds Outstanding. Panel (b) Trust Funds Invested in Loans. Panel (c) Trust Funds Invested in Real Estate

Note: Data for the collective and single RE funds are available only up to June 2020.

Source: CEIC Database.

7.5. Local Government Financing Vehicles

The scope of shadow banking has been significantly enlarged as a result of the RMB4 trillion financial stimulus package in 2008.[28] Since the central government only provided 30% of the package, the local governments had to finance infrastructure projects, as stipulated in the package, by seeking loans from the financial sector. Banks did not want to have these loans on their balance sheets, pretty much like securitizers in the U.S. wanting to lend via securitized instruments. A solution is for the state-owned enterprise (SOE) banks to issue infrastructure loans via Local Government Financing Vehicles (LGFVs), which are themselves SOEs owned by the local governments.[29] The loans are in the form of Municipal Corporate Bonds (MCBs), implicitly guaranteed by the local governments. These bonds could be rolled over by issuing new MCBs, resulting in a snowball-like enlargement of more shadow banking loans because WMPs and trust funds are the main sources of funding. Note that "Corporate" in MCB implies that its credit risk level is the same as corporate bonds.

Onshore LGFV bond issuance in 2021 hit RMB5.9 trillion, equivalent to an annual growth rate of 26%.[30] This is partly due to the refinancing of matured bonds and new issues. It was predicted that the amount in 2022 would be even higher, due to the maturity of an even larger amount of loans as well as the funding needed to support substantial infrastructure projects.[31] Figure 7.11 plots the amount of onshore LGFV bond issuance together with the amount

[28] Chen *et al.* (2018).
[29] Pages 55–56 of Collier (2017).
[30] See LGFV Bond Monitor Fourth Quarter 2021 Report by Moody's Investors Service (2022b).
[31] *Ibid.*

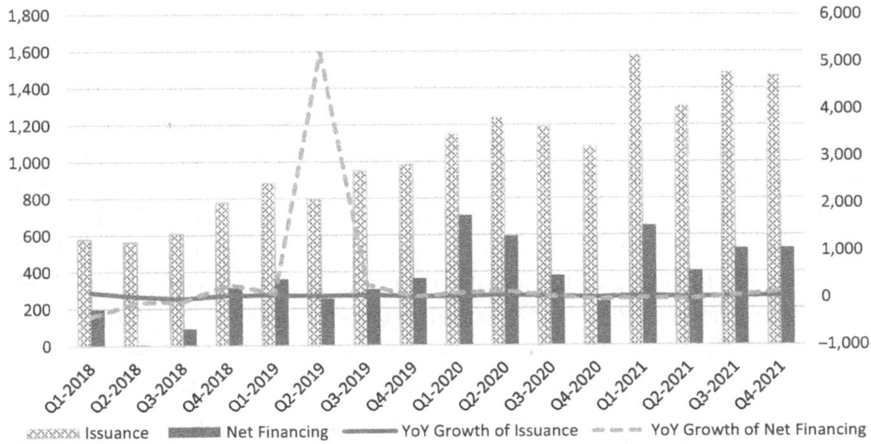

Figure 7.11 On-shore LGFV Bond Issuance (in Billion RMB) and Growth Rates

Note: YoY = Year-on-year.

Source: Moody's Investors Service (2022b).

of net financing. Since net financing refers to new financing, the difference between the two equals the refinancing of maturing bonds. Also plotted are the year-on-year changes in both series.

The spike in the growth of net financing in quarter 2 of 2019 (which is 5,200% in one quarter alone!) has dwarfed the fluctuations in year-on-year growth in issuance. The smooth curve in the figure cannot show that fluctuations ranged from +115% in quarter 1 of 2018 to +25%, −21%, and then +48% in the following three quarters. The weighted coupon rates of these instruments have always been between 4% and 5%, with the highest in quarter 2 of 2019 (at 5%), and lowest in quarter 2 of 2020. Their weighted maturities lie between 3.2 years for bonds issued in quarter 4 of 2021 and 3.62 years for those issued in quarter 2 of 2020. In terms of quality, over half of the LGFV loans are AAA-rated in 2018, but only 34% in quarter 4 of 2021. Comparatively, 27% are rated AA or below, and the rest 26% are AA+. LGFV bond issuance dominates the onshore bond market, accounting for 44% of the overall corporate bond issuance, followed by 31% by the Central SOEs, 21% from regional SOEs, and 4% from privately owned enterprises (POEs).

In addition to the still-rising amount of onshore bond issuance, LGFVs have evolved to become the largest issuers of offshore bonds, especially after the default or near-default of the bonds from the Chinese real estate companies starting from the second half of 2021.[32] However, most of the USD 28.3 billion issuance in 2021 was due to refinancing.[33] Average coupons have dropped to 2.8% by quarter 4 of 2021, despite the increased rates of U.S. bonds. Total issuance is estimated to have hit USD 35.4 billion in 2022. Some of these offshore bonds are held by subsidiaries of Chinese financial institutions, which also hold the onshore bond counterparts. Figure 7.12 depicts the amount of offshore LGFV bond issuance and the year-on-year growth rates as in Figure 7.11. The year-on-year growth rates of issuance here had even bigger swings, with a big spike of 763% in quarter 2 of 2019. The big fluctuations, not surprisingly, are in the growth rates of net financing, which showed a 10-fold increase in quarter 2 of 2018 and then a drop 1 year later, finishing at −814% at the end of 2021.

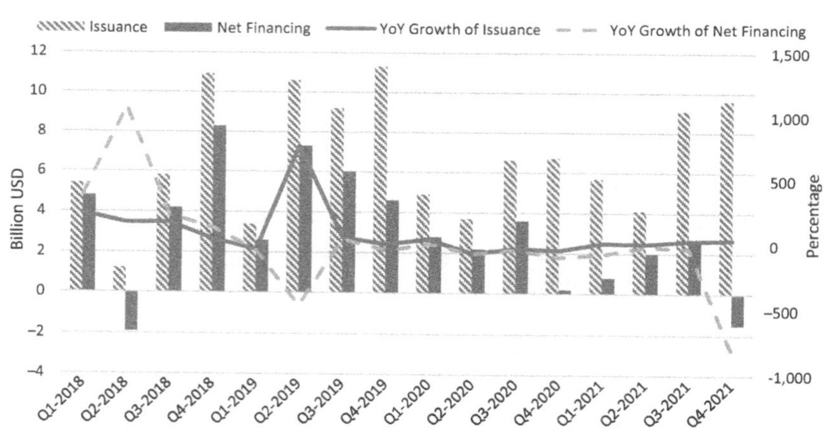

Figure 7.12 Off-shore LGFVs Bond Issuance (in Billion USD) and Growth Rates

Note: YoY = Year-on-year.

Source: Moody's Investors Service (2022b).

[32]South China Morning Post (2022).
[33]Moody's Investors Service (2022b).

7.6. Securitization in China

Unlike the securitization market in the Western world, securitization started in China only in 2005, and the variety of assets being securitized is very limited. The State Council, China Banking Regulatory Commission (CBRC), China Security Regulation Commission (CSRC), and the People's Bank of China (PBoC) are the major regulatory bodies for securitization. CBRC approves products from banks and non-bank financial institutions, while CSRC approves products from corporations such as SOEs and non-SOEs, and financial institutions such as financial leasing companies.[34] The assets backing the securities are largely corporate loans or assets, although mortgages also have their niche. It has been commented that this makes the securities heavily intertwined with the performance of the corporations, and any temporary insolvency of a corporation will spill over to the securities.[35]

7.6.1. Asset-Backed Securitization

Securitization in China started in the early 2000s when non-performing loans (NPLs) held by the Big Four (State-owned banks), accounting for 21.4%–26.1% of their total loans, had gone beyond what was permitted by the Basel Accord.[36] The RMB14,000 billion NPLs were eventually transferred to four asset management companies, which also got themselves in trouble, thus triggering securitizing and selling the loans upon an upgrade in credit ratings for the package, with a tradeoff of increased costs on credit enhancement. It looked like the main purpose of securitization had become getting rid of the NPLs and achieving banking reforms, rather than the usual functions of increasing liquidity and efficiency of assets.[37]

The year 2005 marked reforms and better-quality securitization through the "Some Opinions on Promoting the Reform, Opening and

---

[34]Tang *et al.* (2017).
[35]*Ibid.*
[36]Wei (2007) provides a thorough description of the early development of the asset-backed securitization in China.
[37]Wei (2007). This is not unlike the U.S. government using structured deals to sell off assets from savings and loans that had gone under in the 1980s. See Chapter 9, endnote 2, and https://www.missionsq.org/x3333.html?RFID=W2308.

Steady Growth of Capital Markets" document of the State Council, which saw several maiden launches. The first ABS issued in August 2005 was backed by leasing services of China United Network Communications Group, better known as China Unicom (founded as an SOE), one of the three largest telecommunications companies besides China Telecommunications Corporation (also known as China Telecom) and China Mobile Communications Group (China Mobile). The first collateralized loan obligation (CLO) was launched in December 2005 by the China Development Bank (CDB). As mortgages are in general safe assets, Chinese banks were not interested in issuing mortgage-backed securities (MBS) initially. The first residential mortgage-backed securities (RMBS) of RMB3.1 billion, called the Jianyuan series, was launched by China Construction Bank (CCB), and mainly sold to their affiliated SOEs customers.

Subsequently, there were 26 more asset securitization deals in the following three years, totaling RMB93.3 billion. The securitization market has become quiet since, especially upon the arrival of the GFC, but gained momentum starting in 2011 and experienced a boom in 2014. There was also a sharp increase in CLO issuance. Total issuance involving RMB329 billion in 2014 alone surpassed ten times the sum of the previous years, which is not too surprising if compared to RMB589.06 billion in 2015 alone. This is also the same year when more types of assets backing the securities were added. The boom market also enhanced the fast increase in non-performing loans (NPLs). This is certainly also "helped" by the increased liquidity in the banking sector when the regulatory bodies relaxed lending measures. The securitization of NPLs restarted in 2016 with several successes. In 2020, BMW Automotive Finance (China) sold the first auto loan ABS in China, with double oversubscription.

Currently, possible underlying assets include Residential Mortgage Bonds (RMBs), Commercial Mortgage Bonds (CMBs), NPLs, corporate loans, auto loans, credit card loans, petty loans, and financial leasing credits. All these are credit assets, the so-called credit ABS. Securitization can also be done with corporate assets such as creditor's rights of the corporations and claims on returns of projects and credit assets, which are collectively called enterprise ABS.[38] Securities backed by credit assets are traded in the interbank bond market, while those backed by corporate assets are traded in

[38]More about ABS can be seen in Zong *et al.* (2019).

securities exchanges. There are also asset-backed notes (ABN) for nonfinancial corporations, and insurance asset-backed securities (or insurance ABS), although both occupy a very small fraction of overall ABS issued. BNP Paribas reports that 21.2% of the ABS issued were backed by mortgages, 8.4% by auto loans, and 3.6% by corporate loan receivables.[39] Most ABSs obtained AAA ratings, reflecting their low default risks as the overall delinquency rates tend to be low over the years.

According to MSCI, the Chinese residential mortgage backed securities (RMBS) sector is the fastest-growing asset class and will continue to grow bigger.[40] For instance, RMB50.5 billion of RMBS was issued in the first quarter of 2018 alone.[41] The average term is 12 years, which is the longest of all securitized products in China. Relative to their U.S. counterparts, their yields are generally higher, prepayment rates and default rates are lower, and they have more predictable cash flows. Chinese securitization is also in the international arena, with the first internationally rated RMBS issued by the Postal Savings Bank of China in July 2016. Also according to MSCI, 9 of the 226 Chinese RMBS are rated by Standard and Poors (S&P) Global and Fitch Ratings. International investors can also join the market through the Bond Connect available between Hong Kong and Chinese bond markets.

Figure 7.13 depicts the total amount and the monthly changes of ABS issuance by depository financial institutions since 2016. Unfortunately, the data before 2016 are not available from the CEIC Database, and therefore could not graphically verify the beginning, stagnant, and boom periods of the structured financing market. Interestingly though, monthly new issuance fluctuated a lot until 2019. Before then, the change could be between a drop of 15% and a rise of 28%. That represents RMB82.82 billion and RMB79.41 billion of ABS issuance in quarter 1 of 2017 and quarter 1 of 2018.[42] After 2019, the range of the change was within the range of only plus or

[39]Article from "Market Trends" issued by BNP Paribus on May 29, 2020. Available at: https://cib.bnpparibas/safe-harbours-china-s-abs-market-comes-of-age/.
[40]MSCI published "Chinese RMBS: A Way to Diversify Fixed-Income Portfolios" on July 7, 2021, written by Jian Chen and Yihai Yu. Available at: https://www.msci.com/www/blog-posts/chinese-rmbs-a-way-to-diversify/02614869994.
[41]See Moody's Investors Service (2018).
[42]*Ibid.*

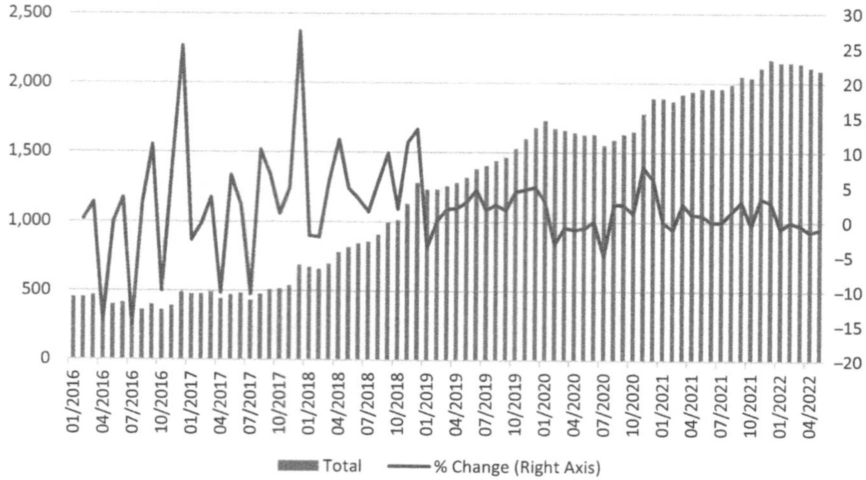

Figure 7.13 Asset-Backed Securities Issued by Chinese Depository Financial Institutions (in Billion RMB)

Source: CEIC Database.

minus 5%. It once again reveals the determination of the Chinese regulatory bodies to promote a healthy development of the securitization market.

7.7. Real Estate Investment Trusts

Despite the development of structured finance, there were no real estate investment trusts (REITs) until 15 years later, in June 2021. Currently, the Chinese REITs cover only infrastructure projects, including projects on logistics, data centers, and sewage and waste treatment. The REITs market therefore has a very high potential to expand. Plans are already laid out for highways and utility projects. This market is also dominated by institutional investors. Appetite has been accumulated from individual investors because of the higher yield relative to government bonds, and low volatility. Figure 7.14 shows the transaction volume in units, the turnover amount in million RMB (both in Panel (a)), the total market value, and market value in circulation (both in Panel (b)). The two curves on Panel (a) are very close visually, but are not really comparable — the left-axis is in the number of units transacted, while the right-axis is the turnover

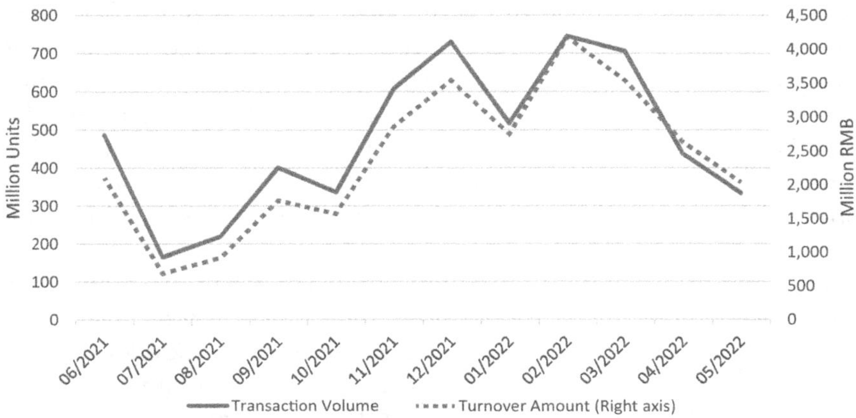

(a)

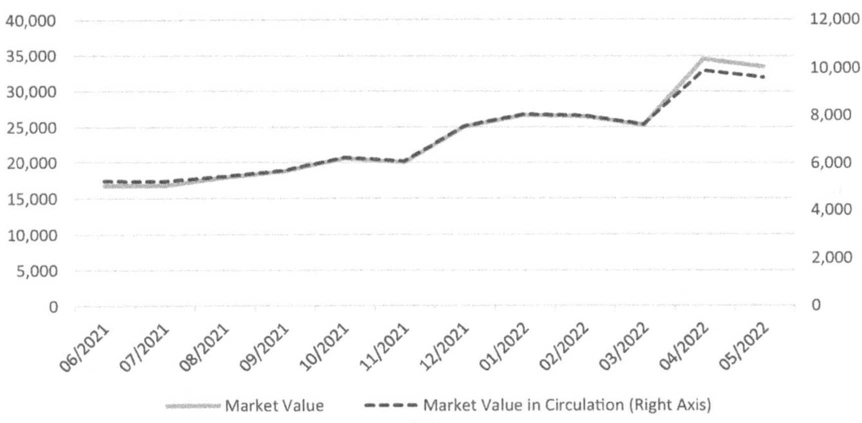

(b)

Figure 7.14 China REITs. Panel (a) Transaction Volume (in Million Units) and Turnover Amount (in Million RMB). Panel (b) Total Market Value and Market Value in Circulation (in Million RMB)

Source: CEIC Database.

amount in million RMB — albeit very highly correlated. The same applies to Panel (b), this time both in million RMB. The right axis showing the market value of circulation is only about one-third of the total market value.

Why did REITs have a late start? A major reason is that the real estate market, particularly the residential housing market, which is a very important tool for the Chinese government to boost economic growth, is also one that draws many household investors, is easily flooded with funding, and is therefore potentially risky. Adding REITs could further flood the real estate market. That said, regulatory bodies are well aware of the functions of REITs for attracting funds, and a way of alleviating debts, which is why infrastructure projects were chosen. There has already been discussion of extending the scope of infrastructure to include affordable rental housing units. Once the inclusion is implemented, the REITs in China will be one step closer to the REITs commonly found in other countries.

Given the massive expansion of Chinese property developers over the past decade, sources of funding confined only to bonds and loans could mean they have high leverage ratios. A good channel is then REITs. Currently, 16 REITs holding 112 properties in China are being traded in Singapore and Hong Kong. Similarly, the first CMBS backed by Chinese commercial properties was issued by Citigroup Global Markets Asia and Macquarie Bank outside of China in 2006.

7.8. Fintech-Led Shadow Banking

In Figure 7.1, there is a shadow banking category called "Others". Items include financial leasing, microcredit, pawn shop loans, peer-to-peer (P2P) lending, ABS, and consumer credit companies. The P2P lending sector has played a crucial part of inclusive finance via fintech in many countries, although the sector is small relative to all other shadow banking channels. An exception is China. However, it also created a big drama in China upon a complete closure of the sector by the end of 2020.

Another group of fintech financing providers is the group of Big Techs, which includes Ant Financial, formerly a subsidiary of Alibaba, and WeBank, a subsidiary of Tencent. We will cover more of these in Chapter 10 as both groups have played significant roles in the credit market boom and busts in China, with some introduction here.

P2P lending platforms are essentially companies offering online platforms for borrowers to match lenders in the types of loans, the borrowers' credentials, terms of the loans, and interest rates. In some cases, the platforms will assess the creditworthiness of the borrowers to determine borrowing rates. In others, there is a "reverse auction" process in which lenders submit their interest rate bids to the platforms for particular borrowers, who then choose the lowest one. Zopa of the U.K. formed the first P2P lending platform in 2005, followed by the more famous Prosper Marketplace and LendingClub in the U.S. P2P lending in Asia started in Korea in 2007, the same year the platform called Pai Pai Dai (which literally means "Auction to Borrow") started in China. However, P2P lending in China did not really grow much until 2010, after which China soon became the largest world market in fintech, reaching a worth of USD 100 billion in 2015, contrasting USD 34 billion in the U.S.

The following figures are all with the data from CEIC Database which provides data only from 2014.[43] Although not starting from the beginning of history, this data series is not bad, considering that not much happened before 2014, both in terms of volume and amount, anyway. Figure 7.15 depicts the situation of the P2P lending market in China for the period of January 2014 to December 2019. Panel (a) provides information about the monthly turnover volume, outstanding balance, and net inflow. Turnover amount and net inflow started slowing down by July 2017. That was also the time when the Chinese regulatory bodies decided to impose much stricter regulations on the previously loosely regulated market. The outstanding balance peak of RMB1,069.17 billion was recorded in May 2018, although the exponential increase also stopped in the last quarter of 2017. Incidentally, funding in the market started to experience a continuous outflow also in May 2018.

Panel (b) plots the number of lenders and borrowers in the market. Interestingly, there were always more lenders than borrowers until 2017, while Panel (c) shows that the average amount that lenders were willing to invest was always around RMB50,000, whereas borrowers could have loans of over a million RMB. The highest average borrowing amount reached RMB0.395 million in February 2014, which then slid to consistently about RMB50,000 after July 2017.

[43]Before the closure of the P2P platforms, all data were readily available from an online platform called Wang Dai Zhi Jia (meaning "Home for Online Borrowing"), which provided very comprehensive data for each loan from 2010. Unfortunately, the closure of the market also marked the closure of this data source.

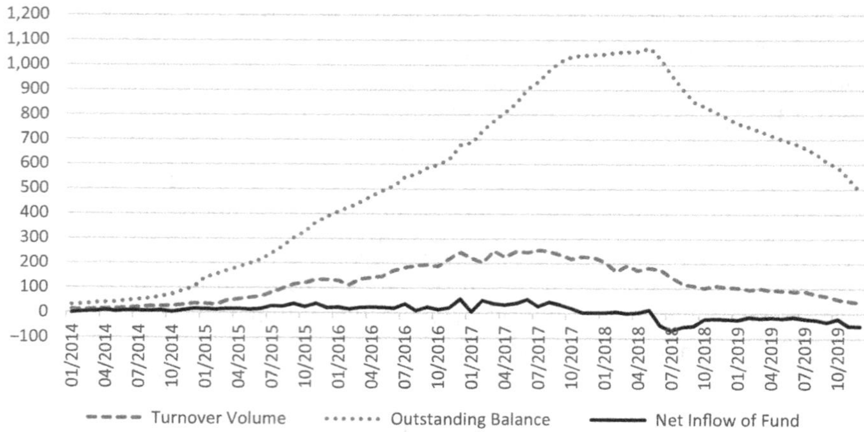

(a)

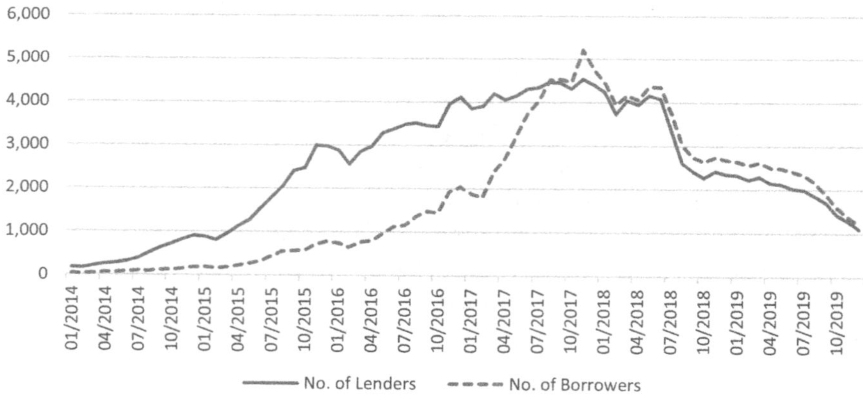

(b)

Figure 7.15 Peer-to-Peer (P2P) Market in China. Panel (a) Monthly Turnover Volume, Outstanding Balance, and Net Inflow (in Billion RMB). Panel (b) Number of Lenders and Borrowers (in Thousand Persons). Panel (c) Amounts of Lending and Borrowing per Person (in RMB). Panel (d) Rate of Return (in %) and Period of Loans (in months)

Source: CEIC Database.

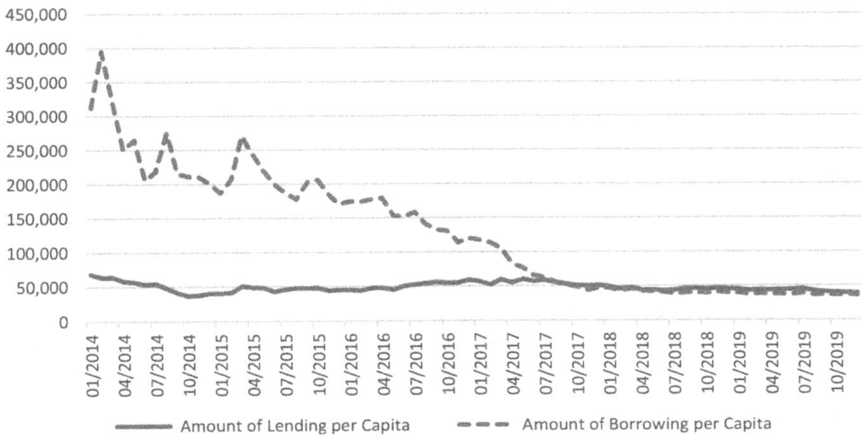

(c)

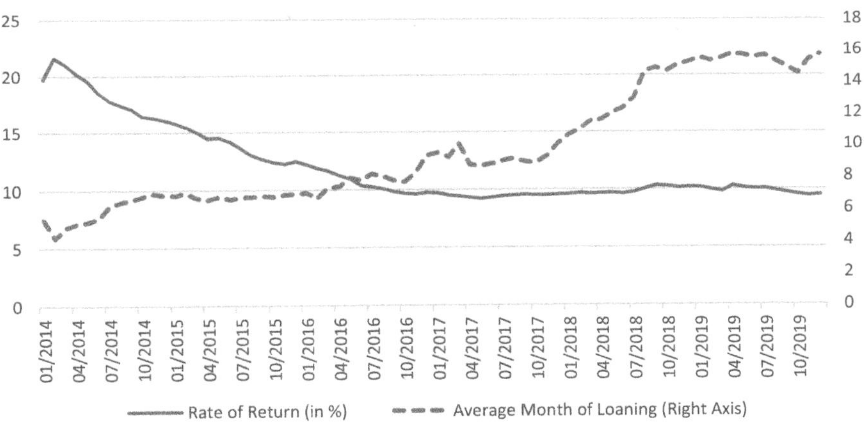

(d)

Figure 7.15 (***Continued***)

Panel (d) plots the annualized rates of returns that lenders could earn and the average duration of the loans in months.

Rates of return as high as almost 22% in February 2014 explain why there were more lenders than borrowers in the first two-thirds of the P2P history. Even after sliding down to an apparently steady rate of about 10%, this rate was still much higher than the rate for bank deposits. If this is the return to lenders, it suggests a big burden for borrowers, which can be further verified by the average number of months of borrowing on the right axis. The average term of the loans has almost tripled by the end of 2019, suggesting that borrowers were not able to return the loans without being given a longer time.

The attractiveness of the market is reflected in how people rushed to establish P2P platforms, with a peak of 3,605 platforms in November 2015 (Panel (a) of Figure 7.16). The boom of new establishments was between quarter 4 of 2014 and quarter 1 of 2015. The number of closures started to grow, with two peaks, in mid-2016 and mid-2018. As mentioned earlier, the P2P sector was completely shut down by the government, in November 2020.

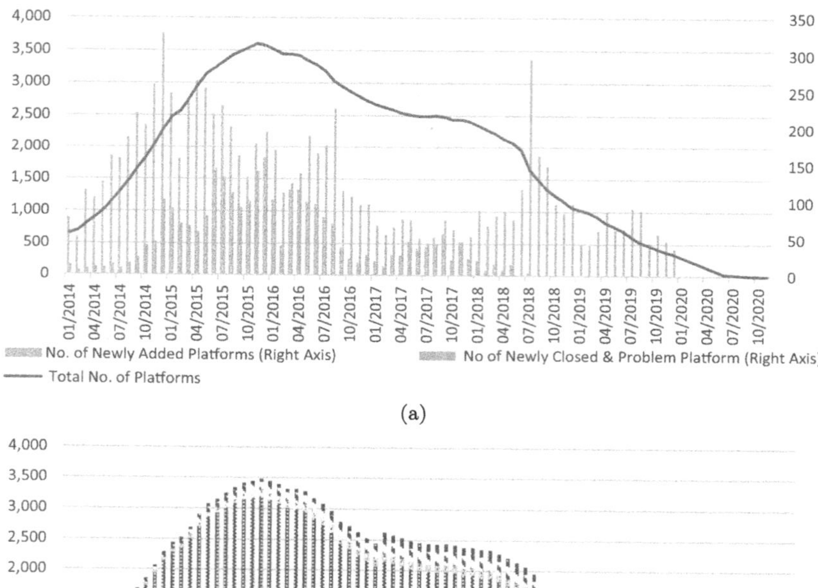

(a)

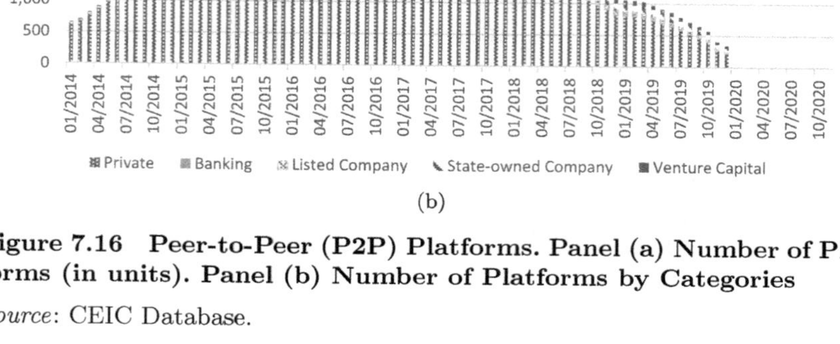

(b)

Figure 7.16 Peer-to-Peer (P2P) Platforms. Panel (a) Number of Platforms (in units). Panel (b) Number of Platforms by Categories

Source: CEIC Database.

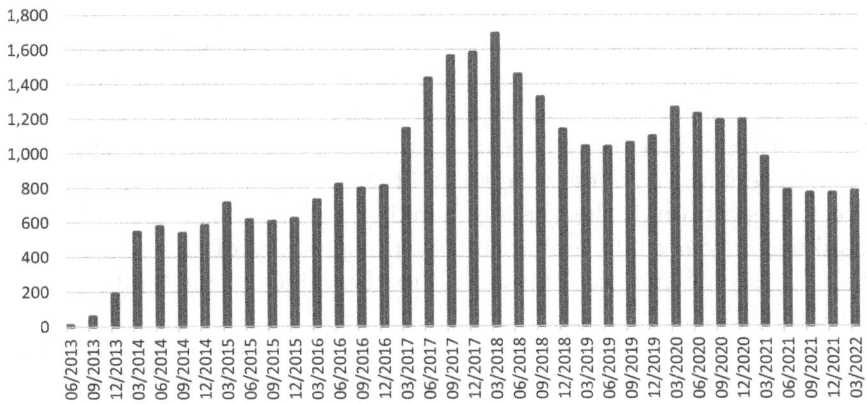

Figure 7.17 Yu'E Bao Net Asset Value (in Billion RMB)

Panel (b) offers some interesting classifications of the platforms into five categories: private, banking, listed companies, state-owned companies, and venture capital. The "banking" category is almost invisible; the values were only between 3 and 5. It is surprising at a glance why banks also form P2P platforms. Unfortunately, no further information about these platforms is available. Most P2P platforms are small "private", perhaps tech, companies.

The last snapshot of fintech financing is the tech giant, Alibaba. Ant Financial is the financial arm of Alibaba, providing all sorts of fintech financing. A very early version called Yu'E Bao (meaning "the treasure from the remaining balance") was established when TaoBao (meaning "digging treasure") attracted so many online shoppers, as the Amazon of China, that it started to offer payment accounts to its customers. The cash balance in the Yu'E Bao accounts earned interest income, albeit very small. Later on, as deposit rates were low anyway, more cash was deposited in Yu'E Bao. Figure 7.17 plots the net asset value of Yu'E Bao. The trend can also reflect the performance of TaoBao as an online consumption platform.

7.9. Is Shadow Banking Good or Bad?: The U.S. and China

Shadow banking in the West has been accused of becoming the origin of the GFC. It sounds like shadow banking is evil, or at least not good, to say the least. Think of how well one knows about what a typical bank does in terms of its value versus risk-taking. Then think of learning about whether corporations do well or are profitable, or their sensitivities to the dynamic economies through their share prices. Analogously, we are able to price the loans and liabilities of commercial banks because some of the securities backed by them are traded through the shadow banking system. Therefore, shadow banking may actually enhance the transparency of the commercial banking sector and price discovery for the values of the banks' assets and liabilities.

Given proper governance and transparency, shadow banking can enhance financing and economic growth by channeling funds to productive uses. The first FSB Report on global shadow banking mentioned several advantages, such as alternative sources of funding, enhanced liquidity, and more efficient credit if some of these shadow banks can do better in specialized credit intermediation.[44] This is especially crucial when the banking sector has to practice monetary tightening due perhaps to macro-prudential policies such as to combat inflation. A disadvantage is its being a source of systemic risk, especially because of its interconnectedness with the regular banking system, after runs on shadow banking providers.

Another criticism of shadow banking goes to the core of what it does — its ability to exploit regulatory arbitrage. Unlike banks that have to follow extensive regulations, shadow banks can provide the banking function like banks under less scrutiny. It is also possible that the regulatory barriers are inefficient, and arbitrage helps. It has been the case that the arbitrage comes from newness and ensuing lack of transparency. Newness makes moral hazard much easier. "Fool me once, shame on you. Fool me twice, shame on me".

One might now be confused about the various forms of shadow banking in both the long and short term and in the U.S. and China. A simplified summary of the different forms of securitization and shadow banking in Table 7.1 might therefore be helpful. In reality, there are cross-overs, in this case among all three, as we discussed in Chapter 5 on U.S. mortgage market structure. Hence, to answer the

[44]Financial Stability Board (2012).

Table 7.1 Comparison of Types of Shadow Banking and Securitization

	China	U.S.	
	Shadow Banks	**Securitization**	**Shadow Banks**
Structure's Life	Ongoing business	One deal at a time	Ongoing business
Mode of Operation	Intermediation	No intermediation	Securitized Banking (pieces of securitization deals)
Credit Risk-Taking	Yes	Credit risk passed through to Investors or Agencies	Yes
Liquidity Provision	Not Much Liquidity; Short and medium-term Debt	Not Much Liquidity for Private Pools	Provide Liquidity with deposit-like debt
Government Support	Probably	No Guarantee for Private pools	Probably Not

question from this section's title, shadow banking is Dr. Jekyll and Mr. Hyde — both good and bad in one body but at different times.

7.10. Summary

Shadow banks can increase the availability of funding in underserved markets. Since they have not had deposit insurance or access to backups from central banks until recently, they have not generally had the option of selecting against the government, although the option of selecting against everyone else exists, enabled by a lack of transparency and options for moral hazard.[45]

There is also the risk that shadow bank risks will spill over to other banks, many of which are considered "too big to fail" (acronym is TBTF) and may have to be bailed out. Furthermore, there is bound

[45]See, for example, Fahri and Tirole (2017) and Martinez-Miera and Repullo (2018).

to be inefficient risk-taking because of implicit subsidies and distortions from moral hazard and agency costs.[46] We will cover how securitization is applied to mortgages in the U.S. housing markets in Chapter 8, and then how the broader shadow banking led to the GFC when linked to the housing markets in Chapter 9. We will also cover in Chapter 10 how a lot has changed since China became the second largest economy, showing that its less market-oriented markets are becoming better developed, but probably neither less risky nor efficient.

[46] See, for example, Acharya and Richardson (2009), and Acharya *et al.* (2013).

Chapter 8

Securitization and Its Discontents

Securitization has allowed a broadening of sources of funds for mortgage lending (and other loans such as car loans, students, etc.) by tapping capital markets and investors, particularly bond markets, and their investors, who already know about long term fixed income securities. Mortgages are now most often written via an *Originate-to-Distribute* model, facilitating entirely separate entities participating in each step of the mortgage process. The borrower makes payments, but need not know who ultimately gets the money or how, or even whether the loan is sold or not. The originator only needs to originate and not fund or service the loans. Instead, the originator can sell a bundle, or pool, of loans into the capital market. Often the originator sells the right to service loans to a third party, a servicer, who is better at collecting money.[1] The underlying credit risk and interest rate risk lie with investors and/or guarantors.

The securitization package is often further unbundled by breaking the pool into pieces or *tranches* designed to appeal to particular investor types. This is rather like carving a chicken so that buyers who prefer chicken breasts do not have to buy chicken thighs as well. We note immediately that this suggests an M–M violation. Recall the pizza problem. That different investors are somewhat inflexible in what they want to hold is the arbitrage for structured deals. But the

[1]There is a very active market in the U.S. for trading servicing rights, which sell at a positive price because of built-in profitability in servicing contracts. This built-in profitability acts as a control on servicing performance because it can usually be transferred to a different servicer.

structures have obstacles to overcome. As discussed in Chapter 5, there is a tradeoff between the benefits of securitization and agency costs from moral hazard.

The moral hazard problem comes from reliance on upstream agents, e.g. originators and servicers, to originate good loans and service them properly and also on guarantors to pay off when they need them. Hence, whoever is taking credit risk needs to align the incentives of originators and servicers with theirs. Otherwise, they'd better have better information about default risk. An important substitute for good information is the ability to use property as collateral, because the owner of the property takes the first hit in a loss situation, limiting losses to investors and incentivizing the seller to do less damage to the buyer in selecting loans. Collateral is rather like ketchup — enough of it can make a bad meal tolerable. Remember? Securitization would be much more difficult without it.

Securitization is a largely American channel for mortgage lending. Mortgage-backed securities (MBS) are generally made up of long-term fixed-rate mortgages. MBS is a more attractive way of funding long-term mortgages, and selling to bond market investors who are interested in fixed-rate assets, than portfolio lending by short-funded banks. In this chapter, we run through various versions of securitization, emphasizing the structures of securitization deals. They look similar in many ways, but can be quite different in terms of handling (sometimes well and sometimes poorly) risk and moral hazard.

We begin with covered bonds, a particular version of securitization that is not really securitization, because they do not entail selling securities. Rather, it is about setting aside a part of a bank's portfolio and borrowing against it. That is, it is hybrid, involving both portfolio lending and selling secured mortgage-back debt that is made up of tradeable securities. We then go on to the real thing, moving from a pure mutual fund type MBS to Agency MBS, to structured Agency MBS (CMOs), and then to PLS and their structuring, and then on to derivative securities that play with the original pool and slices of the pools and make bets on their performance.

A big problem has been the inability to understand what was behind some of the tranches in many of the structures, especially as they became further away from the mortgages behind them all. Structuring made moral hazard easier and made the structures sensitive to shocks such as plummeting house prices. This was behind most of the bank panic, and it is the main strand of the Gorton story. All of this can seem rather bewildering, but the rise and fall of it, particularly the PLS and CDOs and their role in securitized banking, is important.

8.1. On-Balance Sheet Securitization with Excess Collateral: Covered Bonds

Traditionally, mortgages are provided by banks as portfolio lenders as in Figure 5.3. Banks also issue covered bonds. These are regular bonds collateralized by mortgages on the bank's balance sheet and sold to bond market investors (as opposed to depositors). This is similar to securitization (to be explained next), except that it is on the bank's balance sheet. Figure 8.1 shows the corresponding balance sheet structure.

The collateral backing the covered bonds is segmented from other assets, mostly mortgages, and is worth more than the value of the bonds. As such, bond investors have some cushion against losses, similar to the function of bank capital. However, the extra collateral value does not function to secure the other bank liabilities. Thus, if not properly accounted for, some of the bank's capital becomes a subsidy from holders of other liabilities (such as depositors, or those who guarantee them) to the covered bonds. This implies mispriced deposit insurance. That can present a moral hazard for bank owners against deposit insurers and/or other debtholders of the bank.

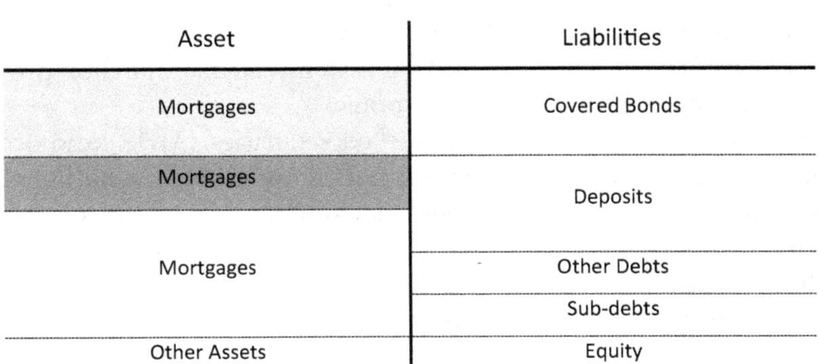

Figure 8.1 Balance Sheet Structure of a Bank Issuing Covered Bonds

To illustrate, the shaded areas (mortgages) in Figure 8.1 represent the collateral backing the covered bonds. Of this, the lightly shaded area represents the excess collateral, which is used twice — once to assuage the investors in the bond, and then counted as an asset for bank capital purposes. This is a straightforward case of regulatory arbitrage if no additional capital requirements are required for banks. The Federal Home Loan Banks in the U.S. lend to member banks via a similar structure.

8.2. Securitization Basics

Securitizing loans, such as mortgages or car loans, or credit card receivables, follows similar processes. We take mortgages as an example, both because that is what the book is about and because of the superior collateral characteristics. The securitized product is a pool of mortgages bought from a bank (or specialized lender like a mortgage bank) and sold in pieces into the bond market. Main actors in the securitization process are:

1. Deal sponsors, who put the deal together and usually act as dealers in the securities.
2. Mortgage originators and brokers, who originate the loans and sell them or who act as agents for mortgage bankers or depositories to sell the loans.
3. Mortgage servicers, who manage the movement of money from the borrower. These need not be the originators.
4. Special Purpose Vehicles (SPVs), which are separate (shell) corporations that are like Trusts; they manage the funds paid by borrowers to the servicers and then to investors, and they provide bankruptcy remoteness to the sponsors.
5. Investors, who buy mortgage-backed securities (MBS) and accept interest rate risk and some credit risk, depending on whether there are outside guarantors (somewhat like deposit insurance).
6. Risk-takers, who might be the investors themselves, perhaps shared with the sponsors, or maybe outside guarantors that act like insurers, taking the risks (e.g. of default) of the loans.

The key difference between securitized loans and covered bonds is the role of the SPV, which takes over ownership of the pool and provides limited liability to sellers of the loans. Although both types

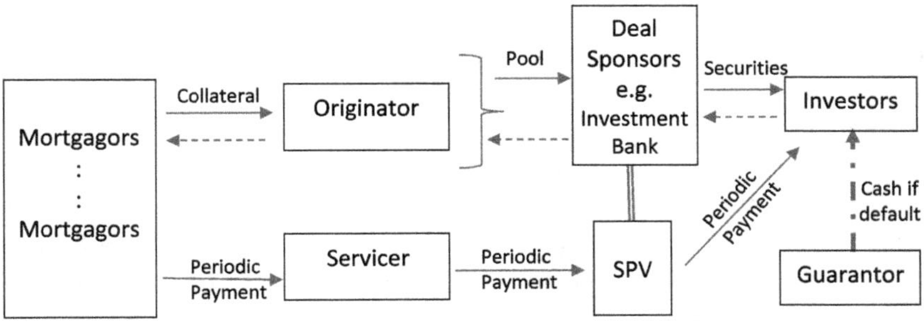

Figure 8.2 Stylized Securitization Flow

provide tradeable securities, the SPV model can do it without the deception about capital adequacy seen in the covered bonds.

A stylized securitization deal with the six groups of players above is depicted in Figure 8.2. The dotted arrows are lump-sum cash for housing purchases. Starting with originating mortgages to homebuyers, an originator will sell the mortgages to the deal sponsors, usually the bank or investment bank, which then bundles and repackages pools of the mortgages into new forms of securities backed by the collateral of the loans, and sells to investors in pieces. The proceeds are ultimately given to homebuyers for their home purchases. They then make periodic payments to the servicer, who then passes the money to the SPV, which pays the investors, according to the rules of the deal.

In case of defaults, the credit risk is absorbed by the investors in the order of rank (AAA investors take losses last), or by a guarantor who pays the investors off (as represented by the big fat dotted-dashed arrow). Deal sponsors bundle debts from many originators. Also, the SPV is linked with the deal sponsor with two thick lines to show that the former is a (shell) corporation of the latter, and therefore only functions to collect and pass money to investors.

As mentioned at the beginning of the chapter, pools of loans are often "tranched" so that investors absorb risk in sequence from those best able to least able to manage and understand risk. In these deals cash flows are prioritized by a sequence of tranches. For instance, the senior tranches are paid first, followed by the intermediate or mezzanine tranches, and finally the equity tranches. In cases of losses, the equity tranche takes the first lost, the mezzanine tranches take losses in sequence and senior tranches are the last in line and get the highest ratings. None of this is special. It is what corporations do when they raise money, with shareholders taking the first hit and various types of debt taking risks down line.[2]

The SPV owns the securities, which protects the seller, although the seller might keep a portion of the deals as part of their investments (on their balance sheets). This gives the pool sponsor "skin in the game" (i.e. the sponsors, e.g. investment banks, also lose and take a first hit) when there is loss from the pools of loans), though this is often too small to matter much. The tranches are sold to funds and other investors, mostly institutional, including investment banks, investment funds, pension funds, and insurance companies, which will hold a majority of the bonds and sell some to individual or retail investors. The riskiest parts are meant to be sold to investors who are willing to take the risks such as maybe hedge funds. As we see below, they are sometimes resecuritized and put pieces into new deals.[3]

Tranches are often rated by credit rating agencies, along the same lines as other bonds, though often less accurately.[4] A big part of the game is to have a deal getting an AAA (or AA) rating as much as possible so it can be sold to institutional investors aiming for high ratings. A consequence of this is a lemons problem because sellers will put together pools that just barely make AAA, so these marginal pools will perform worse than average AAA assets in general. This is a reason to expect (to the extent that investors understand this) that the AAA pieces will have higher interest rates than other AAA securities.

---

[2]An important stimulus to structuring came from the role of the U.S. government (via the Resolution Trust Corporation) using structured deals to sell off assets from savings and loans that had gone under in the 1980s. For a quick summary, see https://www.missionsq.org/x3333.html?RFID=W2308.

[3]Other examples are asset-backed securities (ABS) that are backed by loans with other assets as the collateral, e.g. car loans, or credit card receivables or corporate bonds. In some cases, such as student loans, the securities are backed by Federal guarantees, rather than physical assets as collateral (it is not easy to pledge human capital as collateral). This is the same as for securities guaranteed by the agencies.

[4]An important difference is that corporate ratings tend to be ongoing opinions about the overall credit of the company. Securitization deal ratings on the other hand are considered deal by deal, which means there are a lot of them, and the business is lucrative and more difficult regarding accuracy.

Sales of the deals usually work well when the economy is good, and borrowers continue their periodic payments, such that investors of these financial instruments get paid punctually. Credit enhancement also comes from regional diversification, and pools are made up of securities from different industries. While defaults may be high individually, the overall pool is stable and more manageable when mixed with other low quality mortgages, and with larger AAA pieces. The degree of diversification has been overestimated in the past though, causing more risk than expected to more senior tranches with higher ratings, leading up to the GFC.

8.3. Securitization Structures

Next, we cover the pros and cons of different structures of securitization, how they compete with other modes of doing mortgages, how they fit in, and therefore where their arbitrage is. We cover most of the types of securitization deals. A byproduct of the era leading to GFC is the birth of many acronyms. The names of the deals covered in this Chapter are additional "ingredients" of the "alphabet soup", and they can be as hard to follow as the names in War and Peace.

A major purpose of most securitization deals (aside from the covered bonds) is to move loans off the balance sheets of banks and other portfolio lenders.[5] Here we expand on versions of Figure 8.1. We depict different categories of deals, discussing reasons for their existence and their risks in the following sections. For now, we present the simplest one as an introduction.

The barest version of securitization is a mutual fund that passes through cash flows from pools of securities or mortgages. Its appeal lies in diversification. For example, a pure pass-through from mortgage pools called mortgage-backed securities, MBS, is usually more about geographic diversification and less about diversification across products. Figure 8.3 is a representation of the simplest sort of

[5]We should note that some sales have had buyback provisions, which do not take them off the balance sheet completely. In some cases, quite often with structured deals sponsored by investment banks, the promises were implicit, meaning they could be ignored in a pinch (and need not be considered formally as claims on the sellers' capital). This was sometimes called "pinky-swear" recourse.

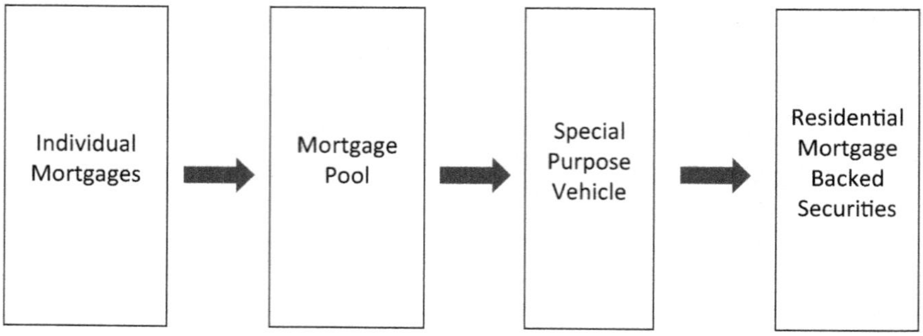

Figure 8.3 Structure of a Pass-Through with No Guarantees

securitization deal. We label this a "Residential Mortgage-Backed Security" (RMBS). Cash flows are shared in a *pro rata* manner by investors. Interest rate risk and credit risk are born equally by all investors, and there is no liquidity risk.

This can increase diversification, which is not readily available to all due to transaction costs. However, unlike stocks which are easier because one can follow their history, mortgages suffer from the Diamond problem of severe information asymmetry. This makes diversification in funds made of mortgages less effective and therefore suggests leaning toward structuring or intermediation. Here we look at structuring.

Banks issue RMBS through their SPVs. Unlike a bank actively managing its portfolio, an SPV just follows instructions given by the deal or pool sponsor (the bank in this case). Securitization incurs little, if any, active management after the pool is formed, and the deal generally lasts only as long as the assets. Some deals are indeed actively managed, such as new assets being added to replace old ones, as is the case with securitized credit card receivables. This is less important for RMBS, but not non-existent.

The securitization deal in Figure 8.3 would be (and has been) hard to sell because regular bond market investors would need a lot of information at the level of individual loans to deduce its risk. They would likely believe that loan originators and/or better-informed investors could select against them. And as in all markets for lemons (explained in Chapter 5), they would tend to avoid buying into the pool, unless there are some sort of credit enhancement.

8.4. Agency Market: MBS with Credit Enhancement

Unlike RMBS issuers mentioned above, Fannie Mae, Freddie Mac, and Ginnie Mae (the Agencies) provide an additional guarantee beyond default insurance that investors will get promised cash flow on time, which is why Agency MBSs dominate the markets in FRMs in which they can operate.[6]

As introduced in Chapter 5, the GSEs, have portfolios that are similar to banks.[7] Their assets include mortgages and MBS and the present value of guarantee fee income and enjoy the value of an implicit guarantee. They have liabilities from their guarantees and their own debt as well as equity. While very similar in structure to bank balance sheets, theirs are different in that their liability holders are not depositors, though sometimes they have been short-term debt-holders. To that extent, they are less like shadow banks than they are like regular banks with guarantees and regulations.

8.4.1. Agency Pass-Through MBS

The securitization business of the agencies is the most interesting part of their activities because it introduced mortgage securitization. Their core business from which they now receive the bulk of their income is simple: they put pools of similar mortgages together, typically FRMs that pay off rather like mutual funds, and sell shares of the pools. Most importantly, they guarantee payments and the securities are more like long term bonds. Figure 8.4 provides a general sketch of a typical Agency pass-through MBS pool. Note that this is not on their balance sheets, as is the case for the bank, but rather in the structure of a separate entity, the SPV, which is a single securitization deal.

The cash flows are run through an SPV (in this case a trust) that gets the money to the investors. The guarantee has effectively taken credit risk off the table for bond market investors, allowing them to focus on the interest rate and prepayment risks, which the

---

[6]See Weicher (1999) for a discussion of some of the history of the secondary market.

[7]Ginnie Mae is a part of the government and does almost nothing but guarantee timely payment on securities. That is why it has a very minimal balance sheet.

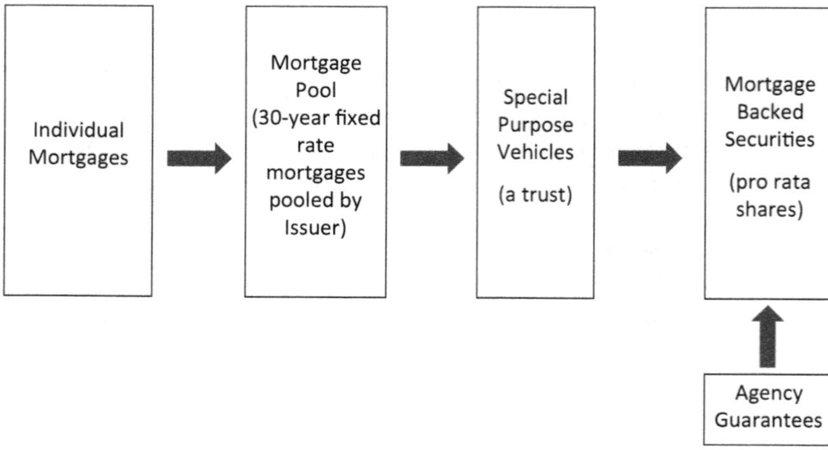

Figure 8.4 Structure of Agency Pass-Through MBS

investors are more familiar with. This has virtually eliminated the moral hazard via credit risk to investors.[8] Note that the agencies or their government guarantors are still subject to moral hazard because of mortgage originators. The credibility of the guarantee by the agencies has greatly enhanced the perception that the agencies are covered by the government if they are unable to pay off. This also creates incentives for adverse selection against the Government, in the form of encouraging risk-taking. Any loss covered by the government opens up the possibility of taxpayers' loss.

The guarantee of agency pass-throughs is a solution to the problem of too little information for investors to buy shares in the structure in Figure 8.3. The set of guarantees and regulation similar to the case with banks are now used in the bond market, which can now focus on managing interest rate risk, which is what it does anyway.

8.4.2. Collateralized Mortgage Obligations: Structuring Interest Rate Risk

But there is more. Pro-rata shares of pass-throughs are not everybody's favorite. Mortgages have unique characteristics that make them different from normal bonds. Among these is uncertainty about

[8]Assuming agencies cannot go bankrupt.

when (and not if, given the guarantee) the principal will be paid back. Many investors like to hold simpler and more transparent liabilities, like deposits, debt, or equity. In the 1980s, the Agencies began developing hybrid pass-throughs which are deals structured in a way that allows investors to hold special parts of the deals to better match what they want, rather like carving up a chicken and letting buyers have an easier choice of breasts versus legs. This is "client-oriented" in the sense of viewing leg fans and wing fans as different clients.

The first of such deals were the collateralized mortgage obligations (CMOs) sold in the 1980s.[9] Pools made up of 30-year FRMs were divided into four tranches that paid off the principle sequentially. Investors could better control the terms of their assets (e.g. banks like shorter time assets, and pension funds might like longer term assets). Most Agency MBS are now put into CMOs. That CMOs have tended to make money has been a strong indicator that the MBS market alone was not enough (see Section 8.6). Otherwise, there should not be opportunities for extra money-making simply by structuring the mortgages (M–M Theorem).

Most CMOs offer some sort of prepayment risk control, such as dividing the tranches further to include one tranche taking the first hit on prepayments, and a much less exposed residual tranche. Although there are other ways of carving up the mortgage pool chicken, the key requirement is that all carved pieces have to add up to one whole chicken. All payoff promises are kept. In the case of Agency CMOs, on top of the original guarantee, there is a guarantee that the deal will work. Given the extent to which the market has expanded into 50 plus tranche deals, this is not a trivial addition to the original guarantee against credit risk.

Figure 8.5 shows a sample Agency CMO with four tranches that receive the principal in sequence from Tranches 1 to 4, with Pieces A and B inside the tranches such that Piece A absorbs most prepayments, allowing some prepayment protection to the holders of Piece B. These structures can involve adverse selection by dumping loans with high prepayment risk. This is largely mitigated by the large size of the pools, which diversifies much, but not entirely, of the risk away.

---

[9]See McConnell and Buser (2011) for a survey that discusses the evolution of CMOs.

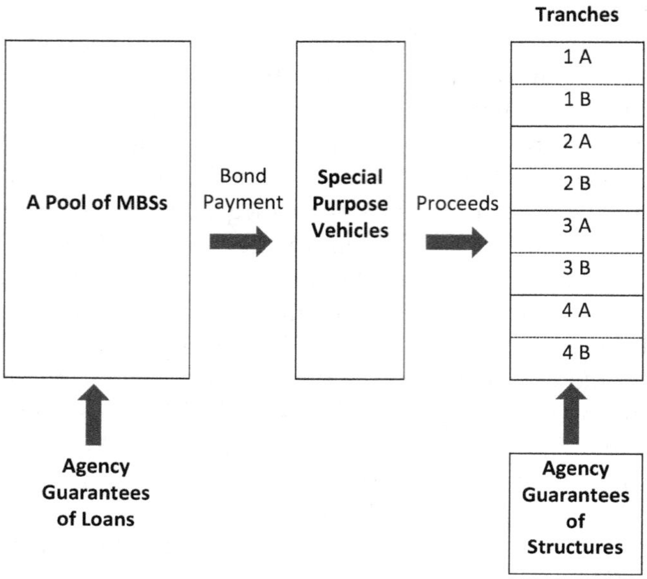

Figure 8.5 Agency CMOs

We next enter the more wild-west version that operates without guarantees or deposit insurance, Private Label (aka Wall Street) securitization.

8.5. Structuring Credit Risk: Private Label Securities

The non-agency private label securities (PLS) market is driven by regulatory arbitrage. It has mostly operated in areas not eligible for the Agencies, initially mainly because the balances of the loans in these markets were too large for agency purchases by regulation. Over time, it became advantageous to securitize riskier "non-prime" loans (subprime loans and low documentation Alt-A loans). That business took off around the turn of the century.

Figure 8.6 depicts a typical PLS deal. Losses flow from the bottom to top, and payments from the top to the bottom. By getting money back first and taking losses last, the top tranche could legitimately have an AAA rating even with risky assets in the pool, as long as the subordination from the lower tranches is big enough. The PLS

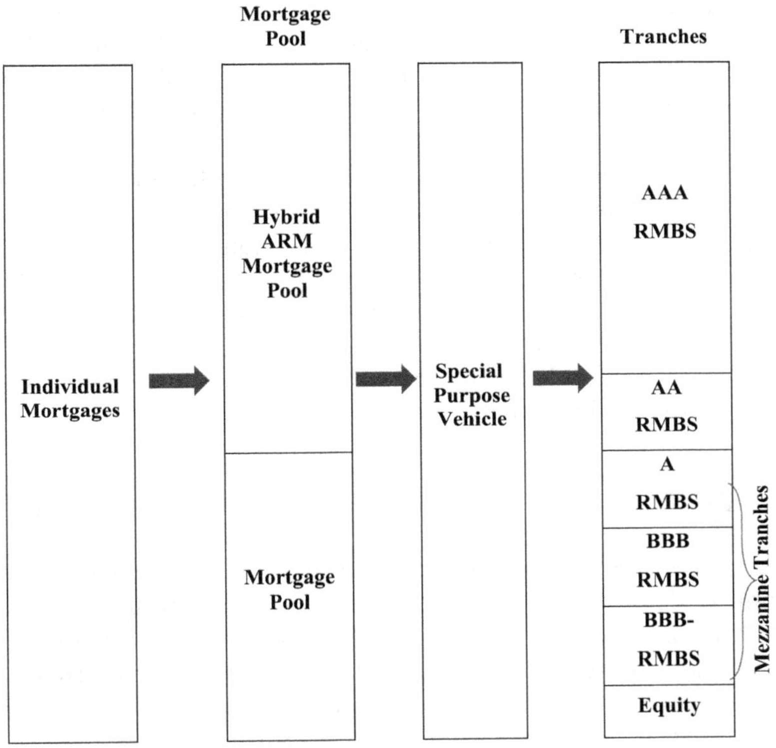

Figure 8.6 Non-Agency (Private Label) RMBS

deal in Figure 8.6 is a representation of a standard six-tranche PLS deal.[10]

This is how you get AAA ratings in subprime deals. It is not because investors were talked into thinking the loans are really AAA, but because of the role of investors who are subordinated to them and take the risk first. For instance, 20% subordination beneath the top tranche is larger than the capital ratio of almost any bank, and therefore could (depending on the underlying assets) be enough to get the top 80% rated AAA. However, it is the *volatility* of the losses in subordinated bits that matters. Even though the 20% subordination

[10]Because of the six tranches, this type of deal is sometimes called a "six pack". Investment bankers do have a sense of humor, even without using French.

is usually more than enough to cover losses, there can be times when losses can be greater than 20%, especially if their losses are highly correlated. Hence, how many of the tranches get AAA depends critically on the correlation among the asset in a pool, as well as asset type.

In the extreme, one could imagine a pool where the loans were perfectly correlated, for instance, 90% of the time none would default and 10% of all of them would. This deal should not have an AAA piece, because the AAA piece, like the rest of the deal, will take losses 10% of the time. Although no deals were this bad, there were deals with pieces that had AAA ratings, and investors and rating agencies did not know the underlying correlations. That was a serious type of moral hazard to the extent the sellers knew.[11]

8.6. Re-Tranching — Collateralized Debt Obligations

AAA pieces are important arbitrages, and deal makers try to maximize their size, but what about the other tranches? Lower-rated tranches can be sold to hedge funds or other investors who are better able to manage the risks. However, an alternative is to "resecuritize" by putting lower-rated pieces of deals in these other tranches together into new deals with senior tranches, which could be rated AAA. These new structures are called Collateralized Debt Obligations (CDOs). Pieces of other deals are put together and structured. The idea, again, is to squeeze out more AAA tranches.

How can it be done? With considerable difficulty and a bit of deception! This has been the most controversial part of the U.S. securitization business. In principle, it is not different from straight RMBS deals with individual mortgages. Indeed, there is potential to increase diversification by mixing pieces of RMBS deals with other assets, such as ABS deals from different industries (e.g. car loan ABS tranches or corporate bonds) and across wider geographies.

[11]This incentive is ubiquitous and is a reason why corporate bonds usually have restrictions on risk-taking of the corresponding companies. Companies in trouble have the incentive to "gamble for resurrection" by changing to risky strategies when they get into trouble.

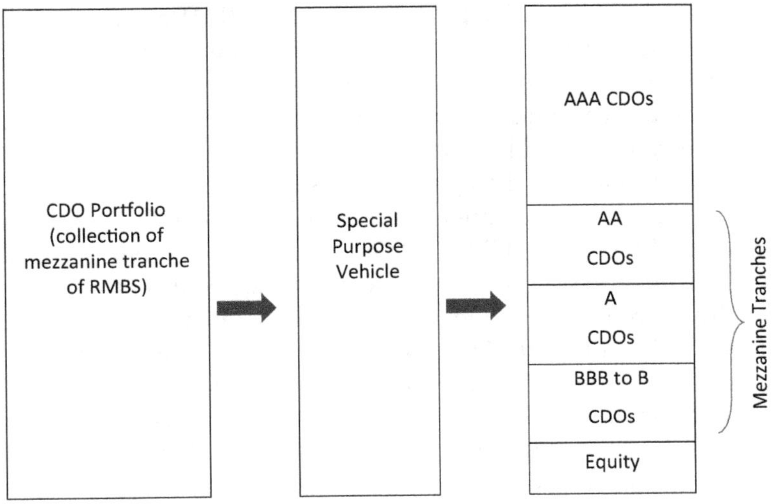

Figure 8.7 A Collateralized Debt Obligation Structure

Consequently, there are more AAA securities in the market, but it is harder for investors to understand the underlying risk because the securities are moved further away from the individual loans in the original deal (e.g. RMBS), and it is possible to overestimate the diversification benefits of pooling and underestimate moral hazard surrounding it. This was partly from problems inherent in measuring the risks of complicated assets and partly from agency costs. Less diversification than investors thought exposes them to cascades of defaults, which is something that the evolution of CDOs brought to the GFC. Figure 8.7 depicts the structure of a regular or "Cash" CDO.

CDOs can be very sensitive to diversification risk. They can entice the issuers, who are also owners of equity pieces, to include highly correlated, and in general riskier, assets. This is similar to the first level structures in Figure 8.6 but with more tools for obfuscation. We shall illustrate how vulnerable even the senior AAA pieces can be in the next section.[12]

CDOs can be resecuritized into structures that are aptly called CDO-squared. The structure is the same as above except that the

[12]See Cordell *et al.* (2012) on problems with CDOs.

collateral is made up of CDOs rather than RMBS, which implies that it is more leveraged. It is hard to see the underlying logic of this other than to squeeze out more AAA-rated pieces, at the cost of larger and harder to guess levels of correlation among assets as there are too many layers and unclear composition of the securities from the individual loans in the original deals.

Another type of instrument that is similar to CDOs is collateralized loan obligations (CLOs). While CDOs are usually backed by personal debts such as mortgages, auto loans, credit card loans, and so on, CLOs are bundled from corporate loans, usually from different industries. The collateral is the assets of these corporations. In this sense, the CLOs are less risky than CDOs not only because their risk is more diversified because they are backed by assets of corporations from different industries but also because they are less linked to banks, less leveraged, and less complex.

8.7. Benefits and Risks from Tranching and Resecuritizing

Asset-backed securities in general, and RMBS deals in particular, are confined to one industry where specialists put the deals together at the first securitization stage. Resecuritization adds diversification that is not possible at the first stage. For instance, most CDOs combined pieces of mortgage deals with pieces of deals from loans to borrowers in different groups or industries. This can add diversification and justify the AAA rating for some pieces. One can imagine resecuritizing in sequence with pieces of pools from different deals until there is a universe of AAA pieces and residual pieces that take the credit risk, acting like insurance companies, with diversified risk. That is the good side. On the downside, deals that do not add diversification can lead to over-leveraging and compounding the risk of securitization.

Securitization is about writing derivatives, like options and futures contracts, in the sense that the values of the products are derived from the underlying assets. The CDOs made up of layer after layer of ABS are similar to compound call options. And like exotic options, it will be very difficult to find analytical solutions. If used as collateral, the CDOs can generate liquidity risk and regulatory arbitrage to the financial systems through maturity transformation in fragile markets. As commented by the Financial Stability Board (Financial Stability Board, 2020, p. 64), a lot of excessive credit risk can be built up through securitization and resecuritization.

We borrow the example from John Hull's classical book on financial risk management (pages 134–136, Hull, 2018) as illustration. We take the simple example as in Figure 8.7, which is similar to Figure 6.5 of Hull's book which, as he describes, is a more realistic securitization example with ABS, ABS CDOs, and CDOs of CDOs, and deduce the values in the same approach as Hull's Table 6.1.

Suppose subprime mortgages are bundled into a portfolio with an arbitrary initial value of 100 to create five tranches of RMBS, namely the AAA-rated, AA, A, BBB, BB+ Not Rated (NR). One can imagine that when a lot of the loans default due to a poorer economy, the amount of payments collected from those who paid might be able to satisfy the payments to the senior tranche, but not all the mezzanine tranche. And if this latter tranche is subsequently bundled, then its senior tranche can get the payment, but not necessarily the mezzanine tranche of this second layer of the bundle. If there have been many layers of bundles, the payments can dry up very quickly after paying back the senior tranche of the first few layers, but not others, even if the investors are holding "senior" tranches of the further layers. It is clear that there is a lot of leverage in the whole securitization story.

Table 8.1 shows the initial values and residual values of the RMBS securities with their proportions in the portfolios, given certain percentages of losses. Also shown are their corresponding losses in values. The AAA-, AA-, and A-rated tranches are then bundled into a second layer of "High-grade RMBS CDO", itself with another six tranches. In reality, this second layer will be bundled together with ABS formed from another mortgage portfolio. At the top of the table is the initial value of the mortgage portfolio of $100. Suppose there is a nationwide decline in property values everywhere, and a sharp increase in mortgage defaults as was the case beginning in the U.S. around 2006 or 2007 (we elaborate on GFC default rates in the later part of this chapter). That would lead to losses in the corresponding RMBS and subsequently the CDOs.

The columns on the right in Table 8.1 list four scenarios of losses. The "Value" next to the "Loss" (representing the percentage of loss)

Table 8.1 Values and Losses in the Securitization Stream with Loss in Subprime Mortgages

Mortgage Portfolio	Share (%)	Value	10% Loss		15% Loss		20% Loss		25% Loss	
			Value	Loss (%)	Value	Loss (%)	Value	Loss (%)	Value	Loss (%)
		100	90	10.0	85	15.0	80	20.0	75	25.0
RMBS										
AAA	80	80	80	0	80	0.0	80	0.0	75	6.3
AA	10	10	10	0	5	50.0	0	100	0	100
A	5	5	0	100	0	100	0	100	0	100
BBB	4	4	0	100	0	100	0	100	0	100
BB, NR	1	1	0	100	0	100	0	100	0	100
High-grade RMBS CDO										
Senior AAA	85	80.75	80.75	0.0	80.75	0.0	80	0.93	75	7.12
Junior AAA	8	7.60	7.60	0.0	4.25	44.1	0	100	0	100
AA	3	2.85	1.65	42.1	0	100	0	100	0	100
A	2	1.90	0	100	0	100	0	100	0	100
BBB	1	0.95	0	100	0	100	0	100	0	100
NR	1	0.95	0	100	0	100	0	100	0	100

in the title row is the value of the mortgage portfolio corresponding to the loss. Down the columns are the value and percentage of loss from the initial value for each of the tranches of the securities in each scenario. For example, 10% of the ABS is in the AA tranche, representing an initial value of $10. In case of a 10% loss in the subprime mortgage portfolio, investors of this tranche can still get back all the $10 investment. However, for example, if the loss is 15%, they will be able to get back only 50% of their initial investment. In the case of the A-rated tranche, investors will get nothing even if there is a 10% loss in the mortgage portfolio. In the case of the high-grade ABS CDO in the next layer, even the junior AAA tranche will lose 44.1% of the investment if there is a 15% loss in the mortgage portfolio value, not to mention higher loss, or other lower tranches. It is obvious here that securities rated as AAA, albeit "junior", are not all that safe. At 25% portfolio loss, even the AAA-rated RMBS and Senior AAA-rated RMBS CDO incurred a loss. One can therefore imagine the big loss at the last layer of a multi-resecuritization, generating $\mathrm{CDO}^{\mathrm{N}}$, even with a small loss in the subprime mortgage portfolio.

8.8. Derivatives of CDOs: Credit Default Swaps as Insurance Policies

Is there any way to hedge the risk of CDOs? Yes, as the Chinese saying goes, "where there is danger, there is always opportunity"! The field of finance has undergone many innovations over time. Financial market participants have found new business opportunities analogous to selling insurance.

The key financial instrument is called the Credit Default Swap (CDS), a variant of the structure above that acts like insurance. These are synthetic (non-cash) CDOs for which the payoffs depend on how "referenced" deals perform, rather like making side bets, instead of having actual assets in the structure. As with insurance, a financial institution can buy CDS against the default risk from pieces of RMBS, CDOs, and other deals that it sells. When payments from a tranche are not enough to cover what has been promised, the CDS buyer can claim a predetermined amount. As with insurance policies, the law of large numbers, along with diversification, makes pool-wide CDO defaults unlikely to change (so long as everything in the economy goes well, that is). The underlying risk is the same as with the cash CDOs described above. The questions are whether diversification is well-estimated and/or hidden and how well the CDS can handle it. The estimated cost will be incorporated in the pricing of the CDS.

CDS enhances the liquidity transformation of the relatively more illiquid bonds.[13] When some bonds are traded with low liquidity, repackaging their default risks into CDS allows bondholders to effectively transfer the credit risks to investors who trade the more liquid CDS, or to portfolio managers who need to diversify portfolio risks. However, unlike the situation of a buyer of car or fire, or life insurance, the buyer of CDS is not necessarily buying protection for its own securities. Instead, it can short the pools, rather like making a side bet on performance.[14] For instance, a trader can pick a pool of CDOs and buy insurance against them even if he does not own the CDOs. The trade is like buying fire insurance against your neighbor's house because you know that the neighbor smokes in bed. That implies a moral hazard problem that is also common with insurance, meaning that CDS can be very risky.

Figure 8.8 shows a version of a CDS structure. As with insurance, the buyer of the CDS buys the protection against the loss in value of the securities (e.g. tranches of RMBS, ABS, CDOs, etc.) in the reference portfolio. An occurrence of a "credit event," such as failure to pay interest or repay principle by the reference portfolio triggers a protection payment. The compensation that the seller pays the buyer depends on the terms stated in the CDS. Note in the figure that there is no arrow coming from or going to the reference portfolio because even though the amounts of cash flows involved (i.e. the "compensation" flows shown by the arrows) are derived from the value of the pools, they are from the seller (insurer), not the investors in the pool.

Sometimes there is just one protection buyer, and sometimes protection sellers buy tranches from a CDS pool so that risk can be prioritized. As with cash CDOs, moral hazard can exist if the buyers

---

[13] As Oehmke and Zawasowski (2015) discussed.

[14] Normally shorting a security means borrowing it for selling, and hoping to buy it back at a lower price later. However, tranches of CDOs do not trade often enough to make this feasible.

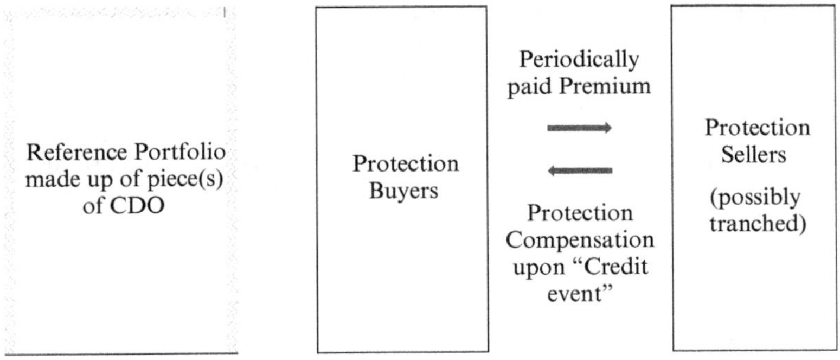

Figure 8.8 A Credit Default Swap Structure

of the protection know more than the CDS sellers. A notorious example of this is the Goldman Sachs Abacus Deal that ended up with Draconian downgrades.[15]

8.9. Summarizing Different Structures for Mortgages

The various types of structures described above, while looking similar, are different not only in risk allocation but also in degrees of moral hazard, agency costs, and regulatory arbitrage. Table 8.2 summarizes the main elements of subsidies and costs, moral hazard, and regulatory arbitrage across structure types.

Many of the deals set up before the GFC were very opaque structures that invited moral hazard. Structured deals with AAA- or AA-rated pieces from MBS and CDOs looked good on paper like they were well capitalized and holding investment quality assets. Investors discovered only later that they were not. Again, a big factor was the inadequate diversification that investors thought the structures had. Many of the deals had subsidies and tax breaks including deposit insurance, implicit GSE guarantees, and Too-Big- (or Too-Systemic-) To-Fail bailouts. All these probably distort resource allocation in the longer run, by providing incentives to

[15]Kent Smetters and Richard Herring wrote "Goldman Sachs and Abacus 2008 — AC1: A Look Beyond the Numbers", posted on *Knowledge at Wharton* on April 28, 2010. Available at: https://knowledge.wharton.upenn.edu/article/goldman-sachs-and-abacus-2007-ac1-a-look-beyond-the-numbers/.

Table 8.2 Differences in Advantages among Different Structures

	Types of Advantage		
Structure Type	**Subsidy/Cost**	**Moral Hazard**	**Regulatory Arbitrage**
Bank	Deposit insurance, Too big to fail (TBTF)	Against deposit insurer (government in case of TBTF)	Exploit deposit insurance
Covered Bond	Excess collateral	Takes bank capital protection away from other stakeholders	Exploits capital regs along with deposit insurance
Agency MBS	Implicit guarantee	Against government	Limits on what banks can do, and guarantee
Structured PLS	Lower cost by separating risks	Against investor or CDS; Opaque, Correlation risk	Agency loan limits and limits on risk-taking
CDO (resecuritizing)	Lower cost by separating risks	More opaque than PLS, Correlation risk	Same as PLS
CDS (insurance)		Moral hazard from insured	Exploits absence of deposit insurance

produce too much housing, at the expense of other investments, as well as to increase house prices, and they did not help to stabilize the financial system in 2008 (or other previous times).

8.10. Summary: Are Structured Deals Good or Bad?

In this chapter, we introduced the process of securitization and the different types of structured deals. All of them contain mortgages and are backed by collateral. But the similarity ends there. Some deals are transparent and/or have guarantees. Others are not transparent and are very distant from the collateral supporting them, with major moral hazards and transparency issues. They turned out to be very sensitive to shocks, both to information/understanding and house price declines. That they were held by shadow banks was a major part of the reason for the silent bank runs in 2008. Their arbitrage morphed into moral hazard. The key in the U.S. was securitized banking, which combined the worst of short-term funding (the shadow banks) with the newness and excessive complications and moral hazard of structured deals and securitized banking.

Are structured deals good or bad? Both. At their best, structured deals share risks with those best able to handle them by taking account of client concerns, and pricing for them efficiently. At their worst, the hidden risks (sometimes in plain sight) in ways that exploit lemons problems, leading to a crash when the misinformation is discovered, like the cat is out of the bag.

Structuring is, in principle, the same thing as businesses raising money from different investors, some of whom want equity while others prefer safer debt or the near certainty of regular income. Where the structures go, how they evolve, and settle down, can be almost random. Many of the cost differences that cause violations of M–M can be small and yet lead to sharp changes in market structure (with small changes in benefits). So, the arbitrage can change, even if the resource allocation coming from the market need not change much, and the other arbitrage, dumping lemons, can emerge.

On the question of how these deals should be regulated, we take a pass for now.

Chapter 9

Housing Markets and Shadow Banking

Part I — The Dark Side of the Force: Securitized Shadow Banking and GFC

To summarize the previous chapter, shadow banking has evolved over the last few decades into a story of regulatory arbitrage in markets where traditional banks are either not allowed or too costly to operate. What this means, and which markets it opens up, varies by country. Shadow banking in the U.S. has been especially about bank-like structures that are short-term collateralized borrowings secured by seemingly highly rated securities, often held by other shadow banks. Two examples are Repos secured with AAA-rated tranches of CDOs and MMMFs backed by commercial paper, both with deposit-like liabilities.

On the other side of the world, shadow banking in China has been less about securitization and structures than about ongoing institutions that are similar to savings banks in terms of intermediating with liabilities that are essentially term deposits. Since the deposits generally could not be withdrawn on demand, runs were less of a problem, although insolvency and inefficient lending remained. So, the two approaches are similar but not identical; and the two countries have similar but different regulatory structures, and economic environments in which to operate, which accounts for most of the differences. As a result, the regulatory arbitrage has been different. We focus on the U.S. here and on China in the next chapter.

Mortgages are logical assets for both securitization and shadow banking because they are backed by real estate as collateral. Here we look at how the combined force of housing bubbles and shadow banking were instrumental in the Global Financial Crisis. In the next chapter, we look at how apparent bubbles associated with the shadow banking system in China turned out to be air leaks rather than bursting bubbles, although that is less clear now.

9.1. When Housing Markets Met Shadow Banking in the U.S.

Shadow banking and securitization met housing markets with good intentions. They were to create a less regulated and less costly way of broadening funding sources. They can stimulate innovation and information about what works and what does not without exposing the traditional financial system to systemic losses, and they introduce flexibility and mitigates losses from imperfect regulations. That housing is good collateral provides investors (depositors and debt holders) security about their investments without the need for default models and loan level information or government guarantees. It turned out to be complicated. And there are dark sides.

That shadow banks do not directly expose the traditional system does not mean there are no systemic problems. That shadow banks do not have deposit insurance or bail-out mechanisms means the shadow system is exposed to "bank-runs". They can exploit poor information structures and rip off investors, deliberately or carelessly, particularly for products without a track record. Free entry into the business with minimal regulation enhances competition, which may lower monopoly profits but enhances incentives for risk-taking and moral hazard. The connection with securitization makes it easier.

More broadly, shadow banks have hard-to-observe options to exploit risk-taking. They may initially be conservative as a way of developing a reputation. But if they get unlucky and start piling up losses, the value of their reputation falls. And if they have less to lose on the downside, they can choose to roll the dice to maximize the upside. This strategy is sometimes referred to as "Gambling for

Resurrection".[1] It comes from limited liability as well as the ability to hide risks for a while if they are taken fast enough. This is especially serious, systemically, for shadow banks because they are not covered by government guarantees or bail-outs that would limit collateral damage.[2]

9.1.1. Bubbles and Bank Runs: Diamond/Dybvig Meets Gorton

As is discussed in Chapter 3, asset prices are said to have bubbles when their prices feed on themselves (i.e. momentum) and grow too rapidly to be explained by fundamentals, and then burst because the growth cannot be sustained. The distinction between momentum and bubbles is fuzzy. A bubble occurs because of momentum. But bubbles are "not really bubbles" until their existence is proven by bursting, i.e. a crash. This makes them hard to be identified before the fact, both in terms of whether there is one or when it will burst.[3] When they do burst, they lower the values of mortgages backed by the houses as well as the net worth of the institutions holding the mortgages.

The housing boom that started in the late 1990s and early 2000s and then broke around 2007 would probably not have led to the GFC by itself. When a bubble gets inflated, and finally leaks or bursts, it needs only create cyclical price movements, not a financial crisis. Even without guarantees on the mortgages, there can still be resolution for financial institutions holding the less valued mortgages by selling off assets or selling the firms, although some others had to go bankrupt. Bankruptcy with banks is more complicated because so much of their assets are deposits that are supposed to be able to be cashed out on demand. The banks almost never have liquidity if

---

[1]As far as we know, this term was first applied in *Thrifts under Siege: Restoring Order to American Banking* by R. Brumbaugh (1988). An excellent discussion is *The S&L Insurance Mess: How Did It Happen?*, by Edward J. Kane (1989). There has been a large literature formalizing this term.

[2]This is not to say that guarantees are unambiguously good. Even though they do have stabilizing effect, they incentivize risk-taking.

[3]A well-known reference for this type of model is Hyman Minsky. See Minsky (1992) for a concise version.

depositors want their money all at once. This is the Diamond-Dybvig model, without deposit insurance.

For instance, none of the bubbles that crashed in real estate markets in the early 1980s, the stock market in 1987, and the tech market in the late 1990s created financial panic. However, the crash during the Great Depression, both in the stock market and real estate market, did lead to a general financial crash. Why the differences? A major reason is that banks made loans collateralized with both stocks and real estate, and not until 1933 did the U.S. have nationwide deposit insurance or "bail-outs" to limit their spillovers, nor were they heavily regulated. As a result, fears of deposits not being withdrawable precipitated mass efforts to withdraw money after bank asset values fell and resolution was slow.

In the cases of the recent bubbles around the GFC, deposit insurance and semi-guaranteed bail-outs ensured that there were almost no bank runs on regular banks. The runs were on the shadow banks/securitized banks. The consensus by now is that the GFC was generated by a combination of housing bubbles, enabled by new financial structures and changes in risk-taking incentives, and the collapse of fragile shadow banks that held pieces of the failed structures. So, it was like 1930 all over again, but this time with shadow banks and silent bank runs.

9.1.2. Other Countries

In the years leading up to the GFC, U.S. households were not alone in trying to enjoy the high returns from price increases. Housing markets in many countries boomed in the early 2000s. Many middle-class households in the U.K., for example, bought holiday homes in sunny places such as Spain. This was also one of the reasons for the soaring house price in Spain. Others used housing as a vehicle for accumulating wealth for retirement. Government policies also played a role. Ireland and Spain had advocated homeownership for a long time. Another boost comes from, for example, by buy-to-rent mortgages in the U.K., which allowed owners of the houses to take on mortgages paid from the rent of the houses.[4]

[4]Chapter 10 of Quinn and Turner (2020) provides a good description of what happened during the boom and bust of the subprime bubble.

Figure 9.1 shows real (i.e. inflation-adjusted) house price indices of selected countries, with all indices set to 100 points in 2015, which is why all curves intersect in year 2015. We group the PIIGS countries together in Panel (a) because of their very poor financial situations during the GFC, resulting in much higher household expenditure on housing after 2007, as mentioned in Section 1.3.1. Also shown in the same graph is the price index of Iceland, which was bailed out by the IMF because of the crisis. The price indices of these countries surged between 2000 and 2008. The index of Ireland doubled from 80 index points in quarter 2 of 1999 to its highest 160 in quarter 1 of 2007, as was Spain, from 80 in quarter 4 of 2000 to 166 points in quarter 3 of 2007. That of Italy was 90 in quarter 4 of 1999, to 136.3 points in quarter 1 of 2008. Greece also doubled its index in 10 years ending quarter 3 of 2007. Portugal is the only PIIGS country that got into trouble, not because of house price increases.

Panel (b) of Figure 9.1 depicts the real price indices for the whole Euro Area and the U.K., with the U.S. as a comparison, also with 2015 as the base year. Hence, the price index for the Euro Area is almost always higher than that of the U.K. does not mean houses in the Euro Area are more expensive. Rather, the flatter curve of the Euro area means that the U.K. prices grew faster. Numerically, the indices for quarter 1 of 2000 are 56.54 and 85.87 points for U.K. and Euro Area, with both jumping to 108.69 (almost doubled) and 112.95 (increased by nearly one-third), respectively, in quarter 3 of 2007. Relatively speaking, the price movement in the U.S. was not all that extreme.[5]

As prices increase, developers are more enticed to build as discussed in Chapter 3. Eventually, for example, 119,000 new houses were built in Ireland in the period of 2000–2008, which is one new house for 0.81 new inhabitants. In the U.K. as a whole, there were 1.78 new inhabitants per new house. This would not be bewildering if households were big and generally cramped in houses. However, the average household in the U.K. has only 2.4 persons. That means either households really like small families or there was a significant oversupply. If these numbers are not astonishing enough, consider

[5]This is actually comparable to the S&P CoreLogic Case–Shiller U.S. National Home Price Index in Figure 1.3 in terms of trend but not magnitudes because their bases for calculation and base years are different.

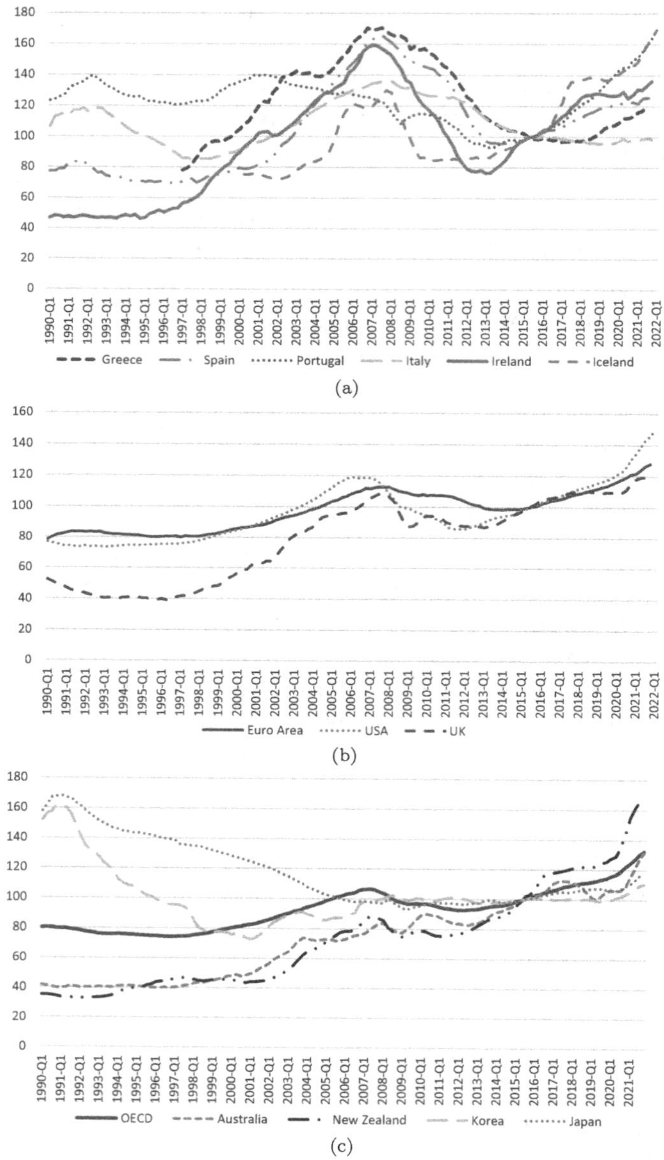

Figure 9.1 Real House Price Indices of Selected Countries (2015 = 100 Index Points). Panel (a) Greece, Spain, Portugal, Italy, Ireland and Iceland. Panel (b) Euro Area, United States, United Kingdom. Panel (c) OECD, Australasia, Japan and Korea

Source: Housing prices (indicator) from OECD (2022). DOI: 10.1787/63008438-en.

Spain alone building as many new houses as in Germany, France, and the U.K. combined.[6] In Ireland, the number of houses finished in 2005–2006 was equivalent to all 10 years in the 1990s. The average sizes of households in Spain and Ireland were only 2.6 and 2.7, respectively. What drove the demand for this housing was the lax credit supply.

The loan-to-value (LTV) ratio could be as high as 125%. That is dangerous. Suppose you begin with a 125% LTV loan. That is, you buy a house, and it comes with 25% extra cash for you, which is supposed to be paid back over time. This means that there is an incentive from the beginning to default and take the 25% right away. Why would the lender make such loans? Most loan originators are paid at least in part by the quantity of originations. Perhaps originations were made to get the borrower to take out a loan, and pass the risk on to investors, without full disclosure. Worse than that, there is an incentive for a borrower and lender to collude and split the extra 25%. These were dangerous.

Mortgage terms could be interest-only or teaser-rate (i.e. very low, or no, payment in the beginning few years) mortgages, both of which can be accompanied by risky balloon payments.[7] This means that, like the U.S., these European markets experienced strong credit expansion, probably stimulated by the house price growth (and vice versa).

Panel (c) depicts the house price indices for two Asian countries — Korea and Japan, and two Australasian countries, for comparison. The index of OECD is also shown here for reference. OECD's experience is very similar to that of the Euro Area. The housing markets of the two Asian countries did not have experiences similar to those of the Western countries. Instead, Korean house prices had been dropping throughout the 1990s, while those of Japan dropped till 2006. Both were then quite steady thereafter. On the other hand, Australia and New Zealand have undergone constant growth throughout the period covered in the figure. The crisis only caused a hiccup in these countries. In fact, Australian prices have grown more than three times, and those in New Zealand have grown by over 400% over 30 years! (Recall that these are after adjusting for inflation!!)

---

[6] Pages 174–175 of Quinn and Turner (2020).

[7] Also from page 175 of Quinn and Turner (2020).

9.1.3. Bubbles and Crashes

Sometimes, housing bubbles start with mortgage rate declines pushing up demand and subsequently prices, and then generating momentum. It was more complicated the last time around. The U.S. housing market bubble leading to the crisis was significantly buoyed and magnified by the induced rise in the PLS market and the shadow banks that took advantage of it. The advent of both just after the beginning of the millennium meant that households with low credit scores and/or poor loan documentation, and/or low downpayments, who would otherwise not be able to obtain mortgages now got mortgages, albeit with higher rates and adjustable rates that were very likely to go up in 2 years. One can imagine how far this was extended when "NINJA" loans, standing for loans to people with No-Income-No-Job-or-Assets became a well-known part of the PLS market. A nanny from New York could have six houses, all with borrowed money.[8]

To have a closer look at what the U.S. housing bubble meant, recall from Chapter 3 that there are hints of a bubble if the price relative to rent continues to increase. Figure 9.2 plots the price-to-rent ratio, together with the corresponding percentage change. Note that the ratio was very stable during 1982–1997, after which it started to climb, and it accelerated at the beginning of 2003, verifying the formation of a bubble starting in 2003. Its peak was at the beginning of 2006, after which it started to deflate in July 2006 (i.e. the percentage change becomes zero). It did not take long to burst — the very steep drop in percentage point changed from 2.54% in April 2005 to −4.02% in July 2008. The price-to-rent ratio finally ended at a steady level of 1.2 as before 1997 only on April 1, 2012, from which it started to rise gradually again.

Moral hazard was certainly a factor for the crisis, especially in the context of the originate-to-distribute model (OTD), which takes away some of the incentives to underwrite properly. There are actually contractual ways of solving a lot of these problems, such as the use of collaterals, outside appraisers, recourse, etc. Even though different forms of the OTD model have been around for a while, it was most likely because OTD combined with the success of property price

[8]Lewis (2010).

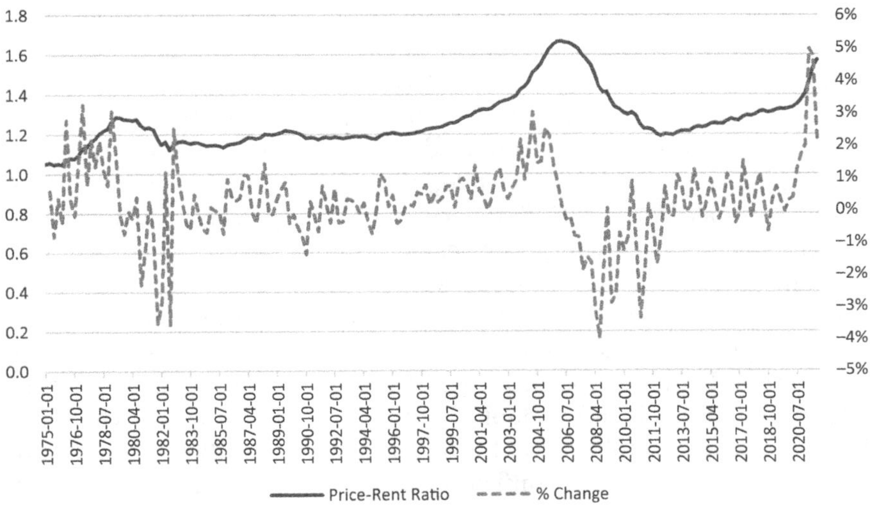

Figure 9.2 Price-to-Rent Ratio and Corresponding Percentage Change for U.S

Source: Federal Reserve Economic Data from the Federal Reserve Bank of St. Louis. Available at: https://fredblog.stlouisfed.org/2018/09/is-the-housing-price-rent-ratio-a-leading-indicator/?utm_source=series_page&utm_medium=related_content&utm_term=related_resources&utm_campaign=fredblog.

growth, and newness attracting newness, induced investors and other players in the market to be careless or devious, or dumb. Optimistic expectations of future house prices boosted demand for housing.[9] Flippers (buyers aiming to sell quickly for profit) also added fuel to the game. The newness and seeming success of the mortgage market innovations contributed to the lure to investors — as well as hubris combined with a dose of P.T. Barnum.

You might be puzzled about why households would buy houses that they could not afford. One reason is that rising house prices suggested they could afford it. If they could not make mortgage payments, they could presumably refinance and take out a bigger loan based on higher property value, and use the excess to get by, or sell

[9]Nevertheless, Cox and Ludvigson (2021) found empirically that credit conditions were the main driver and predictor of the price growth, while beliefs, including widespread exuberance leading to the boom and then shifts to depression leading to the bust, could not predict the price movement much.

the house at prices that would be higher than their purchase prices. This is certainly valid as long as housing prices continue to grow. However, simply keeping prices flat (not even falling) was enough to put many borrowers, who needed equity to grow, in trouble.

Indeed, house price growth did cover up the sour taste of the underlying gruel for a while, though it did not last. To mix metaphors, as Warren Buffet once said, "Only when the tide goes out do you discover who has been swimming naked". The tide was the turn-around in house prices, and the lack of clothing was in the myriad flaws in recently-invented mortgages and their owners.

Some people warned about this early on. Robert Shiller, the Nobel Laureate in Economic Sciences in 2013, is probably one of the earliest who wrote about it in his book, Irrational Exuberance, of which the first edition was published in 2000.[10] But of course, 2000 would have been too early a year to confirm that there was a housing bubble.[11] In any case, it is difficult to admit in advance the existence of a housing bubble, let alone one that was huge, or when it would burst.[12] Economists and bank regulators by and large did not see the crisis coming. For example, as widely reported by media, Alan Greenspan, the chairman of the Federal Reserve from August 1987 to January 2006, only admitted in 2007 that he did not see the U.S. housing market bubble coming until 2005 and 2006.

When the Federal Reserve increased interest rates from 1.03% in June 2004 to 5.25% in September 2006, new homebuyers were faced with higher interest rates.[13] So were those with adjustable rate mortgages. Subprime delinquency rates rose. Remember low-income mortgagors thought they could always sell the houses if they could not pay the mortgage? Not this time! House prices started to level off and then drop, a typical response to interest rate hikes. Homeowners with negative equity could not sell the houses at high enough prices to

[10]Shiller (2000).

[11]One of us was warning, admittedly half-heartedly, in 2002 that then recent rapid house price growth was not sustainable. He/she was wrong 4 years in a row.

[12]Gorton (2012).

[13]As shown in Panel (b) of Figure 1.5, the effective Fed fund rate dropped from the previous peak of 6.04% in December 2000 down to 1.73% on March 1, 2002, and then further down to the lowest at 0.98% on December 1, 2003.

repay the mortgages and lost the houses. Nannies with condos could not refinance their way out. Houses that were foreclosed on and sold had often been unaffordable to the original buyers, who could not afford proper maintenance of the houses, leaving the houses with much inferior conditions at the time of sale. By the end of 2006 and the whole of 2007, the market was flooded with foreclosed properties offered for "fire sale" at "take as is" prices.

In Chapter 4, we illustrated the links between borrowers' default decisions and housing values for the early period of 1975–1985. Here we cover the defaults before, and leading to, the GFC. We use data supplied by the Federal Housing Finance Agency to illustrate the link between defaults with credit scoring. We compare FRMs bought by Fannie Mae and Freddie Mac and those put into PLS to analyze the performance of the loans for different origination years, controlling for two important measures of credit risk, LTV ratios, and borrowers' credit scores measured by FICO score. The four LTV classes include:

- 75 and below, the safest category;
- 75–85, the most common category which clusters around 80 (basic 20% down loans);
- 85–95, high LTV loans, which cluster around 90, and;
- 95, which contains 95 and higher.

FICO stands for Fair Isaac Corporation, which uses consumer data to provide the FICO credit score that index the probability of a borrower making a payment. FICO scores have been widely used in mortgage valuation, ranging from low 500s to 800, and are put into discrete "buckets". A score below 620 is considered quite low. While there is no clear definition of subprime, a reasonable definition for our purposes is that subprime covers a FICO score below 640 and from 640 to 680 with an LTV ratio of over 85%.

Performance is measured by the share of loans that were ever delinquent for 90 days or more (i.e. in serious trouble) during specific years of originations in the data series through 2009. Table 9.1 depicts defaults on loans as percentages of overall mortgages. In particular, the first set of columns is the default rates of loans originated in 2003, a good year whereby property values rose rapidly in the following 3 years. The second set of columns shows the same measure for loans originated in 2006, a bad year with sharply declining housing prices. The final set of columns presents the differences

Table 9.1 Defaults as Percentages of Mortgages in the Crash

LTV Bucket	FICO Bucket				FICO Bucket				FICO Bucket			
	<640	640–680	680–720	>720	<640	640–680	680–720	>720	<640	640–680	680–720	>720
	2003 GSE FRMs				**2006 GSE FRMs**				**Differences: 2006–2003 GSE FRMs**			
<75	6.9%	3.2%	1.6%	0.5%	20.0%	12.7%	8.0%	2.7%	13.1%	9.5%	6.4%	2.2%
75–85	9.6%	5.3%	3.0%	1.1%	24.8%	19.8%	15.0%	6.5%	15.2%	14.5%	12.0%	5.4%
85–95	13.3%	8.0%	4.9%	2.3%	27.5%	21.3%	16.8%	9.3%	14.2%	13.3%	11.9%	7.0%
>95	20.7%	10.7%	6.5%	3.2%	40.1%	25.6%	18.0%	9.5%	19.4%	14.9%	11.5%	6.3%
LTV Bucket	**2003 PLS FRMs**				**2006 PLS FRMs**				**Differences: 2006–2003 PLS FRMs**			
<75	11.0%	5.5%	3.3%	1.4%	31.8%	23.8%	18.9%	9.0%	20.8%	18.3%	15.6%	7.6%
75–85	16.3%	9.7%	6.3%	3.2%	46.3%	42.5%	36.0%	23.3%	30.0%	32.8%	29.7%	20.1%
85–95	18.4%	12.3%	8.8%	5.3%	47.6%	39.4%	32.8%	22.3%	29.2%	27.1%	24.0%	17.0%
>95	25.2%	14.8%	9.9%	6.1%	50.1%	39.0%	31.0%	22.4%	24.9%	24.2%	21.1%	16.3%

between the two, showing the sensitivity of various categories and how they are compared to the mortgage meltdown. We can gather the following insights from Table 9.1:

1. *Looking at the 2003 default rate group*: High LTV meant higher defaults if FICO scores were held constant, but not if the scores varied. For instance, for Agency data, LTV ratios of 95% or greater with varying credit scores (680–720) had about the same default rates as those with LTV below 75% and low credit scores (6.5% versus 6.9%). There is clearly a tradeoff between these two important characteristics. What looks to be worst is not simply high LTV or low FICO, but rather a high LTV combined with a low FICO score. This is an example of risk layering.
2. *The loan channel is important*: Private label securities (PLS) had much higher default rates even controlling for credit score and LTV, and the increases between 2003 and 2006 were bigger.
3. *Economic conditions are very important*: The 2006 vintage had worse defaults than the 2003 vintage for all categories and for both Agency and PLS mortgages. Agency loans originated in 2006 did worse than PLS loans from 2003. The reality is worse than the table suggests because the 2006 loans had only 3 years of exposure until 2009; whereas those from 2003 had six.

9.2. The Global Financial Crisis: Starting with the U.S.

The GFC episode has been widely covered in books written by academics and other authors.[14] The following are some examples, each with different angles. Darell Duffie discusses how the dealer banks like J.P. Morgan and Goldman Sachs were involved in a lot of derivatives and securitization and failed during the crisis.[15] Nicola Gennaioli and Andrei Shleifer explain the crisis from investors' psychological point of view and the fragility of the financial system due to too

[14]Gillian Tett's "Fool's Gold" (Tett, 2009) offers a more novel-like narration of the crisis with less academic details and more storylines. Securitization leading to the crisis is covered in Michael Lewis' "The Big Short" (Lewis, 2010).
[15]Duffie (2011).

much leverage.[16] Gary Gorton gave a bank run perspective, which is our favorite story.[17] There is also a focus on the causes of the crisis from the housing bubbles, particularly the increase in household debts, of which 80% were from mortgages and home-equity debt in 2006.[18] There is also concern about the different fault lines that, when coming together, had almost destroyed the U.S. financial sector.[19] Research studies on its causes and potential remedies, both theoretically and empirically are also in abundance. The Financial Stability Oversight Council of the U.S. Department of Treasury (and more broadly and internationally, the Financial Stability Board) has also periodically assessed and closely monitored the shadow banking system to avoid repeating history. Here we provide a sketch of what happened.

9.2.1. Timing

There was no official beginning date for the crisis. Rather, there was a series of events that built up to it, starting firstly in the U.S. For instance, the Federal Reserve Bank of Dallas documented the subprime mortgage crisis to be during the period of 2007–2010.[20] Others considered 2007–2008 as the crisis period. Nevertheless, at least for the Great Recession, there is consensus that it lasted from December 2007 to June 2009, with a slow recovery thereafter.

It all began with securitization and shadow banking hiding risk and making assessment of risk very costly as in Chapter 6 and this chapter. Even as prices slowed down and started to fall, investors were still confident about the securities because the collateral is mortgages, which are considered to have relatively low risks. Besides, there are guarantees for Agency obligations, and recourse to insurance, e.g. CDS, for PLS. However, a decline in house prices ate into the guarantees and insurance, losing the protection power for the senior tranches. The loss rippled to global financial institutions involved in the securities.

[16] Gennaioli and Shleifer (2018).
[17] Gorton (2010, 2012).
[18] Mian and Sufi (2014b).
[19] Rajan (2010).
[20] Duca (2013).

The first alarm was raised when Northern Rock, a major British mortgage bank, had to be helped by the Bank of England in September 2007. Half a year later in March 2008, Bear Stearns in the U.S. had to be acquired by J.P. Morgan, followed by Washington Mutual Inc. six months later. On September 7, 2008, the U.S. Treasury had to inject funds into Fannie Mae and Freddie Mac. A shocking moment of the crisis was when Lehman Brothers had to file for bankruptcy on September 15, 2008, after the government refused to bail it out. Even AIG, the world's largest insurance company before the crisis, had to be bailed out soon afterward, which came as a surprise because insurance companies were supposed to be really prudent in risk-taking. AIG Financial Products had been extensively issuing CDS for MBSs and CDOs. Obviously, AIG Financial Products was much riskier than AIG, although it shared the same credit rating.

Within a month, the U.S. Treasury opened the Troubled Assets Relief Plan (TARP) Capital Purchase Program to inject capital into the financial system. In the end, 51 institutions joined TARP. This was supplemented by quantitative easing (QE) aka "Large-Scale Asset Purchases" (LSAP), which involved buying long-term securities.[21] This helped lower long-term interest rates, directly lowering mortgage rates. QE2 and QE3 were subsequently launched in November 2010 and September 2012.[22] A major part of the purchases was Agency securities, which directly lowered mortgage rates.[23] For the Fed, it was "all hands on deck".

9.2.2. Exercising the Option to Change Strategy

The notion that moral hazard was at the center of the GFC is now conventional wisdom. Here we look at a slice of it: changes

[21]It has been argued that this was about "printing money". This is misleading. Expansionary policy *always* involves printing money. QE or LSAP was different. Printing money in both cases was to buy long term securities in order to get directly at mortgages and other long-term rates to generate the biggest stimulus.

[22]Board of Governors of the Federal Reserve System, "FOMC statement — November 3, 2010" and "FOMC Statement — September 13, 2012". Available at: https://www.federalreserve.gov/newsevents/pressreleases/monetary20101103a.htm and https://www.federalreserve.gov/newsevents/pressreleases/monetary20120913a.htm.

[23]The Fed was virtually the only purchaser of MBS for much of the period.

in strategy as losses grew. The period 2005–2006 was critical in the evolution of house prices in the U.S. That was the time when non-prime lending reached a peak, subprime default rates began to increase, and house prices were starting to fall. The increase in defaults after 2005 was caused to a large extent by an increase in the supply of subprime lending from 2002 to 2005.[24] Around twenty executives from Fannie Mae and Freddie Mae were interviewed by the Financial Crisis Inquiry Commission and confirmed in their testimony that there was support for a change in strategy around 2005.[25] Both GSEs had internal differences in strategies in 2005 in the face of lost market share during the 2003–2005 period,[26] which led to increases in risk-taking.

An important but somewhat neglected part of the story is second mortgages, which are literally mortgages subordinated to a first mortgage, typically attached to an 80% LTV mortgage. The balance on the second is usually equal to somewhere between 5% and 20% of the loan balance. For instance, an 80% first and a 15% second is equivalent to a 95% loan to the borrower and is similar to an 80% LTV loan to the investor in the first mortgage.[27] This is very much the same as private insurance coverage. Why not just take out a 95% LTV mortgage to begin with? A reason is that an 80% LTV is a "magic number". For regulatory, rating agencies, and investing purposes, an 80% first mortgage is important and costs go up sharply above that. A 95% LTV first mortgage might therefore cost more than an 80% first plus a 15% second, and the second covers losses up to 15%. In principle, second mortgages can be priced with tools similar to those in Chapter 4, if the necessary information is available. Second mortgages had very high default rates and contributed to the failure of banks holding them. Moreover, the second mortgages obfuscated the actual LTV, making the first mortgages easier to sell

[24] Mian and Sufi (2009). Although they do not explicitly consider Alt-A loans, the Alt-A market moved in more or less the same way as the subprime market.
[25] See FCIC (2011, pp. 178–187).
[26] See Chapter 9 of FCIC Final Report: "Fannie Mae and Freddie Mac: Two Stark Choices".
[27] They are not exactly the same because the second mortgage will default first, which may spill over to the first mortgage because of the negative equity combined with high foreclosure costs.

Table 9.2 Composition of Private Label Pools Over Time

Year	CLTV	Full Documentation	For Purchase	Investor Owned	No Prepayment Penalty	Average FICO	Silent 2nd
A. *Alt-A Loans*							
1999	77.5	38.4	51.8	18.6	79.4	696	0.1
2000	80.2	35.4	68.0	13.8	79.0	697	0.2
2001	77.7	34.8	50.4	8.2	78.8	703	1.4
2002	76.5	36.0	47.4	12.5	70.1	708	2.4
2003	74.9	33.0	39.4	18.5	71.2	711	12.4
2004	79.5	32.4	53.9	17.0	64.8	708	28.6
2005	79.0	27.4	49.4	14.8	56.9	713	32.4
2006	80.6	16.4	45.7	12.9	47.9	708	38.9
B. *Subprime Loans*							
1999	78.8	68.7	30.1	5.3	28.7	605	0.5
2000	79.5	73.4	36.2	5.5	25.4	596	1.3
2001	80.3	71.5	31.3	5.3	21.0	605	2.8
2002	80.7	65.9	29.9	5.4	20.3	614	2.9
2003	82.4	63.9	30.2	5.6	23.2	624	7.3
2004	83.9	62.2	35.7	5.6	24.6	624	15.8
2005	85.3	58.3	40.5	5.5	26.8	627	24.6
2006	85.5	57.7	42.1	5.6	28.9	623	27.5

Note: All entries are in percentage points except FICO.
Source: Loan Performance (2007) via Aschraft and Schuerman (2008).

into securitization pools as long as no one found out about the "silent second" mortgage.

Indicators of risk-taking can often be found in the characteristics of pools of loans. Table 9.2 presents summary measures of characteristics of subprime and Alt-A Private Label pools over time, with characteristics of Alt-A in part A and subprime loans in part B. Across the top are pool characteristics: combined LTV, or CLTV, (i.e. adding second mortgage, if any), share of pool with full documentation, share for purchase (rather than refinance), share investor owned, share with no prepayment penalty, average FICO (credit) score and share with a *silent* second mortgage (second mortgage not recorded at closing). The first six items were known by investors at the time of purchase. However, the silent seconds were registered after the fact, and therefore were not known to investors when they bought into a pool. The data are shown by origination year.

Pool composition changed over the period. LTV ratios worsened some, but credit scores slightly improved, and more loans had less than full documentation. Note the silent seconds, which were not recorded until after the pool into which they were put were sold. These increased very sharply. The significance of the silent seconds and the rise of low documentation were traces that sellers were apparently looking for ways of hiding something, pretty much sounding like "Gambling for Resurrection". Observable variables, especially FICO and CLTV, did not increase much, but CLTV was understated by the silent seconds. This is at the same time when homebuyers were tempted by surging house prices and innovative mortgage terms.

9.2.3. Consequences

Figure 9.3 illustrates the extent of the crash in PLS, and particularly CDO, markets for the 2007–2009 period when the U.S. housing

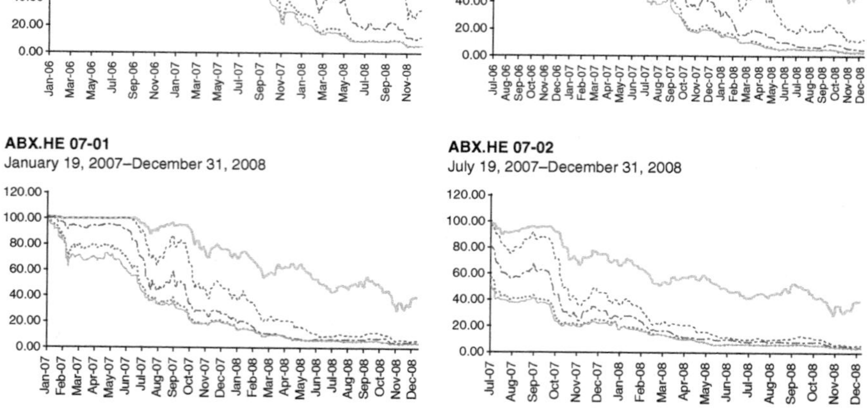

Figure 9.3 Prices of CDOs and CDSs of the U.S. During the Crash Period

Source: Cohen-Cole and Sabry (2012). Markit data.

bubble burst and the Global Financial Crisis followed. The figure depicts prices (discounts from par) of tranches of CDOs over time for different issue times. The prices are derived from the CDSs for CDOs, which are converted from interest rate spreads into up-front prices. Hence, the changes in price in the four quadrants are estimates of average losses in value on CDOs at various times of issuance. The declines were unprecedented. Note particularly how even AAA-rated tranches of CDOs lost half their values. Financial instruments for which these were collateral, e.g. repos, were also bound to crash.

9.2.4. Panic and Silent Runs

We see from Figure 9.3 the timing and depth of CDO price plummets. But what actually happened from the viewpoint of investors? Shadow banks had to sell assets to pay off investors who would not roll over their "deposits". Since investors' withdrawals are usually in cascades under such circumstances, assets were sold under "fire sales". Some of the deals were bailed out by the parent banks (creators of their SPVs). Institutions with cash abundance hoarded it. Others took the so-called "flight to quality". "Credit squeeze" or "credit crunch" were the popular terms for disappearing credits. Eventually, the run on shadow banking spread to the traditional banking system, which affected uninsured deposits and other bank liabilities. Many individual investors were among the last to realize that many of the AAA-rated structured assets they held were toxic. The IMF estimated that large U.S. and European banks lost more than USD1 trillion in these toxic assets between January 2007 and September 2009. The underlying forces that dragged the financial system were the combinations of credit risk, liquidity risk, and price bubbles.[28]

One might ask how come all those elites working in the financial sector did not see a crisis coming, and instead continue to issue structured products like ABS, CDOs, and CLOs. Many books about the crisis mention that the bankers did feel, or expect, the crisis coming. But as with bubbles, it was hard to know when to stop — maybe hold on a little longer while it still looks good. And pass the risk on

[28] Jarrow and Protter (2020).

to someone else? — As long as they were not the last ones to try to sit "when the music stops"![29]

9.3. European Housing Bubbles, and the Debt Crisis

Section 9.1.2 covered what happened in selected countries in Europe in the period leading to the crisis. Here, we present the bubble from another angle, more in line with the fundamental models explained in Chapter 3. Figure 9.4 depicts the price-to-rent ratio of the PIIGS countries plus Iceland for the period of quarter 1 of 1999 to quarter 4 of 2015 with 2015 as the base year of the index. The period covers the turn of the millennium and both the GFC and the European Debt Crisis. The country price-to-rent ratio from the OECD database is the price index divided by the rent index. The fluctuations represent changes in the price-rent ratio over time. In any case, the curves in the figure are interpreted as follows. The peak for Spain at quarter 3

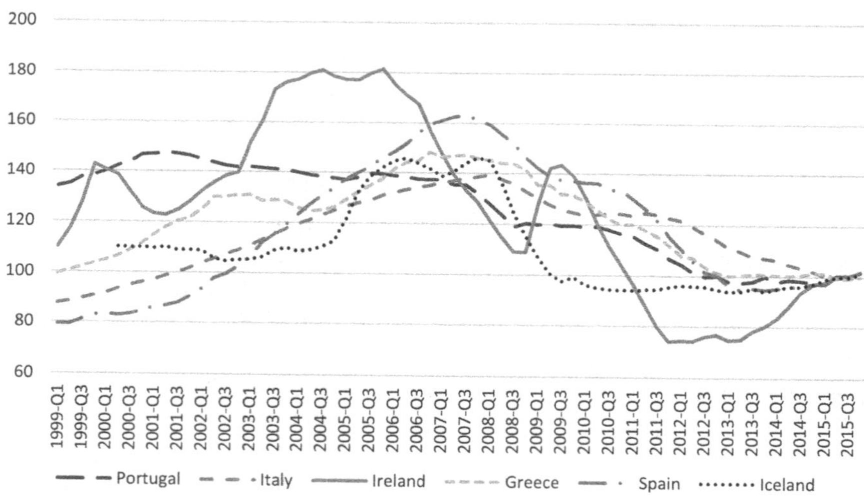

Figure 9.4 Price-to-Rent Ratio of the PIIGS Plus Iceland
Source: OECD.

---

[29] "When the Music Stopped" is the title of Chapter 4 of the excellent book: *After the Music Stopped: The Financial Crisis, the Response, and the Work Ahead* by Alan S. Blinder (Blinder, 2013).

of 2007 at 163 index points means that the price-to-rent ratio is 1.63 times higher than that of 2015. So, for example, if the price-to-rent ratio in 2015 is 17, then that in 2007 would be 27.7, meaning the price of a typical housing unit would be 27.7 times the annual rental payment.

The GFC affected most developed economies and marked the beginning of the European debt crisis, which was a repercussion of the crisis, and lasting from 2008 to 2012.[30] This section offers a brief timeline. After the British government nationalized Northern Rock in 2007, other mortgage banks also needed the rescue.[31] Relief measures launched in October 2008 included the Bank of England taking up illiquid assets of banks and replacing them with Treasury bills, funds to be injected into banks, and guaranteeing interbank lending. Some financially stronger and more stable countries like Belgium, Germany, and France, among others, also have to inject funds into their financial systems and guarantee loans of their banks because many had invested in the AAA-rated ABSs and CDOs, mostly created in the U.S.

For example, BNP Paribas, the largest bank in France, notified its investors that no withdrawals were allowed from some funds invested in U.S. subprime mortgages. Also, IKB Deutsche Industriebank AG and several other very large banks in Germany suffered huge losses from subprime investments funded by borrowing from the asset-backed commercial paper market.[32] Other countries with bigger bubbles and bigger bursts were driven to the edge of bankruptcy. Banks in Iceland had increased their risk-taking significantly before the crisis, and its own systemic financial crisis had resulted in its central bank not being able to act as the lender-of-last-resort (LOLR), and had to be eventually bailed by countries led by the IMF.

Other examples are the PIIGS, namely Portugal, Ireland, Italy, Greece, and Spain as seen in Figure 9.1. Unlike the other four

---

[30]Ashoka Mody (2018) had a very detailed narration of the European debt crisis.

[31]To understand how frenetic the market had become, just take note that even the lead singer of Westlife (a British boyband), Shane Filan, had to declare bankruptcy in June 2012 because of his EUR 5.5 million debt from his Irish property development company; and Colin Farrell, a famous Irish actor, also lost GBP 3 million in Irish properties (McDonald and Dan Milmo, 2012).

[32]Pages 194–195 of Mody (2018).

countries, Portugal's real house price was already dropping well before the crisis, from 2001 until 2013 when it started to climb. The trouble with Portugal was its ever-expanding government size and increasing salaries of civil servants. And when the crisis hit, its sovereign credit rating dropped significantly, and it had to be bailed out by IMF in 2011. Ireland and Spain were both caught in the housing bubble frenzies; their central banks had to bail out their banks, eventually increasing sovereign credit risks. Ireland received a bailout from IMF, the European Commission, and the European Financial Stability Facility (EFSF) in 2010. Hungary followed suit in 2011, and Cyprus and Spain in 2012. Housing bubbles also existed in Greece. But with Greece, another problem is that its tourism industry was also hard hit because of the crisis. The government experienced a huge deficit in 2009 while trying to help out.

Intriguingly, when the Fed started QE (or LSAP), the European Central Bank (ECB) thought the soon-to-be GFC was just a hiccup, and the bigger problem was inflation. And in order to combat it, the ECB had to maintain, if not increase, interest rates, rather than decrease. The problem was escalated because European banks in general had less buffer than their U.S. counterparts, and were more interconnected. Consequently, there was an investors' "flight to quality" and to liquidity and credit squeeze. Reacting to the panic, instead of boosting spending, never mind inflation, the European side promoted austerity measures to reduce government budget deficits and debts in 2010–2011. As a result, the PIIGs interest rate spread was further enlarged, and debt-to-GDP ratios significantly increased, along with declining GDPs.

The austerity programs did not work well — perhaps the wrong timing and magnitude![33] Greece was forced into a deeper recession, leading to an overall unemployment of 28% for most of 2013 shown in Panel (a) of Figure 9.5 (contrasting below 10% before August 2009), with youth unemployment of as high as 60.2% in July 2013 in Panel (b) (compared to below 30% before 2010). Its total unemployment dropped to below 27% only in June 2014. Also shown in Panel (c) is the unemployment for those 25–74 years old for comparison. Spain closely followed Greece. From the same set of graphs in Figure 9.5, the solid curves represent the situations of the EU.

[33]De Grauwe and Ji (2013).

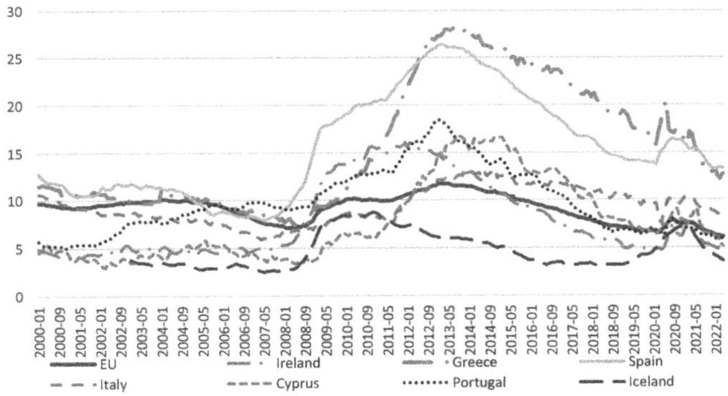

(a)

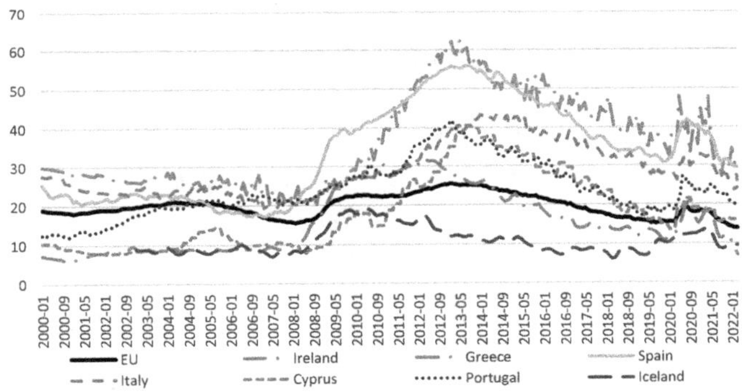

(b)

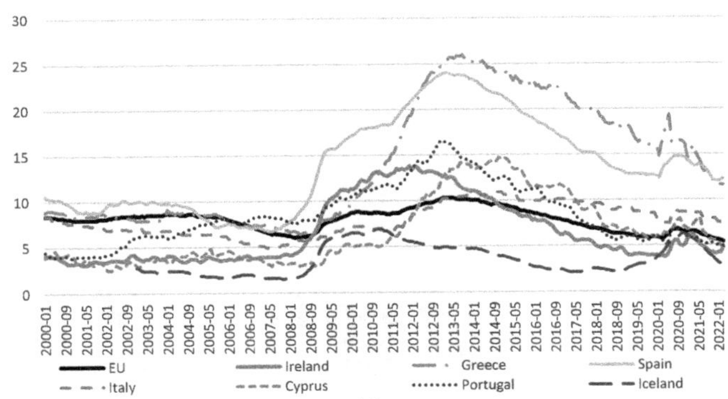

(c)

Figure 9.5 Unemployment in Selected European Countries (Seasonally Adjusted). Panel (a) Total Unemployment. Panel (b) Youth Unemployment (Below 25 Years Old). Panel (c) Unemployment from Age of 25 to 74 Years Old

Source: Eurostat; Seasonally adjusted data. Available at: https://ec.europa.eu/eurostat/databrowser/view/UNE_RT_M__custom_3025798/default/table?lang=en.

Iceland is the only one that has unemployment rates lower than the average, even though it too had to be bailed out. Despite not belonging to PIIGS, Cyprus is also included due to its bad situation in the crisis.

Another way of looking at the Debt Crisis is to check the government deficit/surplus represented by net borrowing/lending as percentages of the GDP of the same set of countries as in Figure 9.6. Quite surprisingly, Greece and Spain were only the second and third worst countries in terms of deficits. Ireland, one that experienced the highest per capita GDP growth at 294% for the period of 2000–2021 (Figure 9.7), had borrowed the most in 2010, amounting to net borrowing of 32.1% of its GDP. That of EU is 1.76 times, Greece is 1.3, Italy 1.38, and the rest are at least 1.6 times.

It was finally Mario Draghi, then ECB president, announcing "whatever it takes" on July 26, 2012, meaning that ECB would be the lender-of-last-resort for government bonds, that stopped the crisis from going further[34]; the sovereign interest spreads quickly shrunk.

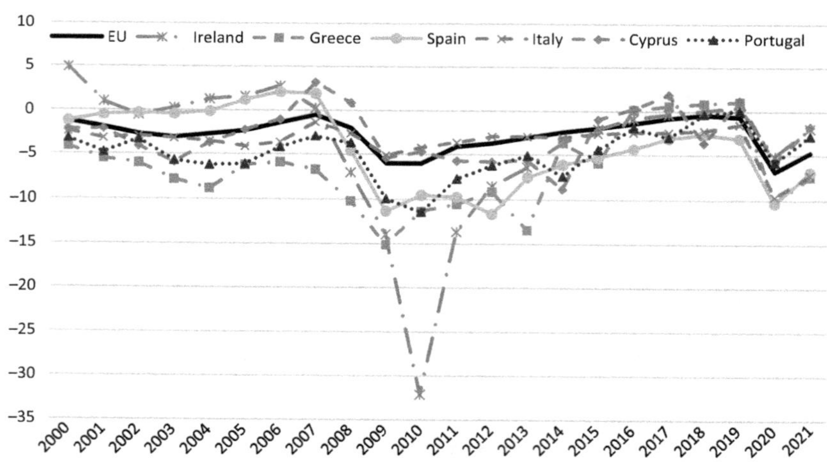

Figure 9.6 Government Deficit/Surplus (Net Borrowing/Lending, as % of GDP)

Source: Eurostat.

[34]From the Verbatim released by the European Central Bank as "Speech by Mario Draghi, President of the European Central Bank at the Global Investment

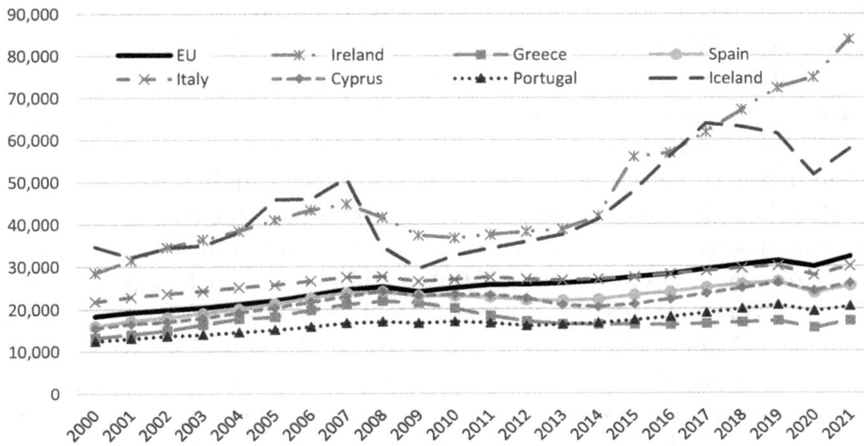

Figure 9.7 GDP per Capita for Selected European Countries (in Euro)

Source: Eurostat.

Subsequently, on September 12, 2012, the ECB launched a permanent bailout fund, namely the European Stability Mechanism. Had the ECB acted sooner, there might not be that much panic, and austerity measures might not be necessary. Clearly, the impact of the crisis was big and persistent; unemployment in all these countries was worse than before the crisis, even up till 2022. Often less discussed was the stunning IMF fund injection from China, complementing the stimulus packages of major countries in combating both crises.

9.4. Interconnectedness, Fragility, and Contagion

The way a crisis moves from one place or sector to another, or from one member to another in the system, has to do with how they are connected. Interconnectedness can probably be better understood via an analogy with the COVID-19 pandemic. A *contagious* virus like the

Conference in London on July 26 2012". Available at: www.ecb.europa.eu/press/key/date/2012/html/sp120726.en.html.

Omicron variant of COVID-19 spreads much faster than the Delta, or earlier, variant. Of course, if the person with the virus happened to be alone on an island, no one else in the world will get it, because there is no *connection*. On the other hand, if this person lives in a small community, those who are less healthy, i.e. more *fragile*, will be more likely to catch the virus. They also have a higher *systemic risk* if they live close to each other. If neighbors like to socialize, there is strong *interconnectedness*. In other words, interconnectedness does not necessarily create a crisis if the neighbors are not fragile or weak. Even if they are fragile and get sick, there will not be a problem if their sickness is not of contagious type. Now consider the people in this community have close ties with other nearby communities located within short distances. *Contagion* in the community will also be spread to other communities because of their strong ties.[35]

More formally, financial interconnectedness is the degree to which financial institutions are linked together through their transactions. The degree of contagion is the speed of fragility from one financial institution to another. Contagion requires financial institutions to be interconnected. Systemic risk refers to how, in the face of unexpected shocks, the fragility of one financial institution can affect the fragility of the whole financial system. Once this happens, it will almost always be followed by an economic downturn. Severity of the downturn depends on the ability of the system to maintain liquidity. In 2008, the traditional banking system had liquidity via deposit insurance; the shadow bank system did not. When one shadow bank is insolvent, other shadow banks that did not initially experience withdrawals will be in trouble too because their investors/depositors will see declining asset values all over, and subsequently initiate withdrawals because they worry about their own banks. Those apparently safe shadow banks had to sell assets rapidly at low prices, realizing losses that they might have kept secret.

To make things worse, the financial markets have been so interconnected that almost every financial institution is holding some of these financial instruments of other financial institutions, while

[35]Perhaps moral hazard can also be included in this analogy if we also consider the person with the virus not honestly informing everyone else about the virus before exploiting them.

simultaneously bundling their own. This spiral and contagious effect eventually carried on throughout the whole shadow banking sector. The collapse of Lehman Brothers is an archetypical example. Lehman Brothers was an investment bank, not a commercial bank. It had repos as the equivalent of deposits. But unlike deposits, they were not insured, and they were eligible for loans from the Fed only in the case of emergency. When it requested help in September 2008, the government thought it was just an individual case, and any help would be a bad example that would encourage moral hazard by other institutions. After unsuccessful searches for an institution to buy Lehman, the Fed and the Treasury let it go. As other intuitions followed, it became clear that many financial institutions had been swimming naked.

The Global Monitoring Report on Non-Bank Financial Intermediation 2021 by the Financial Stability Board[36] (see below) shows concisely how the failure in the shadow banking system (through Non-Bank Financial Intermediation, NBFIs, which include Other Financial Intermediaries, OFIs,[37] and insurance companies and pension funds, ICPFs) can, given their interconnectedness, be contagious to banking sectors, and in an international context. Its Graphs 2-2 and 2-3 are reproduced here as Panels (a) and (b) in Figure 9.8. Note that these graphs are made up of data from the 21 non-Euro area jurisdictions plus the Euro area as a whole. The numbers for earlier years were being updated and therefore not identical to those in earlier reports. There are peaks in 2013 in both panels due to the availability of additional data from the Euro area. If assuming there is no change in the availability of the data, and that the curves continued smoothly past 2013, then Panel (a) shows that bank exposure to NBFIs as a percentage of banks' assets dropped fast and significantly from the nearest peak in 2007. Their use of funding from NBFIs increased, however, and started dropping only after 2010. This is reflected in the increased exposure of NBFIs to banks (Panel (b)) in 2007, which dropped only after 2010. Likewise, the NBFIs' use of

[36]Financial Stability Board (2021b).

[37]OFIs include "investment funds, captive financial institutions and money lenders (CFIMLs), central counterparties (CCPs), broker-dealers, finance companies, trust companies and structured finance vehicles". (Box 0–1 on page 3 of the Report, Financial Stability Board, 2021).

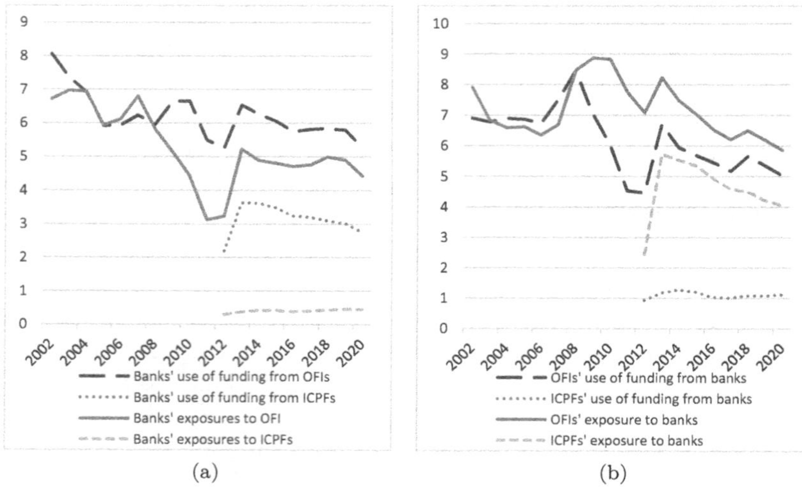

Figure 9.8 Interconnectedness of Banks and NBFIs. Panel (a) Banks on NBFIs. Panel (b) NBFIs on Banks

Note: Banks'/OFIs'/ICPFs' use and exposure of funding are expressed as a percentage of global banks/OFIs'/ICPFs' assets.
Source: Financial Stability Board (2021b). Data available at: https://www.fsb.org/2021/12/global-monitoring-report-on-non-bank-financial-intermediation-2021/.

funding from banks mirrored the trend of banks' exposure to them very closely.

To illustrate interconnectedness further, Figure 9.9 shows the change in the interconnectedness of sovereign funds, banks, and insurance companies before the crisis, and during the European debt crisis, which is extracted from the work of Billio and coauthors.[38] Their paper is about interconnectedness among countries by showing how one country's decision to guarantee a local bank could also mean guaranteeing another country's sovereign debt when the domestic bank also held the foreign country's sovereign debt. In their original graphs, red represents banks (mostly the top half, bounded by the dark rectangle here), blue for insurers (mostly the bottom half, bounded by the dashed gray oval), and black the sovereigns (mostly the left bottom, bounded by the dotted white triangle).

[38]Billio *et al.* (2014), courtesy of Robert C. Merton, Professor Andrew Lo, and their coauthors for permission to include a copy here.

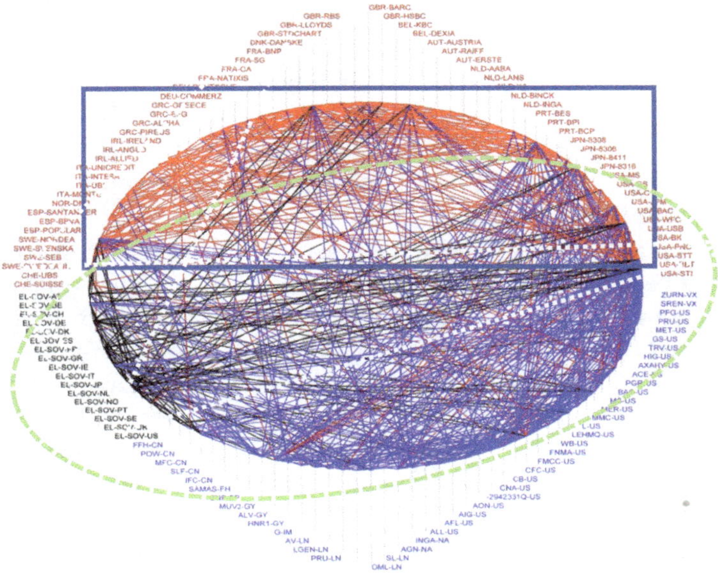

(a)

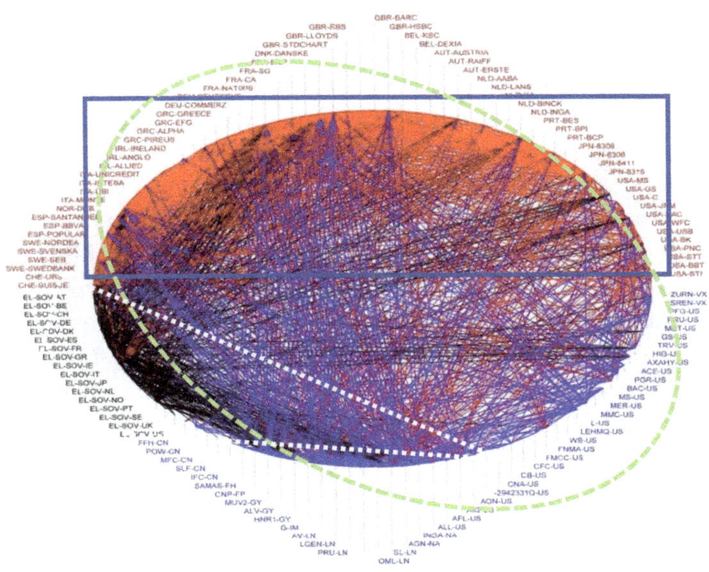

(b)

Figure 9.9 Interconnectedness of Sovereigns, Banks, and Insurance Companies. Panel (a) July 2004–June 2007. Panel (b) April 2009–March 2012

The lines represent significant connections (not in terms of transactions, but the impact on credits). The two graphs clearly show how more connected countries and their financial institutions were after the crisis. As they also emphasized in the paper, higher interconnectedness does not imply a bad influence on the system, although it does indicate probabilities of defaults are highly connected, which means more fragility within the system.

Interconnectedness can intensify systemic risk, leading to contagion.[39] The level of systemic risk depends on the levels of financial fragility and types of banking networks.[40] If a bank is not fragile and is still able to meet its commitments even if its debtors default, its loss will not be contagious to its connected counterparties.[41] This is also why financial institutions like AIG have been called Systemically Important Financial Institutions (SIFIs), because they pose very high systemic risks to the financial system as a whole (i.e. TSTF and TBTF).

Systemic risk has been modeled both mathematically and in words. We summarize a version of a popular model here.[42] A central point of the model is that the interactions between hedging against unsystematic risk (i.e. company-specific risk, also called idiosyncratic risk) and the neglect of seemingly extreme events (often called tail risk) can mask serious financial fragility. Some probability models such as the classic bell curve are not good at handling large (aka *black swan*) risks and are even worse at handling interactions among risks. The neglect of downside risks comes from (1) assuming that, in the worst case, the collateral (such as the mortgages underlying the MBS) can still pay off more than they actually think they can under stress, and (2) that "risk-free" debt is really risk free.

Since all of the financial intermediaries do the same thing, all will tend to fail when one fails; and the increased *systematic* risk is also *systemic* risk. By attempting to diversify risks through buying securities from other peers, financial intermediaries are actually more

---

[39]Studies on this include, for example, Allen and Gale (2007), Gai and Kapadia (2010), Acemoglu *et al.* (2015), and Roukny *et al.* (2018).
[40]See, for example, Elsinger *et al.* (2006) and Acemoglu *et al.* (2015).
[41]Scott, Hal S. (2016) also explains how contagion rather than connectedness is the main element of systemic risk in the financial system.
[42]In the research paper "A Model of Shadow Banking" by Gennaioli *et al.* (2013).

closely linked to each other. So, why would they neglect this risk? One reason is that calculations of the probabilities are usually based on the normal distribution assumption, which is not suitable for joint extreme events. Another is that they did not even have it in mind, as proposed by Daniel Kahneman, who won the 2002 Nobel Prize in Economic Sciences, and his friend, Amos Tversky.[43] The last reason is the inaccurately high ratings of the securities that misled the measures of risk, especially for regulators.[44]

In a nutshell, the story is one of how lax borrowing standards led to more loans, which entered the shadow banking system, got securitized, and bought by financial intermediaries. This eventually got all financial intermediaries more interconnected, with increased fragility (because of the quality of the loans and securities), but with systemic risk at extreme events miscalculated, finally resulting in a global contagion.

9.5. Global Consequences

We have seen in this chapter that there were differences in the impact of the GFC across countries. Regulations and regulatory arbitrage have been largely responsible for shadow banking. Of importance has been the tendency of U.S. shadow banks to fund with deposit-like instruments (e.g. repos again), secured by shaky prices of CDOs, which facilitated panic. Note that the U.S. has been more capital market-oriented, particularly in the housing market (but with more than a few exceptions). Its financial markets have in some ways been *laissez-faire* (in non-prime mortgages and shadow bank structures), and not in other ways. It has provided guarantees and subsidies that promoted certain types of lenders as well as housing and has enabled risk-taking.

---

[43]Kahneman and Tversky (1979). Tversky was not awarded the Nobel Prize because he passed away in 1996.

[44]In the defense of the credit rating agencies, they also did not see this rare event coming. Even if they used the most sophisticated quantitative models and the most comprehensive data, they might still not be able to evaluate this left tail of the probability distribution.

The U.S. reacted to the Crash by providing bailouts to banks and other institutions, but not fast enough, partly due to overlapping regulators and a slow budget process, along with some confusion about balancing short run stabilization with longer run moral hazard. Banks had to operate under closer scrutiny and more stringent regulations after the crash. But while banks were so interconnected and led to the crisis, and many were too large to be left to default (the so-called "too big to fail", TBTF, or "too systemic to fail", TSTF), bailouts and mergers have caused small banks to "join" big banks, resulting in fewer but even bigger banks. The recovery after the crash was steady but slow.

Many European countries were heavily affected by the GFC, followed by more crises, such as the European debt crisis. Figure 9.5 has already shown that unemployment rates of those heavily affected have mostly not gone back to pre-crisis levels, especially for youth unemployment. Not only did the younger generation have to suffer from something they did not cause, but there was more stress and anxiety among people in general after experiencing the "roller coaster ride".[45] Due to delinquencies and foreclosures, the homeownership rates of some countries, e.g. U.K. and U.S., actually declined after the crisis. New housing developments were deserted. This is not dissimilar to the unfinished skyscraper skeletons in Thailand, for example, after the 1997 Asian Financial Crisis. Only this time it was not due to overinvestment and overdevelopment, but boosting homeownership to those who could not afford to be homeowners.

The GFC hit the global economy for an extended period and left effects that dragged on, almost up the COVID-19 pandemic. But to say that the whole globe was as affected as the U.S. and most of Europe is exaggerated. Australia, for example, was not much hit. South Africa was seriously dragged in. Asian countries that were connected to the west (e.g. Hong Kong, South Korea, Japan, and Taiwan) were not greatly affected. The GFC affected the global economy in terms of international trade and currency disruption, as the USD value depreciated relative to other currencies after the Fed expansion.

The GFC affected China differently. Housing markets and shadow banking met in China with somewhat different stories. We proceed to this Part II of their dance in the next chapter.

[45]Page 190 of Quinn and Turner (2020).

Chapter 10

Housing Markets and Shadow Banking

Part II — China: "This One Is Different", with Tiger Parents

China was largely isolated from the GFC. House prices did grow rapidly at about the time of the GFC, and they have been recently showing strong signs of slowing. The reasons for not being in the GFC are because China is not too financially connected internationally, there are controls on the banking system, and especially because of the financial stimulus from the central government to avoid the headwind from the crisis. Let us walk through the Chinese housing story.

10.1. What Has Determined Housing Prices in China?

Increased income is one of two major forces boosting property prices. The other is the lack of alternative investment tools for Chinese households, due to significant home bias. Chinese households do not have much access to foreign investments due to currency controls (except for those who actually found ways to buy real estate abroad). As mentioned in Chapter 2, deposits constitute a considerable amount of their wealth. Otherwise, Chinese stocks and bonds are the two major financial investment vehicles. The total amount of outstanding bonds relative to GDP has been about 50% since 2005, which started to increase in 2014 to about 100% by 2018. This is small when compared to over 200% for the U.S. and Japan. Stock markets in China are also not as big and efficient as those of the U.S. and Japan. Whereas stock market capitalization as a percentage of GDP is 194.49% for the U.S. in 2020, it is only 82.96% in China.[1] The wealth accumulated from selling second homes has financed increases in consumption, which further promotes housing purchases.[2] In fact, about 70% of the wealth of the middle class is invested in property markets.[3]

The lack of diversification into international stocks and bonds implies that the ups and downs of the Chinese economy exert large impacts on Chinese investors, with little smoothing from foreign markets. This is exemplified by the fact that the total value of non-financial assets amounts to USD35.83 trillion as of 2019, of which USD33.32 trillion is in housing, a value larger than that of the U.S.[4] This contrasts the USD46.29 trillion of total financial assets, of which USD16.06 trillion in deposits and USD24.4 trillion in stock and equity. Thus, big swings in the performance of property markets will create big impacts on household wealth.

The mechanisms of the property markets certainly do not help. First, as usual, transactions in property markets were highly illiquid and time-consuming, and corresponding risks are highly undiversifiable. Second, given the high homeownership rate, the residential lease markets are very small, especially before 2000, except in the few big cities where many people move in to find better jobs and living. Rental rates were set artificially low, which was why rental growth was consistently high until after 2001 when it became steady both in rural and urban areas (Panel (a) of Figure 10.1). This means that a second home does not generate much cash inflow from renting

[1]It was 147.66% and 158.12% in 2018 and 2019 in the U.S., but only 45.52% and 59.63% in China in the same years.

[2]Yuan *et al.* (2020) and Li and Zhang (2021).

[3]Nunlist (2017).

[4]Nicholas Borst (2022) released "How Strong Is China's Household Balance Sheet?" on the website of the Seafarer Funds in March 2022.

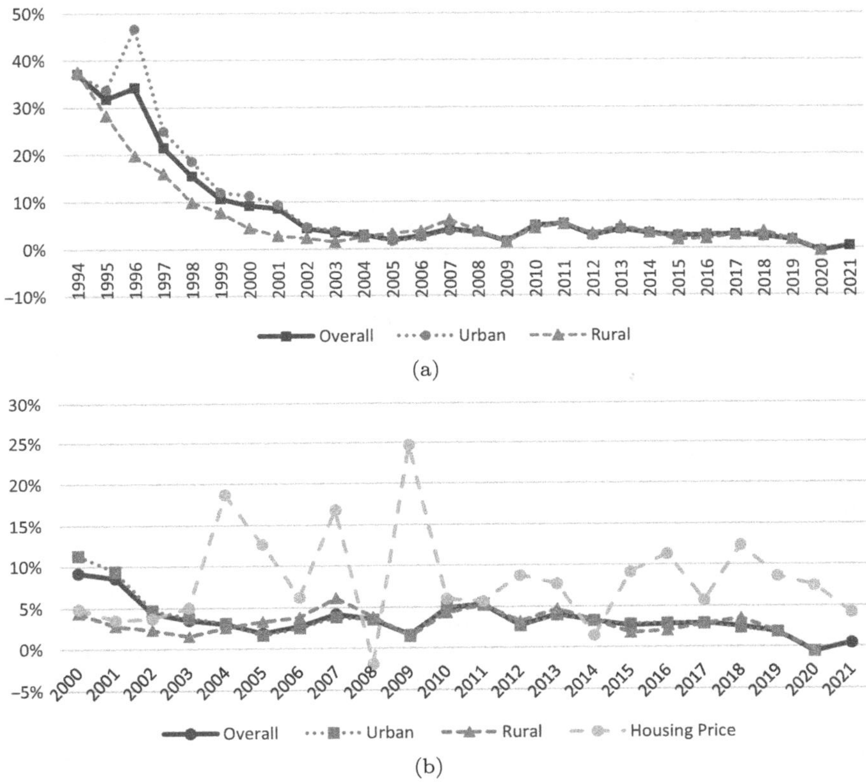

Figure 10.1 Growth Rates of Rents in China. Panel (a) Percentage Changes in Rental Rates for Overall, Rural and Urban Areas. Panel (b) Percentage Changes in Rental Rates and Housing Prices for 2000–2021

Note: The rental rates are presented as rental indices from the CPI, with the previous year = 100 index points. That is, the change in rental rate = index − 100.

Source: National Bureau of Statistics of China.

it out. Interestingly, Chinese households do not seem to mind the second home being vacant.

10.2. The Waltz: The Government and the Markets

Are there really bubbles in Chinese housing markets? Have the property markets posed increasing risks of insolvency for households?

Housing prices used to chase rent (see Panel (b) of Figure 10.1), until 2003 when rental growth could no longer keep up with the growth in price. While rent growth remains steadily below 5% most of the time, with rental markets in both the rural areas and the urban areas mirroring each other since 2006, the growth rate of housing prices has fluctuated significantly.

Buying housing units in China does not mean owning the land on which they sit. Buyers only buy the "use rights" of the use of the national land for a maximum of 70 years, although they own the properties they bought. Development starts with the developer "buying" a parcel of land, which is effectively buying the right to build on that parcel of land from the local government through, for example, land auctions. Sales of rights to land use have therefore become a crucial source of income of as much as 40% for the local governments, significant enough for them to lure developers to continue construction through improving both infrastructure and the business environment, not to mention taxes levied from property development and sales are also attractive sources of income.[5]

At the beginning of the millennium, and after a few years of advocating homeownership, housing prices grew slowly and stably, but that did not last long. The small boom in 2005 triggered a range of regulatory policies such as changes in loan-to-value (LTV) ratios, bank reserve rates, tax rates, land-use right, and supply structure reforms. In particular, the land-use rights reform referred to the right to land use to only be obtained through tender, oral, or listing auctions. Supply policy specified that at least 70% of the newly constructed residential buildings had to be units of 90 square meters or less. This first "noticeable" "overheating" market was trivial compared to what happened later. The Central government decided to cool down the market early on by limiting the loans to developers to 65% of development costs. In 2008, both the downpayment ratio and the mortgage rate increased.[6]

The Central government implemented cool-down measures and intervened when stimuli are needed several times over the subsequent 15 years. For example, in order to avoid "sinking" together with

[5]Wu (2015) and Peng *et al.* (2020).

[6]See for example *Reuters* (2011) for major property policy changes, and Arestis and Jia (2019) for more about the housing price movements in China.

the Western economies after the GFC, the Central government put forward RMB4 trillion, equivalent to about USD586 billion in November 2008, mainly to support new and huge infrastructure and social welfare projects in the attempt to combat the spread of the crisis to the Chinese economy. Almost 40% of the stimulus funds were devoted to infrastructure, such as railways and airport constructions, and other rural development and technology advancement projects. A smaller portion was also poured into promoting energy saving and gas emission cuts. As a result, as previously discussed in Chapter 2, China quickly recovered, and has since surpassed Japan to become the second largest global economy.

Since some of the stimuli have also been used to help construction industries, property market bubbles have been created. The government was quick in implementing new policies in 2010 such as to restrict lending. Other "cool-down" policies less common in other countries included policies that would indirectly approve sales prices and restrictions for second home purchases. Some of these policies, however, were interpreted by residents as signals to "buy", as long as they were qualified.[7] The property market finally cooled down in 2014 (the change in price was almost zero in 2014 in Panel (d) of Figure 2.8). That was not only after the government's aim to curb the markets as in 2008–2009 and 2011–2012, but also because of excess inventory.[8] But then, as a consequence, together with an economic slowdown, China's GDP grew only at 7.4% (see Figure 2.1), the slowest in 24 years, and was worse than the 7.5% that the Central government had targeted. Subsequently, its stock market plummeted by 8% in 1 day in January 2015.[9] Given the sluggish stock market, people turned to the property market for investment, even if the secondary market is not active. The Central government had little leeway but to introduce more aggressive easing measures again. After all, the property and construction sectors collectively make up 25% to 30% of its GDP.

The Chinese government can always find ways to cool down housing markets via regulation when they are overheated and entice more homeownership when there are signs of sluggishness. It has

[7]Nunlist (2017).
[8]Chivakul *et al.* (2015).
[9]Wong (2015).

been commented that while it is the practice in other countries that housing units are built when there is demand, building housing units in China can be for the purpose of consuming steel and cement.[10] After more than two decades of fast growth, President Xi Jinping emphasized clearly in the 19th Communist Party Congress in October 2017 that "houses are for living in, not for speculation".[11] This is an important signal that the government aims at sustained growth with reform in the property markets. Among the latest policies were the resale restrictions such as the prohibition of resale within 2 or 3 years of purchases, depending on the cities in 2017, and then further resale restrictions for both newly bought or second-hand units in mid-2019,[12] amid growing demand again. It is less clear that this is efficient in terms of resource allocation.

Since bubbles are identified only when they have burst, one cannot say for sure that there is or is not a housing bubble in China because nothing has burst yet. In any case, even if bubbles have been forming, they have been very sturdy because of the measures from the Central government. That is still the case unless of course, the government plans to let them go. In contrast, the bubbles in other economies such as the U.S. were thin bubbles ready to pop when expectations cooled off after an unsustainable surge in prices relative to rents. Meanwhile, the government was not good at getting its act together to stabilize housing prices.

10.3. Housing Markets Meeting Shadow Banking in China

As was the case with Western counterparts, shadow banking in China began with good intentions as households need funding, and investors need extra channels for investments. There was also a regulatory arbitrage in housing finance. What is unique in China is that even local governments needed shadow banking.

We have seen from Chapter 7 that shadow banking includes entrusted loans, WMPs, securitized products, LGFVs, and even

[10]Kawate (2021a).
[11]Zhen (2017a, 2017b).
[12]Lan *et al.* (2022).

fintech channels like P2P and Yu'E Bao. Here we shall discuss how they are related to the housing markets (and bubbles).[13] Since fintech channels played an informal and potentially non-trivial role, more discussion will be included in Chapter 11.

10.3.1. Home Purchases

The average price-to-rent ratio in China reached 36 in 2020 in a dataset where a ratio of above 20 signaled booming housing markets, behaving strongly like growth stocks in the sense of capitalizing on rising future benefits or incipient bubbles.[14] Amid the seemingly unaffordable housing prices, there can still be strong demand if households really want to own their own homes and join the bandwagon before it's too late, as long as mortgages are available and their income grows fast enough. After all, prices would not have surged so much without demand going up first. Figure 10.2 replicates the changes in disposable incomes shown in Figure 2.3 and plots against the growth rate of average housing prices. Growth in personal income has apparently outperformed that of housing prices between 2000

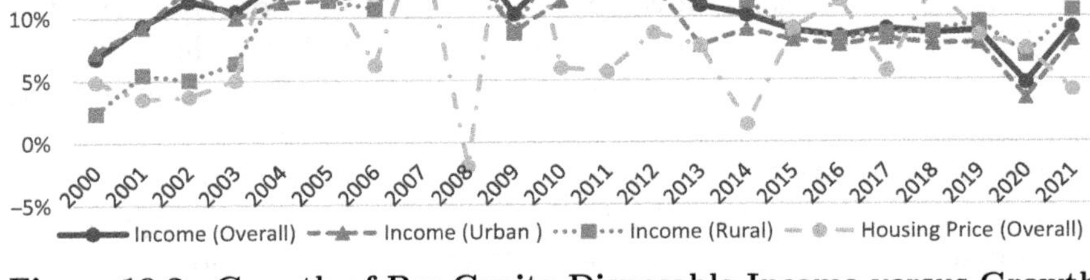

Figure 10.2 Growth of Per Capita Disposable Income versus Growth of Average Housing Price

[13]Lai and Van Order (2019) showed empirically the link between the Chinese shadow banking (using entrusted loans) and housing prices.
[14]Borst (2022).

and 2015, except for 2004 and 2009, but the gap has disappeared in the recent 6 years. This of course does not mean that housing in China has become more affordable, but rather that it is no longer a growth stock. At least it is more certain that the Chinese housing market bubble, even if exists, will not burst like that in the U.S. in 2007–2008.

Almost all the funds used for home purchases are through savings from parents or from mortgages, which constitute the biggest household liabilities. Other sources of funding, although often limited, are crucial, too. Informal loan channels can include loans from relatives, crowdfunding, and other fintech platforms. As personal bank loans are very limited, most of the personal debts are from the shadow banking sector. Peer-to-peer lending has been one of the main sources for small loan amounts, which could be used as part of the downpayments of home purchases.[15]

10.3.2. The RMB4 Trillion Stimulus Package and LGFVs

Another consequence of the RMB4 trillion stimulus package is the establishment of Local Government Financing Vehicles (LGFVs). Since the package demands local authorities to incentivize more infrastructure developments, the amount for infrastructure has to be budgeted locally, accounting for 70–75% of their expenditure. Recall also from Chapter 7 that local governments generate income from "selling" land to developers. Obviously, they cannot sell land every day, and infrastructure development was costly. Consequently, the local governments have become heavily indebted, and have had to raise funds from the LGFVs' Municipal Corporate Bonds, as covered in Chapter 7.

Developers have almost always been encouraged to build,[16] especially because there was always high housing demand. Where did developers get the financing from? Whereas SOE developers obtain loans from the Big Four SOE banks, others have to obtain entrusted

[15]Keohane (2016), which mentioned that such were short-term loans of typical 90 days, and small in size.

[16]This is similar in principle to developers in the U.S. which could get commitments from lenders and may keep a second mortgage.

loans. Small ones in rural areas could approach microfinance companies. All these sources of funding, LGFV bonds, entrusted loans, and microfinance loans, can be financed by individual investors through packaging them as WMPs available from commercial banks or insurance policies.

Problems arose when the heavily indebted LGFVs (with different forms of shadow banking) could not repay their loans. For instance, a small city in Central China called Ruzhou borrowed heavily to build hospitals, auditoriums, and so on, in order to keep the economy growing.[17] The Hohhot Economic and Technological Development Zone Investment Development Group (Hohhot LGFV for short) in Inner Mongolia missed repayment on its bonds in December 2019. Hohhot LGFV was not alone. It was estimated that the total outstanding LGFV bonds by the end of 2019 totaled RMB8.3 trillion, of which RMB71.5 billion were offshore notes.[18] Adding to the trouble is that the local governments would borrow credit from any arrangements, be it trust fund or financial leases, as long as scrutiny from the Central government regulatory policies could be avoided.[19] Incidentally, it is empirically verified that local governments often choose not to default on loans from national lenders, especially if the government leaders are high-rank politicians; that is, banks with weaker political power, usually commercial banks, would be prone to more defaults.[20]

Credit was growing at an average of 20% per annum between 2010 and 2017, obviously way higher than the GDP growth.[21] The total amount of debts amounted to a record 237% of its GDP in the first quarter of 2016, of which USD22.6 billion was rated just one rank above junk by Standard & Poor's.[22] This might have paved the emergence of the next financial crisis.[23] According to the Bank of International Settlements (BIS), China would have had a fiscal

[17]Stevenson and Li (2019).
[18]Zhou (2019).
[19]This is a comment made by Zhiwu Chen, the director of Asia Global Institute at the University of Hong Kong, as reported in Stevenson and Li (2019).
[20]Gao *et al.* (2021).
[21]Reid *et al.* (2017).
[22]Wildau and Weinland (2016) and Tu (2016).
[23]Reid *et al.* (2017).

deficit (8% of GDP) double of what was reported if all the off-balance sheet LGFV loans, including the special purpose bonds, were considered.[24] Corporate loans were also significantly accumulated. A total of RMB120 billion bond payments had been missed in 2018, which was four times the previous year.[25]

What about the accumulation of debt? Relative to western peers, one can say "this one is different" for China, because the huge debt was a deliberate result of the state-driven stimulus package, rather than the passive result of recession, and the Chinese government has been willing to save the systemically important firms and banks.[26] Nevertheless, the stimulus package also created resource-wasting zombie firms, and "gambling for resurrection" via excessive leverage and risk-taking in other cases. A series of articles by Bloomberg and others reported on the Central government's awareness of the threat of shadow banking to the financial system and the economy. A series of measures had been taken, including encouraging banks to lend more by lowering their reserve requirement, enhancing transparency in entrusted loans, and enacting rules to regulate shadow banking products, particularly eliminating the perception of implicit guarantees in WMPs.[27,28] In any case, between its financial isolation and its fiscal stimulus, China got through the economic turmoil and avoided the financial crises that plagued other countries.[29]

---

[24]Springfield (2019).

[25]*Ibid.*

[26]Huang and Bosler (2014).

[27]Bloomberg News on October 10, 2017, entitled "How China Is Tackling Dangers in Its Financial System". Available at: https://www.bloomberg.com/news/articles/2017-10-09/how-china-is-getting-serious-about-financial-risk-quicktake-q-a.

[28]Collier (2017) suggests that the most possible approach taken by the Chinese government is to let the problematic WMPs fail, allowing the small banks to then be saved by merging with bigger banks.

[29]According to the Global Financial Stability Report April 2018: A Bumpy Road (IMF, 2018), profitability of credit allocation to private firms have been improved over the period of 2007–2016, but not so for SOEs. In fact, SOEs have been criticized for not being efficient and profitable, but occupying a lot of credits. In another IMF working paper, Chan and Kang (2018) point out that SOEs, accounting for half of the new credits, generated only half the cumulative value-added growth of the private counterparts.

10.4. The Developers' Saga

One of the major outcomes of the RMB4 trillion stimulus package was overbuilding of housing units, creating "ghost towns". The package translated into a remarkable annual economic growth of 13.1% in the period of 2003–2013[30] and a 4.4% annually compounded land price growth rate for the 35 major cities during 2004–2014, or 54.2% in total.[31] This chain effect translated into higher housing prices, enticing more developers to build, and then more people to buy for investments. As a result, an average of 5.5 million apartments were built each year.[32] An even more striking result is the generation of high vacancy rates, with at least 20 billion square feet of empty housing, eventually generating ghost towns. The resources consumed in producing this large amount of housing could have been used for something of more immediate value.

10.4.1. Ghost Towns

No doubt some of these ghost towns will sooner or later be occupied given enough time for cities to develop. An example is Pudong in Shanghai. When one of us was brought to see the "New Development in Pudong" project in Shanghai in 1995, it was literally nothing but an endless land of mud. Almost in no time, it has become the most important financial district of China, hosting the Shanghai Stock Exchange and the Shanghai World Financial Center, to name a few. Apart from Pudong, however, there have been more "ghost towns" than successful transformation.

The Kangbashi District in Ordos, Inner Mongolia, was a very famous ghost town as a result of the stimulus package. The development started in 2003 and peaked after 2009 with apartment prices for over RMB 8,000 per square meter. But prices dropped from RMB 3,000 to RMB 5,000 when the extra supply led to too many housing units. Many buildings were half-finished. Peter Day of BBC even

[30]Glaeser *et al.* (2017).
[31]Wu *et al.* (2016).
[32]Glaeser *et al.* (2017).

cited it as the largest ghost town in China in 2012.[33,34] A problem with the Kangbashi District is that it is 25 kilometers away from the center of Ordos, called Dongsheng, and even though there were facilities with beautiful architecture, like the new library and the opera house, people would still prefer to live in Dongsheng and commute to the District to work. Interestingly, however, most of the housing units in the District have been sold, mostly to people who plan to move there one day, perhaps after retirement, or for their children to live in when married, or simply for investment. This can be seen as adjusting household portfolios in the face of limited investment opportunities (otherwise why not invest the money in stocks or bonds and sell them later to pay for housing later?).

What happened after 10 years? To stimulate the "life" of an empty city, the government has moved the best schools to Kangbashi District. And because of the regulation that the parents of the would-be students of a school in any district must own a housing unit in the district, the existence of good schools will naturally attract strong purchases. Consequently, the price of a square meter of the apartment was worth RMB 15,000, even though Ordos as a whole experienced an economic downturn in 2019 and 2020. New housing developments have started again.[35]

For China, there is always a way to eliminate ghost towns, either through natural city expansion or by playing another waltz — the government can speed up occupancy through the relocation of good schools, as in Kangbashi District. For example, as reported, the Chinese Premier, Li Keqiang, announced a plan for "Further de-stocking with city-specific measures" at a National People's Congress meeting in 2016.[36] But "de-stocking" (i.e. reducing empty units) bears costs.

---

[33] "Ordos: The Biggest Ghost Town in China", by Peter Day, BBC, March 17, 2012. Available at: https://www.bbc.com/news/magazine-17390729.

[34] One might challenge what level of emptiness constitutes a "ghost town". As Shepard (2015) stated, even Beijing, a Tier 1 city that is considered to have very inelastic supply, has 20% housing units unoccupied. And yet, it is far from being considered as a ghost town.

[35] Kawate (2021a).

[36] Keohane (2016).

10.4.2. The Crackdown in 2021 — Troubled Chinese Developers

The housing market continued to grow after more than a decade of different measures aiming to curb the very heated housing markets, some more effective than others. The lockdown in the first quarter of 2020 due to the COVID-19 pandemic only froze the market for a short period. According to the National Bureau of Statistics of China, investment in real estate development has grown by 38.3% just in the first 2 months of 2021, although the aggregate growth in the first 3 months dropped to 25.6%. The growth in sources of funds for real estate development enterprises amounted to 51.2% and 41.4% in the same two periods.[37]

The markets continued to heat up from strong demand for both accommodation needs and investment. There were at least 65 million vacant housing units, which was one-fifth of all housing units in China, enough for the whole population in France.[38] Put differently, the size of the Chinese housing market according to Goldman Sachs Group Inc. was USD52 trillion in 2019,[39] while the total value of homes in the U.S. amounted to USD43.4 trillion in 2021 according to Zillow.[40] While these two figures are not directly comparable, they provide a good idea of how big the Chinese housing market is. Direct investment in real estate reached USD1.18 trillion in 2020 alone, which is 7.4% of the GDP that year according to the People's Bank of China.

New policies to slow down the market were then launched. For instance, caps for housing prices and rental rates were implemented, and long-planned property taxes would be levied. Mortgage lending was available only to a maximum LTV ratio of 32.5%. Land had to be sold centrally, rather than by local governments. The long-term goal was to divert investments from property markets to other sectors. To do this, not only must loans to property developers be

---

[37]Press Release entitled "National Real Estate Development and Sales in the First Nine Months of 2021" on October 19, 2021 by the National Bureau of Statistics of China.

[38]Batarags (2021).

[39]Xie and Bird (2020).

[40]Manhertz (2022).

strangled or not renewed, but there could also be no bailouts from the Central government. A reason for this is the negative global impact it might create because 10% of outstanding loans to non-financial borrowers worldwide had been invested in the Chinese real estate sector.[41]

Consequently, the last quarter of 2021 was a devastating period for major developers. The most noticeable one is Evergrande Group, the most indebted property developer in the world that has been on the verge of default, rippling to other major developers with bond and loan defaults.[42] Note that at the end of the RMB4 trillion financial stimulus, there was issuance of high-yield bonds by the Chinese property developers in 2013, many of which were three to 5 year high-yield bonds to offshore investors. That is, the next round of refinancing was between 2021 and 2022. The amount of offshore bonds maturing in 2022 reached USD40 billion, while those of the domestic market reached RMB165 billion.[43] According to Goldman Sachs, the estimated default rate of Chinese property-backed high-yield bonds in 2022 was 19%, down from 28% in the previous year. However, if there was slower policy easing than expected, the default rate could be as large as 31.6%.[44] This poses a big problem for financial stability in China because real estate loans constituted 27.4% of total bank loans even in 2020.[45]

Why were the developers short of funds and paying high rates? It all started in August 2020 when policies for curbing the housing markets included the establishment of recommended property selling price indices, land sales exclusively through auction, and most importantly, reducing debt in the property sector through the "three red lines". These three "red lines" require developers to have (i) an asset-liability ratio of no less than 70%, (ii) a net debt ratio of no

[41]Buchholz (2021).

[42]This is part of the strategy to promote Common Prosperity, which has shaken the technology sector, also in the last quarter of 2020.

[43]"Strategies for Dealing with Distressed Debt in China's real Estate Sectors" by FTI Consulting Asia Pacific on March 28, 2022.

[44]From "Outlook for China's Property Sector" in Goldman Sachs Briefings on March 3, 2022 newsletter.

[45]From "Explainer: What's Going on in China's Property Market?" by China Briefing on January 14, 2022. Available at: https://www.china-briefing.com/news/explainer-whats-going-on-in-chinas-property-market/.

more than 100%, and (iii) a cash to short-term debt ratio of at least 100%, before they can refinance. At the time of enacting this rule, none of the developers met the requirement.

An immediate consequence was a decline in housing prices, and 80% of the developers could not meet their sales target in 2021. This is not the beginning of the winter for the market though. Back in September 2021, it was found that 27% of the land put up for land auction by local governments had no bidders. When there were bidders, they were not the usual participants but rather State-owned developers such as China Overseas Property Ltd.; their participation is often interpreted as regaining confidence in very depressed markets.[46] Two-thirds still could not meet the criteria by the end of October 2021.[47] In fact, according to the National Bureau of Statistics of China, contrasting the high growth at the beginning of 2021, the growth rates of sources of funds for real estate development enterprise and investment in real estate development for the first 9 months were only 11.1% and 8.8%, respectively (from 51.2% and 38.3% made up in the first 2 months). As a gesture of disappointment, authorities demanded a "controlled demolition" of 39 of Evergrande's developments in Hainan province, claiming that the building permits were not legal.[48] This was not the first of its kind. The stunning 45-second "controlled demolition" of the fourteen semi-completed estates (idled since 2013) surprised the world on August 27, 2021 (although this was ordered by the developer which took over the estate for redevelopment rather than the official).

Gradually, most developers could meet the criteria and refinance, with the exception of Evergrande, which has accumulated more than USD300 billion liabilities, including USD19 billion overseas bonds. Note that Evergrande alone employed 200,000 people, and was indirectly linked to another 3 million jobs. It still had about 800 unfinished projects by the end of 2021,[49] which cast a big problem because it relied heavily on preselling the housing units to obtain liquidity.

---

[46] From "How China's Housing Market Landed in the Deep Freeze" by Caixin Global on October 18, 2021. Available at: https://www.caixinglobal.com/2021-10-18/cover-story-how-chinas-housing-market-landed-in-the-deep-freeze-101787754.html.

[47] Tam (2021).

[48] He (2022).

[49] Stevenson and Li (2021).

Finally, the panic died down (at least temporarily) after Xu Jiayin, the Chairman of the group, was asked to resolve some of the debts with his own wealth,[50] and subsequently carried out many rounds of negotiations with corresponding creditors. Kaisa Group is another one that could not find refinancing at an affordable interest rate at the end of 2021. As a result, its market capitalization went from USD3.078 billion on 1/1/2020 to USD0.728 billion on 7/1/2022.

The Central government has made it clear that Evergrande is not "Too Big to Fail". Half-expectedly, all those developers that had defaulted on the loans found their ways to negotiate with their creditors for postponing repayments (creditors certainly did not want to see defaults, if at all possible). It is "expected" because big issues like this, and with politically connected top leaders, almost never end in mayhem; "half" because the debt amount issue is really huge. There has been discussion about whether Evergrande will be the Lehman Brothers of China, causing big contagion in the Chinese financial system. The answer was "no", because the problem with Evergrande had existed for some time, and the Chinese government had a good grasp of how far it had gone, and the Chinese government has always been able to regulate markets directly. As long as the housing market does not experience a slump, the Evergrande issue could be solved by restructuring, albeit perhaps taking years.[51] Given the importance of real estate development to the overall economy, it is important to solve the distressed debt and liquidity crunch issues in order for China to pick up its growth engine again.

It is very clear that the government did not consider any of the developers too big to fail. How did this affect the values of the developers, particularly the very large ones? Table 10.1 lists the top ten developers in China. We chose the year 2006 because the few years before it formed the period of booming of many small-scale developers; market participants became relatively stable thereafter. The rankings in 2 other years, 2020 and 2022, together with the market capitalization (in billion USD) on June 30, 2022 and January 1, 2022, show the impact of the strong government policies on particular developers and the industry as a whole. The list in 2006 is quite different from those in 2020. A few "veterans" were ousted, and new

[50]Wang (2021).
[51]Oi (2021).

Table 10.1 Top 10 Developers in China at Different Times

Rank	June 30, 2022*	Market Capitalization in Billion USD 30/6/2022	Market Capitalization in Billion USD 1/1/2022	April 2, 2020†	March 31, 2006‡
1	China Resources Land Ltd.	33.61	33.09	Evergrande Group	China Vanke Co. Ltd.
2	China Vanke Co. Ltd.	33.20	39.43	Country Garden Holdings Co.	China Overseas Land & Investment Ltd.
3	Longfor Group Holdings Ltd.	27.22	31.19	China Vanke Co. Ltd.	Hopson Development Holding Ltd.
4	Poly Developments and Holdings Group	24.54	30.29	Sunac China Holdings Ltd.	Beijing Capital Development Holdings Co. Ltd.
5	Country Garden Holdings Co.	13.30	20.01	China Overseas Property Ltd.	Poly Real Estate (Group) Co. Ltd.
6	China Merchants Shekou Industrial Zone Holdings	12.49	17.53	Poly Developments and Holdings	Evergrande Group
7	Seazen Holdings Co. Ltd.	7.81	11.17	Longfor Group Holdings Ltd.	Dahua (Group) Co. Ltd.
8	Fosun International	7.56	8.95	Seazen Holdings Co.	Greentown Real Estate Group Co. Ltd.
9	Greenland Holdings Corporation	7.13	9.09	China Resources Land Ltd.	China Merchants Property Development Co. Ltd.
10	Sunac China Holdings Ltd.	3.18	6.87	Guangzhou R&F Properties Co. Ltd.	Forte (Group) Co. Ltd. (Fosun buyout)

Note: *The ranking is according to the market capitalization as at June 30, 2022, with the corresponding exchange rates (1 HKD = 0.1274 USD and 1 RMB = 0.1493 USD) on the same day.

Sources: †The ranking is from *China Daily*, April 2, 2020. Available at: https://global.chinadaily.com.cn/a/202004/02/WS5e851841a310128217283bc0_11.html. ‡The ranking is from *China Daily*, March 31, 2006. Available at: https://www.chinadaily.com.cn/bizchina/2006-03/31/content_557217.html.

members joined. Back some 15 years ago, Evergrande was still the sixth largest and had gone up to be the largest developer in 2020 due to its unique business strategy of investing in Tier 2 and 3 cities where other major developers did not reach.

The reshuffling in the 2022 rankings in Table 10.1 highlights the devastated year 2021. If considering market capitalization on January 1, 2022, China Vanke Co. Ltd. was on the top. Half a year later, however, it was China Resources Land Ltd., of which the market value was almost constant. All the others experienced various degrees of value reduction. China Vanke Co. Ltd., one of the few veterans in the top 10, had its value reduced by 15.81%. The last on the list, Sunac China Holdings Ltd., lost 53.7% in just 6 months. One can tell it was in quite big financial trouble, with its rank dropping from top fourth to tenth. Two observations are in order here (but not reported in Table 10.1). First, China Railway Group should be ranked fifth in the 2022 list, but it was eliminated because its main business is neither in construction nor real estate. Second, and more interestingly, the 11th largest developer omitted here is actually Evergrande Group, with a market capitalization of USD2.78 billion on June 30, 2022 (USD2.928 billion on January 1, 2022), down from USD37.89 billion on January 1, 2020.

10.5. Finale: U.S. and Chinese Markets — Bubbles or Not?

We have covered the latest boom and bust of the housing markets in the U.S. and the bubbly Chinese housing markets that have not really burst (yet). We know that the momenta come from different sources, but both are because of boosting ownership, and readily available lending, a lot of which comes from shadow banking. How alike are these bubbles? We have previously researched this question using econometric models called mean group (MG) estimation and pooled mean group (PMG) estimation.[52,53] In particular, we studied the sales price and rent indices of 44 metropolitan statistical areas

---

[52]Lai and Van Order (2020).

[53]We will not cover the lengthy methodologies here. Interested parties can read the various research papers due to Hashem Pesaran and his coauthors: Pesaran and Smith (1995), Pesaran *et al.* (1999) and Pesaran and Shin (1999).

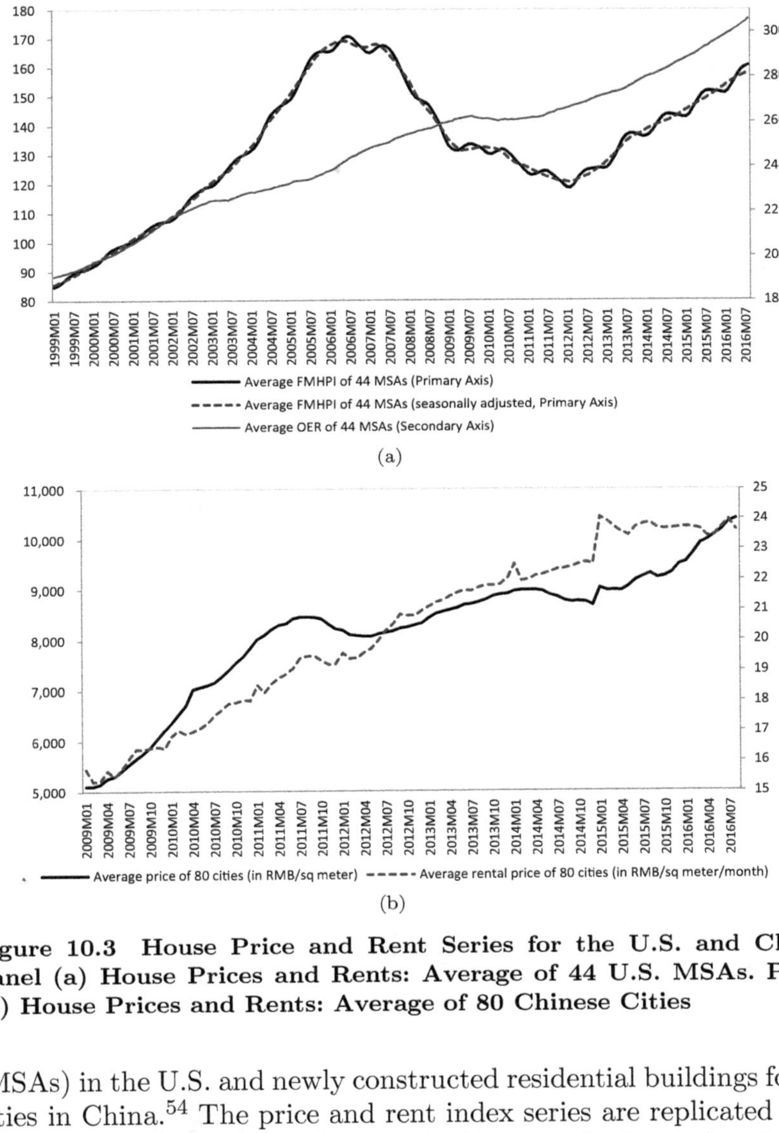

Figure 10.3 House Price and Rent Series for the U.S. and China. Panel (a) House Prices and Rents: Average of 44 U.S. MSAs. Panel (b) House Prices and Rents: Average of 80 Chinese Cities

(MSAs) in the U.S. and newly constructed residential buildings for 80 cities in China.[54] The price and rent index series are replicated here in Figure 10.3, while the average growth rates of price and rent, and

[54]US house price indices are from Freddie Mac House Price Index (FMHPI) and rent series are from the Owners' Equivalent Rent of Primary Residence (OER) from the Bureau of Labor Statistics. Chinese housing data are available from the National Bureau of Statistics of China and CityRE Data Technology Co. Ltd.

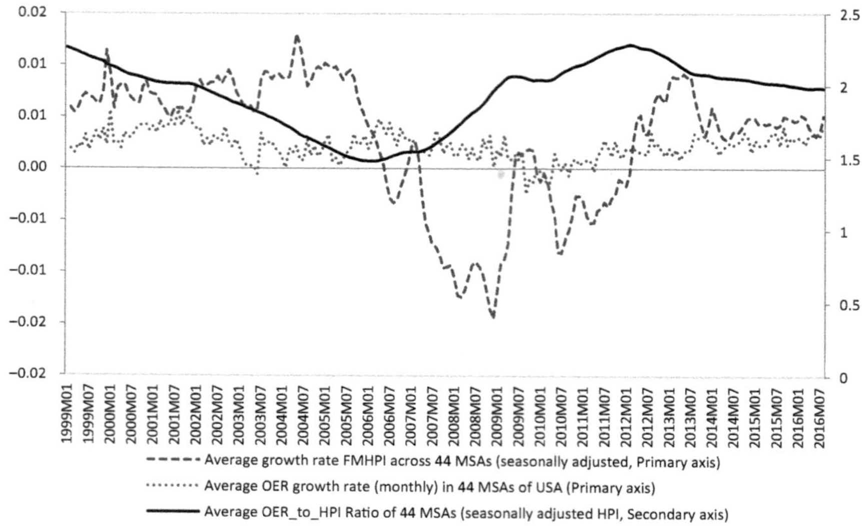

(a)

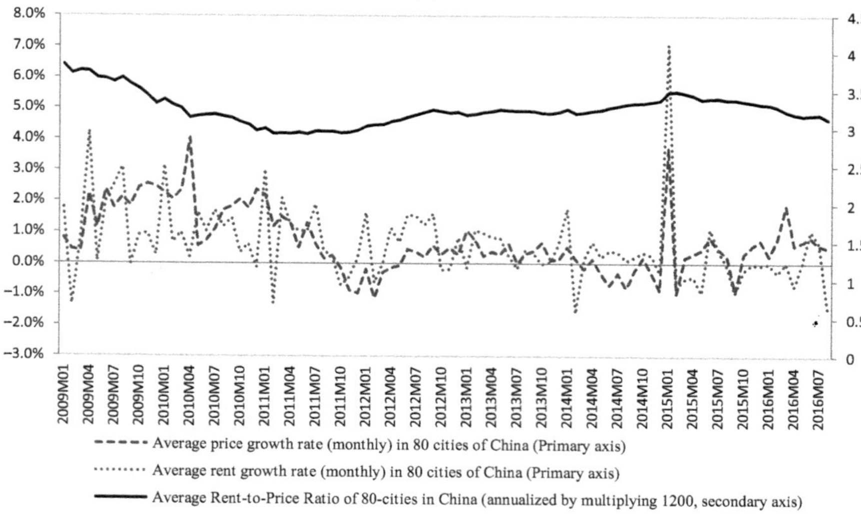

(b)

Figure 10.4 Average Rent-to-Price Ratio, Price Growth Rate, and Rent Growth Rate. Panel (a) U.S. MSAs (Seasonally Adjusted Data). Panel (b) 80 Chinese Cities

the price-to-rent ratios are duplicated in Figure 10.4. Note that the price series and price-to-rent ratios of the U.S. here are different from those shown in Figure 9.1 Panel (b) and Figure 9.2 because of the different cities/MSAs covered, although the trends are comparable.

We used PMG to estimate parameters of equations like equation 3.24 in Chapter 3. The estimates were generally in line with what our theory suggested and the story implied by Figures 10.3 and 10.4.[55] Controlling for factors such as interest rates, credit spreads, inflation, and accounting for borrowing costs with corresponding riskiness at real prices, we found two stand-out features that suggest the differences in the housing markets of both countries. First, both markets had similar price upsurges, approximately doubling at the beginning 7 years of the bubble period. Second, the U.S. markets show a clear tendency for price growth much faster than rent growth. Conversely, that of China looks more like prices chasing past rents and/or anticipating future rents. In fact, we do not see much evidence of bubbles in China: any deviation from the fundamental movement quickly reversed to equilibrium.

However, our econometric models cannot identify whether the Chinese economy is structured in a way that is less prone to bubbles than the U.S., or if the different results reflect that the Chinese policymakers have been good at stabilizing economic turmoil. If that is the case, then there is inherent risk from changes in policy regimes.

10.6. Summary and Comments

Unlike many Western economies that were dragged down by the GFC, the Chinese economy was unaffected by it. China was less connected financially with the U.S. and Europe, and its thick-skinned housing bubble was not really a bubble. It was based on a modest amount of momentum along with the scarcity of space as people moved to cities, and it was stabilized by government policy. So, if a bubble existed, it was deflated but not burst.

Bubbles or not, shadow banking in China has become well-established, with different types of structures and institutions from

[55]See Lai and Van Order (2010, 2017) for the estimation details.

those of its western peers. Its system has spiraled into extensive debts, mostly due to the LGFVs, corporate bonds, and loans. However, the shadow banks are mostly not funded with demand deposits, but rather with term deposits and other debt that take time to withdraw. This lessens, but does not eliminate, the probability of a run. It does not lessen the risk of bankruptcy.

Major financial institutions in China are government-owned and regulated. The shadow banks, however, are market-based institutions competing for funds and are capable of being in trouble. China has some advantages of an authoritarian approach to policy in that it can change regulations fast and act fast to stabilize markets. But the stabilization is heavy-handed at times, and it lacks many of the benefits of markets as an allocation mechanism. A prime example is the ghost towns, which have been put to place by local authorities for budgetary reasons, and not where housing is best built, or whether it needs to be built (relative to other demands on the economy). A good guess is that it is less likely to achieve the best housing results in the medium to long run.

Chapter 11

Ten Years After

The Legacy of the GFC

This chapter covers the developments since the GFC. First, we cover housing markets and assess whether we have been seeing bubbles. The short answer to the recent slowdown is that interest rate increases, triggered by inflation and Fed policy (e.g. high mortgage rates), have caused house prices to turn, but not bubbles leaking air. Second, we focus on new forms of shadow banking, with increased use of technology. We discuss China separately because of the different evolution of markets after the crash and its wide range of new ways of lending.

11.1. Housing Markets After the GFC

Most places have had house price booms since the GFC. Many have shown steady momentum, but not bubbles (as yet). This was in spite of the survival of shadow banks, which had made risky loans before the GFC. At the same time, the changing structure of mortgage markets has moved lending away from riskier products. The U.S. has shifted away from subprime and low downpayments, and there are almost no low-doc loans. Of the new mortgages in the U.S. in quarter 1 of 2022, only 2% were to subprime borrowers.[1] Delinquency

[1]Federal Reserve Bank of New York (2022). Total Household Debt Increases in Q1 2022, Driven by Mortgage and Auto Balances, Press Release, May 10, 2022.

rates dropped to 3.2% in February 2022, which is the lowest since January 1999.[2] It looks like the interactions of house price growth, shadow banking and securitization have not been as strong lately as in the run up to the GFC. In the following, we shall take a look at the general picture since the GFC and what the COVID-19 pandemic brought to the housing markets.

11.1.1. The Picture Since the GFC

Figure 11.1 provides information for the post-GFC recovery period. The left side (Panels (a1), (b1), and (c1)) has price-to-rent ratios (P/R Ratio), and the right side (Panels (a2), (b2), and (c2)) has price-to-income ratios (P/I Ratio). The ratios are of indexes, not actual prices and rents, and they are not for the same types of household groups. This is because we only have grouped data rather than loan-by-loan data, which means that the numbers in the numerator and the dominator represent different household groups. Homeowners tend to have higher than average incomes, perhaps because of tax advantages of ownership that go to higher income households. Hence, average incomes in a country are generally lower than those of homeowners. Using the indexes makes comparisons across countries easier, although they have to be handled with caution.

In particular, a price-to-income ratio index of 100 in 2015 does not mean that income is enough to cover price. It only means that the ratio is normalized to 100, so that subsequent index values can be interpreted as growth if they are higher than 100. This allows us to have comparable data on how rapidly these ratios are changing. Perhaps the following example might clarify. Suppose the price-to-income ratio and price-to-rent ratio in 2015 are 4 and 12, respectively. As 2015 is the base year, both become 100. Now suppose the two ratios are 120 and 130 after some years. That means the

Available at: https://www.corelogic.com/intelligence/u-s-delinquencies-drop-to-lowest-level-in-more-than-23-years-in-february/; https://www.newyorkfed.org newsevents/news/research/2022/20220510#:~:text=Housing%20Debt,average%20seen%20between%202003%2D2007.

[2]CoreLogic (2022). U.S. Delinquencies Drop to Lowest Level in More Than 23 Years in February: Loan Performance Insights Report Highlights: February 2022, May 10, 2022.

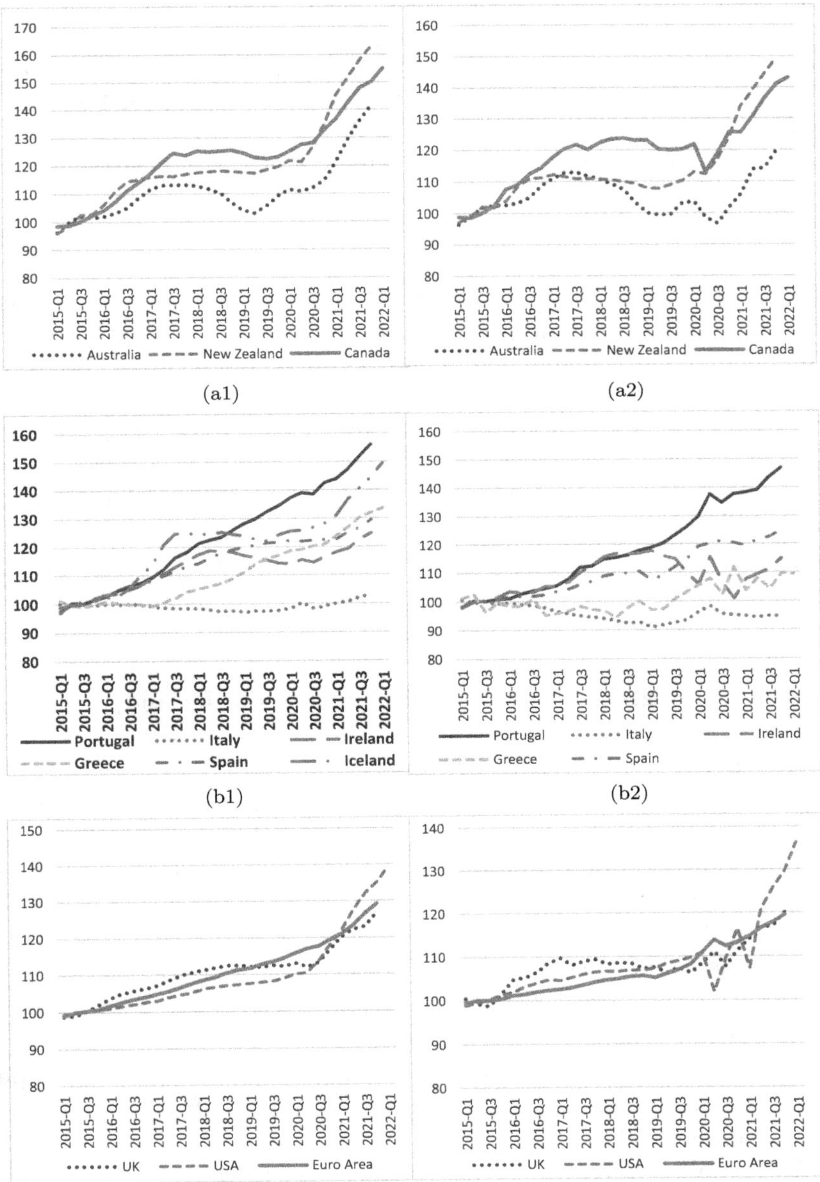

Figure 11.1 (*Continued*)

Figure 11.1 Housing Affordability of Various Countries. Panel (a1) P/R Ratio – Group 1. Panel (a2) P/I Ratio – Group 1. Panel (b1) P/R Ratio – Group 2. Panel (b2) P/I Ratio – Group 2. Panel (c1) P/R Ratio – Group 3. Panel (c2) P/I Ratio – Group 3

Note: P/R Ratio is price-to-rent ratio; P/I Ratio is price-to-income ratio.
Source: OECD.

price-to-income ratio and the price-to-rent ratio have increased by 20% and 30% over those few years. In other words, the actual price-to-income ratio has gone up to 4.8 while the price-to-rent ratio has gone up to 15.6, implying that household income is even less adequate for home purchases if housing is already expensive.

Three groups of countries are included in Figure 11.1. Group 1 includes the "world's bubbliest countries": Canada, Australia, and New Zealand.[3] Group 2 are the PIIGS countries plus Iceland. Group 3 are the leading countries: U.K., U.S. and the Euro Area. Chinese data are not available. Its story is different anyway; we will discuss it in the next section. The dataset begins in 2015. Combining it with the series in Figure 9.4 gives a price-to-rent series for PIIGS and Iceland all the way from 1999 to quarter 1 of 2022. Data for quarter 2 of 2022 are available only for Canada, Iceland, U.S., and Greece.

The price-to-rent ratios of Group 1 increased in the range of 40–60 index points from 2015, with New Zealand climbing the most after the pandemic outbreak. Panel (a2) shows that although household incomes in New Zealand and Canada were picking up, as their price-to-income ratios did not grow as fast as the price-to-rent ratios, price is still growing faster than income (otherwise, the index would drop). Australia's price-to-income ratio and price-to-rent ratio in quarter 4 of 2021 are 120 and 140, respectively. That is, price relative to rent increased faster than price relative to income. Except for Portugal, all countries included in the figures have apparently experienced some hiccups in 2016–2017 but picked up after the outbreak of the pandemic.

Almost all countries have had increases in price-to-income ratios, and housing costs are eating into income. Italy is the only country

[3]Curran (2022).

Table 11.1 Housing Affordability by Selected Countries in Mid-Year of 2022

Rank	Country	Price-to-Income Ratio	Price-to-Rent Ratio, City Center	Mortgage Payment as % of Income	Cost-of-Living Index (New York = 100)
4	Hong Kong	42.59	61.94	266.62	76.55
6	China	38.43	61.31	309.62	40.31
12	South Korea	26.51	123.73	184.39	66.95
28	Singapore	16.78	38.87	103.02	79.09
49	Portugal	12.97	19.25	79.61	42.18
55	Greece	12.08	23.74	90.05	50.23
69	Italy	11.1	26.69	65.34	58.47
75	Japan	10.49	39.6	60.22	62.77
83	Canada	8.91	27.74	71.34	68.78
90	New Zealand	8.01	23.07	58.69	68.96
91	United Kingdom	7.99	21.21	53.51	60.42
95	Spain	7.49	19.85	46.72	47.51
98	Ireland	6.97	13.31	47.93	66.73
100	Iceland	6.8	18.8	54.84	86.59
106	Australia	5.6	19.59	37.63	72.27
109	United States	4.58	12.84	37.41	69.92

Source: Numbeo.

that had modest changes in both ratios. Even so, its price-to-rent ratio was slightly tilted on the upside after quarter 3 of 2021, and its price-to-income ratio did not really move after coming down slightly from peak in quarter 2 of 2020. Portugal's housing price ratios are among the lowest; both ratios are almost monotonically increasing. The situations in the U.K. and the U.S. are similar; both ratios soared at similar rates and from similar index points when the pandemic hit them.

Table 11.1 presents recent data on affordability across countries.[4] Aside from the countries included in Figure 11.1, we also include those with astonishing housing price growths, namely Hong Kong,

[4]Data in Table 11.1 are all from Numbeo. Even though Numbeo is a private online provider, it has been widely cited by global media. Available at: https://www.numbeo.com/property-investment/rankings_by_country.jsp.

South Korea, Singapore and Japan. It lists the price-to-income ratio, price-to-rent ratio (for housing at the city center), mortgage payments as a percentage of personal income, and the relative cost-of-living index. As with Figure 11.1, because we do not have loan-level data, the price ratios portray affordability for the average household, which represents the affordably of ownership for renters, and not the rent burden of an average owner.[5] "Mortgage Payment as % of Income" is the average monthly mortgage payment relative to the average monthly salary, on a 20-year, 100% LTV ratio mortgage for a 90 square meter (sq.m.) house/apartment sold at the average price/sq.m. Price-to-rent ratios for housing outside of city centers are lower than those in the city center for the countries included in Table 11.1.[6] The cost of living index is set relative to the cost of living in New York City, which is set to equal 100.[7]

Not surprisingly, the most expensive housing (relative to average income) is in Hong Kong, with price-to-income a bit above China and a ratio 1.6 times more than the third row, South Korea. Hong Kong is famous for *nano-flats*, which means the benchmark apartments in the table is more representative of luxury flats, which would be unaffordable for most households. Countries even more unaffordable than Hong Kong are (not shown in the table) Syria, Ghana and Sri Lanka, all with varying degrees of political unrest.

A total of 112 countries are included in the source. The ranks of Australia and the U.S. at 106 and 109, imply that their housing is relatively affordable.[8] Of course, both countries are big enough to simultaneously contain cities with sluggish demand and those with soaring demand. Another interesting observation is that China was

[5]For instance, in the U.S., the usually quoted payment-to-income ratio is more like 20%–25% for average homebuyers. However, the table shows a ratio of 37% because homeowners tend to have higher incomes than renters.

[6]It should be noted that Hong Kong has been separately listed by the source even though it is the Special Administrative Region of China because of the different legislatures.

[7]Note that there is always a risk of loss of accuracy and representativeness from evaluating with a common currency unit, the index.

[8]Note our discussion in Chapters 1 and 3 (Sections 1.2.3 and 3.2.4, respectively) of affordability versus user cost. Here, we are not considering investment or tax dimensions.

ranked behind South Korea in the beginning of 2022. It only took a half year for China to jump up to the sixth rank, before South Korea (which ranked 10 a half year ago). In addition, Hong Kong was third at the beginning of 2022, with a price-to-income ratio of 46.93, evidence of the beginning of a slowdown in the Hong Kong property market in the first half of the year.

The four columns give inconsistent and incomplete signals. The high value of one number, such as the price-to-income ratio, does not mean housing is expensive. For example, the price-to-income ratio of Canada is lower than that of Japan. So is the price-to-rent ratio. But how does that square up with the higher payment-to-income ratio in Canada?

Here is one explanation, using what we know about the two countries and what we have from the discussion of user cost in Chapter 4. Recall that the price-to-rent ratio is analogous to price–earnings ratio for a stock. High values indicate higher expected growth. Japan's housing has had a high growth rate for some time, and so we should expect higher expectations and a higher price-rent ratio. Canada has, however, had higher nominal interest rates, which is consistent with a high ratio of mortgage payments to income. We cannot tell from the table which country is more affordable, in the sense of payment burden, because while Canada has higher mortgage rates, Japan has higher prices. A good guess though is that given the small size of flats in Japan, Canada is most likely more affordable. This would be clearer if we had data with comparable houses in the two countries.

The cost of living in China is the lowest, although housing price to income is almost the highest, and mortgage payment as a percentage of income is ridiculously high. This sounds strange at first glance, but not quite. China's cost of living is indeed low, with low basic food and transportation costs. It also has quite a significant proportion of households with low income. Regarding homeownership, many households had already purchased their homes from their employers in the 1990s, which resulted in a high homeownership rate. Since these homeowners have finished with their payments, they do not have to consider mortgage costs in their cost of living.[9] Another

[9]They probably do consider user cost, which is probably low because of appreciation.

reason is that a noticeable proportion of homeowners have enough wealth to either pay the price in full, or with a high downpayment, leaving the average mortgage costs low. Chinese are famous for saving a lot, remember?

But for the general lower-income new homebuyers-to-be, housing can be quite unaffordable. The annual disposable income per capita in urban areas was RMB47,412 (or USD7,112) in 2021.[10] This is RMB3,951 per month. If the average household has two people, then the average household income per month is RMB7,902 (or RMB11,774 with a household size of 2.98 in 2021). With an average sales price of RMB10,500 per sq.m. in the same year, a 90-sq.m. apartment as in Table 11.1 will require a mortgage monthly payment of RMB4,058, assuming the mortgage rate is 5% per annum. Depending on the size of the households, this suggests that despite lower costs of living in general and high expected home price appreciation, the cash flows prospects for homeownership for households that are currently renters are low because mortgage payments will constitute a high percentage of their income unless their units are extremely small. Unfortunately, there is almost always enough demand that developers do not really need to trim the sizes of the units so that they could become more affordable.

Real house prices in many countries rose over the period of 2020–2021.[11] Shown in Figure 11.2 are percentage changes in real house prices for the various countries discussed so far — the PIIGS, USA, UK, Iceland, and China, as well as the European Area in general. U.S. has the highest price upsurge (although Turkey, New Zealand, Czech Republic, Luxembourg, and Australia surpassed U.S., in descending order of percentage increase, as shown in footnote 2 of the McKinsey & Company article).

---

[10] Source is Statista. Available at: https://www.statista.com/statistics/278698/annual-per-capita-income-of-households-in-china/.

[11] McKinsey & Company (July 5, 2022). How Inflation is Flipping the Economic Script, in Seven Charts. Available at: https://www.mckinsey.com/featured-insights/inflation/how-inflation-is-flipping-the-economic-script?cid=other-eml-alt-mip-mck&hdpid=47252fc8-f7be-4565-86a8-3c510163dcc4&hctky=12069925&hlkid=4c90e3924e4f401fbc3038a58001014d.

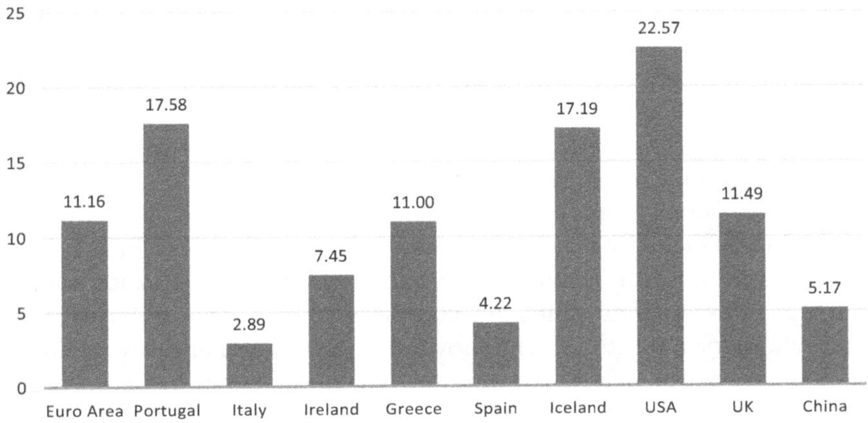

Figure 11.2 Growth (in %) in Real Housing Prices between 01/2020 and 12/2020 for Selected Countries

Source: OECD.

11.1.2. Housing Markets and The Pandemic

We have talked about affordability from Table 11.1 and that housing in the U.S. is relatively affordable, but not in other countries. What has changed since the pandemic?

The first officially reported COVID-19 case started in Wuhan, China, December 31, 2019. China was the first country to be hard hit by the pandemic outbreak, with the whole of Wuhan, the capital city of Hubei province with a population of about 11 million, under strict lockdown, followed by other cities in the province, and then other provinces in the country. For the first time, people were prohibited from traveling during the very important Chinese New Year period when a lot of them had planned to go back to their hometowns to celebrate the once-a-year family gathering. The virus soon traveled everywhere in the world.

People were stranded at home for days, then weeks, and then months. Soon, the "new normal" has become "work from home" ("WFH", a new member of the alphabet soup). They started to have online meetings. Before long, people realized that they could extend the meetings to regional offices, international offices, and their clients all over the world. It turned out that WFH was not all that bad.

The longer people stayed at home, the more they realized space and ambiance are both very important. They did not have to worry too much about "location, location, location" commanding them to live as close to work as possible, so as to save commuting time and hassle. People started to spend more time decorating their homes, focusing on their families and getting closer to nature. WFH has led people to rethink about their housing units, such as whether they should move to places farther away from cities so that they can have bigger and cheaper housing. This lowered relative house prices, inside versus outside cities, without much of a clue as to whether that will reverse if and when normal sets in. The move to housing farther away signaled an increase in the overall demand for residential space but a decrease in the demand for office space.

A consequence of WFH is downtown restaurants finding demand for lunch lower and unpredictable, leading them to downscale their operations, while takeaways and chain restaurants have found a new business niche; even high-end restaurants had to consider various takeaway businesses. Ironically, these also happen most in the cities with an increase in job opportunities.[12] Offices had to provide flexibility and a sense of human connection.[13] More intriguingly, more people quit their jobs after the pandemic because they soon realized that instead of feeling miserable losing their jobs, they could make use of the internet to set up their own businesses, which would provide them with more flexible workhours and workdays, which would be especially valuable for parents who could take care of their kids while working.

The "Great Resignation" (or the "Big Quit"), which started in early 2021, occurred in many countries, especially in Europe (although Australia and China are alike). Major reasons for this include safety concerns of the pandemic, stagnant wages, and job dissatisfaction; some people were still grieving from loss of loved ones. But the most obvious reason is the choice of more "self" time, cost of living, and flexibility of remote working and baby boomers retiring early. All this new "normal" has changed the demand for homes in terms of space, style, location, and amenities. No one knows how long this will last.

[12]Anderson (2022).
[13]Chiarella *et al.* (2022).

As a result, the brief period of negative sentiment in 2020 ended up with higher housing prices. Figure 1.2 shows that the homeownership rate in the U.S. started to rise in 2016, with a local maximum in 2020. The Case–Shiller U.S. National Home Price Index in Figure 1.3 shows a sharp increase since May 2020 (the end of May was also the reopening of economic activities after the "stay at home" choices as well as mandates in some states in the U.S.), all the way to early 2022. Aside from a long period of low production and a relatively small stock of houses, one reason for house price increases in the U.S. is the shortage of labor. For example, according to the U.S. Bureau of Labor Statistics, there was a shortage of 402,000 construction positions in October 2021 even though wages have already significantly increased after the pandemic. This shortage was a result of job and labor mismatch and in part due to the reasons mentioned above regarding the Great Resignation.[14]

The latest statistics from the Bureau of Labor Statistics of the U.S. Department of Labor show that 4.53 million workers left their jobs in March 2022. Resignation has passed 4 million for 11 times between June 2021 and May 2022.[15] Figure 11.3 uses data from a McKinsey & Company article to depict the average growth of wages in different sectors in the U.S. for the 2 years before the COVID-19 pandemic (12/2017–12/2019), and the pandemic (12/2019–2/2022).[16] Wages grew sharply in the second period. It looks like the shortage of labor has become a contributor to inflation as well as a result of inflation.[17]

On the other side of the world, according to the Residential Property Price Index released by the Central Statistics Office of Ireland, the annual housing price index in Ireland has grown 15.2% in March 2022, the highest since January 2016, although it has gone

[14] Hovnanian *et al.* (2022).

[15] According to Anthony C. Klotz, creator of the term "Great Resignation", Klotz (2022).

[16] With reference to Exhibit 2 of Basar *et al.* (2022).

[17] This is discussed by David Autor, the Ford Professor of Economics at MIT, at the podcast interview by McKinsey Global Institute in February 2022, entitled "Forward Thinking on Pandemic Paradoxes, Labor Market Myths, and 'Cowboy Capitalism' with David Autor". Available at: https://www.mckinsey.com/featured-insights/employment-and-growth/forward-thinking-on-pandemic-paradoxes-labor-market-myths-and-cowboy-capitalism-with-david-autor.

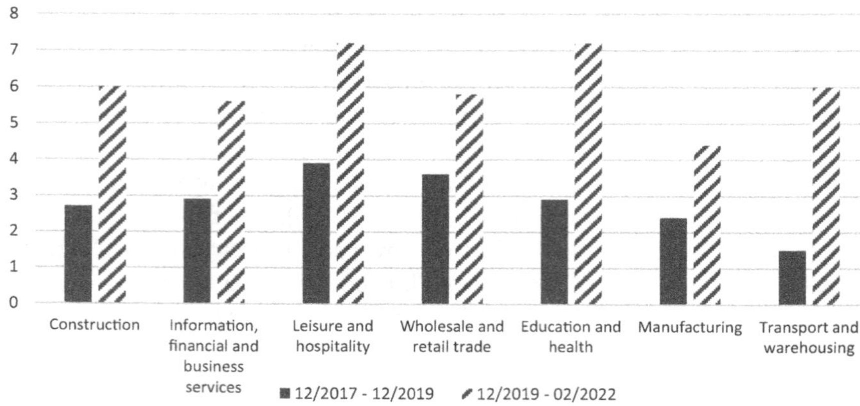

Figure 11.3 Private-Sector Wages in the U.S. Before and During COVID-19

Source: Basar *et al.* (2022).

down to 14.4% in May 2022.[18] The last peak was at 13.4% in April 2018. It was never positive for the period of June–November 2020. The lower growth in May 2022 does not mean a slowdown, however. The monthly change for May 2022 was actually 0.8%, compared to 0.7%, 0.5%, and 0.4% in February, March, and April, respectively. Interestingly, while the price in Dublin, the capital, grew at an annual rate of 11.7% in May, it was 16.6% outside Dublin. That is evidence of people moving out of the city center. Another example is Switzerland. Apartments and single-family houses there had seen prices increase by 7.3% and 6.9%, respectively, in 2021. All these changes point to housing needs due to the pandemic as well as economic growth.[19]

Finally, according to the UBS Global Real Estate Index 2021, real house prices have grown by 6% between mid-2020 and mid-2021 for the cities.[20] As with Ireland, this is also the largest increase since

[18]Accessible at: https://www.cso.ie/en/releasesandpublications/ep/p-rppi/residentialpropertypriceindexmay2022/.

[19]This is from a report by SWI (a branch of Swiss Broadcasting Corporation) on January 4, 2022, entitled "Pandemic Pushes Swiss House Prices Higher". Available at: https://www.swissinfo.ch/eng/pandemic-pushes-swiss-house-prices-higher/47236452.

[20]UBS (2021).

2014. A city is said to be prone to bubble risks if its real estate bubble index scores higher than 1.5. Nine cities have index points higher than this threshold, including (in descending order of scores) Frankfurt, Toronto, Hong Kong, Munich, Zurich, Vancouver, Stockholm, Paris, and Amsterdam. Frankfurt has an index of 2.16, denoted as most at-risk. Toronto and Hong Kong are runner-ups scoring 2.02 and 1.9, respectively.[21]

Thus, housing demand has been building up in many cities around the world. Key findings are still that prices increased faster outside of cities due to pandemic-related restrictions and WFH arrangements. As demands are expanded, prices might deviate from rent again, affordability will worsen, and a mortgage might become more burdensome. It can easily become a potential for a bubble (and a crisis).

11.1.3. China and Its Policy

China was the first country to have a COVID-19 pandemic outbreak and city-wide lockdowns, which ended by the end of March 2020 for most cities in China, and in early April for Wuhan. The only exception was Urumqi in Xinjiang, which started in mid-July and ended in late August 2020. To combat financial instability due to the COVID-19 pandemic lockdown in 2020, the People's Bank of China (BOC) reduced the required reserve rate (RRR), and the economy responded positively, although its growth rate was still slow relative to its recent history.

Business everywhere was much better than before the pandemic. It was apparently the case that consumers started "revenge spending" (i.e. significant increase in spending after an extended period of restricted consumption) after being locked down for two whole months. Its retail sales grew by 34.2% in March 2021, although consumption has slowed significantly since, and was only 2.5% in August of the same year, which was lower than the 7% annual growth estimate.[22] China was the only country that generated positive growth in GDP by 2.3% in 2020.

---

[21]Statista also reported the global real estate bubble index scores, with the same values, on February 18, 2022.
[22]Lau (2021).

So was the housing market. It was reported that over 30% of the economic growth in 2020 was attributed to investment in the real estate sector.[23] But unlike the Western countries, housing demand increased not because of WFH. Local governments were keen to revive the economic growth after the pandemic. This has however resulted in an oversupply of housing units in lower-tier cities, extending the prolonged episode of over-heated housing markets with ghost towns, coupled with many young people in Tier 1 cities not being able to afford housing. At the same time, the relaxation of monetary policy to keep the economy afloat amid the impact of the pandemic has resulted in excess liquidity. Housing prices, and speculation, continued to increase into 2021.

11.2. Shadow Banking and Its Fellow Travelers

Continuous assessment from the Financial Stability Board (FSB) shows that there was a lot of capital inflow into emerging economies after the GFC because global funds left advanced economies where interest rates were low to seek for higher returns. This also induced vulnerabilities due to the growth of liquidity mismatch and currency mismatch. More collateralized loan obligations (CLOs) have been issued in 2014 than before the GFC. Non-bank financial intermediation has been increasingly important in these emerging economies, especially in the debt markets, and has become even more vulnerable after the COVID-19 pandemic in terms of liquidity mismatches, interconnectedness, and leverage. FSB has been analyzing the systemic risks of NBFI, forming policies necessary for its cross-border nature, and learning from the market turmoil in March 2020.[24]

In the U.S., even though many of the old structures are still around, they are generally not collateralized by risky assets like pieces of CDOs as they were before the GFC. The subprime and Alt-A markets have more or less disappeared. Repos are still important, as are securitized commercial papers, but are generally secured by Treasury or Agency securities. There are still structured deals, such as CMOs and credit risk transfers (CRTs, which are structured deals

[23]Kawate (2021b).
[24]Financial Stability Board (2021a, 2022).

like synthetic CDOs that sell credit risk in pieces), typically from pools of Agency loans.

An opinion article in the *Financial Times* best described how far shadow banking has gone after the GFC: that there would always be some financial crises somewhere in the world whenever the Fed increases rates.[25] Shadow banking has drawn attention again because of the speedy increase in interest rates by the Fed starting in quarter 2 of 2022. In the article are also the following acute comments:

> ...[investor told Sharma]: swing a stick in Manhattan these days and you are bound to hit someone involved in private lending, ... The next financial crises are thus likely to arise in new areas of the markets, where growth has been explosive, and regulators haven't yet arrived.

However, private lending and platforms supporting shadow banking are not the same as those discussed in Chapter 6. Private conduit lending has the "shadow" in the sense of connecting lenders to borrowers but not the "banking" because there is no intermediation, margin requirements or obligation of paying off "depositors".

More recently, new forms of shadow banking involving extensive technology to financing loans have evolved. We may think of these "fellow travelers" as shadow *conduits* (or *shadow market makers*) and shadow bank *intermediaries.* In what follows, to keep the notation simple, we shall refer to both types as shadow banking and differentiate them based on context. More broadly, shadow banks are best defined by what they are not: They are not traditional banks or Agency securitization deals. They are banking with the equivalent of deposits, making them susceptible to runs. Chinese shadow banks tend to be banks but with term deposits, which are less susceptible to runs. Peer-to-peer (P2P, which is direct lending via an online platform) conduits, for example, are basically market-makers.

In the following section, we discuss these new travelers of shadow banking with technology and how the pandemic has nudged the speedy development of financial technology (fintech).

---

[25]Sharma (2022).

11.2.1. Peer-to-peer Lending

According to the FSB,[26] of the 19 jurisdictions surveyed in 2021, the most common non-bank financial intermediation conduit is peer-to-peer (P2P) lending. The platform acts as a market-maker, a kind of cyber auctioneer. Those in the U.S. and Europe are relatively well regulated and are alternatives to bank lending. These markets are in general quite small, certainly much smaller than their Chinese counterparts. In the U.S., due to the stringent regulations aiming to protect retail investors, only Prosper Marketplace and LendingClub, the two largest platforms, have survived, and their fund providers are mostly institutional investors, meaning their issuance of notes does not violate regulations.

In Asian markets, South Korea passed its first law for marketplace lending (alternative term for P2P lending) in October 2019. Malaysia started only in 2016, with 11 platforms in total so far. Unlike other countries, its platforms only lend to SMEs. P2P lending is also performing well as alternative finance in Indonesia, Japan, Australia, New Zealand, European countries, and others.

The U.K. market is similar to that in the U.S. in the sense of abundant regulations. It has at one time more than one hundred platforms, but mostly small, except Zopa, Funding Circle, and Ratesetter. Zopa is the very first P2P platform on earth, aiming at the personal loan market. Funding Circle is the largest, loaning to small businesses, while Ratesetter does both types of loans. However, Zopa closed its P2P business in December 2021 and instead focuses only on its banking business. Similarly, Funding Circle closed its P2P arm in March 2022 to focus mainly on commercial lending. Funding Circle has gone public in 2018, while Zopa intends to do so at the end of 2022. Ratesetter was bought by Metro Bank in 2020 and closed down the P2P arm in April 2021. This means that all the three main P2P platforms in the U.K. have exited the market. Currently on top of the list are Assetz Capital, Folk2Folk, and CrowdProperty, in descending order of market size, all lending to SMEs and smaller property developers.[27]

[26]Box 0–2 on Innovations in NBFI, Page 4 of Financial Stability Board (2021b).
[27]https://p2pfinancenews.co.uk/2022/04/01/uk-p2p-sector-more-than-doubles-in-size-as-new-big-three-emerges/.

P2P lending platforms can make markets for loans to homebuyers and small developers. Some purposely focus on lending for real estate purchases and developments. For instance, in the U.K., there are 19 platforms serving the real estate sector. LendInvest is the oldest, founded in 2008. Some offer loans backed by properties or land, or loans specific for mortgages. Others set up investment portfolios, such as for buy-to-let projects or specifically for commercial properties, for retail investors. Some specify that the borrowers are property professionals, which include developers.

In the U.S., some P2P lenders focus on mortgage and mortgage refinancing loans. Interestingly, these are not the biggest P2P platforms. The largest LendingClub is only starting to plan for it. P2P platforms can make use of artificial intelligence (AI) and big data systems to obtain soft information about the borrowers, complementing traditional mortgages offered by banks by lending to homebuyers who are creditworthy but rejected by incumbent banks with higher loan documentation standards. Since they are online platforms, their lower operating costs imply lower borrowing rates and transaction costs conditional on the level of risk. P2P lending is therefore suitable for first-time homebuyers who do not have enough savings to cover the downpayment, but have stable jobs and can make the periodic mortgage payments.

As always, there is an issue of moral hazard via dumping loans with hidden risks. The technology-driven credit evaluations are akin to credit scoring models, albeit with big data sets. It is not clear if the modeling is sound and/or cannot be gamed by clever players who reverse-engineer them, not unlike the reverse engineering of rating agencies by pool sellers, and dumping the worst of the loans that are not well modeled.

11.2.2. Crowdfunding

Crowdfunding is basically a securitized version of P2P market-making. Online platforms pool funds from a crowd for investment opportunities in return for interest (like loans) or dividends (like in equities), and in some cases, for charity purposes, or for supporting some invention or movies, like venture capitalists (VCs). The more general for-profit ones can be in the form of loans with interest payments or equity receiving dividends. The platform often pools small amounts from retail investors, similar to P2P lending. The difference is in the "crowd". Whereas P2P lending is one investor choosing which borrower to lend to, crowdfunding is a group of investors pooling money together for a project or loan (like securitization). Of course, a P2P platform would be similar to a crowdfunding platform when several investors individually choose to fund the same project/portfolio of the P2P platform. Another difference is that crowdfunding platforms usually use social media such as Facebook and LinkedIn to attract investors.

Real estate crowdfunding aims to pool capital through online platforms to fund projects secured by real estate. The project can be a mortgage of a homebuyer, or "flipping", i.e. redevelopment of a torn or abandoned property. It can also be a portfolio of (good or distressed) mortgages. In the U.S., crowdfunding has higher default risk than P2P lending, probably because the types of underlying projects are riskier. In any case, the availability of funds outside of the banking sector will always be beneficial to homebuyers, while also offering another channel for retail investors.

This, of course, is subject to the same concerns about moral hazard as in traditional shadow banking. Furthermore, both crowdfunding and P2P lending likely have as yet unobserved risks.

11.2.3. Cryptocurrencies, Decentralized Finance, and DCEP

The availability of smartphones has significantly changed how people live and enhanced the development of fintech. Just consider scanning the QR code when entering shops during the pandemic, or getting to the website without the need to type the webpage URL (for *uniform resource locator*, the address of the website). Using digital devices is like inborn skills for Generation Z (Gen-Z) and beyond. But even many baby boomers have learned mobile banking options. China, for example, is almost totally cashless in daily living, to the extent that it is less inconvenient to lose an identity card than a mobile phone.

Decentralized finance (DeFi) is the idea of eliminating money transfers through a centralized unit, like a bank. Funds are transmitted directly between two parties through blockchain. This is similar to cryptocurrencies (or cryptos) except that it uses *stablecoins*, which are pegged to fiat money, exchange-traded commodities, or even some cryptocurrencies. It is this backing by something (probably) valuable that distinguishes them from cryptos. Of course, if they are backed by highly volatile cryptos, they may not be very stable. Examples of stablecoins are Tether and USDC. Stablecoins are still privately issued, meaning they can still serve the original purpose of cryptos in disrupting financial services, enhancing financial inclusion, and reducing payment friction. Unfortunately, they also share most downsides of cryptos, except perhaps less volatile.

While DeFi is still under development, the IMF emphasizes that digital money/currencies supplied by both the public and private sectors can enhance cheaper, faster, easier, and more available financial inclusion not only locally, but internationally, albeit also posing a lot of crucial challenges. As much as people want decentralization from DeFi, there are always significant benefits from economies of scale, perhaps by a few organizations/authorities. Furthermore, it will be difficult to calculate tax because transactions cannot be traced by one single "central" party. Similarly, regulations have to be well set in order to avoid money laundering because of the lack of "central" party, and because different jurisdictions run separate regulations, it would be quite difficult, if not impossible, to internationalize DeFi. In mortgage markets, it is difficult to see a legitimate use for it except for hiding information.

China was the first to implement DeFi through digital currency central payment (DCEP), using its central bank digital currency (CBDC) (see Section 11.3.2). The idea of DCEP is to avoid too many versions of digital money for daily consumption, which might end up with total reliance on particular fintech companies (like Ant Financial), resulting in a system that is too interconnected. What are the advantages of CBDC and DCEP if cryptocurrencies such as Bitcoins and Ethereum have created so much drama, over the past few years?[28] For one, DCEP can facilitate international monetary systems if there is mutual acceptance across countries. For instance,

[28]Bitcoin's price dropped from its peak of USD68,789 on November 10, 2021 to USD17,708.62 on June 18, 2022, without a solid reason explainable by fundamental finance theory, unless of course "animal spirit".

the People's Bank of China has been seeking to collaborate with other central banks in establishing a system that adopts monetary compliance and standards in order to facilitate cross-border transactions. That way, e-RMB can become an international currency. This might take some time though.

The European Central Bank also launched the digital euro project in July 2021. At least something like Euros, used by 19 of the 27 European Union countries, might be in place soon. The crucial issue is the establishment of sets of regulations that facilitate the ecosystem in ensuing and ensuring consumer protection, anti-money laundering, data protection, anti-market manipulation, financial stability, and tax compliance.

DCEP, cryptos and stablecoins are payment methods and can be used to move money around by buying and selling quickly. However, unless there are good markets for hedging,[29] they are not good assets to hold because of instability. How are they related to shadow banking and housing markets? It turns out that houses have been sold with cryptos in the U.S. as early as 2014. There were also transactions in Columbia and Mexico. In fact, many Latin American countries accept bitcoins for housing purchases. Other countries include U.K., United Arab Emirates, and Estonia. The first transaction in Europe, via bitcoins, was a three-bedroom apartment in Braga, Portugal, bought with 3 bitcoins on May 5, 2022. That is equivalent to 110,000 EUR.[30] This is considered a big leap for digital economy in Europe because deals with cryptos in the past meant converting to, for example, Euros or USD, before trading.

The first house sold in the U.K. (at 82.55 bitcoins) was transacted in Essex in December 2017, for a price of GBP375,000. New details emerged when closing the deal. For instance, it is important to know where the money is from and the identities of both the buyer and the seller (to avoid issues of money laundering; the seller certainly does not want to be in a lawsuit), the tax and other procedures as this transaction would not have the same documentation regarding the financing part. Not all European countries accept cryptos for

[29] Such markets have been developing. A well-known one is FTX, which is a platform for trading crypto derivatives. Its recent collapse was not inherent in the nature of the assets traded.

[30] Idealista (2022).

selling houses. For example, the cryptos have to be converted into Euros before the purchase in Spain. In the U.S., some mortgage lenders also allow borrowers to collateralize their mortgages with bitcoins.[31]

One can be dubious about all these. A problem with promising bitcoins as future payments is that the price of bitcoins (and similar vehicles) can be extremely volatile, making them poor bets unless a future price can be locked in.[32] It is highly probable that more of the real estate purchases will be completed with digital currencies in the near future, perhaps in faster pace than expected, although it is much less clear whether they will be used as forward payments. The payment mechanisms are essentially speedy ways of writing checks, which is nice, but not essential for trading properties. The main use is likely to be to hide transfers, for instance, to escape real estate taxes.

In what ways are cryptos like shadow banking? Note that traders can have "wallets", which are entries on blockchain ledgers and are like accounts, but the exchange is not obligated to pay the "depositors". A "run" can happen if the depositors fear changes in the value of the coins. If the empty wallets are owned by shadow banks (and other institutions), this can cause a problem for the banks. This is more like the sell-off of CDO pieces in 2007 or stocks in 1929. Institutions like FTX, which facilitate crypto trading do not create cryptos, but have clients who have accounts used for trading. That is, they are essentially shadow banks running accounts like broker-dealers. What can happen? FTX filed bankruptcy in early November 2022, losing its customers' USD8 billion.[33]

---

[31]In the May 26, 2022 article of the *Bitcoin* Magazine, "Can You Buy a House with Bitcoin?", it was stated that Freddie Mac allows "the use of bitcoin to secure a mortgage loan under certain circumstances". But it is also stated that Freddie also updates the guidelines frequently. From the Freddie bulletin, to which the article is linked, there are no specifics about the use of cryptos for mortgages. The two websites are, respectively, https://bitcoinmagazine.com/business/can-you-buy-a-house-with-bitcoin and https://my.sf.freddiemac.com/updates/guide/bulletin~2021-36#cryptocurrency.

[32]As discussed above in footnote 29, there are evolving markets for crypto futures and swaps.

[33]Chow (2022).

11.2.4. PropTech

Property Technology, or PropTech, applies technology to various segments regarding real estate properties from research to design. A step-by-step story can start with a developer or homebuyer finding the right location using big data about the area and the vicinity.[34] Step 2 would be finding the source of financing, such as through crowdfunding; the fund provider can also use big data to analyze the credentials of the potential borrower and the property to be developed. Step 3 involves the design and construction stage in which computer-aided technology and other software, and 3D printing, can be used for the design and robotics for construction. Drones can be used for monitoring the process too. Step 4 for developers would be to find a real estate agent online platform startup. Potential buyers can do virtual tours of the properties with virtual reality (VR) applications. Step 5 covers the deal-making, in which case mortgages will be needed. All these can be assisted with online applications. For example, the deal could be totally based on cryptos, and/or with digital contract. Finally, in the last step, the home occupier can make use of the Internet of Things (IoT) to set up a smart home to enrich their lifestyle, managed by some PropTech asset management firms.

Leading asset managers and developers have already used different forms of PropTech for their assets and portfolios. High-end real estate properties, including, but not limited to, houses and offices, incorporate state-of-the-art security systems, climate control sensors, remote control lighting, and so on. Home occupiers can use their mobile phones to open the doors, turn on the air-conditioning at home when they are about to leave their office or send a QR code to their friends who could then open the car park gates and doors to the buildings when visiting them. Lifts of a smart office building can be programmed to bring all people waiting optimally to their required floors in the shortest time without being too cramped in the lifts.

Another example is Amazon Go, the self-service store that you can grab and go without the need to check out at a cash register. Some of these applications involve the IoT, AI, big data, and machine learning. Others are just simple technologies that have been around

[34]This complete real estate cycle story is with reference to the Real Estate Sector Report by CaixaBank Research (2018).

for some time. In any case, good data are crucial in supporting the development and usage of PropTech.[35]

More formally, CBRE, a global real estate firm, defines a real estate company as a PropTech firm if it attempts to increase efficiency, visibility, experience, flexibility and productivity using technology.[36] Another good classification suggested by a research team from the University of Oxford is that PropTech can intersect with fintech to provide real estate fintech, while PropTech itself also includes smart real estate, which has nothing to do with fintech, and shared economy, with a little overlap with fintech.[37] In the 2017 report by the research team, PropTech includes listing and search services, software for leasing management, P2P and crowdfunding, information and data, valuation and analytics, occupier services, brokerage with tech, tech for asset management, agent matching, sales and marketing, and agency services. They further refined the definition in 2020 to include ConTech and LegalTech.[38] The former is computer-aided design (CAD), which embeds smart real estate (or smart buildings). The latter provides technological support on legal matters, bridging real estate and fintech, and therefore facilitates, for instance, smart contracts.

All these subsectors (real estate fintech, sharing economy, smart buildings and Contech) need none, one, or more of the three drivers: information, transactions/marketplace, and management/control. For example, of the 600 plus companies, 51.2% are in the real estate fintech subsector, of which 12.9% focus on information technology, while the remaining 38.3% focus on technology related to trading, i.e. sales and leasing (see Figure 11.4).

PropTech has developed rapidly, just like fintech and other modes of digital disruption. An application used in China is signing the sales and purchase agreements online. When the developer and the buyer arrive at all terms of the transaction, the developer will input all the details of the purchase agreement in the system so that both parties will e-sign the agreement, which will then be recorded in the government database. When approved, usually after a few days, the

---

[35]Braesemann and Baum (2020).
[36]CBRE (2019).
[37]Baum (2017).
[38]Figure 11.2 of Baum *et al.* (2020).

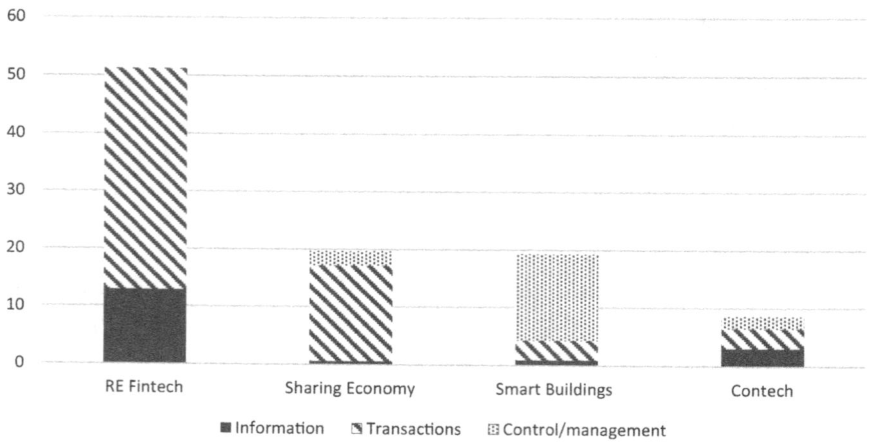

Figure 11.4 PropTech Subsectors and Drivers

Source: Data from Table 4 of Baum *et al.* (2020).

two parties complete the legal purchase process in the traditional way. The purpose is to protect the buyers by registering the sales right away to prevent the housing unit from being sold to multiple buyers, and correct data are recorded. Such arrangements are not common PropTech applications in that the contract signing system is not run by a tech startup. The management of such data and process, and the assurance of compliance of the parties with technology, is run by RegTech, for regulation technology.

Like fintech, which developed much faster during, and due to the pandemic, the growth of PropTech has also accelerated. People demand more and better use of their homes. The same is true for offices. That means more data and information about the properties from different angles in different areas have to be collected. According to Unissu, a company providing data, resources and tools to property professionals, there were almost 9,000 PropTech firms as of July 2022.

Leasing and mortgage tech are two particular PropTech applications closely linked to shadow banking, besides P2P and crowding. Leasing here is really about renting housing units, rather than the more general financial leasing, which is a branch of fintech shadow banking. Financial leasing involves the owner of, for example, some equipment leasing to someone who needs to use, but does not have the money to buy and own, it. While leasing is not new, the recent development is to do the leasing through online fintech platforms to make use of big data and technology.

Several types of PropTech can be related to leasing. First, retail investors can join startups with expertise in buy-to-rent projects using technology. Then, there are platforms with which renters can search for their ideal rental units without involving an agent and agent commissions and fees. There are open banking platforms that renters can use for paying rents more efficiently and conveniently. As for mortgages, incumbent banks offering the mortgages can use the same technology to check the accuracy of any available information related to the loan. Their competitors are fintech companies offering speedier mortgage approvals, which are not necessarily associated with higher default rates. That mortgage lending conduits use new technologies to make markets and to evaluate credit quality most likely implies improved efficiency and availability in mortgage lending.[39]

Other fintech companies involved in mortgages include firms that help with finding or accumulating the deposit necessary for starting a mortgage and other firms that help find the most suitable financing products, which is especially crucial to entrepreneurs or self-employed people who have more difficulty getting a mortgage. Some platforms help people evaluate the costs between leasing and buying. A related type of PropTech is the technology provider of automated mortgage underwriting, which streamline the evaluation process of mortgage application approvals using robotic process automation, AI and machine learning. Such systems provide more thorough data verification, analysis and appraisals (both on the borrowers and the properties), less fraud incidents, and cost reduction.

There are other technologies that help change the way housing market trading and setups are dealt with, but perhaps in more subtle ways. Bank of China Hong Kong, for example, started using blockchain technology for real estate appraisals back in 2018.[40] Jones Lang LaSalle (JLL), Spain, also used blockchain technology to gather information about a property reliably, and making modification of

[39]Fuster *et al.* (2018).
[40]JLL (2018).

the information impossible. Virtual reality can also be employed in PropTech applications. One application is to enhance design, such as presenting to the investor of the property the viability of some scenarios of the design. A more popular application is for international investors to have a preview of the properties without being physically there.

11.2.5. The Metaverse

As a side story, real estate markets are also hot in the metaverse, a totally virtual world that has made up a second world for the avatar (aka digital twin) of those who join in. Properties are transacted as non-fungible tokens (NFT) with cryptos. Not only are people buying land and houses, they even plan to "rent" them.

Although there is no formal or official data, a total sales value of USD9 billion of land has been transacted in the top ten metaverse platforms. The most expensive piece so far was transacted at USD5 million. Sales in January 2022 alone reached USD85 million. It is expected to reach USD1 billion in the whole 2022 and increase by USD5.37 billion in the 5 years leading to 2026.[41] Should the metaverse continue to grow, then there will be a whole set of avatar property markets, with their own housing or real estate bubbles, and because capital is needed, albeit in cryptos, there will be shadow banking avatars sooner or later, too. How intertwined this is with the real financial sector is yet to be determined. At least for now, HSBC and PricewaterhouseCoopers (PwC) have already purchased some virtual land.[42]

11.2.6. Impacts of The Fellow Travelers

How is the plunge of cryptos in 2022 related to shadow banking and/or housing markets? First, they can be potentially huge sources of funding for mortgages. Second, the timing of the plunge actually more or less coincides with the time of fund dry-up of the venture capital (VC) business in general. VC funding surged in 2021, especially on tech startups. Unfortunately, starting from the quarter 1 of 2022,

[41]Frank (2022) and Mariotti (2022).
[42]Bidar and Patterson (2022).

many tech startups had to lay off people; their stock prices dropped significantly. Even big techs like Netflix and Robinhood had to lay off people.[43] VC funding to startups had shrunk a lot in 2022. Vision Fund of SoftBank Group Corporation of Japan (SoftBank in short), the world's largest venture capital fund focusing on technology, has slowed down funding tech startups significantly, not to mention that its founder, Masayoshi Son, has lost as much as USD25 billion.[44] SoftBank's stock price plunged more than 40% between April 2021 and April 2022.

That a lot of PropTech, fintech and regtech firms are startups and lack funding implies slower tech-related development in housing markets. For instance, a startup for home loans called Knock expanded its business from 14 to 75 cities in 2021. Then in 2022, instead of going public through a special purpose acquisition company (SPAC) as originally planned, and after failing to be acquired by a larger company in December 2021 at half the initially planned price, it had to lay off 250 employees and raise funds from existing investors as well as obtain a loan; its value as at May 2022 was only half of what was planned to go public. Another example is Blend Labs, which is a fintech startup on mortgages originally worth USD3 billion, plummeted by two-thirds and has to lay off 10% of its staff in May 2022.[45] The lesson learned from these rollercoasters is that the abundant amounts of VC funds in 2021 are not indicative of the startup values in the near future.[46]

11.3. China and Shadow Banking: Carrying On

China still has the largest shadow banking sector in the world, which is equal in size to 60% of its GDP, while those in Ireland and Luxembourg have been expanding between 8% and 10%.[47] The asset-backed securities (ABS) market of China has also become the second largest

[43]Kunthara (2022).
[44]Lee *et al.* (2022). According to another source, Kharpal (2022), the loss even amounted to USD27.4 billion.
[45]Griffith (2022).
[46]Carson (2022).
[47]Sharma (2022).

in the world since its establishment in 2005. As of the end of 2021, its green bond market had become the world's second largest by both annual issuance and total issuance, amounting to RMB440.1 billion and RMB1.3 trillion, respectively, of which more than half were issued by non-financial corporates for the first time since 2016 when the first green bond was launched.[48] Of this, 18.6% are being traded offshore.

Fintech-enhanced shadow banking has also extensively developed in China. Some areas are even leading the world market, but which are also considered too big by the government. A lot has happened to the fintech industry in China starting in 2020. Many fintech reports point to China as a good example to learn from as its world's largest P2P market had gone through a full and dramatic cycle from formation to death in less than 15 years. Another big story is on the Big Techs.

Stepping into 2022, due to the pandemic, market crackdowns, government policies, and economic slowdown, different shadow banking markets have been quaked. Unsecured CLOs backed by micro and small enterprises (MSEs) loans will be more vulnerable, although ABSs on auto loans and RMBSs will be relatively stable.[49] The relatively new Chinese REITs market, mainly on infrastructure, was discussed in Chapter 7. While it is understandable that permission to launch REITs for property developments at this time might be too risky given the heavy debt profiles of the property developers (to be discussed soon), REITs could be a good source of funding for property developers after this round of clearing of their overleveraged issue. Hence, it would not be too wrong to be optimistic about the growth of the REITs market in China.

11.3.1. Developers and LGFVs Still Fighting Against Loan Defaults

After the outbreak of COVID-19 pandemic in 2020, because of tightened regulatory policies on lending and then a round of rectification of the industry in 2021, Chinese property developers experienced an

[48]Deng *et al.* (2022).
[49]Moody's Investors Service (2022a).

unprecedented housing market slowdown and surge in debt defaults, all alarmed investors because of the spread of news about the overly indebted Evergrande. We have seen from Table 10.1 how much the values of the developers' shares have plummeted even within the first six months of 2022. Investors have simply lost confidence; bank loans and other instruments like trust funds have been much harder to obtain.

A recent S&P report stated that even though the central government has started to support housing purchases with lower mortgage rates and higher loan-to-value ratios, there was still an unprecedented slowdown in household loans.[50] A related problem explained in the report is the contagion risk arising from the increasing joint venture projects of the developers. When one developer is delinquent, banks and trust companies freeze the funding, such that other developers in the joint venture would also be affected. It is also estimated that, at the extreme, as much as 20% of the developers will eventually become insolvent (or 40% if there needs to be a fire sale of land banks and assets).

Adding to the episode was homebuyers refusing to pay mortgages for presale units in the fear that the heavily indebted developers would leave the projects unfinished. The scope has gone up to over 100 projects in more than 50 cities. It was estimated that incomplete presale projects sum up to 1% of all mortgages, constituting up to RMB388 billion non-performing loans if all such buyers default.[51] This is not only an issue for housing markets, but also the shadow banking market. Note that RMBS have always been considered as low-risk investments with which mortgagors' default rates have been very low. Newly issued RMBS in 2021 alone amounted to RMB499.3 billion, from a total new mortgage amount of RMB1,400 billion. Delinquent mortgages affect the income stream of RMBS, in which a lot of WMP investment money lands.

Other causes of slow housing demand are the supply of government-funded affordable housing and the city-wide lockdowns due to the COVID-19 pandemic.[52] The property sector is estimated to be in deep winter, marking a year-on-year drop in home sales by

[50]Liu and Tsang (2022).
[51]Bloomberg (July 14, 2022).
[52]Tan *et al.* (2022).

20% every month since the middle of 2021, while the overall home and land sales in 2022 would drop by 10% and 20%, respectively. The impact will highly likely ripple to the banking sector, with declining credit quality, especially for small banks.[53]

Another issue is on the local governments and therefore the LGFV sector. The central government started to check on the real estate markets in big cities in January 2021 to once again emphasize that "houses are for living, not for speculation".[54] After a few months of market regulation, housing prices for new homes grew 3.8% in September 2021, the slowest of the first nine months in 2021.[55] In August 2021, President Xi Jinping also put forth the "Common Prosperity" to aim at "sharing the opportunity to be wealthy", i.e. shrinking the wealth gap.[56] That was a prelude to the wider policy change to regulating the property markets, which had already piled up mounting debts. In reports released by S&P Global, 2022 is a year in which corporate default risk in China is still high, and it is believed that there will be a soft landing in the real estate sector as the government has made it clear that no property developer is too big to fail.[57,58] Investors have lost confidence. Property sales dropped 26–28% in 2022.[59]

---

[53]Zhengzhou in Henan was under international spotlight on July 11, 2022 because of the big scene of security agents attacking people who protested at the People's Bank of China in Zhengzhou to claim back their money, a lot of which were lifetime savings, deposited in four rural banks via online third-party platforms to transfer the funds illegally for illegal activities (Wang and Ramzy, 2022). Finally, the Henan Banking and Insurance Regulatory Bureau and the Henan Provincial Local Financial Supervision Bureau jointly announced one day later that depositors will be repaid RMB7,000 for those account of RMB50,000 or less (Reuters, July 11, 2022). No further information about the rest of the deposits was released.

[54]Of course, the difference between speculating and wealth-building is the eye of the beholder.

[55]Gao and Woo (2021).

[56]Mullen (2021) and Bloomberg (2021b).

[57]Chang (2022).

[58]S&P Global keeps track of the performances and risk levels of 1800 LGFVs, and evaluates the risk levels by cities. An example is "A Closer Look at China's LGFVs — Hebei". Available at: https://www.spgchinaratings.cn/insights/articles/commentary_hebei-lgfvs_24july2020_en.pdf.

[59]RatingsDirect (November 20, 2022). China Property Is Heading for a Transformation, And Maybe A Turnaround. S&P Global Ratings.

After the glamorous land sales by local governments, with a year-on-year surge of 11.7% at the end of 2020, land sales plunged 24.4% in the first 11 months of 2022, with SOEs and LGFVs constituting almost 80% of the sales; private developers had mostly disappeared.[60] LGFVs had lost the niche for new investors. During the last period of shortage of funds from banks in 2012–2015, LGFVs could turn to shadow banking instruments such as WMPs and entrusted loans for rolling over their maturing municipal corporate bonds (MCBs) written in 2009 due to the stimulus plan.[61]

The same strategy does not seem to have worked this time, as seen from the non-increasing, or even shrinking, amounts of WMPs and entrusted loans in 2021 in Figures 7.1, 7.3, and 7.9. At the same time, however, due to the relatively sluggish economy, the central government will probably increase infrastructure investment again. Local governments could be forced into widened fiscal deficits, especially since refinancing has become more challenging amid less availability of offshore financing.[62] What is worse is that, from an IMF study, 80–90% of the LGFV spending is on new external financing, meaning very limited operating cash inflows; the extent of inefficient use of LGFV funding is just astonishing. Note that restraining LGFV funds implies less local investment and therefore economic growth and eventually less resources to local firms. The feedback loop can pose a tremendous negative impact on the local economy.

That said, there is still a belief that the central government is credible in preventing contagion from both the property market and LGFVs, and the latter would be buoyed by plenty of liquid onshore refinancing.[63] Another way of getting out of the debt spiral is to transform the LGFVs into investment holding companies. Successful cases have already happened in Anhui, Shanghai and Guangdong.[64]

---

[60]Oriental Daily (January 2, 2023) Local governments financial difficulties, Land Sales Shrunk 24%. (in Chinese). Available at: https://orientaldaily.on.cc/content/%E7%94%A2%E7%B6%93/odn-20230102-0102_00202_025/%E5%9C%B0%E6%96%B9%E6%94%BF%E5%BA%9C%E8%B2%A1%E5%9B%B0-%E8%B3%A3%E5%9C%B0%E6%94%B6%E5%85%A5%E7%B8%AE24.

[61]Chen *et al.* (2018).

[62]Tan *et al.* (2022).

[63]Chang (2022).

[64]*Ibid.*

Stronger LGFVs can also change their sources of financing from trust funds to bank loans to restore credibility.

Related to both developers' loans and LGFVs are the structured financial products. Shadow banking products increased for the first time after 2.5 years by RMB100 billion in quarter 1 of 2020, but then shrank again by RMB540 billion in quarter 1 of 2021, making it 55.4% of GDP.[65] Again, due to the pandemic lockdown, the production chain and the logistics chain were severely affected, and SME borrowers were under severe liquidity stress, thus pushing up the delinquency rates of the structured products. It had been difficult for SME owners to pay the wages to their employees amid suspension of production and shipping the products abroad.

Added to this episode were the worsening productivity and business dynamics of private firms, particularly the younger ones.[66] Furthermore, SOEs should also be managed, particularly since a third of those are related to the property sector. Research has shown that zombie firms are highly related to SOEs, of which 30% are more likely to stay zombie in the following year, demonstrating overcapacity and misallocation of resources.[67,68] IMF suggests the removal of implicit guarantees of the SOEs.[69]

According to a recent survey, credit exposure started in 2020, and asset quality was affected once moratoria on loan repayments, government guarantees, and the pandemic-related measures were retreated.[70] This is especially true for new debts under public guarantee scheme (see Exhibit 1 of the report). Expected credit loss has increased while borrowers' resilience decreased after the pandemic.

[65] "Moody's — Chinese Shadow Banking Activity Grows for First Time Since 2017 as Economy-Wide Leverage Rises", June 24, 2020, and "Moody's — China's Shadow Banking Sector Falls Further Amid Regulatory Tightening", June 28, 2021, both as Research Announcements, Moody's Investor Service.
[66] Cerdeiro and Ruane (2022).
[67] According to Lam *et al.* (2017), firms are classified as "Zombies" when they have three consecutive years of losses, heavily leveraged, cannot meet environmental and technological standards, suspended production for six months or more, and unpaid utility bills.
[68] Lam *et al.* (2017).
[69] IMF (2022d).
[70] Bagaria *et al.* (2022), in the McKinsey & Company report on Risk & Resilience Practice.

As commented in the World Economic Outlook of April 2022, the continuous tightening policies on the highly leveraged developers and the strict city lockdowns aiming for zero-COVID policy would significantly slow down the Chinese economy.[71]

Actually, even before the pandemic, there had already been a default of SOE offshore bonds in December 2019 — Tewoo Group Co. Ltd. wholly owned by the city of Tianjin and Qinghai Provincial Investment Group Co. Ltd. wholly owned by Qinghai Province. In the same month, Inner Mongolia's LGFV also defaulted its onshore bond.[72] S&P Global also estimated that the offshore bond defaults had surged to 3.3%, and would be higher towards the end of 2022, at the peak of maturity of those bonds, although recovery from SOEs would be more likely than from private-owned enterprises (POEs), partly also because more of the POE bonds are in the real estate sector with deeper trouble.[73] Face values of bonds were indeed not paid. Defaults were replaced by negotiated extensions of the maturities.

Over two-thirds of the defaulted offshore bonds (106 of a total of 147) in 2020–May 2022 were from the real estate sector, which contrasted to only 1 out of 34 or 7 out of 43 in the period before 2015 and in 2015–2019, respectively. The situation of the onshore bonds is slightly better, with 58 of 237 bonds for the period 2020–May 2022 (compared to 0 before 2015 and 11 in 2015–2019).[74] IMF even considered the slowdown in China, due mainly to the risks from high leverages of property developers, high local government liabilities, high household debts, and therefore fragile banking system, is one of the reasons for a downside world economic outlook.[75] COVID-19 also adds to financial vulnerabilities.[76]

As analyzed in the "Global Banking Outlook — Midyear 2022" by the S&P Global, the Chinese economy's risk was adjusted from "positive" to "stable", as its property sector-related non-performing loans were forecasted to rise from 2.5% in 2021 to over 5% in 2022,

---

[71]IMF (2022c). In fact, similar comments from IMF have been made in various World Economic Outlook in previous quarters.
[72]Chu (2020).
[73]Chang *et al.* (2022).
[74]*Ibid.*
[75]IMF (2022c).
[76]Chapter 1 of IMF (2022e).

resulting in the largest amount of bank credit losses in the world, although the ratings of its banks were still stable.[77] Trouble ahead? If so, local or Global?

11.3.2. DCEP in China

China was the first mover in central bank digital currency (CBDC) and digital currency central payment (DCEP) with digital yuan, or e-CNY or e-RMB (yuan, RMB, and CNY, denoting Chinese Yuan, are always used interchangeably). What are the differences between CBDC, DECP, and digital yuan? Digital yuan is the Chinese CBDC, which is used for DCEP. CBDC is backed by the country's currency. Different from the general concept of CBDC, e-RMB is issued by the state-owned banks rather than its central bank, the People's Bank of China (PBOC). The CBDC project was started in 2014 by the PBOC, but has its pilot use only in 2021 in Shenzhen, Suzhou, Chengdu and Xiong'an, strategically covering the south, east, southwest, and the north east. Xiong'an is coined as a state-level new area in the southwest of Beijing, serving the Beijing–Tianjin–Hebei economic triangle. CBDC was later extended to other cities, including Shanghai.

The pilot test was experimented in selected physical stores like Starbucks and McDonald's, as well as online shopping platforms like JD.com. A big step in the pilot test was in the 2022 Winter Olympics in Beijing on virtually all transactions for everyone in the Olympic Village. More cities have been gradually included.[78] There are also an increasing number of online platforms and physical outlets joining the usage of e-yuan by using QR codes, and Near Field Communication (NFC) protocols, for electronic devices from both sides of the transaction. A transaction amount at the end of 2021 was just shy of RMB87.57 billion.[79] DCEP is not a direct constituent of shadow banking. It however is the medium for people to store value, which is linked to shadow banking, just like Alipay linked to Ant Financial.

[77]Released on July 21, 2022. Available at: https://www.spglobal.com/_assets/documents/ratings/research/101563908.pdf.
[78]Xinhua News Agency (2022).
[79]Ma *et al.* (2022).

11.3.3. The Death of P2P and the Issue of Big Techs

China's P2P sector used to be the largest in the world, and it only took 10 years to experience growth, exponential growth, a short maturity period, and then fast dying, to complete extinction. A totally different sector, but also within fintech is the expansion of the Big Tech, including their e-wallets, similar in usage to DCEP. These e-wallets are not problems in themselves. However, their extensive market penetration has caused high alert of the central government. What are these to do with the housing market? It turns out that both are sources of funding for partial downpayments. This is why both deserve to be discussed here.

11.3.3.1. *A run on P2P platforms*

The P2P platforms attracted funds from investors by paying high returns of as much as 4% per month in some cases. In the earlier years when there were very limited (if any) regulations, such as in 2013–2014, some of these platforms even loaned out like loan sharks to highly risky projects and charged very high double-digit rates and then guaranteed principal plus interest returns of 15% to investors (the average return rate in 2013 was as high as 21.3%, according to Wangdai Zhijia, the online platform database of all P2P platforms). Some of them used the funds to repay their own loans or invest in their own projects. Eventually, there was a run on these platforms in October 2013, resulting in a collapse of 75 platforms. Others operated a Ponzi scheme, attracting new funds to pay back existing lenders. This "new covers old" scheme went on and on, leading to losses for many investors. The infamous case of Ezubao at the end of 2015 was linked to 900,000 investors, lending more than RMB4 trillion each year in the preceding years. Subsequently, Minsheng Bank was the first to establish a bank P2P fund custodian platform in February 2015. Other platforms followed suit to put their funds with custodian institutions to increase credibility with investors.

Due to the economic downturn, many borrowers were not able to return the money, and more platforms defaulted or closed due to the newly enacted regulations in July 2015. Then in 2018, all platforms were required to register with a newly established uniform standard, which extended to 2019 when all platforms must be either national or regional platforms, according to the levels of paid-up capital thresholds. As more regulations were put in place (better late than never), the number of platforms decreased almost exponentially, especially after 2018, as seen in Chapter 7. By the end of 2019, there were only 343 platforms. Eventually, provincial governments were required to reduce the number of institutions and the scale of the sector. Finally, all P2P platforms completely vanished in mid-November 2020, ending a 10-year P2P history in China.[80]

11.3.3.2. *Crackdowns on Big Techs being too-big-to-fail*

Big techs in China, including Alibaba, Tencent, JD.com, DiDi, and Meituan, for example, have been driving extensive innovation, technology and e-commerce retail sales. Although there are other big techs, such as Huawei, Xiaomi, ByteDance and Baidu, we choose to focus on those providing mostly online platforms for transactions with monetary values and harder hit by the Chinese regulations in the last quarter of 2021.

We mentioned Ant Financial in Chapter 7. Tencent is another big tech, initially focused on interactive video games and social communication platform, WeChat. It later stretches into other sectors, such as cloud computing and fintech. JD.com is the largest online retailer in China. DiDi, the short form of DiDi Chuxing (Chuxing means “going out” in Chinese, “DiDi” is the sound of car honking its horn) started as the Chinese version of Uber. Etcetera, etcetera.

Several of them are related to shadow banking because their businesses facilitated personal deposit accumulation accounts. Examples that have been discussed are Yu’E Bao and WeChat red packets (or the TenPay, WeChat Pay which is also known as Weixin Pay, and QQ Wallet, all belonging to Tencent). Given the huge population in China, and the successful penetration of mobile payment, these accounts have gathered big funds that could be invested as WMPs. These big techs partner with both incumbent banks and other non-bank financial intermediaries (NBFIs) to offer WMPs and other financial products. It looks like the big techs can offer safe investment opportunities to their customers with minimal risks because their business profiles are much diversified, and they partner with major banks.

[80] Chong and Xie (2020).

Issues arise when one considers how much data and information they have held. Due to the large customer database from their e-tailing, they can fully utilize the big data to analyze customer preferences, financial backgrounds, creditworthiness, and personal details, very efficiently and effectively with their technologies that are supposed to be few of the best on earth. The upside is the soft information of clients is useful in evaluating creditworthiness, for instance, the downside is too much personal information. Ant Financial even stretched to financial inclusion by offering financing and consumption opportunities to remote areas in China.

Similar to the 16-month-long investigation by the U.S. House Judiciary Committee's antitrust panel on the "monopoly power" and data privacy of the big tech giants in the U.S., the Chinese government has also started tighter scrutiny on its big techs at about the same time when it cracked down the P2P industry in the last quarter of 2020. First, there are clear resolutions of fintech standards, business structure, and risk management, with the aim of governing mobile payments, fintech financing, and digital money. Ant Group, and its parent, Alibaba Group, as well as Tencent, were immediately affected. The would-be world's largest IPO of Ant Financial of USD37 billion in Hong Kong was halted just two days before its launch in November 2020, for reasons of regulatory compliance, regulatory arbitrage and antitrust. Alibaba was fined RMB18.23 billion (or USD2.8 billion) on April 10, 2021, due to antitrust.

The IPO suspension and then the anti-monopoly regulations offer very strong signals from the central government to govern the big tech sector, particularly because Alipay and WeChat Pay collectively dominated the online payment market, suggesting that they are "too big to fail" and possess high potential for substantial systemic risk. As a result, their stock prices slid. Within the 2 years thereafter, different big techs were subject to newer scrutinized regulations. On April 13, 2021, the regulatory bodies demanded Tencent, ByteDance, and 32 other internet platforms to perform comprehensive reviews and improvement plans on antitrust law. Tencent's blow was on its video games. Then, in August 2021, new rules were released to crack down on celebrity worships by teens; Douyin, the Chinese TikTok, was right on target. The last chronicle was on DiDi, with its IPO in the US stock market on June 30, 2021 halted.

Apparently, the central government is keen to suppress the power of the big techs and assure their proper service provision and innovation. After all, they all possess direct and indirect relations with the economy, either because they provide financial services through their fintech arms or they are targets of NBFI investments; any bailout will be very costly and will definitely quake the financial sector. It should nonetheless be noted that such a wave of scrutinizing policies coupled with the financial stresses from the property developers have posed increased uncertainty to the economic development.

11.4. What's Next?

We have seen what has happened over the past two decades, the first half leading to the Global Financial Crisis as covered in Chapter 9, and the second half up until the turn of the 2020s. While the COVID-19 pandemic is still defining the "new normal", the Russian invasion of Ukraine is not yet over, the Chinese debt issue and economic slowdown seem to be on the brink of losing control, and the western economies are facing potential stagflation (not to mention the prolonged and more frequent heatwaves due to global warming), we end this book by opining on the "collaboration" between housing markets and shadow banking in the near future. Will they move further from each other after the incidents in the past two decades? Or will they continue to get along well?

11.4.1. Housing

Housing markets in Europe encountered similar situations to those in the U.S. People found that there is a new shift in appreciation of homeownership amid remote working. The pandemic also caused households to save more. Simultaneously, supply cannot pick up also for reasons resulting from the pandemic. However, property prices are on the surge in several countries for another reason. Large institutional investors, many from overseas, have turned away from offices and retail to target residential investments. Many other countries in Asia, North, Central and South America, and Australasia, have also undergone price surges to record levels in 2020.[81]

---

[81] Arnold *et al.* (2021).

As reported by OECD, households in the current generation have paid much more to be homeowners relative to previous generations. Similar comments have also been given by Demographia. Of course, this is before the interest hikes by the Federal Reserve — seven times with a total increment of 4.25% in just 2022 — and before many governments have to combat the serious inflation and perhaps stagflation.

Housing markets in China are cooling off, in part because of the government policies and also because of lower demand. It might be due to (un)affordability in top-tier cities or loss of confidence that the heavily indebted developers could eventually complete the construction and deliver the presale units. It might also be the case of high homeownership rate. A research paper found that 90% households own at least one property and 35% own more.[82] When the market is almost saturated and the aging population continues to expand, there will not be much room for new demand. Due to the pandemic, China has already announced in May 2022 monetary and fiscal measures that amount to USD5.3 trillion, which is one-third of its GDP, albeit smaller than the stimulus in the first round of the pandemic outbreak in 2020.[83]

11.4.2. Will Housing and Shadow Banks Stay Together?

The interactions of house price growth, shadow banking and securitization have not been as strong or as dangerous lately as they were in the run up to the GFC. Shadow banking is still mostly about regulatory arbitrage. Housing and shadow banking get together as long as arbitrage related to housing lasts. Housing has been a sector open to shadow banking around the world, primarily because it is usually good collateral within a sound legal structure but not always well-served by traditional banks.

In the U.S., for example, market regulations made subprime loans profitable despite not having access to deposit insurance.

---

[82]Wheatley (2020).

[83]Bloomberg (2022). China's Stimulus Tops $5 Trillion as Covid Zero Hits Economy, May 20, 2022. Available at: https://www.bloomberg.com/news/articles/2022-05-19/china-s-stimulus-tops-5-trillion-as-covid-zero-batters-economy#xj4y7vzkg.

The subprime market has mostly crashed and not resurged. Along with it are the related structures, like CDOs, that are either gone or supported by safer assets. It is not likely that shadow banks will return for housing any time soon. Currently, almost all mortgage lending has access to deposit insurance or guarantees of some sort, making bank runs unlikely. The next GFC will most likely be triggered from somewhere else.

The verdict is still out in China, where shadow banks are about the same and continue to fund housing. Overall, shadow banking in China is very regulation-driven. From the years of ensuing and ensuring economic growth amid the GFC when different forms of shadow banking instruments and vehicles such as WMPs and LGFVs were heavily promoted, to the P2P sector that was allowed to grow freely in the 2010s, and then its total eradication by end of 2020, and from the blow to the big techs with antitrust rules in October and November of 2020 following the "common prosperity" policy, to the regulations aiming to crack down real estate market speculation that led to shortage of funds to property developers in 2021. Any government policies scrutinizing either shadow banking or the housing sector will impact the other, and then the economy. For example, regulating the housing markets had shaken shadow banking (e.g. LGFVs), and local economies, which in turn had to be resolved by the government. Obviously, a difference between the Chinese story and the rest is the heavy involvement of the central government all along, not just at the end when there would be problems.

What has come together, post pandemic, in both the West, particularly the U.S., and China is shadow banks' fellow travelers, i.e. conduits that use technology to bring buyers together and to evaluate risk. They produce risks that are not too different from those of shadow banks earlier. One risk is obfuscation. Modelers, using mathematics and technology (particularly IT), can often complicate simple structures, making them into something seemingly profitable, but are too complicated for their risk levels to be assessed by laymen or even seasoned investors. The second, which is related to the first, is that there is still plenty of potential for moral hazard. If something seems too good to be true, it probably is!

Finally, this book has covered the "housing markets meet securitized (shadow) banking" story, how they danced and how they have evolved. We posted a preview in the Introduction with the U.S. playing Pink Floyd's "we don't need no education", echoing the ignorance and arrogance that came to housing finance at the turn of the millennium, and then evolved into something closer to Sinatra, calmer and steadier (as the economy grew steadily for over a decade). However, "one more for the road" signals that maybe there is still danger ahead.

In China, it was a steady three-step waltz that avoided bubbles and crashes. Then there were changes in instruments, forming new channels, new tools and new support for shadow banks. More recently, however, the music has become somewhat discordant as the shadow banks began to look like trouble. It will be up to the central government to play the music that leads the dance.

Epilogue: 2022

Leftovers from the Pandemic and New Surprises

2008 is a number that appeals greatly to Chinese. "2" sounds like "easy" in Cantonese, "love" in Mandarin (or Putonghua); "0" being "miraculous"; "8" is, the most well-known, "making a fortune". Leading to 2009, "9" means "long-lived", again superstitiously good. But 2008–2009 was far from good! It marked the Global Financial Crisis, leading to the European Debt Crisis. Fast-forward to February 2, 2020! How often can a date be beautifully written as 2020 0202 or 0202 2020? Unfortunately, while still within the Chinese New Year, this date was already part of the massive COVID-19 lockdown in China. Fast-forward again, this time to February 24, 2022. Still looking quite beautiful in writing, this is the day the Russian Invasion of Ukraine started. Oh well!

The world economy is in turmoil as we wind up the book. Worldwide output is slowing, if not falling; inflation has risen sharply. Housing markets in the U.S. and Europe develop differently from that of China once again. What then are the prospects beyond 2022 for the housing and financial markets, amid the winding down of the pandemic and the advent of the Ukraine war? The war that has shaken the globe is behind surging prices for oil, energy, metal, and crops. Meanwhile, China, the only major economy having positive GDP growth in the pandemic year 2020, has evolved into one sticking to a zero-COVID policy for three whole years, then having credit risk problems, with big property developers at the edge of default, and an economy-wide slowdown. The U.S. economy is also in a slowdown and may be headed for a recession, but it is also in the midst of a strong labor market (3.5% unemployment rate).

Do current problems resemble the GFC? Here, we take a brief look, with focus on background information from recent events as they might "set the table" for what happens next. Key data points are the rising inflation almost everywhere, except in China, and the seeds of a recession in the U.S. and slower growth in China. However, at least in the case of the U.S., this is not because of a fragile financial structure as in 2007, but rather because of high interest rates raised by the Fed in response to the inflation. Its labor market continues to be strong and inflation is slowing at the beginning of 2023, but the verdict is out on how bumpy the landing will be. While China does not have much inflation, it is also undergoing an unusual slowdown, relative to its recent history.

2022

February 2022 is the month when Russia started shelling Ukraine.[1] Countries of the European Union, the U.K., the U.S., and several others started their economic sanctions on Russia. The war in Ukraine had further pushed food, grains, metal, and energy prices up. March is the month when most countries around had opened up their borders for international traveling, while Shanghai, China, experienced a massive lockdown for 2 months. It would be hard to imagine such an important city being forced to a standstill, causing another round of supply chain crisis, at least in China. When more countries started to pick up in the summer of 2021, China started to undergo slowdown in August.[2] The National Bureau of Statistics of China estimated that economic growth was 2.5% for the first half of 2022, of which Quarter 2 was only 0.4%, the lowest since the beginning of the

[1]The Annexation of Crimea started almost the same day 8 years ago.

[2]As reported by Lau (2021), fixed-asset investment grew by 10.3% in the first 7 months in 2021, but 8.9% in the first 8 months.

COVID-19 pandemic in January 2020. As of July 2022, an annual growth of 5.5% for the whole of 2022 was considered to be a challenging target.[3] What else happened?

The Ukraine War

At the beginning of the Russian invasion of Ukraine, not many people expected that it would last for more than a few months. About 2 months after the war began, McKinsey & Company reported a survey in five European countries (Germany, France, UK, Italy, and Spain) that the COVID-19 pandemic was only the third problem that people worried about.[4] The first far more worrying problem was the rising prices, followed by the war. Respondents were pessimistic about economic development, with the degree of pessimism higher than the big hit by the pandemic. When the same survey was done again in June, COVID-19 went down to be the fifth concern.[5] The most worrying concerns were still rising prices, followed by the war, with the U.K. having the most worries about rising prices among the five countries. But the third and fourth had become unemployment and extreme weather. For real estate, though, the perception was that rent and mortgage expenditures were relatively stable. Then inflation accelerated. It is now the case in the U.S. that rents have been increasing faster than prices in general.

---

[3]2022 is a year with some remarkable events. One event that is not related to either the housing market or shadow banking, but a big one, is the assassination of Shinzo Abe, the longest serving prime minister of Japan who once led Japan out of a two-decade stagnation (his policies in reviving the economy was called Abenomics).

[4]McKinsey & Company survey on "How Inflation and the Conflict in Ukraine are Impacting European Consumers" released on May 26, 2022. Available at: https://www.mckinsey.com/business-functions/growth-marketing-and-sales/our-insights/survey-european-consumer-sentiment-during-the-coronavirus-crisis.

[5]McKinsey & Company survey on "European Consumers Increasingly React to the Stress of Rising Prices" released on July 14, 2022. Available at: https://www.mckinsey.com/business-functions/growth-marketing-and-sales/our-insights/survey-european-consumer-sentiment-during-the-coronavirus-crisis?cid=other-eml-alt-mip-mck&hdpid=b9d44e54-fb73-4c99-b0cc-512f766579a7&hctky=12069925&hlkid=4311bfac5b9c4a1cb776f28de1a89405.

The war has induced supply-side shocks that have likely caused most of the recent inflation, and relative slowdowns in several European countries that rely on Russia for crude oil and natural gas. Ukraine alone supplies over 40% of sunflower oil, double-digit percentage of wheat, barley and maize, which are the crucial food of many European, Middle East, and African countries, especially those poor economies.[6,7] In addition, Russia and Ukraine also export fertilizers composed of nitrogen, phosphorous, and potassium, making up 28% of the global supply.[8] Natural gas is needed to make fertilizer. This implies less food produce because of less fertilizers and higher food prices for the same reason. The supply chain crisis caused by the COVID-19 pandemic had already caused a surge in food prices by 28% in 2020 and then 23% in 2021. The war has caused a rise of 17% in February and March 2022 alone.

What many people had not expected was that the war has also affected the production of chips for digital devices and electric vehicles. Ukraine supplies most of neon, krypton, and xenon, which are gases needed for the production of chips. This is on top of the shortage of chips supplied globally during and after the pandemic. One can imagine its impact in this digital world where our daily lives and AI cannot be separated. Another story is the shortage of nickel, lithium and other materials that are needed to produce batteries for electric vehicles. Platinum and palladium are needed for parts of combustion engines of cars that reduce the concentration of air pollutants for producing vehicles running on hydrogen. Not only has the war delayed the net-zero transition as a result, but it has also affected global trade. For example, BMW and Audi were not able to send their new cars to their customers in China because of fear of car damages due to the war or confiscation by Russia using the railway passage for shipment in April 2022.[9] Overall, countries have found

---

[6]McKinsey & Company survey on "How Inflation and the Conflict in Ukraine are Impacting European Consumers" released on May 26, 2022.

[7]IMF (2022f) more precisely stated that Ukraine and Russia together supply more than half of sunflower oil, 25% of global export of wheat, and one-fifth of barley and maize.

[8]Domm (2022).

[9]Reuters, "BMW, Audi suspend shipments by train to China due to Ukraine war", April 26, 2022. Available at: https://www.reuters.com/business/autos-transportation/bmw-audi-suspend- shipments-by-train-china-nikkei-2022-04-26/.

it harder to meet the COP26 targets against global warming and to tackle messy logistics along with inflation.

China and the Pandemic

The Chinese Zero-COVID policy has turned from a successful beginning to a less successful ending. China was the only major economy having positive GDP growth in 2020. But city-wide lockdowns even with minimal outbreaks for three whole years had exhausted the public everywhere in the country. However, unlike many other countries that have moved to "business as usual", China was hit by a new and much more contagious wave of COVID-19, which was why it was determined to achieve a "Zero-COVID" policy. The omicron variant caused a complete lockdown in Shenzhen for 1 week in March 2022 and then in Shanghai for 2 months starting on March 28, 2022, pausing a lot of commercial activities and the logistics industry. This had further held back growth. As some economists joked, "We have not had a haircut for 3 months. I will not make it up by having three haircuts within the next month! The foregone business of hairdressing would never be made up".

The predictable slowdown of housing markets has certainly not helped developers solve their maturing loans in Quarter 2 of 2022. This time, however, the central bank did not cut the Required Reserve Rate (RRR) by as much. Also, other measures to stimulate the economy such as subsidies to rental markets or housing provident funds and loans to SMEs in 2020 were very minimal and not widely implemented across the country in 2022, although there was a stimulus package tailored to support the worst-affected sectors on May 31.[10]

As Kristalina Georgieva, the Chair and Managing Director of the IMF, addressed at the opening of the Boao Forum for Asia Annual Conference 2022, a prolonged slowdown of this second largest economy posed significant spillover effect to other countries.[11] To see the

---

[10] Moody's (2022). Government Policy — China: Credit Pressure Rises for Wide Range of Issuers as Omicron Outbreak Hurts Growth, Moody's Investors Service, June 14, 2022.

[11] Speech by Kristalina Georgieva for the Opening Plenary at the Boao Forum for Asia Annual Conference 2022 on April 20, 2022. Available at: https://www.imf.org/en/News/Articles/2022/04/20/sp042022-boao-forum-for-asia-annual-conference-2022.

importance of China's economic growth, again according to IMF, each additional 1% growth in China can bring about 0.3% additional growth in other countries.[12] In 2021, the Chinese GDP growth was 8.1%, a sharp contrast to other developed countries hard hit by the COVID-19 pandemic. However, IMF had to adjust the estimated GDP growth of China for 2022 downward from 4.8% on 28 January to 4.4% on 19 April and to 3.2% on November 23, 2022.[13]

In response, the People's Bank of China started a series of reductions in the prime loan rate (LPR). Funds were spared to help housing developers. At the same time, home-purchase regulations were loosened, and lockdowns were more focused on buildings rather than cities. However, multinational corporations have been reluctant to continue locating main offices in China. International trade has also been affected as international corporations could no longer wait for the Chinese factories to be reopened from repeated lockdowns; they had to find substitutes in other Southeast Asian countries.

The negative sentiment from the very unpleasant lockdown experience and the psychological impact have helped build a negative atmosphere for the economy. Policymakers were well aware of the rapidly increasing leverage and speculation and had to worry about debt and financial instability. Their main focus was on infrastructure and supporting technology and innovation. The greatly pressured local governments in maintaining economic growth meant that the LGFV loans were also under stress of refinancing, like the property developers. Unfortunately, the negative energy is unlikely to be boosted with the strategy of easing the housing market which worked well in the past. The costly 3-year zero-COVID policy was brought

[12] IMF news article, "China's Economy is Rebounding, But Reforms Are Still Needed", by Diego A. Cerdeiro and Sonali Jain-Chandra, February 3, 2023. Available at: https://www.imf.org/en/News/Articles/2023/02/02/cf-chinas-economy-is-rebounding-but-reforms-are-still-needed#:~:text=China's%20economy%20is%20set%20to,boost%20to%20the%20global%20economy.

[13] The January estimate is reported in "IMF Says China's Economic Imbalances Have Worsened" by *Wall Street Journal* on January 28, 2022. Available at: https://www.wsj.com/articles/imf-says-chinas-economic-imbalances-have-worseened-11643356801. The estimate in April and November are from the IMF website: https://www.imf.org/en/Countries/CHN.

to an end when there were (rarely seen) massive protests in different cities in late November 2022 after tragic incidents of virus-infected and sick people not being saved in time because of lockdowns. The previously stringent policies were gradually relaxed or removed. The Chinese border was eventually opened in January 2023.

Financial Conditions

Stock markets have performed poorly, mostly down by 15% or more in the first half of 2022. S&P 500 even plummeted by 21%, which is the largest half-year loss in over 50 years, sharply contrasting the rally in 2021.[14] Another signal is the U.S. inverted yield curve — the 2-year and 10-year Treasury note yields were 3.23% and 3.03%, respectively, on July 20, 2022, which usually suggests expectations of a weakening economy.

Goldman Sachs releases the Global Financial Conditions Index, while the Financial Stability Board also releases Global Financial Conditions. Figure 1 depicts the latter in the April 2022 Global Financial Stability Report (GFSR) on the top left, which approximates the Goldman Sachs Global Financial Conditions Index on the bottom right. The two series are not directly comparable both in terms of measures and units. Nevertheless, they can provide some idea of the worrisome financial conditions leading to 2022. For the GFSR index, positive values imply tightening economic conditions. Similarly, a higher Goldman Sachs Index value refers to more economic tightening. Both exhibit high (i.e. tightening) values in 2020, mostly from the first quarter due to the pandemic, and then slid down in most of 2021. The sharp increase of the Goldman Sachs Index completes the story of recent tightening, which has continued in 2022.

Overall, as described in the World Economic Outlook 2022 (IMF, 2022a), the COVID-19 pandemic and the Ukraine war have widened the wealth gap between the advanced economies and the emerging and poorer ones. Vaccines, for one, have not been evenly distributed. The shortage of food and energy made the developing economies

---

[14] Jackson (2022).

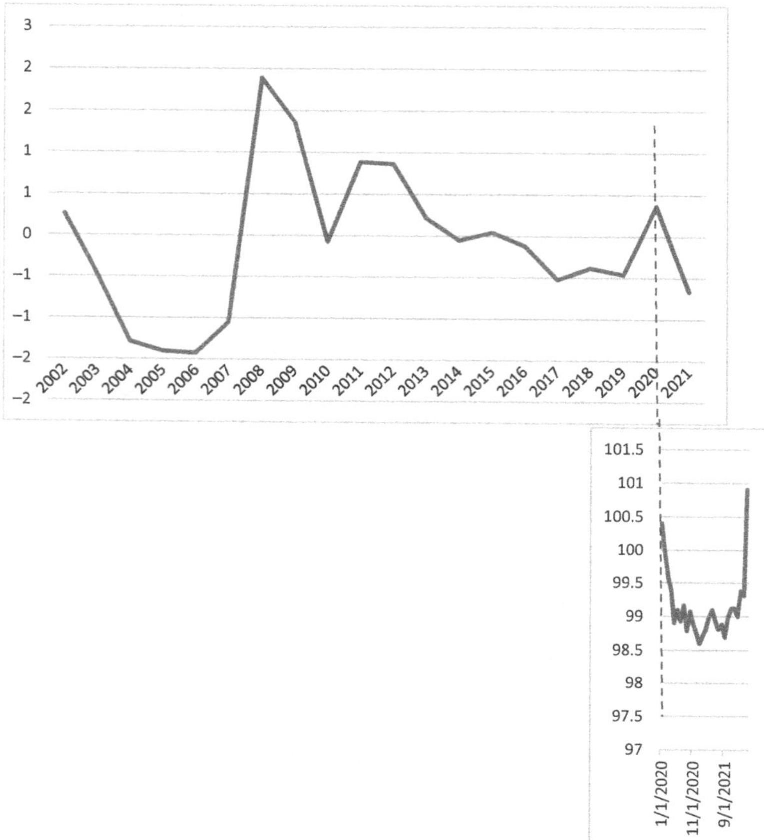

Figure 1 Global Financial Conditions
Note: The top graph is from the Global Financial Stability Report, while the bottom one is from the Goldman Sachs Global Financial Conditions Index.

more susceptible to shocks. China's frequent lockdowns had also disrupted the global supply chains, even if temporary.

Housing and Housing Finance

What were the changes in mortgage markets? Defaults have increased and will probably continue increasing as house prices growth slow and may even fall. There have been some institutional/market changes as well, which we cover here.

Mortgages

Lending has continued to become more conservative. Of the new mortgages in the U.S. in the first quarter of 2022, only 2% were to subprime borrowers.[15] Delinquency rates (i.e. mortgage payments due for 30 or more days) also dropped in February 2022 to 3.2%, which is the lowest since January 1999.[16] Defaults probably will go up, not because of the structure of loans, but because of the monetary policy of raising rates, complicating affordability. This is common across countries.

Two-thirds of Canadians already considered housing unaffordable in their communities in a recent survey.[17] That was before the interest hike of 0.5% on June 1, 2022, and then another "big" 1% on July 13, 2022, in reaction to the high inflation, bringing the Bank of Canada overnight rate to 2.5% in August 2022.

The housing market in the U.K. continued to be hot in June 2022, with a growth rate up 9.3% from the same month the previous year, after six consecutive monthly increases (even though housing prices in Scotland and Wales had started to drop).[18] The price hike was due to lack of supply. However, interest rate increases have

---

[15]Federal Reserve Bank of New York (2022). Total Household Debt Increases in Q1 2022, Driven by Mortgage and Auto Balances, Press Release, May 10, 2022. Available at: https://www.corelogic.com/intelligence/u-s-delinquencies-drop-to-lowest-level-in-more-than-23-years-in-february/; https://www.newyorkfed.org/newsevents/news/research/2022/20220510#:~:text=Housing%20Debt,average%20seen%20between%202003%2D2007.

[16]CoreLogic (2022). U.S. Delinquencies Drop to Lowest Level in More than 23 Years in February. *Loan Performance Insights Report Highlights*, February 2022, May 10, 2022. Available at: https://www.corelogic.com/intelligence/u-s-delinquencies-drop-to-lowest-level-in-more-than-23-years-in-february/.

[17]Canadian Press (2022). Nearly 1 in 4 Homeowners Say They'd Have to Sell Home If Interest Rates Rise More, According to Survey, June 13, 2022.

[18]Howard and Michael (2022), referring to the study by Rightmove, the largest online real estate website in the UK.

caused 20% increases in monthly mortgage payments for new home-buyers relative to that at the beginning of the year. In September and October, U.K. has undergone three prime ministers within seven weeks (and five prime ministers in 6 years!). By the end of the year, U.K. narrowly avoided a recession, and housing prices dropped slowly month-on-month, but not by much. U.K. house prices have fallen for five straight months, and expectations are glum.

China — Solutions from the Government, Again

Systemic risk from the less regulated shadow banking sector is still a concern in China. The striking incident of the four rural banks in Henan and Anhui Provinces that rejected depositors' withdrawals and turned into a protest (see footnote 54 of Chapter 11 for more information) is one of the alarms that shadow banking activities in more suburban areas far away from the central government might have brought a lot of problematic operations to light. It has been revealed that depositors' money was drawn by online platforms from everywhere in the country, in response to high deposit rates, to support possibly excessively risky lending projects, some of which even belong to criminal gangs.

In June 2022, the central government gave a green light for Ant Financial to process its IPO again.[19] Another piece of news released on July 25, 2022, is the plan for establishing a real estate fund worth up to USD 44 billion, to be initially funded by China Construction Bank (one of the four the state-owned bank) and the People's Bank of China, to help the property developers to resolve their debt crisis.[20] The initial amount would be about USD 7.3 billion from the China Construction Bank and USD 4.4 billion from the People's Bank of China. It was also speculated that other banks will also join to chip in to the trust fund sooner or later, as the amount needed to save the property developers is huge. Other non-bank financial institutions might also join in, and the rescue would take a few years to complete. Which developers to help, on top of those ten biggest ones,

[19] Zhu (2022).
[20] Jim (2022).

will have to be decided by the local governments. Then on November 21, 2022, the People's Bank of China and the China Banking and Insurance Regulatory Commission (CBIRC) jointly launched an RMB200 billion loan quota scheme to support the completion of presold projects.[21]

These pieces of news are gestures from the central government to boost the economy. In the case of saving the developers, there is a new problem. Consumers have been losing appetite for new housing units and instead opt for second-hand units amid the bad experience from the almost defaulting developers. Demographics with slow or negative population growth also suggest low demand for new houses. Finally, the big policy dilemma is the tension between regulating markets to keep them stable and letting markets work to allocate resources better. China has been moving away from market solutions.

Monetary Policy

The U.S., along with most of the rest of the world, has become quite concerned about inflation. The Fed has been raising its policy rate (the Fed Funds rate) in an effort to combat the worst inflation since the 1980s before it becomes embedded in market expectations, and therefore harder to bring down. Though the labor market is still hot and unemployment is still low, high interest rates will slow it down. Due to interest rate hikes, the rate on 30-year fixed-rate mortgages has already gone up to over 6%, more than doubled since December 2021. Residential construction costs went up 19%. Typical monthly mortgage payments climbed 45% in 2021, and have further increased in 2022, according to the National Association of Realtors.

Figure 2 shows the 30-year FRM, the 15-year FRM, and the 5/1 ARM rates for the year before the first massive hike of 0.5% on May 4, 2022.[22] The last one represents a hybrid mortgage made up of a fixed rate for the first 5 years, and an adjustable-rate mortgage (ARM) thereafter. The mortgage market has responded to news about the

[21] S&P Global Webinar on "China's LGFV Land Grab: Things That Can't Last Won't" on November 23, 2022.

[22] The first raise on 17 March was 25 basis points. It was speculated that there would be another 0.75% in 2023.

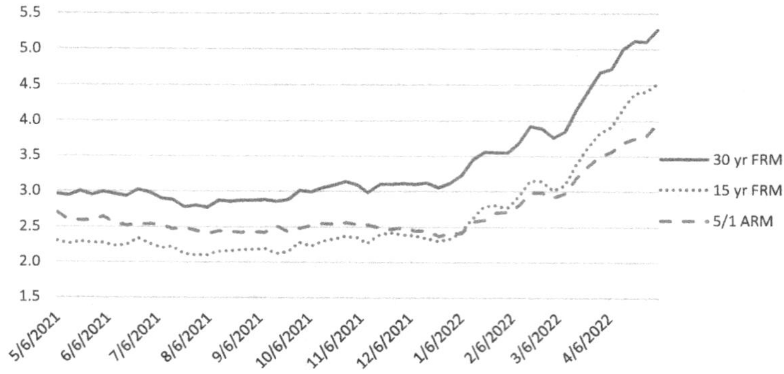

Figure 2 U.S. Mortgage Rates in the Year Before the May 2022 Interest Rate Hike

Source: Freddie Mac.

interest hikes even before they actually happened. The 5/1 ARM is the closest among the three to the ARM that follows the market rates closely. The increased gap between the 30-year rate and the 5/1 ARM probably comes from the expectation that high rates are likely to fall later, which makes the prepayment option more valuable and increases the spread relative to less-callable bonds (see Section 4 of Chapter 4).

Recall in Chapter 3 how higher mortgage rates mean that rents (real and imputed) are discounted at higher rates, causing a decline in prices, followed by a decline in production over time. Note that longer-term assets are more sensitive to interest rate changes. This kind of monetary policy is a classic (and disruptive) way of slowing down both inflation and the economy through housing markets.

The Fed raised Fed Funds rate seven times in 2022 to 4.50%. This has indeed slowed down home sales, the size of the mortgage market and housing production, and house prices are falling, as expected. Figure 3 is a count of the number of central banks worldwide that changed interest rates throughout 2022. Obviously, inflation has hit both advanced and emerging economies. Although not every country increased rates, no advanced economy cuts rates.

Another Crisis? Or Not?

The mid-2010s saw housing markets worldwide starting to pick up, and creating momentum again towards the end and leading to 2020.

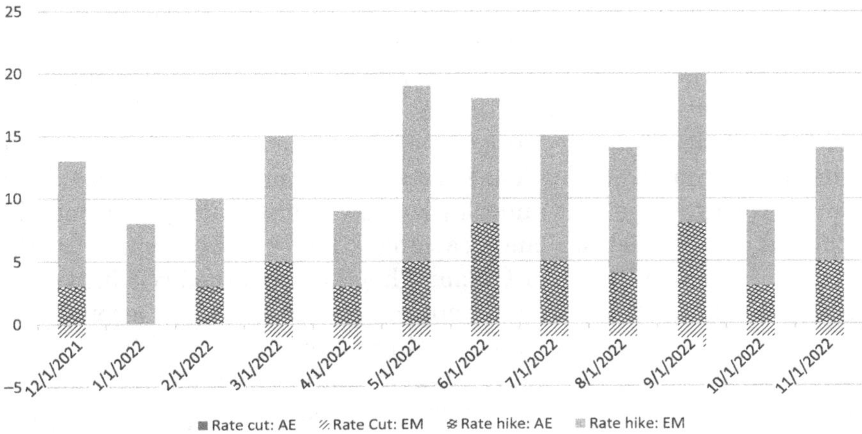

Figure 3 Number of Central Banks Changing Rates

Note: AE = Advanced economies; EM = Emerging Markets.

Source: IMF. Available at: https://www.imf.org/en/Blogs/Articles/2022/12/16/the-global-economy-turbulent-year-in-five-charts?utm_medium=email&utm_source=govdelivery.

Are bubbles building up again? Will there be another crisis? If so, are we ready? Is this time different?

This time probably is different. First, the housing bubble before the GFC was generated by lax lending standards and overly optimistic markets, subsequently defaulting in the face of a turnaround in the housing market, and by shadow banks, which were sources of moral hazard. Subprime mortgages constitute a much smaller portion now, and shadow banks are no longer much of an issue. Second, the previous boom resulted in oversupply. That is not the case this time (at least not when the time this book is completed) as production has lagged for a decade.[23] At any rate, there has been house price momentum, but not a bubble yet.

The Ukraine war and its side effects have indeed set the table for a recession, but the table is different. This time the downturn will not be due to the financial system, which is mostly operating as it should, albeit at higher levels of interest rates. It is higher interest rates coming from the policy decision to go after inflation that threatens housing. What we have been seeing is not much about

[23]Keys (2021).

increased demand from easy lending. It is more like a result of supply shocks that raised prices and lowered growth.

As far as shadow banking is concerned, two considerations for the near future stand out. First, at least for now, global non-bank financial institutions have lower leverage and improved liquidity and funding.[24] Second, shadow banking is less incentivized this time. The regulatory arbitrage that underlay shadow banks in the past is mostly gone due to regulations and learning about what does not work. Shadow banks still exist in China. They have experienced increased credit losses and are becoming more regulated. As they become regulated, they are less of shadows and more of banks.

What is left is technology-based market-making and underwriting. We do not know their risks yet. The recent collapse of FTX suggests that moral hazard is a non-trivial problem. However, it is not a big part of the housing finance story. What is left in the U.S. is a more stable housing finance system with the Agencies and insured

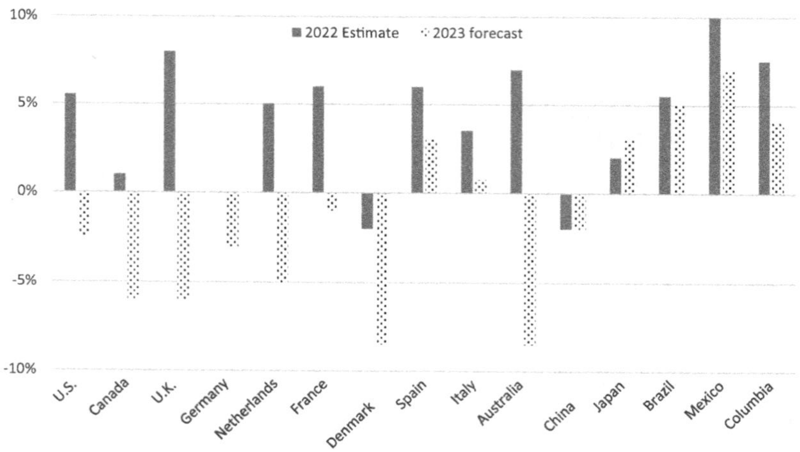

Figure 4 Nominal Changes in Home Prices — 2022 Estimates and 2023 Forecasts

Note: The 2023 forecasts are midpoints between high and low forecasts.

Source: Fitch Ratings "Global Housing And Mortgage Outlook — 2023", December 2022.

[24]Fitch Ratings 2022 Mid-Year Outlook: Global Non-Bank Financial Institutions, report released in June 2022.

banks taking the bulk of the risks. While this may or may not be the most efficient way of allocating resources, it does not signal instability. In China, there are risks to institutions (shadow banks) along with a considerable increase in the use of technology. But the main problem with the Chinese system is the tendency to overregulate and misallocate capital.

None of this looks like anything close to the GFC. With hindsight, it looks like the interaction among housing, shadow banks and risky securitization deals was just an episode. Perhaps predictable, it is certainly one that has run its course for now. Something similar may well occur later, probably in a different financial context, but not just yet.

We close with Figure 4, which shows the 2022 estimates and 2023 forecasts of changes in home prices in various countries.

References

Acemoglu, Daron, Asuman Ozdaglar, and Alireza Tahbaz-Salehi (2015). Systemic Risk and Stability in Financial Networks, *American Economic Review*, 105(2), 564–608.

Acharya, Viral V., and Matthew Richardson (Ed.) (2009). *Restoring Financial Stability: How to Repair a Failed System*, An Independent View from New York University Stern School of Business, John Wiley & Sons, March 2009.

Acharya, Viral V, Thorsten Beck, Douglas D Evanoff, George G Kaufman and Richard Portes (Ed.) (2013). *The Social Value of the Financial Sector: Too Big to Fail or Just too Big?*, World Scientific Studies in International Economics, World Scientific Publishing Company.

Adams, Brian, Lara Loewenstein, Hugh Montag, and Randal J. Verbrugge (2022). Disentangling Rent Index Differences: Data, Methods, and Scope. Working Paper No. 22–38. Federal Reserve Bank of Cleveland. Available at: https://doi.org/10.26509/frbc-wp-202238.

Akeroff, George A. (1970). The Market for "Lemons": Quality Uncertainty and the Market Mechanism, *The Quarterly Journal of Economics*, 84(3), 488–500.

Allen, Franklin, and Douglas Gale (2007). *Understanding Financial Crises*, Clarendon Lectures In Finance, Oxford University Press, Oxford.

Allen, Franklin, Yiming Qian, Guoqian Tu, and Frank Yu (2019). Entrusted Loans: A Close Look at China's Shadow Banking System, *Journal of Financial Economics*, 133(1), 18–41.

Anderson, Brett (2022). The Business Lunch May Be Going out of Business, *New York Times*, July 11, 2022. Available at: https://www.nytimes.com/2022/07/11/dining/business-lunch-restaurants.html?te=1&nl=updates-from-the-newsroom&emc=edit_ufn_20220715.

Andersson-Manjang, Simon K., and Nika Naghavi (2021). *State of the Industry Report on Mobile Money 2022*, GSMA, London, United Kingdom.

Arestis, Philip, and Maggie Mo Jia (2019). Financing Housing and House Prices in China, *Journal of Financial Economic Policy*, 12(4), 445–461.

Arnold, Martin, Colby Smith, and Matthew Rocco (2021). House Prices Climb to Record Levels in US and Europe, *Financial Times*, June 23, 2021. Available at: https://www.ft.com/content/3082fe00-cdb7-4eb9-ab2d-2309b9848114.

Ashcraft, Adam, and Til Schuermann. (2008) Understanding the Securitization of Subprime Mortgage Credit, *Foundations and Trends in Finance*, 2(3) (July 2008).

Asian Development Bank (2014). *Access to Finance: Microfinance Innovations in the People's Republic of China*, Asian Development Bank, Philippines.

Awanis, Arame, Christopher Lowe, Simon K. Andersson-Manjang, and Dominica Lindsey (2022). *State of the Industry Report on Mobile Money 2021*, GSMA, London, United Kingdom.

Bagaria, Avani, Juan Antonio Bahillo, Radhika Chopra, Andreas Kremer, Mario Nargi, Kris Ramana, Olivier Salome, and George Sotiropoulos (2022). *IFRS 9 Models in Financial Instruments and Impairment Regulations: The New Reality and Lessons Learned*, McKinsey's Risk & Resilience Practice, McKinsey & Company, May 2022.

Balding, Christopher, (2013). How Badly Flawed Is Chinese Economic Data? The Opening Bid Is $1 Trillion, August 14, 2013. Available at SSRN: https://ssrn.com/abstract=2307054 or http://dx.doi.org/10.2139/ssrn.2307054.

Basar, Joe, Casper Bel, Roman Belotserkovskiy, Ezra Greenberg, Marta Mussacaleca, Juan Sarmiento, and Jan Vandaele (2022). *Full-Potential Procurement: Lessons Amid Inflation and Volatility*, McKinsey & Company, April 2022.

Batarags, Lina (2021). China Has at least 65 Million Empty Homes — Enough to House Population of France. It Offers a Glimpse into the Country's Massive Housing Market Problem, *Business Insider*, October 14, 2021. Available at: https://www.businessinsider.com/china-empty-homes-real-estate-evergrande-housing-market-problem-2021-10.

Baum, Andrew (2017). *PropTech 3.0: The Future of Real Estate*, Said Business School, University of Oxford, Oxford, United Kingdom, April 2017.

Baum, Andrew, Andrew Saull, and Fabian Braesemann (2020). *PropTech 2020: The Future of Real Estate*, Said Business School, University of Oxford, Oxford, United Kingdom, February 2020.

BBC (2022). China Ride-Hailing Giant DiDi Fined $1.2 Bn after Probe, *BBC News*, July 22, 2022. Available at: https://www.bbc.com/news/business-62248513.

Bidar, Musadiz, and Dan Patterson (2022). Virtual Land Rush Is Driving up the Cost of Space in the Metaverse, *CBS News*, May 6, 2022. Available at: https://www.cbsnews.com/news/metaverse-real-estate-companies-land-rush/.

Billio, Monica, Mila Getmansky Sherman, Dale F. Gray, Andrew W. Lo, Robert C. Merton, and Loriana Pelizzon (2014). Sovereign, Bank and Insurance Credit Spreads: Connectedness and System Networks, Systemic Risk Tomography (SYRTO) Working Paper Series, Working Paper No. 8.

Black, Angela, Patricia Fraser, and Martin Hoesli (2006). House Prices, Fundamental and Bubbles, *Journal of Business Finance and Accounting*, 33(9–10), 1535–1555.

Black, Fischer, and Myron Scholes (1973). The Pricing of Options and Corporate Liabilities, *Journal of Political Economy*, 81(2), 637–654.

Blake, David P. (2022). The Great Game Will Never End: Why the Global Financial Crisis Is Bound to Be Repeated, *Journal of Risk and Financial Management*, 15(6), 245. DOI: https://doi.org/10.3390/jrfm15060245.

Blinder, Alan S. (2013). *After the Music Stopped: The Financial Crisis, the Response, and the Work Ahead*, The Penguin Press, London.

Bloomberg (2021a). China to Overhaul Education Sector 'Hijacked by Capital', Bloomberg Asia Edition, July 26, 2021. Available at: https://www.bloomberg.com/news/articles/2021-07-25/china-to-overhaul-private-education-sector-hijacked-by-capital.

Bloomberg (2021b). China's Xi Says Common Prosperity Doesn't Mean Full Equality, *Bloomberg News*, October 15, 2021.

Bloomberg (2022). More Chinese Homebuyers Refuse to Pay Mortgage Loans Amid Contagion Fears, *Bloomberg News*, July 14, 2022.

Borst, Nicholas (2022). How Strong Is China's Household Balance Sheet? Prevailing Winds, Seafarer Funds. Available at: http://www.seafarerfunds.com/prevailing-winds/chinas-household-balance-sheet/.

Bradley, Chris, Wonsik Choi, Jeongmin Seong, Ben Stretch, Oliver Tonby, Patti Wang, and Jonathan Woetzel (2020). *The Future of Asia: Decoding the Value and performance of Corporate Asia*, McKinsey Global Institute, May 2020. Available at: https://www.mckinsey.com/~/media/mckinsey/featured%20insights/asia%20pacific/the%20future%20of%20asia%20decoding%20the%20value%20and%20performance%20of%20corporate%20asia/the-future-of-asia-decoding-the-value-and-performance-of-corporate-asia-july-2020.pdf.

Braesemann, Fabian, and Andrew Baum (2020). PropTech: Turning Real Estate into a Data-Driven Market? Oxford Future of Real Estate Initiative, Working Paper Version 1.3, April 16, 2020, University of Oxford, Oxford, United Kingdom.

Brennan, Michael J., and Eduardo S. Schwartz (1977). Convertible Bonds: Valuation and Optimal Strategies for Call and Conversion, *Journal of Finance*, 32(5), 1699–1715.

Brumbaugh, R. Dan (1988). *Thrifts under Siege: Restoring Order to American Banking*, Ballinger Pub Co., Pennsacola, Florida.

Buchholz, Katharina (2021). *Chinese Housing Boom Slowed Outside Main Cities*, China Housing Market, Statista, September 13, 2021.

Carson, Biz (2022). Lessons from Times the Bubble Burst, Protocol, July 23, 2022. Available at: https://www.youtube.com/watch?v=SXByV6FdtWQ.

Case, Karl E., and Robert J. Shiller (1989). The Efficiency of the Market for Single-Family Homes, *American Economic Review*, 79(1), 125–137.

Case, Karl E., and Robert J. Shiller (1990). Forecasting Prices and Excess Returns in the Housing Market, *Real Estate Economics*, 18(3), 253–273.

CBRE (2019). What real estate investors should know about Proptech in 2019, 24 September, 2019. Available from: https://www.cbre.co.in/insights/articles/what-real-estate-investors-should-know-about-proptech-in-2019.

Cerdeiro, Diego A., and Cian Ruane (2022). China's Declining Business Dynamism, International Monetary Fund, IMF Working Paper WP/22/32.

Chan, Sally and Joong Shik Kang (2018). Credit Booms — Is China Different? International Monetary Fund, IMF Working Paper WP/18/2, January 2018.

Chang, Charles (2022). *Credit FAQ: China's Soft Landing May Come with Surprises, Comments*, S&P Global, New York, March 11, 2022. Available at: https://www.spglobal.com/ratings/en/research/articles/220311-credit-faq-china-s-soft-landing-may-come-with-surprises-12259622.

Chang, Charles, Jenny Chan, Chang Li, and Lucy Li (2022). *China's Surging Defaults Test Courts and Bond Recovery, Webinar Slides*, S&P Global, New York, Ratings, May 2022. Available at: https://www.spglobal.com/ratings/en/research/pdf-articles/220505-china-s-surging-defaults-test-courts-and-bond-recovery-101550631.

Chen, Jie, William Hardin III, and Mingzhi Hu (2020). Housing, Wealth, Income and Consumption: China and Homeownership Heterogeneity, *Real Estate Economics*, 48(2), 373–405.

Chen, Wei, Xilu Chen, Chang-Tai Hseih, and Zheng (Michael) Song (2019). A Forensic Examination of China's National Accounts, *Brookings Papers on Economic Activity*, Spring, 77–141.

Chen, Zhuo, Zhiguo He, and Chun Liu. (2018). *The Financing of Local Government in the People's Republic of China: Stimulus Loan Wanes and Shadow Banking Waxes.* ADBI Working Paper 800, Asian Development Bank Institute, Tokyo. Available at: https://www.adb.org/publications/financing-local-government-pr c-stimulus-loan-wanes-shadow-banking-waxes.

Chen, Zhuo, Zhiguo He, and Chun Liu (2020). The Financing of Local Government in China: Stimulus Loan Wanes and Shadow Banking Waxes, *Journal of Financial Economics*, 137, 42–71.

Chiarella, Daniele, Federico Marafante, and Robert Palter (2022). *Workplace Real Estate in the COVID-19 Era: From Cost Center to Competitive Advantage*, McKinsey & Company, May 2022.

Chivakul, Mali, W. Raphael Lam, Xiaoguang Liu, Wojciech Maliszewski, and Alfred Schipke (2015). Understanding Residential Real Estate in China, IMF Working Paper WP/15/84, International Monetary Fund, April 2015.

Chong, Koh Ping and Yu Xie (December 9, 2020). China Hails Victory in Crackdown on Peer-to-Peer Lending, *Wall Street Journal*. https://www.wsj.com/articles/china-hails-victory-in-crackdown-on-peer-to-peer-lending-11607515547.

Chong, Tze Ning (2020). China Tightens Rules for Microfinance Companies, S&P Global — Market Intelligence, September 17, 2020.

Chow, Andrew R. (2022). Where Did FTX's Missing $8 Billion Go? Investigators Offer New Clues, Time, December 21, 2022. Available at: https://time.com/6243086/ftx-where-did-money-go/.

Chu, Susan (2020). Credit FAQ: Are Bailouts On the Way Out for China's Local and Regional SOEs?, S&P Global Ratings, February 4, 2020. Available at: https://www.spglobal.com/ratings/en/research/articles/200204-credit-faq-are-bailouts-on-the-way-out-for-china-s-local-and-regional-soes-11330488.

Cohen-Col, Ethan and Faten Sabry (2012): *United States: The Use of ABX Derivatives in Credit Crisis Litigation. 2012* NERA Economic Consulting. Available at: https://www.mondaq.com/unitedstates/credit-crisis-and-the-emergency-economic-stabilization-act/160294/the-use-of-abx-derivatives-in-credit-crisis-litigation.

Coleman IV, Major, Michael LaCour-Little, and Kerry D. Vandell (2008). Subprime Lending and the Housing Bubble: Tail Wags Dog, *Journal of Housing Economics*, 17(4), 272–290.

Collier, Andrew (2017). *Shadow Banking and the Rise of Capitalism in China*, Palgrave Macmillan, Singapore.

Cordell, Larry, Yilin Huang, and Meredith Williams (2012). Collateral Damage: Sizing and Assessing the Subprime CDO Crisis, Federal Reserve Bank of Philadelphia, Working Paper No. 11-30/R, May 2012. Available at: https://www.philadelphiafed.org/-/media/frbp/assets/working-papers/2011/wp11-30.pdf.

Cox, John C., Jonathan E. Ingersoll, and Stephen Ross (1985). A Theory of the Term Structure of Interest Rates, *Econometrica*, 53(2), 385–407.

Cox, Josue, and Sydney C. Ludvigson (2021). Drivers of the Great Housing Boom-Bust: Credit Conditions, Beliefs, or Both? *Real Estate Economics*, 49(3), 843–875.

Cox, Wendell (2022). *2022 Demographia International Housing Affordability Report*, Urban Reform Institute and the Frontier Centre for Public Policy, March 2022. Available at: http://www.demographia.com/dhi.pdf.

Culp, Christopher L. and Compass Lexecon (2013). Syndicated Leveraged Loans during and after the Crisis and the Role of the Shadow Banking System, *Journal of Applied Corporate Finance*, 25(2), 63–85.

Curran, Enda (2022). The Worlds' Bubbliest Housing Markets are Flashing Warning Signs, *Bloomberg*, June 22, 2022. Available at: https://www.bloomberg.com/news/features/2022-06-21/cooling-real-estate-markets-in-us-uk-risk-deeper-global-economic-slump?cid=other-eml-onp-mip-mck&hlkid=0314b299ad30409aaa1bfbe89ce61ffd&hctky=12069925&hdpid=01230236-ca45-4c75-9c44-c90ee8c85c4c#xj4y7vzkg.

Da Costa, Pedro, and Kristina Cooke (2009). Crisis May Be Worse Than Depression: Volcker, *Reuters*, Business News, February 21, 2009. Available at: https://www.reuters.com/article/us-usa-economy-volcker-idUSTRE51J5JM20090220.

De Grauwe, Paul and Yuemei Ji (2013). From Panic-Driven Austerity to Symmetric Macroeconomic Policies in the Eurozone, *Journal of Common Market Studies*, 51, 31–41.

Demirgüç-Kunt, Asli, Leora Klapper, Dorothe Singer, and Saniya Ansar (2022). The Global Findex Database 2021: Financial Inclusion, Digital Payments, and Resilience in the Age of COVID-19, World Bank Group.

Deng, Manshu, Wenhong Xie, and Jin Shang (2022). China Green Bond Market Report 2021, Climate Bonds Initiative, May 2022. Available at: https://www.climatebonds.net/files/reports/cbi_china_sotm_2021_0.pdf.

Deng, Yongheng, John Quigley, and Robert Van Order (2000). Mortgage Terminations, Heterogeneity and the Exercise of Mortgage Options, *Econometrica*, 68(2), 275–308.

Diamond, Douglas, and Philip Dybvig (1983). Bank Runs, Deposit Insurance, and Liquidity, *Journal of Political Economy*, 91(3) 401–419.

Domm, Patti (2022). A Fertilizer Shortage, Worsened by War in Ukraine, Is Driving Up Global Food Prices and Scarcity, *CNBC*, April 4, 2022. Available at: https://www.cnbc.com/2022/04/06/a-fertilizer-shortage-worsened-by-war-in-ukraine-is-driving-up-global-food-prices-and-scarcity.html#:~:text=Russia%20and%20Ukraine%20together%20export,prices%20are%20rising%20even%20more.

Donaldson, Dave and Adam Storeygard (2016). The View from Above: Applications of Satellite Data in Economics. *Journal of Economic Perspectives*, 30(4), 171–198.

Dougherty, Ann and Robert Van Order (1982). Inflation, Housing Costs, and the Consumer Price Index, *American Economic Review,* 72(1), 154–164.

Du, Xiaoshan (2010a). The Current Situation and Future Prospects for Microfinance in China, *Microfinance in China*, World Microfinance Forum Geneva.

Du, Xiaoshan (2010b). The Current Supply of Microfinance Services in China, *Microfinance in China*, World Microfinance Forum Geneva.

Duca, John V. (2013). Subprime Mortgage Crisis: 2007–2010, Federal Reserve History, Federal Reserve Bank of Dallas, November 22, 2013. Available at: https://www.federalreservehistory.org/essays/subprime-mortgage-crisis.

Dudley, William C., and Jan Hatzius (2000). The Goldman Sachs Financial Conditions Index: The Right Tool for a New Monetary Policy Regime, *Global Economics Paper 44*, Goldman Sachs, New York.

Duffie, Darrell (2011). *How Big Banks Fail: And What to Do about It*, Princeton University Press, Princeton and Oxford.

Elsinger, Helmut, Alfred Lehar, and Martin Summer (2006). Risk Assessment for Banking Systems, *Management Science*, 52(9), 1301–1314.

Fabozzi, Frank J., ed. (2001) *The Handbook of Mortgage-Backed Securities*, 5th edn. McGraw-Hill, New York.

Farhi, Emmanuel and Jean Tirole (2017). Shadow Banking and the Four Pillars of Traditional Financial Intermediation, NBER Working Papers 23930, National Bureau of Economic Research, Inc.

Feng, Rebecca (2022). Chinese Banks Lose a Mortgage Safety Net as Developers Slide Into Distress, *Wall Street Journal*, September 9, 2022. Available at: https://www.wsj.com/articles/chinese-banks-lose-a-mortgage-safety-net-as-developers-slide-into-distress-11662715801.

Financial Crisis Inquiry Commission (FCIC) (2011). The Financial Crisis Inquiry Report: Final Report of The National Commission on the Causes of the Financial and Economic Crisis in the United States, January 2011.

Financial Stability Board (2012). *Global Shadow Banking Monitoring Report 2012*, November 18, 2021. Available at: https://www.fsb.org/wp-content/uploads/r_121118c.pdf.

Financial Stability Board (2018). *Global Shadow Banking Monitoring Report 2017*, March 5, 2018. Available at: https://www.fsb.org/2018/03/global-shadow-banking-monitoring-report-2017/.

Financial Stability Board (2019). *Global Monitoring Report on Non-Bank Financial Intermediation 2018*, 4 February 2019. Available from: https://www.fsb.org/wp-content/uploads/P040219.pdf.

Financial Stability Board (2020). *Global Monitoring Report on Non-Bank Financial Intermediation 2019*, January 19, 2020. Available at: https://www.fsb.org/wp-content/uploads/P190120.pdf.

Financial Stability Board (2021a). Enhancing the Resilience of Non-Bank Financial Intermediation Progress Report, November 1, 2021.

Financial Stability Board (2021b). *Global Monitoring Report on Non-Bank Financial Intermediation 2021*, December 16, 2021. Available at: https://www.fsb.org/wp-content/uploads/P161221.pdf.

Financial Stability Board (2022). US Dollar Funding and Emerging Market Economy Vulnerabilities, April 26, 2022.

Fitch Ratings (2022). Chinese WMP's Growth Moderates, Contagion Risks, Non-Rating Action Commentary, March 16, 2022.

Frame, W. Scott, Andreas Fuster, Joseph Tracy, and James Vickery (2015). The Rescue of Fannie Mae and Freddie Mac, *Journal of Economic Perspectives*, 29(2), 25–52.

Frank, Robert (2022). Metaverse Real Estate Sales Top $500 Million, and Are Projected to Double This Year, *CNBC*, February 1, 2022. Available at: https://www.cnbc.com/2022/02/01/metaverse-real-estate-sales-top-500-million-metametric-solutions-says.html.

Fuster, Andreas, Matthew Plosser, Philipp Schnabl, and James Vickery (2018). The Role of Technology in Mortgage Lending, Federal Reserve Bank of New York Staff Reports, No. 836, February 2018.

Gai, Prasanna and Sujit Kapadia (2010). Contagion in Financial Networks, *Proceedings of the Royal Society A*, 466, 2401–2423.

Gan, Nectar (2022). Shanghai Fears New Lockdowns as Millions Test for Covid Amid Sweltering Heat, *CNN*, July 13, 2022. Available at: https://edition.cnn.com/2022/07/13/china/china-covid-shanghai-lockdown-heat-wave-intl-hnk/index.html.

Gao, Haoyu, Hong Ru, and Dragon Yongjun Tan (2021). Subnational Debt of China: The Politics-Finance Nexus, *Journal of Financial Economics*, 141(3), 881–895.

Gao, Liangping and Ryan Woo (2021). China's New Home Prices Stall Amid Crackdown on Speculation, *Reuters*, October 19, 2021. Available at: https://www.nasdaq.com/articles/chinas-new-home-prices-stall-amid-crackdown-on-speculation-2021-10-20.

Gennaioli, Nicola and Andrei Shileifer (2018). *A Crisis of Beliefs: Investor Psychology and Financial Fragility*, Princeton University Press, Princeton and Oxford.

Gerardi, K, A. Lehnert, S. Sherlund, and P. Willen (2008). Making Sense of the Subprime Crisis, *Brookings Papers on Economic Activity*, 2008.

Glaeser, Edward, Wei Huang, Yueran Ma, and Andrei Shleifer (2017). A Real Estate Boom with Chinese Characteristics, *Journal of Economic Perspectives*, 31(1), 93–116.

Global Times (2022). Strict Regulation Puts Brake on China's $75B Online Education Sector, *Global Times*, May 31, 2021. Available at: https://www.globaltimes.cn/page/202105/1224981.shtml.

Gorton, Gary B. (2010). *Slapped by the Invisible Hand: The Panic of 2007*, Oxford University Press, Oxford.

Gorton, Gary B. (2012). *Misunderstanding Financial Crises: Why We Don't See Them Coming*, Oxford University Press, New York.

Gorton, Gary B. (2015). *The Maze of Banking: History, Theory, Crisis*, Oxford University Press, Oxford, New York.

Gorton, Gary B. (2020). The Regulation of Private Money, *Journal of Money, Credit and Banking*, 52(S1), 21–42.

Gorton, Gary B. and Andrew Metrick (2010). Regulating the Shadow Banking System. *Brookings Papers on Economic Activity*, (Fall), 261–297.

Gorton, Gary B. and Andrew Metrick (2012). Securitized Banking and the Run on Repo, *Journal of Financial Economics*, 104(3), 425–451.

Griffith, Erin (2022). Fear and Loathing Return to Tech Start-Ups, *New York Times*, May 11, 2022. Available at: https://www.nytimes.com/2022/05/11/technology/tech-start-ups.html.

Hachem, Kinda (2018). Shadow Banking in China, *Annual Review for Financial Economics*, 10, 287–308. Available at: https://www.annualreviews.org/doi/abs/10.1146/annurev-financial-110217-023025.

Haliassos, Michael (Ed.) (2013). *Financial Innovation: Too Much or Too Little?* The MIT Press, Cambridge, Massachusetts.

Hayre, Lakhbir (2001). A Concise Guide to Mortgage-Backed Securities (MBSs), in Lakhbir Hayre (ed.), *Salomon Smith Barney Guide to Mortgage-Backed and Asset-Backed Securities.* John Wiley & Sons, New York, pp. 9–68.

He, Guangwen (2010). An Analysis of Microfinance Demand in China, *Microfinance in China*, World Microfinance Forum Geneva.

He, Laura (2022). Evergrande Has Been Ordered to Demolish 39 Buildings in Chinese Resort, *CNN Business*, January 4, 2022. Available at: https://edition.cnn.com/2022/01/04/investing/evergrande-stock-gain-resume-trading-intl-hnk/index.html.

He, Zekai, Jingjing Ye, and Xiuzhen Shi (2020). Housing Wealth and Household Consumption in Urban China, *Urban Studies*, 57(8), 1714–1732. DOI: 10.1177/0042098019844410.

He, Zhiguo and Jian Li (2022). Intermediation via Credit Chains, Working Paper, January 2022.

Hovnanian, Garo, Ryan Luby, and Shannon Peloquin (2022). *Bridging the Labor Mismatch in US Construction*, McKinsey & Company,

March 28, 2022. Available at: https://www.mckinsey.com/business-functions/operations/our-insights/bridging-the-labor-mismatch-in-us-construction.

Howard, Laura and Andrew Michael (2022). House Prices — Latest News, *Forbes*, July 20, 2022. Available at: https://www.forbes.com/uk/advisor/personal-finance/2022/07/20/house-prices-updates/

Hu, Joseph (1997). *Basics of Mortgage-Backed Securities,* Frank J. Fabozzi Associates, New Hope, PA.

Huang, Yukon and Canyon Bosler (2014). *China's Debt Dilemma: Deleveraging While Generating Growth, Carnegie Endowment for International Peace*, September 18, 2014. Available at: https://carnegieendowment.org/files/china_debt_dilemma.pdf.

Hull, John C. (2018). *Risk Management and Financial Institution*, 5th edn., John Wiley & Sons, New Jersey.

Hull, John and Alan White (1990). Pricing Interest-rate Derivative Securities, *Review of Financial Studies*, 3(4), 573–592.

Hwang, M., J. Quigley, and J. Son. (2006). The Dividend Pricing Model: New Evidence from the Korean Housing Market, *Journal of Real Estate Finance and Economics,* 32, 205–228.

Idealista (2022). A Property in Braga Is Sold for 3 Bitcoins: The 1st 100% Crypto Transaction in Portugal, May 13, 2022. Available at: https://www.idealista.pt/en/news/financial-advice-in-portugal/2022/05/13/5003-house-in-braga-sold-for-3-bitcoins-1st-100-crypto-transaction-in-portugal.

IMF (2017a). Global Financial Stability Report: Getting the Policy Mix Right, Washington, DC, April.

IMF (2017b). 2017 Article IV Consultation with the People's Republic of China, IMF Country Report No. 17/247, August 2017.

IMF (2018). Global Financial Stability Report April 2018: A Bumpy Road. Available at: https://www.imf.org/en/Publications/GFSR/Issues/2018/04/02/Global-Financial-Stability-Report-April-2018.

IMF (2021). The Rise of Digital Money — A Strategic Plan to Continue Delivering on the Fund's Mandate, IMF Policy Paper, April (Washington: International Monetary Fund).

IMF (2022a). World Economic Outlook. Update: Rising Caseloads, a Disrupted Recovery, and Higher Inflation, January 2022.

IMF (2022b). IMF Executive Board Concludes 2021 Article IV Consultation with the People's Republic of China, Press Release No. 22/17, January 28, 2022.

IMF (2022c). World Economic Outlook: War Sets Back the Global Recover, April 2022.

IMF (2022d). 2021 Article IV Consultation with the People's Republic of China, January 28, 2022.

IMF (2022e). Global Financial Stability Report: Shockwaves from the War in Ukraine Test the Financial System's Resilience, April 2022.

IMF (2022f). War Fuels Food Crisis, Finance & Development, June 2022.

Jackson, Anna-Louise (2022). July Stock Market Forecast, Forbes Advisor, July 1, 2022. Available at: https://www.forbes.com/advisor/investing/stock-market-outlook-and-forecast/.

Jarrow, Robert and Philip Protter (2020). Credit Risk, Liquidity, and Bubbles, *International Review of Finance*, 20(3), 737–746.

Jim, Clare (2022). China Plans to Set Up Real Estate Fund Worth Up To $44 Bln, Reuters, July 25, 2022. Available at: https://www.reuters.com/world/china/china-plans-set-up-real-estate-fund-worth-up-44-bln-redd-2022-07-25/.

JLL (2018). Blockchain Technology is Gradually Making Inroads into the Real Estate Valuation Process, Simplifying and Accelerating Investment, Jones Lang LaSalle article, August 21, 2018.

Jones Lang LaSalle and Ashurst (2018). *Asia Pacific Property Investment Guide 2019*, 7th edn., Jones Lang LaSalle and Ashurst. Available at: https://ashurstcd.azureedge.net/-/media/ashurst/documents/news-and-insights/legal-updates/2018/oct/asia-pacific-property-investment-guide.pdf?rev=ea526d5e192a4592a9df706fb333084d.

JLL (2021). *Decarbonizing the Built Environment*, Jones Lang LaSalle Research, June 20, 2021.

Kahneman, Daniel and Amos Tversky (1979). Prospect Theory: An Analysis of Decision under Risk, *Econometrica*, 47, 263–292.

Kane, Edward J. (1989), *The S&L Insurance Mess: How Did It Happen?* The Urban Institute Press, Washington, DC.

Kaplan, Greg, Kurt Mitman, and Giovanni L. Violante (2020). The Housing Boom and Bust: Model Meets Evidence, *Journal of Political Economy*, 128(9), 3285–3345.

Kau, James, and Donald Keenan (1995) "An Overview of Option-theoretic Pricing of Mortgages," *The Journal of Housing*, 6(2), 217–244.

Kawate, Iori (2021a). China's Largest 'Ghost City' Booms Again Thanks to Education Fever, Nikkei Asia, April 19, 2021. Available at: https://asia.nikkei.com/Spotlight/Society/China-s-largest-ghost-city-booms-again-thanks-to-education-fever.

Kawate, Iori (2021b). China Cracks Down on Property Speculation, Nikkei Asia, August 14, 2021. Available at: https://asia.nikkei.com/Business/Markets/Property/China-cracks-down-on-property-speculation.

Kaysen, Ronda (2022). What's Up With the Crazy Housing Market? *New York Times*, July 12, 2022. Available at: https://www.nytimes.com/2022/07/08/realestate/housing-market.html?te=1&nl=updates-from-the-newsroom&emc=edit_ufn_20220714.

Keohane, David (2016). China Property, Tier-1 vs the Rest, *Financial Times*, March 10, 2016. Available at: https://www.ft.com/content/91be381f-5b18-3e41-bd80-63e9fa3d0fa1.

Keys, Benjamin (2021). Why the U.S. Housing Boom Isn't a Bubble, Knowledge at Wharton, Wharton School of the University of Pennsylvania, October 12, 2021. Available at: https://knowledge.wharton.upenn.edu/podcast/knowledge-at-wharton-podcast/why-the-u-s-housing-boom-isnt-a-bubble/.

Kharpal, Arjun (2022). SoftBank Vision Fund Posted Record $27 Billion Loss as Tech Stocks Plummet, *CNBC*, May 12, 2022. Available at: https://www.cnbc.com/2022/05/12/softbank-vision-fund-posts-record-27-billion-loss-as-tech-stocks-dive.html .

King, Brett (2013). *Bank 3.0: Why Banking Is No Longer Somewhere You Go, But Something You Do*, John Wiley & Sons Singapore Pte. Ltd., Singapore.

King, Brett (2019). *Bank 4.0: Banking Everywhere, Never at a Bank*, John Wiley & Sons Ltd., Chichester, U.K.

Klotz, Anthony C. (2022). The Great Resignation is Still Here, but Whether It Stays Is up to Leaders, The OECD Forum Network, June 3, 2022. Available at: https://www.oecd-forum.org/posts/the-great-resignation-is-still-here-but-whether-it-stays-is-up-to-leaders.

Krugman, Paul. (2022). Wonking Out: Lies, Damned Lies and 'Underlying' Inflation, *New York Times*, December 16, 2022. Available at: https://www.nytimes.com/2022/12/16/opinion/underlying-core-inflation.html.

Kunthara, Sophia (2022). Tech Layoffs in 2022: The U.S. Companies That Have Cut Jobs, *Crunchbase News*, July 21, 2022. Available at: https://news.crunchbase.com/startups/tech-layoffs-2022/.

Lan, Hao, Fernando F. Moreira, and Sheng Zhao (2022). Can a House Resale Restriction Policy Curb Speculation? Evidence from a Quasi-Natural Experiment in China. Available at: https://ssrn.com/abstract=4010450 or http://dx.doi.org/10.2139/ssrn.4010450.

Lai, Rose Neng and Robert Van Order. (2010). Momentum and House Price Growth in the U.S.: Anatomy of a Bubble, *Real Estate Economics*, 38(4), 753–773.

Lai, Rose Neng and Robert Van Order. (2017). U.S. House Prices over the Last 30 Years: Bubbles, Regime Shifts and Market (In)Efficiency, *Real Estate Economics*, 46(2), 259–300.

Lai, Rose Neng and Robert Van Order (2019). Shadow Banking and the Property Market in China, *International Real Estate Review*, 22(3), 361–399.

Lai, Rose Neng and Robert Van Order. (2020). A Tale of Two Countries: Comparing the US and Chinese Bubbles Housing Markets, *Journal of Real Estate Finance and Economics*, 61(3), 505–547.

Lam, W. Raphael, Alfred Schipke, Yuyan Tan, and Zhibo Tan (2017). Resolving China's Zombies: Tackling Debt and Raising Productivity, International Monetary Fund, IMF Working Paper WP/17/266.

Lau, Yvonne (2021). China's "COVID-zero' Policy Hit Its Economy in August. Now a New Delta Outbreak Poses Another Threat", *Forbes*, September 15, 2021. Available at: https://fortune.com/2021/09/15/china-covid-zero-cases-economy-retail-sales/.

Lea, Michael (1986). Dueling Guarantees. *Secondary Mortgage Markets*, 3(3), 22–8.

Lee, Yoojung, Pei Yi Mak, Venus Feng, and Min Jeong Lee (2022). SoftBank Founder Son Loses $25 Billion Tech's Brutal Winter, *Bloomberg*, March 16, 2022. Available at: https://www.bloomberg.com/news/articles/2022-03-15/softbank-founder-son-loses-25-billion-in-tech-s-brutal-winter#xj4y7vzkg.

Lewis, Michael (2010) *The Big Short: Inside the Doomsday Machine*, W.W. Norton & Company, New York.

Li, Cheng and Ying Zhang (2021). How Does Housing Wealth Affect Household Consumption? Evidence from Macro-data with Special Implications for China, *China Economic Review*, 69, 1–14.

Lin, Justin Yifu (2011). China and the Global Economy, in Reuven Glick and Mark M. Spiegel (eds.), *Asia's Role in the Post-Crisis Global Economy*, Asia Economic Policy Conference 2011 sponsored by the Federal Reserve Bank of San Francisco, pp. 213–229.

Ling, David C., Joseph T.L. Ooi, and Thao T.T. Le. (2015). Explaining House Price Dynamics: Isolating the Role of Nonfundamentals, *Journal of Money, Credit, and Banking*, 47(S1), 87–125.

Liu, Esther and Ricky Tsang (2022). China's Property Downcycle Won't End with Policy Easing, S&P Global, April 7, 2022. Available at: https://www.google.com.hk/url?sa=t&rct=j&q=&esrc=s&source=web&cd=&cad=rja&uact=8&ved=2ahUKEwifyIy8ie74AhWxR2wGHW-uDb8QFnoECAMQAQ&url=https%3A%2F%2Fwww.spglobal.com%2Fratings%2Fen%2Fresearch%2Farticles%2F220407-china-s-property-downcycle-won-t-end-with-policy-easing-12327035&usg=AOvVaw0PsSyYccCqECTwcyTogldC.

Lyman, Timothy, Leesa Shrader, and Olga Tomilova (2015). Inclusive Finance and Shadow Banking: Worlds Apart or Worlds Converging? *CGAP Brief*, Consultative Group to Assist the Poor (CGAP), September 2015. Available at: https://www.cgap.org/sites/default/files/Brief-Inclusive-Finance-and-Shadow-Banking-Sept-2015.pdf.

Ma, Xiaocheng, Tine Ye, and Yingru Meng (2022). Chinese Embrace Digital Yuan as China Further Promotes Pilot Program, Xinhua News Agency, May 14, 2022. Available at: https://english.news.cn/20220514/18c29e06fb264f00a6d85672104d2c31/c.html.

Mariotti, Tony (2022, August 5). Metaverse Real Estate Statistics, RubyHome, https://www.rubyhome.com/blog/metaverse-real-estate-stats/.

Martinez-Miera, David and Rafael Repullo (2019). Markets, banks, and shadow banks, No 2234, Working Paper Series, European Central Bank.

Manhertz, Treh (2022). U.S. Housing Market has Double in Value since the Great Recession, Gaining $6.9 Trillion in 2021, Zillow Research, January 27, 2022. Available at: https://www.zillow.com/research/us-housing-market-total-value-2021-30615/.

McConnell, John and Stephen A. Buser (2011). The Origins and Evolution of the Market for Mortgage-Backed Securities, *Annual Review of Financial Economics*, 3(1), 173–192.

McDonald, Henry and Dan Milmo (2012). Westlife Singer Shane Filan Declared Bankrupt, *The Guardian*, June 14, 2012. Available at: https://www.theguardian.com/music/2012/jun/14/shane-filan-boyzone-declared-bankrupt.

McMorrow, Ryan (2022). SEC Investigation Chinese Ride-Hailing Group Didi's $4.4 bn US IPO, *Financial Times*, Beijing, May 4, 2022. Available at: https://www.ft.com/content/923ba655-3967-4ae7-8cf1-b16b4fa75a85.

Merton, Robert C. (1973). An Intertemporal Capital Asset Pricing Model, *Econometrica*, 41(5), 867–887.

Merton, Robert C. (1974). On the Pricing of Corporate Debt: The Risk Structure of Interest Rates, *Journal of Finance*, 29(2), 449–470.

Merton, Robert C. (1989). On the Application of the Continuous-Time of Finance to Financial Intermediation and Insurance, *The Geneva Papers on Risk and Insurance*, 14(52), 225–261.

Merton, Robert C. (1990). Capital Market Theory and the Pricing of Financial Securities, In *Handbook of Monetary Economics*, 497–577. Amsterdam, Netherlands: North-Holland Publishing Company.

Mian, Atif and Amir Sufi. (2009). The Consequences of Mortgage Credit Expansion: Evidence from the U.S. Mortgage Default Crisis, *Quarterly Journal of Economics*, 124, 1449–1496.

Mian, Atif and Amir Sufi. (2014a). What Explains the 2007–2009 Drop in Employment? *Econometrica*, 82, 2197–2223.

Mian, Atif and Amir Sufi (2014b). *House of Debt: How They (and You) Caused The Great Recession, and How We Can Prevent It From Happening Again*, The University of Chicago Press, Chicago and London.

Minsky, Hyman P. (1992). The Financial Instability Hypothesis, The Jerome Levy Economics Institute of Bard College, Working Paper No. 74, May 6–8, 1992.

Mittal, Sachin and James Lloyd (2016). *The Rise of FinTech in China: Redefining Financial Services*, Ernst & Young Global Limited and DBS Bank Ltd., Singapore.

Modigliani, Franco and Merton H. Miller (1958). The Cost of Capital, Corporation Finance and the Theory of Investment. *The American Economic Review*, 48, 261–297.

Mody, Ashoka (2018). *Euro Tragedy: A Drama in Nine Acts*, Oxford University Press, New York.

Moody's Investors Service (2017). *Quarterly China Shadow Banking Monitor Report*, August 7, 2017.

Moody's Investors Service (2018). Announcement of Moody's: China RMBS Issuance Exceeds All Other Securitization Classes in Q1 2018, Moody's Investors Service Announcement, May 24, 2018.

Moody's Investors Service (2021). Research Announcement: Moody's — Chinese Banks Made Good Progress in De-risking Wealth Management Business, but Adjustment Risk Remains, June 24, 2021.

Moody's Investors Service (2022a). *Quarterly China Shadow Banking Monitor Report*, April 1, 2022.

Moody's Investors Service (2022b). *LGFV Bond Monitor Fourth Quarter 2021*, March 30, 2022.

Mozur, Paul, and John Liu (2022). China Fines Didi $1.2 Billion as Tech Sector Pressures Persist, *New York Times*, July 21, 2022.

Mullen, Andrew (2021). Explainer: What Is China's Common-Prosperity Strategy That Calls for an Even Distribution of Wealth?, *South China Morning Post*, August 26, 2021. Available at: https://www.scmp.com/economy/china-economy/article/3146271/what-chinas-common-prosperity-strategy-calls-even?module=perpetual_scroll_1&pgtype=article&campaign=3146271.

National Bureau of Statistics of China (2022). Households' Income and Consumption Expenditure in 2021, Press Release, January 18, 2022. Available at: http://www.stats.gov.cn/english/PressRelease/202201/t20220118_1826649.html.

National Association of Realtors (2020). Home Affordability Index Ranking and Payroll Job Growth, November, 2019.

Nneji, Ogonna, Chris Brooks, and Charles Ward (2013). Intrinsic and Rational Speculative Bubbles in the US Housing Market: 1960–2011, *Journal of Real Estate Research*, 35(2), 121–151.

Nunlist, Tom (2017). China' Housing Market: The Iron Bubble, Cheung Kong School of Business (CKGSB) Knowledge, July 31, 2017.

O'Brian, Sarah (2022). 43% of Homeowners Have Delayed Home Improvements and Maintenance due to Inflation. Here's Why That's Risky, *CNBC*, June 17, 2022. Available at: https://www.cnbc.com/2022/06/17/homeowners-delay-big-purchases-improvement-projects-due-to-inflation.html.

OECD (2021). HC.1.5. Overview of Affordable Housing Indicators, OECD Affordable Housing Database. Available at: http://oe.cd/ahd.

OECD (2022). Household spending (indicator). DOI: 10.1787/b5f46047-en. Accessed on May 17, 2022.

Oehmke, Martin and Adam Zawadowski (2015). Synthetic or Real? The Equilibrium Effects of Credit Default Swaps on Bond Markets, *Review of Financial Studies*, 28(12), 3303–3337.

Oi, Mariko (2021). Evergrande: China's Efforts to Contain Its Lehman Moment, *BBC News*, December 20, 2021. Available at: https://www.bbc.com/news/business-59605130.

Peng, Zhiwei, Ziliang Yu, and Huifu Nong (2020). Inter-Type Investment Connectedness: A New Perspective on China's Booming Real Estate Market, *Global Economic Review*, 49(2), 186–204. DOI: 10.1080/1226508X.2020.1744465.

Pesaran, Hashem M. and Ron Smith (1995). Long run Relationships from Dynamic Heterogeneous Panels, *Journal of Econometrics*, 68, 79–113.

Pesaran, Hashem M. and Yongcheol Shin (1999). An Autoregressive Distributed Lag Modelling Approach to Cointegration Analysis, in S Strom (ed.), *Econometrics and Economic Theory in the 20th Century: The Ragnar Frisch Centennial Symposium*, Chapter 11, Cambridge University Press, Cambridge.

Pesaran, Hashem M., Yongcheol Shin, and Ron Smith (1999). Pooled Mean Group Estimation of Dynamic Heterogeneous Panels. *Journal of the American Statistical Association*, 94, 621–634.

Quinn, Willian, and John D. Turner (2020). *Boom and Bust: A Global History of Financial Bubbles*, Cambridge University Press, Cambridge.

Rajan, Raghuram G. (2010). *Fault Lines: How Hidden Fractures Still Threaten the World Economy*, The Princeton University Press, Princeton and Oxford.

Reid, Jim, Craig Nicol, Nick Burns, and Sukanto Chanda (2017). Long-Term Asset Return Study: The Next Financial Crisis, Deutsche

Bank Markets Research, September 18, 2017. Available at: http://www.tramuntalegria.com/wp-content/uploads/2017/09/Long-Term-Asset-Return-Study-The-Next-Financial-Crisis-db.pdf.

Reuters (October 18, 2017). China's Xi Says to Maintain Principle Property Is Not for Speculation. Available at: https://www.reuters.com/article/us-china-economy-property-idUSKBN1CN0B5.

Reuters (July 11, 2022). Update 2 — Two Chinese Provinces to Make Some Repayments after Bank Deposit Protests. Available at: https://www.reuters.com/article/china-banks-henan/update-1-chinese-provincial-authorities-promise-payments-after-bank-protests-idINL1N2YS13F.

Reuters (2011 April 14). Factbox: Key Changes in China's Property policy. Available at: https://www.reuters.com/article/us-china-property-policy-idUSTRE73D48820110414.

Riecke, Jeffrey (2014, September 23). China's Microfinance Landscape: Nonprofits, Microcredit Companies, Rural Financers, and Alibaba, *Center for Financial Inclusion*, https://www.centerforfinancialinclusion.org/chinas-microfinance-landscape-nonprofits-microcredit-companies-rural-financers-and-alibaba.

Roukny, Tarik, Stefano Battiston, and Joseph E. Stiglitz (2018). Interconnectedness as a Source of Uncertainty in Systemic Risk, *Journal of Financial Stability*, 35(C), 93–106.

Sablik, Tim (2013). Recession of 1981–1982, Federal Reserve History, Federal Reserve Bank of Richmond, November 22, 2013. Available at: https://www.federalreservehistory.org/essays/recession-of-1981-82.

Saiz, Albert (2010). The Geographic Determinants of Housing Supply, *Quarterly Journal of Economics*, 125(3), 1253–1296.

Scott, Hal S. (2016). *Connectedness and Contagion: Protecting the Financial System from Panics*, MIT Press, Cambridge.

Shan, Chenyu, Dragon Yongjun Tang, and Andrew Winton (2019). Do Banks Still Monitor When There Is a Market For Credit Protection? *Journal of Accounting and Economics*, 68(2–3), 1–25.

Sharma, Ruchir (2022). How Shadow Banks Threaten the Global Economy, *Financial Times*, May 23, 2022. Availably at: https://www.ft.com/content/d22ec352-a4a4-4f4c-832a-cb05af5110f1?shareType=nongift.

Sheng, Andrew and Ng Chow Soon (2016). *Shadow Banking in China: An Opportunity for Financial Reform*, Fung Global Institute Limited, Hong Kong.

Shepard, Wade (2015). *Ghost Cities of China: The Story of Cities without People in the World's Most Populated Country (Asian Arguments)*, Zed Books, London.

Shepard, Wade (2016). An Update on China's Largest Ghost City — What Ordos Kangbashi Is Like Today, Forbes, April 19, 2016. Available at:

https://www.forbes.com/sites/wadeshepard/2016/04/19/an-update-on-chinas-largest-ghost-city-what-ordos-kangbashi-is-like-today/.

Shiller, Robert J. (2000). *Irrational Exuberance*, 1st edn., The Princeton University Press, Princeton and Oxford.

Shiller, Robert J. (2007). Understanding Recent Trends in House Prices and Home Ownership. NBER Working Paper Number 13553.

Shiller, Robert J. (2008). Historic Turning Points in Real Estate, *Eastern Economic Journal*, 34, 1–12.

South China Morning Post (2022). China's LGFV Bonds to Top Offshore Dollar Debt Issuers in 2022 as Market Grows Tired of Defaults and Delayed Payments by Developers, May 9, 2022. Available at: https://www.scmp.com/business/banking-finance/article/3177036/chinas-lgfv-bonds-top-offshore-dollar-debt-issuers-2022.

Springfield, Cary (2019). How Much of a Concern Is China's Debt Problem, International Banker, April 29, 2019. Available at: https://internationalbanker.com/banking/how-much-of-a-concern-is-chinas-debt-problem/.

State Council (1998). The Circular of the State Council on Further Deepening the Urban Housing System Reform and Accelerating Housing Construction, No. 23.

State Council (2003). The Circular of the State Council on Promoting the Continuous and Healthy Development of the Real Estate Markets, December 8, 2003. CLI.2.49316.

Stevenson, Alexandra and Cao Li (2019). How Band Is China's Debt? A City Hospital Is Asking Nurses for Loans, *New York Times*, November 10, 2019. Available at: https://www.nytimes.com/2019/11/10/business/china-debt-hospitals.html.

Stevenson, Alexandra and Cao Li (2021). What to Know About China Evergrande, the Troubled Property Giant, *New York Times*, December 9, 2021. Available at: https://www.nytimes.com/article/evergrande-debt-crisis.html.

Stratford, Kate and Arianna Cowling (2016). Chinese Household Income, Consumption and Savings, *Reserve Bank of Australia Bulletin*, September Quarter 2016.

Sun, Guofeng (2019). China's Shadow Banking: Banks' Shadow and Traditional Shadow Banking, BIS Working Papers No. 822, Bank for International Settlements.

Taipalus, K. (2006). A Global House Price Bubble? Evaluation Based on a New Rent-Price Approach. Bank of Finland Discussion Papers, 29.

Tam, Olivia (2021). Two Thirds of China's Top Developers Breach State's 'Red Line' on Debt, *Bloomberg*, October 31, 2021.

Tan, Eunice, Terry E. Chan, Louis Kuijs, Vincent R. Conti, KingEng Tan, Rain Yin, Susan Chu, Harry Hu, Charles Chang, Chang Li, Laura C. Li, WenWen Chen, Jerry Fang, and Christine Ip (2022). China's COVID Policy to Further Weigh on Economy, Credit, Comments, S&P Global, May 16, 2022. Available at: https://www.spglobal.com/ratings/en/research/articles/220516-china-s-covid-policy-to-further-weigh-on-economy-credit-12373139.

Tang, Ya, Daixi Chen, Jing Chen, and Jianguo Xu (2017). The Rise of China's Securitization Market, *Financial Markets, Institutions & Instruments*, 26, 279–294.

Tett, Gillian (2009). *Fool's Gold: How Unrestrained Greed Corrupted a Dream, Shattered Global Markets and Unleased a Catastrophe*, Free Press, New York.

Tu, Lianting (2016). *China Has $23 Billion in Debt That Could Be Cut to Junk*, Bloomberg, February 3, 2016. Available at: https://www.bloomberg.com/news/articles/2016-02–02/fallen-angels-incoming-as-23-billion-of-china-bonds-near-junk#xj4y7vzkg.

UBS (2021). UBS Global Real Estate Bubble Index 2021, Chief Investment Office GWM Investment Research, October 2021.

Van Order, Robert (2000). The U.S. Mortgage Market: A Model of Dueling Charters, *Journal of Housing Research*, 11, 233–255.

Van Order, Robert (2008). Modeling and Evaluating the Credit Risk of Mortgage Loans: A Primer, *Journal of Risk Model Validation*, 2(2), 63–82.

Wall, Larry D. (2014). Have the Government-Sponsored Enterprises Fully Repaid the Treasury? *Notes from the Vault*. Federal Reserve Bank of Atlanta. March 2014.

Wang, Selina (2021). Evergrande's Billionaire Founder Has Been Bailing Out the Business. That Can't Continue, *CNN Business*, November 10, 2021. Available at: https://edition.cnn.com/2021/11/09/investing/china-property-crisis-evergrande-bail-out-mic-intl-hnk/index.html.

Wang, Ya Ping (2007). From Socialist Welfare to Support Home Ownership: The Experience of China, in Murie A., R. Groves, and C. Watson (eds.), *Housing and the New Welfare State,* Ashgate, Aldershot, pp. 127–154.

Wang, Ya Ping and A. Murie (1996). The Process of Commercialisation of Urban Housing in China, *Urban Studies*, 33(6), 971–989.

Wang, Ya Ping and Lei Shao (2014). Urban Housing Policy Changes and Challenges in China, in Doling J. and Ronald R. (eds.), *Housing East Asia*. Palgrave Macmillan, London, pp. 44–70.

Wang, Songtao, Su Han Chang, and Bohua Xu (2012). The Estimation and Determinants of the Price Elasticity of Housing Supply: Evidence from China, *Journal of Real Estate Research*, 34(3), 311–344.

Wang, Zixu and Austin Ramzy (2022). Security Forces in China Attack Protesters Seeking Frozen Funds, *New York Times*, July 11, 2022. Available at: https://www.nytimes.com/2022/07/11/business/china-bank-protest.html?te=1&nl=morning-briefing%3A-asia-pacific-edition&emc=edit_mbae_20220712.

Wei, Yuwa (2007). Asset-Backed Securitization in China, *Richmond Journal of Global Law & Business*, 6(3), 225–243. Available at: http://scholarship.richmond.edu/global/vol6/iss3/2.

Weicher, John C. (1999). The Development of the Housing GSEs, in Peter J. Wallison (ed.), *Fannie Mae and Freddie Mac: Public Purposes and Private Interests*, Volume 1, American Enterprise Institute, Washington, DC.

Wheatley, Jonathan (2020). China's Debt Problem is Really an Asset Problem, *Financial Times*, March 12, 2020. Available at: https://www.ft.com/content/17943d46-62fa-11ea-b3f3-fe4680ea68b5.

Wildau, Gabriel (2015). China Shadow Bank Regulation Shows Results, *Financial Times*, February 2, 2015. Available at: https://www.ft.com/content/01022e62-a207-11e4-aba2-00144feab7de.

Wildau, Gabriel and Don Weinland (2016). China Debt Load Reaches Record High as Risk to Economy Mounts, *Financial Times*, April 24, 2016. Available at: https://www.ft.com/content/acd3f2fc-084a-11e6-876d-b823056b209b.

Wong, Christine (2011). The Fiscal Stimulus Programme and Public Governance Issues in China, *OECD Journal on Budgeting*, 11/3, 1–21. Available at: http://dx.doi.org/10.1787/budget-11-5kg3nhljqrjl.

Wong, Li Anne (2015). China Economy Grow at Slowest Pace in 24 Years, *CNBC*, January 20, 2015. Available at: https://www.cnbc.com/2015/01/19/china-economy-grew-74-in-2014.html#:~:text=China's%20economy%20grew%20at%20its,from%207.7%20percent%20in%202013.

Wu, Jing, Joseph Gyourko, and Yongheng Deng (2016). Evaluating the Risk of Chinese Housing Markets: What We Know and What We Need to Know, *China Economic Review*, 39, 91–114.

Wu, Xun (2015). An Introduction to Chinese Local Government Debt, mimeo MIT.

Xiao, Kairong (2020). Monetary Transmission through Shadow Banks, *Review of Financial Studies*, 33(6), 2379–2420.

Xie, Stella Yifan and Mike Bird (2020). The $52 Trillion Bubble: China Grapples with Epic Property Boom, *Wall Street Journal*, July 16, 2020.

Available at: https://www.wsj.com/articles/china-property-real-estate-boom-covid-pandemic-bubble-11594908517.

Xinhua News Agency (2022). China to Pilot Digital Yuan in More Cities, The State Council, The People's Republic of China, April 3, 2022. Available at: https://english.www.gov.cn/statecouncil/ministries/202204/03/content_WS6248d79cc6d02e5335328b06.html.

Yan, Zan, Ying Fan, and Liqing Zhao (2018). A Reexamination of Housing Price and Household Consumption in China: The Dual Role of Housing Consumption and Housing Investment, *Journal of Real Estate Finance and Economics*, 56, 472–499.

Yoon, Frances (2021). Alibaba Pledges $15.5 Billion as Chinese Companies Extol Beijing's 'Common Prosperity' Push, *Wall Street Journal*, September 3, 2021. Available at: https://www.wsj.com/articles/alibaba-pledges-15-5-billion-as-chinese-companies-extol-beijings-common-prosperity-push-11630587923.

Yu, Sun (2020). China Crackdown on Shadow Banking Sector Prompts Warning, *Financial Times*, August 6, 2020. Available at: https://www.ft.com/content/04a0a603-9f08-419b-a54f-1cfb0922acc8.

Yuan, Xiaojun, Yinjie Shen, and Haigang Zhou (2020). House Price and Household Consumption in China: Evidence from Micro-level Data, *International Journal of Housing Markets and Analysis*, 13(3), 475–501.

Zhang, Hong, Linjun Li, Eddie Chi-Man Hui, and Vera Li (2016). Comparisons of the Relations Between Housing Prices and the Macroeconomy in China's First-, Second- and Third-Tier Cities, *Habitat International*, 57, 24–42.

Zhang, Jane (2021). Alibaba Elaborates on How It Will Use Its 100 Billion Yuan 'Common Prosperity' Fund — Pointing to 'High Quality Growth' for All, *South China Morning Post*, September 1, 2021. Available at: https://www.scmp.com/tech/big-tech/article/3148334/alibaba-elaborates-how-it-will-use-its-100-billion-yuan-common.

Zhang, Joe (2014). *Inside China's Shadow Banking: The Next Subprime Crisis?* Enrich Professional Publishing. Inc., Honolulu.

Zhen, Summer (2017a). What President Xi's Congress Message Means for China's Housing Market, *South China Morning Post — Business*, October 24, 2017. Available at: https://www.scmp.com/business/article/2116621/what-president-xis-congress-message-means-chinas-housing-market?module=inline&pgtype=article.

Zhen, Summer (2017b). China's Xi Says to Maintain Principle Property Is Not for Speculation, *Reuters*, October 28, 2017. Available at: https://www.reuters.com/article/us-china-economy-property-idUSKBN1CN0B5.

Zhou, Ina (2019). China Local Government Unit Escapes Default with Late Payment, *Bloomberg*, December 10, 2019. Available at: https://www.bloomberg.com/news/articles/2019-12-10/china-lgfv- secures-investor-approval-on-late-bond-repayment.

Zhu, Julie (2022). Beijing Gives Initial Nod to Revive Ant IPO After Crackdown Cools, *Reuters*, June 10, 2022. Available at: https://www.reuters.com/markets/europe/exclusive-beijing-gives-initial-nod-revive-ant-ipo-after-crackdown-cools-sources-2022-06-09/.

Zhu, Ning, Ding Ding, and Chi Zhang (2019). Tapering Implicit Guarantees in the Bond Market, in Schipke, Alfred, Markus Rodlauer, and Longmei Zhang (eds.), *The Future of China's Bond Market*, International Monetary Fund, Washington.

Zong, Jun, Bo Li, and Laura E. Kodres (2019). Asset-Backed Securities, in Schipke, Alfred, Markus Rodlauer, and Longmei Zhang (eds.), *The Future of China's Bond Market*, International Monetary Fund, Washington.

Index

C

D

E

F

G

J

K

L

M

T

Z

www.ingramcontent.com/pod-product-compliance
Lightning Source LLC
Chambersburg PA
CBHW070702011025
33323CB00004B/269